# Globalisation, the Global Financial Crisis and the State

Published by
Edward Elgar Publishing Limited
The Lypiatts
15 Lansdown Road
Cheltenham
Glos GL50 2JA
UK

Edward Elgar Publishing, Inc.
William Pratt House
9 Dewey Court
Northampton
Massachusetts 01060
USA

A catalogue record for this book
is available from the British Library

Library of Congress Control Number: 2012946683

This book is available electronically in the ElgarOnline.com
Economics Subject Collection, E-ISBN 978 1 78100 943 7

FSC www.fsc.org MIX Paper from responsible sources FSC® C018575

ISBN 978 1 78100 942 0

Typeset by Servis Filmsetting Ltd, Stockport, Cheshire
Printed and bound by MPG Books Group, UK

# Globalisation, the Global Financial Crisis and the State

*Edited by*

John H. Farrar

*Emeritus Professor of Law, Bond University, Australia and Professor of Corporate Governance, University of Auckland, New Zealand*

and

David G. Mayes

*BNZ Professor of Finance and Director, Europe Institute; Joint Director, NZ Governance Centre, University of Auckland, New Zealand and Visiting Professor, University of Buckingham, UK*

**Edward Elgar**

Cheltenham, UK • Northampton, MA, USA

# Contents


| | |
|---|---|
| *List of figures* | vii |
| *List of tables* | viii |
| *List of contributors* | ix |
| *Acknowledgement* | xiii |

1 Globalisation, the crisis and the state: introduction — 1
*John H. Farrar and David G. Mayes*

PART I INTERNATIONAL PERSPECTIVES

2 Modernising the state: the New Zealand experience — 21
*Margaret Wilson*

3 Rebuilding state systems post-GFC: the South African case — 42
*Laurence Boulle*

4 Chinese multinationals and the state: an institutional perspective — 72
*Xiaohua Yang and Clyde D. Stoltenberg*

5 The EU and the member states: Germany and supranationalism in times of financial crisis — 94
*Jürgen Bröhmer*

PART II COMMERCIAL PERSPECTIVES

6 Corporatisation in Australia: a Queensland perspective — 117
*Tahnee Booth and Adrian Noon*

7 Putting 'why' before 'how': evaluating the rationales for partial privatisation of state-owned enterprises in New Zealand — 140
*Chye-Ching Huang, Susan Watson and Jenny Chen*

8 Public project procurement and the case for public–private partnerships — 172
*Michael Regan*

9 Rethinking the state through the lens of regulatory governance 197
*Graeme A. Hodge*

10 Developments in central banking after the GFC: central banks, the state, globalisation and the GFC 218
*Louise Parsons*

11 The euro crisis 243
*David G. Mayes*

12 The governance and regulation of sovereign wealth funds and foreign exchange reserves in a post-GFC world 272
*Mohamed Ariff and John H. Farrar*

*Index* 295

# Figures


| | | |
|---|---|---|
| 4.1 | China OFDI flow and stock (US dollars million) | 73 |
| 4.2 | Number of Chinese firms investing in OECD and non-OECD countries | 78 |
| 8.1 | A typical PPP contractual arrangement | 176 |
| 9.1 | The regulatory tools of government | 201 |
| 9.2 | Cumulative annual creation of regulatory agencies (RA) across 48 countries and 16 sectors over 88 years: 1920–2007 | 203 |
| 11.1 | Debt and fiscal balance in the euro area (medians) | 252 |
| 12.1 | Asset values in US$ of sovereign wealth funds, 2011 | 276 |
| 12.2 | Foreign reserves of 12 largest holders each with above US$200 billion | 280 |
| 12.3 | Corporate governance | 283 |
| 12.4 | The governance of SWFs | 283 |

# Tables


| | | |
|---|---|---|
| 4.1 | Phases of China's OFDI policy | 76 |
| 6.1 | Returns to government | 121 |
| 6.2 | GOC financial information and financial performance | 125 |
| 8.1 | Procurement performance, United Kingdom and Australia | 183 |
| 11.1 | Euro area government debt/GDP (%) | 251 |
| 12.1 | Compliance with the Santiago Principles by principle | 287 |

# Contributors

**Mohamed Ariff** is a Professor of Finance at Bond University, Australia. Previously, he held the Chair in Finance over ten years and was discipline Head of Finance at Monash University, Australia for six years. His internationally published scholarly books and peer-reviewed journal articles on banking and capital markets, liberalisation, exchange rates, privatisation and tax-compliance costs, all in the Asia-Pacific region, are widely cited in the respective literature. He has won several competitive research fellowships. He has worked as a visiting scholar, fellow and professor in several universities: Boston, USA; Harvard, USA; Melbourne, Australia; Tokyo, Japan (twice); and University College Dublin, Ireland (twice). He served in 2004–06 as the elected President of the Asian Finance Association. He is a recipient of four Australian Research Council (ARC) research grants, the latest a large ARC Linkage grant (with two others) on banking research.

**Tahnee Booth** is a Principal Treasury Analyst in the Office of Government Owned Corporations (OGOC) within Queensland Treasury, Australia. She has worked in OGOC since 2004, primarily on policy, legislative and governance matters.

**Laurence Boulle** is Professor of Law at Bond University, Australia and Adjunct Professor at the University of the Witwatersrand, Johannesburg, South Africa where he was previously Director of the Mandela Institute and Issy Wolfson Professor of Law. He has published in constitutional and administrative law, mediation and alternative dispute resolution (ADR), and globalisation and investment. He has also conducted a consultancy practice in negotiation, dispute resolution and conflict management for over 20 years and has worked extensively throughout Australia and New Zealand, the Asia-Pacific and Africa. He chaired the advisory council to the Australian government on dispute resolution policy and practice and was a part-time member of the National Native Title Tribunal in Australia. He was awarded the Order of Australia (AM) in 2008.

**Jürgen Bröhmer** is Professor and Dean of the Law School at Murdoch University in Western Australia. Previously he was Professor at the University of New England, USA in 2006, then Head of the Law School from 2007–11. He received his law degree from Mannheim University in Germany and his doctorate and post-doctoral habilitation from Saarland University in Saarbrücken, Germany where he worked at the Europa-Institute of Saarland University before coming to Australia. His areas of expertise are German constitutional, European Union and public international law. Jürgen has authored two and co-authored one monograph in specific areas of public international, constitutional and European Union law, edited a number of other books, and published numerous articles and book chapters.

**Jenny Chen** is a Research Assistant at the Commercial Law Department, University of Auckland Business School, New Zealand. She has assisted in various research projects concerned with company and securities law, and has published in the area of disclosure in securities regulation.

**John H. Farrar** is Emeritus Professor of Law at Bond University, Australia. He is also Professor of Corporate Governance and Joint Director of the New Zealand Governance Centre at the University of Auckland, New Zealand. He was Dean of Law at the University of Canterbury, New Zealand (1985–88), Bond University, Australia (1993–96) and the University of Waikato, New Zealand (2004–08). Professor Farrar is the author of a number of books and papers on company and commercial law and corporate governance. He has also been active in law reform in the United Kingdom, New Zealand and Australia, and was a member of the Legislation Advisory Committee of New Zealand (2004–08). In 2008 he was made an Honorary Life Member of the Australian Law Teachers Association for services to legal education in Australia and New Zealand.

**Graeme A. Hodge** is a Professor of Law and Director of the Centre for Regulatory Studies, Monash University, Australia. He is a leading policy analyst on regulation, privatisation and public–private partnerships. Graeme is an internationally recognised scholar, having published 12 books and 100 papers in management, social and economic policy, public administration, and regulation. He has worked with the Organisation for Economic Co-operation and Development (OECD), the European Commission, the United Nations, the Asian Development Bank and the Commonwealth Secretariat as well as serving as a special adviser to several parliamentary committees and inquiries. He has acted as a consultant on matters of regulatory governance in Australasia, Europe, Indonesia, the Philippines, China and the United States.

**Chye-Ching Huang** is Senior Lecturer in Commercial Law, University of Auckland Business School, New Zealand. She has interdisciplinary research interests in areas including tax, corporate law and governance, law and economics, public law, and fiscal and economic policy.

**David G. Mayes** is the BNZ Professor of Finance at the University of Auckland, New Zealand. He is Joint Director of the NZ Governance Centre. He is also Director of the Europe Institute. Previously David has held senior positions in the Bank of Finland, the Reserve Bank of New Zealand, the National Institute of Economic and Social Research and the National Economic Development Office in London, UK. He is a former Director of the NZ Institute of Economic Research in Wellington. His main research has been on the problems of economic, financial and monetary integration, particularly in Europe. His most recent work has been on the implications for financial regulation of the global crisis.

**Adrian Noon** is Chairman, Lanoon Pty Ltd, and former Executive Director of the Office of Government Owned Corporations (OGOC), Queensland Treasury, Australia 2006–12. Prior to this appointment, he was the Deputy Chief of Staff for the Queensland Premier, the Honourable Peter Beattie MP, from July 2005 to July 2006, and before that, the Special Advisor for Treasury in the Office of the Deputy Premier, Treasurer and Minister for Sport of Queensland, the Honourable Terry Mackenroth MP in Australia from February 2001 to July 2005. In his previous role, he had responsibility for overseeing all the government-owned corporations (GOCs) from a shareholder perspective, covering all strategic, commercial and governance aspects of ownership of these corporations.

**Louise Parsons** is Assistant Professor of Law and PhD Candidate at Bond University, Australia. Before joining Bond University, she was in-house counsel in the South African Reserve Bank for 11 years.

**Michael Regan** is Professor of Infrastructure and Head of Infrastructure and Project Management, Institute of Sustainable Development and Architecture at Bond University, Australia. He has extensive commercial experience in corporate advisory and finance in Australia and overseas. Formerly Director of the Australian Centre for Public Infrastructure at the University of Melbourne, his responsibilities include supervision of the postgraduate research and coursework programmes in project finance, infrastructure economics and project procurement including relationship contracting and public–private partnerships.

**Clyde D. Stoltenberg** is the W. Frank Barton Distinguished Chair, Associate Director of the Center for International Business Advancement and Professor at Wichita State University, USA. Previously, Dr Stoltenberg served as Professor and CIBER Co-Director at the University of Kansas, Executive Director of the East Asia Business Program at the University of Michigan, and Director of International Business Programs at the University of Texas, San Antonio and California State University, Long Beach, USA. He has been a Visiting Professor at Nankai University, China and the University of Hong Kong, and an invited speaker on trade in services at conferences organized by the Law Institute of the Chinese Academy of Social Sciences and the Chinese Ministry of Justice. He is on the editorial board of the *Journal of Asian Business* and served as Editor-in-Chief of the *American Business Law Journal*.

**Susan Watson** is a Professor of Law in the Faculty of Law at the University of Auckland, New Zealand. She researches and teaches in the areas of corporate law and corporate governance focussing on directors' liabilities and duties and the theory of the corporation. She has published in those areas both within and outside New Zealand. Susan is joint Editor of the *New Zealand Business Law Quarterly*, New Zealand's leading business law journal, and is Deputy Director of the New Zealand Governance Centre.

**Margaret Wilson**, DCNZM, is Professor of Law and Public Policy at the University of Waikato, New Zealand. She was a Member of Parliament 1999–2008 in New Zealand and held several ministerial appointments including Attorney-General, Minister of Labour and Minister responsible for Treaty of Waitangi negotiations. She is a former Speaker of the New Zealand Parliament 2005–08. Positions held include that of Director of the Reserve Bank, Law Commissioner, Foundation Dean, Waikato Law School and President of the New Zealand Labour Party.

**Xiaohua Yang** is Associate Professor at the University of San Francisco, School of Management, USA. She heads the Globalization of Chinese Enterprise program in the School of Business and Professional Studies at the University of San Francisco, USA. She specialises in international research and development (R&D) strategic alliances, internationalisation of Chinese firms, international human resources (HR) management, corporate social responsibility in multinational firms, and foreign market entry strategies. Dr Yang is particularly interested in understanding forces driving Chinese enterprises to expand overseas and determinants of their operation and performance abroad, especially in biotech industry and life sciences. Widely published in international journals, she is currently the Associate Editor of the *Journal of Asia Business Studies*, among other editorial credentials.

# Acknowledgement

We thank Rosa Riedl at Bond University for all the hard work she contributed in dealing with the authors and publishers throughout the various draft stages of the book, as well as at the conference where we brought the authors together. Without her help there would be no book.

# 1. Globalisation, the crisis and the state: introduction

**John H. Farrar and David G. Mayes**

The global financial crisis (GFC) has challenged much of conventional wisdom. Our conception of globalisation has been called into question. In particular, the Washington Consensus with its emphasis on deregulation and the shrinking of the state has been undermined. Instead, the importance of the state as regulator, investor and indeed economic saviour has been emphasised. We need then to readdress the relationship between globalisation, the crisis and the state, and this is the main objective of this book.

The purpose of this chapter is firstly to give an overview of the main issues arising from the relationship between globalisation, the GFC and the modern state, and secondly to outline the contents of the other chapters.

## 1.1 GLOBALISATION

'Globalisation' is a word whose usage dates back to the 1960s and connotes internationalisation and, to some extent, standardisation. It is mainly thought of in economic terms but can refer to social, political and other cultural matters. Some aspects of globalisation have been around for over 3000 years. The Silk Road enabled international trade to take place between East and West. A distinction is drawn between globalised localism and localised globalism. An example of the first would be the ubiquitous McDonald's, and an example of the second Rio Tinto's operations in Africa.

Professor Harry Arthurs, the distinguished Canadian academic, has referred to 'globalisation of the mind'. He argues that it 'involves a change in our social values and in our fundamental understandings about what role law does play and should play in society. Globalisation is, in other words, an ideology' (Arthurs, 2009, p. 632). He argues that beneath this ideology lies a bedrock assumption that governments which interfere with the free flow of goods, services, capital and information (but not people) impair their capacity to maintain a dynamic economy.

As a concept, globalisation filled a gap in the policies of the Clinton administration and was identified substantially with United States (US) hegemony and the Washington Consensus after the end of the Cold War. The result was that the role of the state, particularly in small countries, was constrained by membership of the global community, which reduced the ability to chose domestic policies in the face of standards of international agreements, increased competition and a degree of convergence mandated by international markets and credit rating agencies.

The complex processes currently summed up in the word 'globalisation' have their antecedents in imperialism, another ideology, and some writers see a conceptual overlap. Although there were earlier empires, the phrase is normally associated with the colonial expansion of European powers in the eighteenth and nineteenth centuries. Imperialism was regarded by Lenin as the highest stage of capitalism. He relied substantially on the book *Imperialism* by the English Fabian writer J.A. Hobson who had reported the Boer War for the *Manchester Guardian*. Hobson drew attention to the astonishing fact that the United Kingdom (UK) in the course of a single generation added an area of 4 754 000 square miles and a population estimated at 88 million to its domains. He also referred to the actions of other European powers and the late entry of the US. The second surprising fact was that the UK's imperial policy had no appreciable influence on the determination of its external trade. Indeed the greatest increase was with its industrial enemies and fellow colonisers. The import trade with the US alone was greater than that of the whole of the colonies. At the same time imperialism was an outlet for the migration of populations, but he thought this could be exaggerated. 'The new Empire is even more barren for settlement than for profitable trade'. How then was the UK induced to embark upon such an unsound business? Hobson thought that the business interests of the nation as a whole were subordinated to those of certain sectional interests, for private gain. It was good business for certain classes and certain trades, in particular the City of London and capital investment. 'The growing cosmopolitanisation of capital is the greatest economic change of this generation'. Every advanced industrial nation was tending to place a larger share of its capital outside the limits of its own political area in foreign countries or in colonies, and to draw a growing income from this source. The modern foreign policy of the UK was primarily a struggle for profitable markets of investment. The same was true of the other countries mentioned, including the US (Hobson, 1938 [1902]).

The US engaged in some of these activities in Puerto Rico, Hawaii and the Philippines, but operated under the illusion that it did not 'do empire'. This was a firm belief of Franklin D. Roosevelt who, as a Harvard student, had sponsored the Boer Relief Fund and had a deep antipathy to European colonialism, unlike his cousin and predecessor as President, Theodore Roosevelt. This antipathy strongly influenced his policies in the Second World War. Nevertheless the dominant role of the US in the Cold War after 1945, and particularly after 1990, has represented a hegemony resembling imperialism in some ways. It is this latter-day hegemony that has led to a US-dominated view of globalisation before the GFC. The US legitimated this by asserting that everyone was a winner from globalisation, whereas the GFC showed that there are winners and losers and that the West can end up on the losing side. This was obscured for a time by the rhetoric of G.W. Bush. The term 'new imperialism' has been used to describe the 'neo-con' approach of the G.W. Bush administration after 11 September 2001, and caused the US to lose legitimacy in the war on terror. It also contributed to the growth of an anti-globalisation movement.

An interesting recent development has been the communist literature in the West about 'The Rise of Chinese Imperialism':

> China has turned the crisis of US and EU finance capital and the global recession into an opportunity to export its own finance capital and to establish imperialist spheres of influence. As a result, China is now entering directly into competition with the existing imperialist powers as an emerging imperialist rival, in particular posing a major challenge to the US, the UK, Germany and France and Japan. (Humanist Workers for Revolutionary Socialism, 2010)

The advantage of China over rivals is said to be that China is able to develop its imperialist character from its ability to use the Chinese people as a super-exploited proletariat. The Chinese government rejects this argument by maintaining that the collective welfare of the country is more important than individual citizens' rights. The party-controlled All-China Federation of Trade Unions is supposed to protect workers' rights, and independent trade unions are illegal. Reforms of workers' rights have been carried out but the enforcement is problematic. Nevertheless there has been dramatic improvement in the lives of hundreds of millions of Chinese. To do this in a large developing country with a population of over 1.3 billion is a massive and complex economic and political task. Jiang Zemin (2001) said in 2000:

> To raise the living standard of the people constantly is the basic starting point and the final goal of all work of our Party. With the constant improvement of their livelihood the people will support the leadership of the Chinese

> Communist Party and the socialist system even more wholeheartedly, and devote themselves to the reform and opening-up and the modernization drive with even more confidence, and the ruling foundation of our party will be increasingly consolidated.

The GFC has undermined some of the Washington Consensus and led to a more multipolar world characterised by the G-20. Hence there is no longer one globalisation but several. Added to this is the reality that the world is no longer only a world of nation states and regional groupings of states, but also a world where multinational enterprises are often larger than many states. Some states now have sovereign wealth funds which are a puzzling hybrid that sometimes lack transparency.

The Seoul Consensus of 2010 put the emphasis on development. The six core principles of this Consensus are:

- focus on economic growth;
- global development partnership;
- global or regional systemic issues;
- private sector participation;
- complementarity; and
- outcome orientation.

The effect of recent events has been, firstly, to refute the determinist fallacy that was linked with US hegemony which involved confusing the causes of globalisation with its effects. Secondly, it marks a redefinition of North and South as centres of influence. We shall return to these points later but let us look at the GFC in more detail.

## 1.2 THE GLOBAL FINANCIAL CRISIS

The GFC arose out of the US subprime mortgage crisis. This social policy of the US was well intentioned but the dangers were underestimated by government and the financial sector. The risks of such loans were thought to be mitigated by the practice of securitisation. This took place at a time of extensive deregulation which had facilitated financial innovation and the use of complex derivative products. Again the risks were underestimated. The result led to both contagion and collapse of some US and UK financial institutions, as well as central bank and government intervention to prop up the system. These reactions were widely transmitted to other countries through the global financial and economic system. This experience has given rise to a reconsideration of the role of central banks and their relationship with governments.

There was a need for action at an international as well as domestic level and this led to the formation of the G-20 and the reconstitution of the Financial Stability Forum as the Financial Stability Board (FSB), as well as action by the International Organization of Securities Commissions (IOSCO).

On an international level, the FSB fulfils a critical role. It has been positioned (by the G-20) to be at the centre of both international and national dialogue, and it provides a point of connection for governments and international bodies of experts (for example IOSCO), as well as institutions such as the International Monetary Fund (IMF) and the World Bank.

Since the beginning of 2010, the FSB has been very productive and has progressed significantly with the tasks imposed on it by the G-20. In April 2011, the FSB issued a progress report on the implementation of G-20 recommendations for strengthening financial stability. It reported the following:

- implementation of reforms to bank capital and liquidity standards;
- addressing systemically important financial institutions (SIFIs);
- regulatory measures for 'shadow banking';
- improving the over-the-counter (OTC) and commodity derivative markets;
- development of macroprudential frameworks and tools;
- progress towards convergence on strengthened accounting standards;
- strengthening adherence to international supervisory and regulatory standards; and
- FSB regional consultative groups to include FSB member and non-member groups.

The FSB's April 2011 report also noted its progress on addressing the financial stability in emerging markets and developing economies, consumer finance protection, reducing reliance on credit rating agencies (CRAs), addressing data gaps, as well as market integrity issues. The FSB Chairman Mario Draghi suggested:

> The ongoing international programme of financial reforms is strengthening the robustness of the global financial system. However, pockets of weakness in the banking system remain and sovereign and banking risks are closely intertwined in some countries.

While there is much more to be accomplished, the general direction appears to be set towards strengthening oversight and regulation. The measures relate primarily to ensuring that structure and operation of financial systems and financial firms are much less likely to be crisis-prone, but they also relate to ensuring that any problems that do occur, especially in large institutions, can be handled swiftly and with limited real consequences for the community at large.

In this context it is important to point out that the representatives of member countries at the G-20 are the finance ministers and the governors of central banks. Whereas central banks may increasingly be responsible for domestic financial stability, the GFC has highlighted the fact that national financial stability can no longer be the only focus and, because of globalisation, financial stability at international level should be ensured.

## 1.3 THE ROLE OF THE STATE

The traditional roles of the state have been:

- to maintain social order or declare war;
- to define property rights;
- to provide for administration of justice;
- to provide public goods;
- to regulate markets;
- to tax; and
- to redistribute wealth through welfare programmes (Farrar and Parson, 2012).

The growth of the modern welfare state resulted in an increased role for the state which has led to increased taxation.

The Washington Consensus, a product of US hegemony, and conceptions of globalisation advocated by bodies such as the IMF and the OECD before 2008, fostered the idea of a retreat of the state. This manifested itself in the following ways:

- privatisation;
- outsourcing;
- public–private partnerships;
- a race to the bottom by cutting taxes and deregulating;[1]
- the impacts of global finance on domestic economies;
- the impact on global systems of production;
- the bypassing of central governments;
- the transfer of policy-making in certain areas to supranational bodies; and

- the emphasis on self-regulation, particularly in the field of corporate governmence.

The role of the state shifted to meta-governance of the economy in the sense of steering, resourcing and assuming accountability in state-owned enterprises and matters such as competition.

The Washington Consensus taken up by the IMF, World Bank and OECD led to a commercialisation of the state. New Zealand accepted this more than Australia did. A federal system tends to be more conservative. On the other hand, necessity has forced the New South Wales and Queensland State Governments to consider privatisation in often controversial circumstances. It was thought that greater efficiency and reduced cost would result from this commercialisation. At the same time, global systems of production and the power of the resources sector undermined the state's power to regulate the market.

In the early 1990s writers such as Kenichi Ohmae (1995) argued that nation states were becoming the local authorities of the global system. They were increasingly subject to the decisions and movement of international capital. This was a pro-business, anti-politics agenda and represented a temporary triumph of neoliberalism following on from the mixed experiences of monetarism in the 1980s.

In the decade since 11 September 2001, the West has been distracted by the war against terrorism and the costly invasions of Iraq and Afghanistan. Coupled with deregulation and tax reductions for the rich, the result has been an increase in debt, considerable errors of judgement and a dangerous state of affairs.

In the GFC, central banks and the state have had to intervene with the result that there has been quasi-nationalisation of some financial institutions and absorption of toxic debt by the state. At the same time there has been state capitalism in some parts of the world as well as the growth of sovereign wealth funds. These have the size to swing or stabilise markets yet lack transparency and may threaten national security. In spite of the resurgence of the state there has been a manifest need for international cooperation to deal with the crisis. The recent reforms of the US and UK have somewhat cut across development of international solutions.

Asian countries had learned the lessons of the Asian financial crisis and built up reserves as well as pursuing more cautious policies. It was the West which was affected most by the crisis which has led to a reconsideration of the relationship between China and the US, since China is now a major creditor of the US. Doubt has been cast on US hegemony and the Washington Consensus version of globalisation. At the same time the US still has military dominance.

The main lessons that we can learn from the GFC are:

- no two crises are exactly alike;
- the first step in a crisis is to ensure stability of the system;
- regulators must be flexible to respond to an emerging crisis while recognising that they cannot manage it;
- regulators need to develop a global early warning system to identify asset bubbles and excesses in domestic and/or international markets and the systemic risk implications;
- there needs to be improved cross-border data sharing and cooperation;
- regulators must take into account the global nature of the present system and its complications;
- regulatory reform must not overreact or be overambitious;
- derivatives need special attention in terms of regulation, disclosure and risk management;
- the boundary of regulation and supervision needs to be pushed out to cover almost all of the financial sector including credit rating agencies; and
- the FSB as the place where all the regulators and other important role players meet has an important role as an international coordinating body. (Farrar et al., 2009, p. 37)

These lessons lead to the need for new institutions, or new functions for existing institutions, and a new approach to regulation.

The idea of a new Bretton Woods Agreement has not been pursued. Instead there has been a strengthening of existing institutions, notably the FSF (now the FSB) and IOSCO. There appears to be no departure from the principles of the system prior to the GFC, and no change to the conceptual framework or philosophy, but only improvements to existing infrastructure and legislative frameworks. The main themes of the new approach to regulation after the GFC appear to be:

- a greater focus on macro-prudential risks across the financial system which takes account of banks, shadow banks and private capital;
- greater emphasis on shared information on financial markets;
- a campaign to reduce regulatory arbitrage;
- some greater regulation of hedge funds;
- standardisation of credit derivatives markets and central clearing systems;
- agreed action against uncooperative tax havens;
- improved standards for valuation of financial instruments; and

- more effective oversight of credit rating agencies. (Farrar et al., 2009, p. 38)

The so-called Washington Consensus contained a significant rhetorical element designed to combat the strong forces for personal and sectoral interests to appropriate the gains from liberalisation and inhibit their spread to the rest of the population. Since the 1950s it had been appreciated that a careful scheduling of the removal of barriers to economic development was needed, otherwise the forces of international competition could wipe out the fledgling sources of increasing value added in developing countries and emerging markets. Similarly, some intervention by the state is required to ensure an acceptable degree of redistribution of benefits across the population as a whole.

However, by the 1980s the view had altered and it was thought preferable to try to bring about change wherever it could be achieved, otherwise there would be little progress. In part it was felt that this would provide the pressure for other changes. This was very much the approach in New Zealand, for example. Liberalisation in product markets would lead to greater flexibility in labour markets and so on.[2] Also barriers at the world level had fallen, as a result of over three decades of negotiation, and hence there was more global openness to adhere to. The richer countries undoubtedly made use of their bargaining power and it was only in the 1990s that the balance became more even with the result that there has been very limited progress on further agreement since then.

This change in view was typified by the advice given to the ex-communist countries, where gradualism was discouraged, in part for fear that there could be the ready means of return to an authoritarian regime. The success of some of the countries which ignored the advice, combined with the experience of the Asian crises, meant that the more extreme views were already outdated by the time of the GFC and what was required was the shock to bring the new orthodoxy into effect. The biggest feature tipping the balance was the continuing success of China. Much of the previous approach to policy was based on the appropriate response of a small country. China was large enough to affect the world on its own and hence could manage to maintain restrictions and absorb imbalances to an extent that would be largely impossible elsewhere, except India. Other countries, primarily in Asia, could therefore follow a similar course and opt out of some of the Western conventions.

At the same time, the maintenance of light regulation in the financial sector was largely an Anglo-Saxon phenomenon, not shared by continental Europe nor indeed elsewhere. The European Union (EU) with its quest for harmonisation has been a steady regulator, concerned to have comprehensive regulation rather than simply responding to market failure in the Anglo-Saxon tradition.

However, some aspects of US hegemony reflected through Washington consensus were more subtle though effective. The monopolisation of economic ideas was a case in point, where theory triumphed over pragmatism and simplified ideas based on unrealistic assumptions had considerable primacy. The example of dynamic stochastic general equilibrium models, without a role for money or credit, in the run up to the GFC in some central banks is a case in point. However, not all such errors were based on theory. In retrospect, one of the most important contributions to the GFC was the belief on the one hand that it was difficult to determine when financial bubbles were occurring rather than soundly based price growth, and on the other that the damage caused when bubbles burst could be limited by substantial rapid action by the authorities. This became known as the 'Greenspan standard' (Blinder and Reis, 2005) and contributed to easy money, overconfidence and a massive build-up of asset prices.

What the GFC did was provide the jolt which pushed countries and more importantly the global community into taking actions that they had been able to put off or ignore in the relatively benign economic circumstances of the late twentieth and early twenty-first centuries. The need for global cooperation to deal with global financial institutions was obvious. Disquiet with self-regulation, particularly regarding corporate governance, had led to a series of attempts at reform. In the UK, self-regulation of the financial sector ended in 1997 with the setting up of the Financial Services Authority – regrettably with flaws shown up by the GFC. Very little that the GFC threw up was new. Almost all of the issues took the form of problems that were well known in advance but thought to be of low probability despite their potential high impact. A large feature of the 'consensus' was simply that nothing had gone badly wrong for a long period of time and hence systems which were adequate in good times were not revealed as being disastrous in a crisis until the crisis struck.

## 1.4 THE APPROACH IN THIS BOOK

The subsequent chapters in the book approach the topic of globalisation, the GFC and the role of the state from a variety of perspectives. Chapter 2 by Margaret Wilson, for instance, looks at it from the point of view of a lawyer in parliament and in government and hence needing to debate and decide upon the legislative challenges that globalisation and the GFC have thrown down. This gives an excellent position from which to reflect on the changing role of the state. The chapter deals with New Zealand, which has implemented a huge programme of change, very much in line with the Washington Consensus since 1984. However, these changes were made not because of outside pressure, but from the conviction of the government of the day that the previous approach of substantial protection and government intervention in the economy was just not working. These changes were made, not by a government of the right, but by a Labour government. However, as the benefits of the rejuvenation of the economy did not spread to all parts of society and inequality increased, enthusiasm waned. Although the process picked up speed again with the election of a National Party government in 1990, Wilson shows how since 1993 there has been more questioning of globalisation.

In many respects New Zealand provided a test bed for the ideas and the early period was widely labelled the 'New Zealand experiment'. In addition to removing barriers to foreign trade and eliminating industry subsidies, many aspects of the economy were subject to 'light-touch' regulation. This did not include the labour market where the Employment Contracts Act replaced a strong role for trade unions. The GFC has shown that much of that light touch, certainly in respect of the finance company sector and also in aspects of corporate governance, has not worked. The tide has turned, with *inter alia* the extension of the powers of the Reserve Bank and the creation of the Financial Markets Authority.

Wilson provides a thorough review of the nature of the state in New Zealand, including the unusual complication of the Treaty of Waitangi and the relationship between Maori and the Crown. This special relationship can affect decisions such as privatisation and the sale of state assets. One feature of the New Zealand system which is of widespread interest is the new management of the public sector, whose impact is still being debated. However, perhaps the biggest challenge to globalisation has come simply through the democratic process. New Zealand has a rather participative democracy and with the introduction of proportional representation following a referendum it has become much more difficult to push policies through. While the balance between globalisation and social welfare has moved back somewhat towards the latter, New Zealand's scope for action has been reduced by the force of international law.

Wilson's very comprehensive and thought-provoking analysis provides the basis for the study of other countries. Laurence Boulle, in Chapter 3, shows how the GFC has affected the post-apartheid South African state. Recent decades have witnessed the increasing integration of Africa into the global economy and South Africa has been a major beneficiary but this sometimes clashes with the political processes and constitutional values. The construction of the post-apartheid state in itself has altered the system substantially, *inter alia* introducing more positive duties on the

South African state to provide social services under the 1996 constitution. Not surprisingly as an emerging economy, South Africa has much more in common with the BRIC countries (Brazil, Russia, India and China) which it has now joined, with a much more substantial role for the state and more interventionist approach following what Boulle describes as the 'Seoul Consensus' for such countries. With the move to the G-20 as the grouping for dominating international cooperation, such countries are now able to have some real influence on international developments in a way that was not true before the GFC.

While Chapter 4 by Xiaohua Yang and Clyde Stoltenberg deals with China, it focuses on the changing relationship of Chinese multinationals and the state since the GFC. The advanced countries have been viewing with some concern the increasing involvement of Chinese companies with state backing in purchasing companies abroad while values are low as a result of the GFC, especially as these companies have benefited China's exchange rate management and limits to inward investment. The chapter documents the extent of their activities and explains that this is very much a deliberate strategy, focused on key industries, particularly where they are difficult to relocate. What these Chinese firms appear to be succeeding in is a form of state capitalism, where the firm is given sufficient independence to take commercial decisions but where the state provides the overall vision and assists financing and competitive advantage.

With an increasing focus on research and development (R&D) and innovation, Chinese firms are acquiring more of the value-added and developing their competitive position. While the state is not loosening its hold over the system, arrangements are evolving and civil society arrangements are developing. Its sheer size gives China a powerful position that it is steadily developing both in the Asian region and in international organisations. As Yang and Stoltenberg conclude:

> We expect that the future landscape for China and Chinese firms will be far from dull and unimaginative. While the role of the state will by no means recede and Chinese multinationals will become ever more active and visible on the global scene, other actors, such as civil organisations and associations, will inject new energy and visibility into the landscape.

A different facet of the challenges to the state comes from the EU where member countries have voluntarily agreed to delegate a number of key areas of decision-making, regulation and policy to the supranational level. The boundary is naturally contentious and the working relationship has obvious challenges. In Chapter 5, Jürgen Bröhmer describes the experience of Germany in the EU and its critical role in the euro crisis. Germany in particular has found itself having to take on a more major role in handling the consequences of problems in other member states than it wants, leading to a tension between narrow and broader interests in the successful development of the EU. Germany is, however, particularly interesting in this regard because of its federal structure. There are thus pressures on the nation state from both the EU and the *Land* levels. In some other EU member states, the subnational level sees the EU as a possible partner in gaining greater autonomy – Scotland and Catalonia for example.

These first few chapters in Part I, therefore, do not merely set up a framework for the analysis of how globalisation and the GFC have been affecting the role of the state, but they also illustrate the practice with respect to four countries. In Part II which follows, we look at the way in which the role of the state is changing in the realm of commercial activities. We have already noted the case of China. In Chapter 6 Tahnee Booth and Adrian Noon look at the case of Queensland and argue that its experience with state-owned companies has been good. Careful governance arrangements encourage efficient operation. International evidence suggests that for such efficient operation, companies need similar governance structures to the private sector, need to have to raise their own funds directly on the market and face competition in their activities. Such companies need to be clearly separate from direct influence from politicians but require a clear route of accountability and incentives for their performance. Booth and Noon argue that these companies have played a major role in the development of infrastructure in Queensland, which would not have been achieved through a purely private framework.

These characteristics for successful state-owned companies set out by Booth and Noon also apply to the companies set for partial privatisation in New Zealand, thus making the chance of gains from the change in ownership smaller. This forms the topic of the analysis by Chye-Ching Huang, Susan Watson and Jenny Chen of the case of New Zealand in Chapter 7. New Zealand is particularly interesting at present as the government has decided to privatise some of its key state-owned enterprises in the energy sector, and the national airline. These privatisations will be only partial, with the government retaining control. Furthermore the airline has already been privatised once before but had to be repurchased following disastrous losses.

The chapter considers the possible rationales for such privatisations and concludes that the case that can be made under most headings is rather weak, but so also is the case against such privatisations. Although the government made this an election issue in November 2011, the debate has not gone away and its principal coalition partner, the Maori party, is opposed to the sales. The government has a clear need to raise funding in the short run in order to halt the climbing debt that the GFC has caused; however it regards the sales as being of long-run benefit not just simply to the fiscal balance from having the companies better managed but also from better operation of capital markets and dynamic spillover effects. However, it is debatable whether the companies are inefficient despite their state ownership.

Chapter 8 by Michael Regan looks at a different way in which the state can interact with the private commercial sector by considering the growth of public-private partnerships (PPPs). While much of the literature on PPPs points out the problems which have occurred with them, Regan considers the successes. More importantly he evaluates their success not against some ideal but against the plausible alternatives, which would be sole state or private provision. In this light PPPs tend to show up rather better as all normal routes to designing, financing, constructing and running such projects have their drawbacks. Not all projects are suitable for PPP but where both parties cannot achieve their full objectives without the other a joint project stands a much greater chance of success. PPPs as a mere attempt to get round hard financial constraints on the public sector are unlikely to be particularly successful.

In Chapter 9 Graeme Hodge takes a much wider view of the role of the state as regulator, suggesting that we can view much of the way in which the government seeks to control the workings of the economy and society as 'regulatory governance'. Thus rather than providing some services itself it regulates how others do it. The range of regulation is considerable, including licensing, planning and environmental controls, a framework of corporate law, competition and restrictive practices regulation, procurement, PPP and rules on disclosure and intellectual property. All of this operates with the parallel framework of taxes, subsidies and services which can provide further influence and direction. All of this is a political activity. There is no single way of operating so the framework can evolve steadily, reflecting the views of different governments and popular pressure. The one feature which is painfully obvious is the enormous growth rate of this activity, with the pages of new regulation setting records each year despite occasional attempts to deregulate or, more frequently, reregulate.

Globalisation operates in this framework through a number of routes. There are all the examples of international agreement and the increasing openness of markets has to some extent altered the power of major players. Clearly there is substantial debate about the degree to which the state is the victim of market forces rather than the controller of them, but the idea of unfettered markets is not a description of reality despite the rhetoric.

Complementing the previous chapter, Hodge uses PPPs as his detailed example. Hodge is cautious about PPPs to say the least and is critical of many of the arrangements that have taken place in Victoria. Because of their contractual nature PPPs tend to offer little democratic recourse after signature. He is also cautious that the relationships are dressed up in words that sound good, such as 'partnership', without there being much in the way of tangible gains to back this up.

In Chapter 10 Louise Parsons considers the role of central banks and the state in dealing with the GFC. The rise of independent yet accountable central banks has been one of the notable features of the last 25 years. One of the means of assisting the achievement of price stability has been to elevate it above party politics and make it the goal of an institution that can be judged independently on its technical competence over the medium term. Leaving monetary policy as the direct responsibility of ministers runs the risk of it being subject to short-term considerations which would introduce just the volatility that policy seeks to avoid. Central banks have been very transparent in their actions and reasoning, so they can be judged. In the years up to the GFC these arrangements seemed to have been highly successful with the fall in inflation and much smoother economic development – famously labelled the 'great moderation' by the current Chairman of the Board of Governors of the Federal Reserve System, Ben Bernanke.

With the GFC this view has begun to look rather complacent as generally speaking central banks did not foresee the problems and still less did they take adequate action. The moderation has been replaced by the most substantial financial crisis since the 1930s and the pendulum of political independence is likely to swing back – certainly from its most extreme example, the Eurosystem where the Governing Council has been able to decide itself what constitutes price stability, without a 'government' to decide on objectives beyond what is laid down in the Maastricht Treaty and maintained in the subsequent revisions.

The rise of these new bodies or the change in the independence of bodies derived from what would previously have been government departments is a pervasive phenomenon in recent years. Frank Vibert (2007) describes this as 'the rise of the unelected'. However, such bodies may actually increase the ability of both parliament and society at large to exert democratic control over the actions of government, as these bodies are separated out and can therefore be addressed directly, rather than having to wrap up the whole of a government's actions in a vote at a general election. Furthermore only a proportion of these agencies are executive bodies and others are monitors and supervisors of executive agencies and hence bring independent and objective powers of oversight, thereby easing the role of parliament as overseers of the conformity of government actions with parliamentary decisions. Similarly, openness and the requirement to consult locally may bring these bodies closer to popular control and not further as initial worries suggested.

The relation between the financial regulators and the GFC is developed further by David Mayes in Chapter 11 where he focuses on the issues behind the euro crisis and their implications for increased integration. The euro area was set up very much as a fair-weather system which worked well if it was not subject to severe adverse shocks. Although the euro area was far from an optimal currency area it was expected that it would slowly grow closer together and restructure steadily so that it was more able to withstand shocks – as illustrated by the case of Finland for example, which has changed markedly in the last 20 years and survived a heavy external shock in the early part of the GFC. The big mistake, however, was to bend the rules for entry and allow countries with high public debt ratios, such as Greece, to enter and then to fail to enforce the Stability and Growth Pact that should not merely have stopped indebtedness increasing but helped it fall to safer levels. The GFC has demonstrated the interconnectedness of economies particularly through the banking system. While other member states may be reluctant to lend to those in difficulty through fear of making losses, they are aware at the same time that a refusal to lend will result in bank failures and hence domestic losses through a different route. Hence the GFC is inevitably bringing countries closer together in Europe, through the agreements on much closer fiscal surveillance and the increased lending and the realisation that problems with the weaker affect all.

In the last chapter, Mohamed Ariff and John Farrar deal with the governance of sovereign wealth funds and foreign exchange reserves, their role in the GFC and the relationship with the modern state. Sovereign wealth funds highlight the tension between market capitalism and state capitalism and the contradictions in the latest permutations of globalisation. Countries that are less open are able to buy important stakes in the economies of the more open, which may lead to a response on the fairness of the international system. At the same time the build-up of foreign exchange reserves and the keeping of exchange rates artificially low, often by the same countries, are creating serious imbalances in the world, which are not merely inhibiting the recovery of some of the countries most affected by the GFC but offering a much greater chance of another crisis or the prolongation of the present crisis, as occurred in the 1930s.

As these chapters show, the power of the state has indeed changed substantially and continues to change, affected *inter alia* by the forces of globalisation. What the GFC has done by imposing a severe adverse shock is to expose the weaknesses of the changes that have taken place over several decades. In the future these weaknesses are likely to be addressed, probably with an increased role for the state and a more pragmatic approach to economic management, with greater emphasis on social and political concerns.

## NOTES

1. In practice deregulation was selective and in general detailed regulation increased, particularly in the EU.
2. Not that all countries followed this precept. New Zealand's near neighbour Australia for example, decided to take the change more slowly and does not seem to have suffered as a result. More recently Finland decided that it needed the pressure of monetary union to get more flexible labour markets, while its neighbour Sweden with a similar economic position decided it should work on flexibility directly. Fifteen years later both countries have a similar performance. There does not appear to be a single recipe.

## REFERENCES


Arthurs, H. (2009), 'Law and Learning in an Era of Globalisation', *German Law Journal*, **10**, 629.

Blinder, Alan S. and Ricardo Reis (2005), *Understanding the Greenspan Standard*, accessed 15 March 2012 at http://www.kc.frb.org/publicat/sympos/2005/pdf/blinderreis.paper.0804.pdf.

Farrar, John H. and Louise Parsons (2012), 'Globalisation, the Global Financial Crisis and the Reinvention of the State', *Singapore Academy of Law Journal*, **24**, 367.

Farrar, John H., Louise Parsons and Pieter I. Joubert (2009), 'The Development of an Appropriate Regulatory Response to the Global Financial Crisis', *Bond Law Review*, **21**(3), 1.

FSB (2011), Financial Stability Board Press Release, Ref no:11/2011, 5 April, accessed September 2012 at http://www.financialstabilityboard.org/press/pr_110405.pdf.

Hobson, John (1938 [1902]), *Imperialism, A Study*, 3rd edn, ed. John Atkinson, London: George Allen & Unwin.

Humanist Workers for Revolutionary Socialism (2010), 'The Rise of Chinese Imperialism – How it has Exacerbated the Decay of World Capitalism and its Implications for the Class Struggle Today', accessed 9 March 2010 at http://www.humanistsforrevolutionarysocialism.org/Publications/China_Pamphlet.pdf.

Jiang, Zemin (2001), *On the Three Represents*, Beijing: Foreign Languages Press.

Ohmae, Kenichi (1995), *The End of the Nation State – The Rise of Regional Economies*, New York: Harper Collins Publishers.

Vibert, F. (2007), *The Rise of the Unelected: Democracy and the New Separation of Powers*, Cambridge: Cambridge University Press.

# PART I

# International perspectives

# 2. Modernising the state: the New Zealand experience

**Margaret Wilson**

## 2.1 INTRODUCTION

Globalisation has not only changed the nature and operation of the financial and economic systems, it has also affected the nature and role of the state and the relationship between state institutions and citizens. Much has been written about the affect of globalisation on the state from the perspective of international relations experts. Susan Strange's seminal work *The Retreat of the State* (1996) analysed the influence of global markets, transnational companies and technology on the power and influence of the state. Although Strange observed that 'the casting of vote from time to time becomes a symbolic act', she also noted, 'The shift from state authority to market authority has been in large part the result of state policies' (1996, pp. 44, 197). In the New Zealand context I would challenge the first observation which implies that the individual has no influence or power over the decisions of their governments, but would agree with the second observation and offer New Zealand as a case study of a state embracing and promoting the institutions, policies and ideology of globalisation from 1984 to 1996. Since that initial enthusiastic embrace of globalisation, New Zealand has embarked on a process of trying to find a balance between reconciling the reality of the free market with adherence to the concept of social protection for all citizens.

This chapter will not focus on the various academic analyses of the relationship between the forces of globalisation and the nation state. It accepts the reality of both globalisation and the state. The recent financial crisis and following economic recession have demonstrated the consequences of a global market failure and reliance on both the state and international institutions to reconstruct a global and domestic regulatory framework (Farrar et al., 2009). Anne-Marie Slaughter (1996) in her analysis on the influence of globalisation persuasively argued that the state was not disappearing but disaggregating and that 'Its component institutions – regulators, judges, and even legislators – are all reaching out beyond national borders in various ways, finding that their once "domestic" jobs have a growing international dimension' (1996, p. 31). She argues for a form of global governance founded on government networks that have been created through globalisation and governed by a set of norms that provide benchmarks against which these global institutions can be held accountable (1996, pp. 244–260).

The current financial and economic crisis provides a practical test for her analysis and the strength of international institutions and comity. The relevance of Slaughter's analysis for New Zealand is that it is a small, geographically distant, economically dependent country that has participated within international institutions since the formation of the International Labour Organization (ILO) and the League of Nations in 1919. While New Zealand is an active international citizen, the question is how much influence or power it has to ensure that globalisation protects and furthers the well-being of New Zealand citizens. It will be argued that while the reality is that New Zealand has little control over global market forces, it does retain some power over the impact of those forces on the people of New Zealand. How this state power is exercised depends on both the constitutional institutions through which state power is exercised and the engagement of New Zealand citizens with government decision-making.

New Zealand has been a dependent economy since colonisation and for some people globalisation is another form of colonisation. Jim McAloon (2009) has argued that in the complex interplay between the forces of Britain and New Zealand settlers may be described as a 'managed globalisation' (2009, p. 197). Geoff Bertram (2009) who reviews the New Zealand economy 1900–2000, also argues that New Zealanders have been constantly engaged in negotiating global forces. While world market forces were a constant in the New Zealand economy, so was the role of the state. He argues (2009, pp. 537, 552):

> The state played a central role in sustaining the institutional and attitudinal underpinnings of each era's political economy. Interestingly, the election of a reformist political party was a reflex settler response in all of the three transitions discussed above: the Liberals in 1890, Labour in 1935 and Labour again (albeit a very different Labour) in 1984. Post-crisis consolidation of hegemony and legitimacy fell to conservative parties representative of (and/or responsive to) the newly ascendant economic elites.

Although the current manifestation of globalisation is not a new phenomenon for New Zealanders, its affects have been comprehensive and required a fundamental rethinking about the respective roles of the market and the state in the lives of New Zealanders. The process of reconciliation between the demands of globalisation for free markets and the expectation of the people for social protection began in earnest from 1984 and have continued since that time. The progress to date may be summarised as follows. Economically New Zealand has survived the forces of globalisation so far, including the current economic recession, but its economy is still fragile with low growth, low productivity and a level of debt that is uncomfortable in the current environment (New Zealand 2011 Budget; see English, 2011). Socially the evidence would indicate that there is growing inequality in a country that has prided itself on being egalitarian and providing a level of well-being for all citizens (Wilkinson and Pickett, 2010; Nolan, 2007). Politically, globalisation has contributed to major changes in the electoral system and the distribution of political power. Importantly however, the people are still engaged with the political system.

I shall first address questions of definitions of both globalisation and the state in the context of the New Zealand experience. The purpose of this section is not to provide a scholarly treatise on these important concepts but rather to reflect how these terms are used in practice and as a frame of reference for policy changes in New Zealand. The chapter will then briefly review the domestic adoption of the neoliberal policy framework of globalisation and the effect of this radical policy change on the notion of the social welfare state that had traditionally characterised New Zealand.

## 2.2 GLOBALISATION IN THE NEW ZEALAND CONTEXT

The arguments surrounding globalisation are often polemical and heavily dependent on perceptions of globalisation rather than academic definitions (Hay, 2006). Often perceptions influence political decision-making, rather than an objective assessment of the evidence available. How globalisation is perceived depends on your position and circumstances in society. As Peter Mandelson (2011) has observed in a speech to launch the Institute of Public Policy research project on the future of globalisation:

> Modern economic life seemed to me to be characterised pretty simply: new opportunity for many, new uncertainty for most . . . Because it seemed to me that there were two very different globalisations: the economic version, the 'seen from 10000 feet' version of new opportunity and aggregate growth. And a more personal and individual one, in which jobs are being lost and real wages stagnating and from which only a relatively small elite seem insulated.

Harry Arthurs (2009), a distinguished legal academic, in an article on the implications of globalisation for the law and legal education notes: 'Globalisation is, in other words, an ideology'. His characterisation of globalisation as ideology is particularly apt in the context of New Zealand. Given the deep if suppressed ideological divide in New Zealand politics, globalisation soon came to describe two different worldviews. Globalisation represented either freedom from the regulatory controls of the state and therefore enabled individuals to pursue their self-interest without restraint from the state, or it removed the necessary social protection from individuals who through their economic and social status required state support to pursue their well-being. Globalisation is also associated with a value system that is centred on the rights of the individual as opposed to a value system centred on the individual as part of a community. The response to the policies of globalisation depends very much on the individual's capacity to cope with the changes, and in particular to protect themselves and their family from its negative effects, such as no state-provided social protection.

The recent demonstrations in Greece and Spain and the Occupy movement highlight the political implications of the policies of globalisation. There is increasing concern about whether national governments can represent the interests of their people against the power of the multinational and transnational companies. Globalisation is also often linked to the increasing disengagement of the people from the electoral process and is thereby undermining the democratic process because of the perceived inability of national governments to affect real change. In New Zealand, it is argued, the people are still engaged in defence of the democratic process, but their ability to influence decisions made globally is questionable.

The continuing viability of the state as the primary provider of social protection is at the heart of the political narrative over the influence of globalisation on the state. Both internationally and nationally, the question of the level and form of social protection to be provided by the state is an issue of concern (UN System Chief Executives Board for Coordination, 2009). The dilemma is that while social protection can be costly, without it economic growth is slow or impossible (International Labour Organization, 2011). New Zealand faces the same problem of finding the appropriate balance between economic and social policy that is economically sustainable and politically acceptable to the people. In policy terms the debate has centred on the reconstruction of the social protection system (Boston et al., 1999; Easton, 2008).

The radical nature of the neoliberal policy framework introduced by the Fourth Labour government in 1984 surprised many New Zealanders. While the Labour Party had signalled that there was a need for change in their election manifesto, the details of the changes were not disclosed to the public. The reasons for the non-disclosure were twofold. Firstly, there was a major ideological debate within the Labour Party prior to the election as to the direction of the policy. One faction supported the neoliberal agenda, the other faction wanted a more conservative, balanced approach to change. With the election of David Lange as leader of the Labour Party in 1983, the neoliberal faction led by Roger Douglas won a political advantage, though the details of the policy debate continued within the Party. The second reason for the failure to provide full disclosure of the policies was the unexpected announcement of an early election by the National Prime Minister Robert Muldoon. This curtailed the debate within the Labour Party that went into election mode and the campaign committee decided on a short election policy statement rather than making public the more extensive policy document (I was Vice-President of the Labour Party at the time and involved in both the policy discussions and preparation of the election manifesto).

The non-disclosure of the full policy agenda was to cost the Labour government electoral support at the 1990 election and provided the basis for the electorate's sense of grievance that the politicians had misled the people. It was therefore surprising that the incoming National government in 1990 had not learned this political lesson and also introduced policies that had not been clearly revealed to the electorate. The National government continued the neoliberal agenda of the Fourth Labour government but applied it more vigorously to social policy with attempts to start to reconstruct the social welfare state. While the Fourth Labour government also sought changes to social policy, opposition within the Labour Party made this extension of the policies very difficult (Wilson, 1989; Clark, 1992, 2005, 2008).

Treasury and Reserve Bank officials, who were concerned at the lack of response from the governments in the 1960s, 1970s and early 1980s to the reality of globalisation, drove the neoliberal policy agenda. Their prescription for the New Zealand economy was contained in the Treasury briefing document to the incoming Labour government in 1987 (Treasury, 1987). Key members of the Fourth Labour Cabinet, in particular the Minister of Finance Roger Douglas, endorsed this policy prescription. Alan Bollard (1994, p. 73) has given a succinct and accurate description of the elements of the new policy framework and the implementation of the policy from 1984 to 1991. He identifies the key elements of the 'Washington Consensus' economic reform programme and the application of this prescription for economic reform in New Zealand.

The result was fundamental economic liberalisation of New Zealand that opened its economy to the world with the removal of regulatory constraints on the free flow of goods and services. This required a radical restructuring of New Zealand business with some sectors surviving to become internationally competitive while some businesses, particularly in manufacturing, were unable to compete with the introduction of cheaper goods so went out of business. This restructuring created unemployment that continued throughout the 1990s. Bollard concludes with this assessment of the reforms as (1994, pp. 103–104):

> The timing was rushed and little attention was paid to sequencing. Consequently, despite some major achievements, a long transitional recession was encountered. The adjustment period was longer then envisaged, with beneficial results taking up to eight years to emerge. It is ironic that, in 1993, as the country is at last starting to feel the benefits of liberalisation, the public appears to have lost its appetite for further reform.

Allan Bollard correctly identified one of the major problems with the incorporation of globalisation policies into New Zealand, which was that little was done to assist the people through the transition from a social welfare state to a free market state. This disruption to the lives of many people therefore resulted in a sense of grievance and betrayal. Unemployment in particular created a sense of uncertainty and insecurity and was seen as being alien to New Zealand, which had prided itself on its low levels of unemployment. Easton (2008) noted that in 1952 two men were on the Department of Social Security's unemployment benefit, while the 2006 census reported that 106 000 were unemployed.

Unease amongst Labour Party members resulted in an organised economic debate within the party where the ministers were required to explain the policies to members of the party and receive an alternative view from economists and trade unionists. The general public however continued to support the government, which was returned with an increased majority in the 1987 election. The debate over the policies at the time descended into rhetoric, with globalisation being characterised as the salvation of New Zealand or the destruction of the New Zealand social welfare state (Kelsey, 1994).

The full effect of the new policy framework on the people was not apparent until after the financial crisis of 1987 and the extension of the policy framework to social policy in the form of social protection reform by the National government after 1990. By 1990 however, the globalisation agenda was firmly entrenched in New Zealand public policy and the reconstruction of the social protection system was under way. Easton (2008) sums up the position of New Zealand after the introduction of the neoliberal policy agenda as follows:

> Thus as the economy has changed, the labour market adapted, and the welfare state has changed too. In particular the increased openness of the New Zealand

> economy as it responded to the opportunities and changes in the world economy – to globalisation – has dramatically changed the welfare state as it was known fifty years ago.
>
> Nostalgia will not take us back to that state, nor do the nostalgic evidently want to give up the benefits of the opening up – especially the wider range of goods and services and opportunities that it has made possible.
>
> Of course we need to be aware of the downsides of globalisation – not everyone in the labour market is a beneficiary in the short, or, even the medium term. The challenge remains as how to minimise the resulting social distress, while maintaining the dynamism and flexibility in the labour market that is necessary to seize the opportunities that globalisation offers.

In the next section I shall address the affect of the globalisation on state institutions.

## 2.3 NEW ZEALAND CONCEPTION OF THE STATE

Attempts at a definition of the state have occupied many distinguished theorists and practitioners. Professor Bob Jessop (2006) argues that no single theory can capture the complexities of the state, but that no understanding of the state can be gained without an understanding of the society within which the state is situated, and concludes (2006, pp. 111, 129):

> Finally, it is increasingly recognised that an adequate theory of the state can only be produced as part of a wider theory of society. But this is precisely where we find many of the unsolved problems of state theory. For the state is the site of a paradox. On the one hand, it is just one institutional ensemble among others within a social function; on the other, it is peculiarly charged with overall responsibility for maintaining the cohesion of the formation of which it is a part. As both part and whole of society, it is continually asked by diverse social forces to resolve society's problems and is equally continually doomed to generate 'state failure' since many problems lie well beyond its control and even be aggravated by attempted intervention.

New Zealand is a good example of the state as a paradox with its lack of a formal written constitution, fragile constitutional institutions, and a commitment to pragmatic political and constitutional decision-making. Professor Jessop (2006, p. 124) also observes:

> the exercise and effectiveness of state power is a contingent product of a changing balance of political forces located within and beyond the state and that this balance is conditioned by the specific institutional structures and procedures of the state apparatus as embedded in the wider political system and environing societal relations.

In the context of the influence of globalisation, New Zealand provides an interesting case study of the interrelationship between the nature of political decision-making that resulted from fragile constitutional arrangements and the social forces within society on political decision-making.

The state in New Zealand is a fluid concept but is best understood as an initiative relationship between the people and political institutions. The relationship is direct and real and constantly evolving. Fundamental to the relationship between the people and the state is the notion and reality of a representative democracy expressed principally through the sovereignty of the institution of the parliament. The unicameral nature of the parliament provides for the directness of the relationship, and the fact one parliament cannot bind another results in a dynamic and uncertain relationship.

## 2.4 CONSTITUTIONAL FRAMEWORK

New Zealand has a fragile constitutional legal architecture. The Constitution Act 1986 describes the roles and function of the central constitutional institutions: the Head of State (the Queen of New Zealand and her representative, the Governor-General); the House of Representatives; the Executive, which must be appointed from elected members of parliament; the parliament that comprises the House of Representatives and the Sovereign; and the judiciary. There is no upper chamber, with the Legislative Council voting for its own demise in 1950 after the government of the day perceived that it offered little value to the governance of New Zealand. A promise to review the decision was never honoured and subsequent attempts to revive the notion of a second chamber of review have all failed.

The Constitution Act is not entrenched and can be amended or repealed by a simple majority in the House of Representatives (except for the term of government which requires a 75 per cent majority). The same formula is used with the Bill of Rights Act, the Human Rights Act and the Electoral Act (with the exception of specific provisions in s. 268 relating to elections that require a 75 per cent majority in parliament or a majority in a national referendum). In theory the legal constitutional framework can be changed at any time and the convention of parliaments not being bound by the decisions of previous parliaments provides the potential for instability. In practice, New Zealanders are reluctant to approve radical constitutional change. The speed with which the Fourth Labour government was able to implement the structural adjustment programme demonstrated the fragility of the constitutional institutions when providing a check on a government from exercising political power without restraint. The abuse of executive power by the Muldoon government in the 1970s is another example of the inability of the state institutions to provide a constraint of the power of the executive. It was obvious by the 1980s that New Zealand had a structural problem in its constitutional arrangements when it came to checking the power of the executive (Palmer, 2006, p. 1).

There is an aspect of New Zealand's notion of the state that is fundamental to its legal and constitutional structure but is often not recognised and that is the notion of the Crown. Although the Crown is often seen as a fig leaf to disguise the nature of political power residing in the state, McLean (2008) makes a powerful case for recognition of the fact the Crown affects all aspects of the state and its relationship with the people (2008, pp. 35, 37). Any change in the nature of the state, such as a move to becoming a republic, or moving to a closer relationship with Australia, would require a legal disengagement of some complexity, including a clarification of the rights and obligations under the Treaty of Waitangi. While these matters may appear to be of domestic nature only, if the forces of globalisation require closer relationships with other states or further international trade agreements, the notion of the Crown may provide an impediment to such a move either through a challenge in the courts or by invoking the Treaty of Waitangi obligations. Jane Kelsey (1999) has noted that the government was forced to negotiate with Maori over the Multilateral Agreement on Investment to ensure that Maori interests would be protected in accordance with the obligations under the Treaty of Waitangi (1999, pp. 339–342). The notion of the Crown highlights that New Zealand has always been connected to the world and influenced by it. For many, globalisation is just another form of colonisation and therefore just another challenge to preserving the sense and reality of national identity and control of decisions that affect New Zealanders.

## 2.5 THE PUBLIC SERVICE

New Zealand's constitutional, institutional and legal state framework is supported by a public service that is professional and independent of the government but, like other state institutions, lacks formal constitutional and legal recognition. John Martin (1990), a distinguished public servant and public sector commentator, has described the public service prior to globalisation as having three fundamental characteristics (1990, p. 123):

> It was *apolitical* (in the sense that hiring and firing was on merit and independent of political intervention); by and large, the system protected the *anonymity* of individual officials; and employment was predicated on a forty-year *career*

> in a unified service. Senior public servants were expected to provide 'free and frank', disinterested policy advice within the Westminster convention of ministerial responsibility and to administer departments 'efficiently and economically' within the rules laid down by the 'control agencies' – notably the State Services Commission (SSC) and the Treasury. The notion of the 'public interest' informed much of what was done. Within that framework, the activities of the State (and thus the bureaucracy) extended into new fields over the decades; the numbers employed and the share of national resources also expanded greatly.

This succinct description of the public services pre-globalisation sums up much of what was considered in need of reform by the advocates of the new public management theorists. The public service was a primary target for reform as much as the economic and social policies because it provided infrastructure support for the state's role of the delivery of social protection. Globalisation then influenced both policies and institutions of the state.

The globalisation programme for reform of the public sector included: selling state assets and privatising state activity; commercialising state activities through state-owned enterprises; and introducing the new public sector management that was based on an analytical framework grounded in public choice theory, managerialism and the new economics of organisations, in particular agency theory and transaction cost analysis (Treasury, 1987). Boston et al. (1991, p. 23), in his overview of the theoretical underpinnings of the public sector restructuring, concluded:

> Nevertheless the impact of the four bodies of theory examined here has been considerable. Not merely have they changed the language of political discourse, but they have also altered the way in which policy issues are defined, analysed, and understood. As a result, the policy agenda has been dominated in recent years by issues relating to the design of incentive structures and contracts, the analysis of alternative governance structures, the avoidance of interest group capture and bureaucratic capture, the pursuit of contestability and external contracting, the application of agent-principal models to a variety of relationships, the minimization of transaction cost and agency cost, and the specification of outputs and outcomes.

Although the public sector reforms have been much admired and discussed they did not fulfil their primary objective: to take the politics out of public policy. They were based on a fundamental distrust of politicians and the people who were assumed to always work in their self-interest. Basically the new public management policies, although designed to make the use of public resources more efficient, were in reality anti-democratic in their assumption that only an elite cadre of officials could be entrusted with making policies for the people. It was unsurprising then that since the 'high' period of globalisation in 1984–96, public sector management has been reviewed with a view to providing a better structure and theoretical framework that reflected the reality or the culture and history of New Zealand.

In 1996 the Schick Report was commissioned to provide a review of the public sector reforms. The review produced a mixed report on the success of the reforms at time when there was growing criticism of the public sector's role in the implementation of the globalisation framework (Kelsey, 1993, 1996). The Fifth Labour government in 2001 instituted a Review of the Centre that identified three priorities for change as being: a better-integrated, people-focussed service delivery; reducing fragmentation and improving the alignment of public services; and enhancing the people and culture in the state sector (Ministers of State Services and Finance, 2001). The changes made by the Fifth Labour government had significantly changed the neoliberal public sector reforms in an attempt to align them with the government's attempts to maintain an efficient public service while reintroducing social balance into policy-making (Boston and Eichbaum, 2007; Chapman and Duncan, 2007). The change of government in 2008 has seen a reversion to the notion of a 'small public sector' with cutbacks in staff and services. This policy has been introduced to address the affects of the 2008 economic recession and it is too soon to conclude whether they are part of an ideological swing back to the National government policies of the early 1990s.

## 2.6 THE LEGAL SYSTEM

Although the affects of globalisation have often focussed on the institutions of government and the public sector, they have also had an influence on the other important state institution: the legal system. For the legitimacy of the constitutional arrangements, the legal system must not only have the values of autonomy, transparency, accountability and efficiency, but it must also have stability and certainty to retain the confidence of the people who rely so heavily on it as a check against the power of the executive. The relationship between the executive, parliament and the courts has long been a contested area that has been characterised by many as a struggle over who makes law – the courts or parliament. Frequently this debate is constructed around the notion of the sovereignty of parliament that is strongly entrenched in New Zealand constitutional thinking.

Globalisation has raised the question whether parliament is the only source of law-making. International conventions, human rights declarations and international trade agreements are amongst the instruments that create legal obligations on citizens and organisations. Although international obligations require incorporation into New Zealand law, there is a practice for New Zealand to ratify through legislation (Kingsbury, 2008). While treaty-making is the prerogative of the executive, it is parliament that incorporates the international obligations and rights into domestic law. The courts however have played a significant role in ensuring that New Zealand acts consistently with its international obligations whether or not these have been incorporated into domestic legislation. Lord Cooke in *Tavita v Minister of Immigration* ([1994]) 'ushered in a new era in judicial use of international human rights obligation by New Zealand courts' (Geiringer, 2004). It was Sir Kenneth Keith however, who clearly articulated the principle for interpreting international obligation in his statement in *New Zealand Air Line Pilots Association Inc v Attorney-General* ([1997]) that:

> We begin with the presumption of statutory interpretation that so far as its wording allows legislation should be read in a way which is consistent with New Zealand's international obligations . . . That presumption may apply whether or not the legislation was enacted with the purpose of implementing the relevant text . . . In that type of case national legislation is naturally being considered in the broader international legal context in which it increasingly operates.

The development of domestic law incorporating human rights and civil and political rights has also raised the question of whether the courts can challenge legislation enacted by parliament that is inconsistent with those obligations. This increasing 'activism' by the courts cannot be directly attributed to globalisation but the more assertive approach of the courts in the protection of individual rights became apparent in the 1980s at around the same time as the neoliberal policy framework was enacted. The then Sir Robin Cooke in 1987 asserted:

> From the point of view of an appellate judge hearing cases day by day it seems more than a decade since the pretence of legal formalism was abandoned and much more open emphasis began to be placed on working out a philosophical approach – to use a somewhat pompous term to describe conscious value judgments . . .
>
> Direct debate of policy considerations, and with an eye to interests transcending those of the immediate parties has become commonplace. Without exaggeration it may be said to be regular fare in the Court of Appeal.

However it was the legal challenge to the State-Owned Enterprises Act by the Maori Council on the grounds it was contrary to the obligations under the Treaty of Waitangi that marked the beginning of a serious challenge to the sovereignty of Parliament (*Attorney-General v New Zealand Maori Council*, [1987]).

The effects of globalisation on the judicial system can also be assessed through institutional change, in particular the establishment of the New Zealand Supreme Court as the final court of appeal. The abolition of appeals to the Privy Council and the establishment of a final court of appeal was criticised as effecting a major constitutional change with implications for the relationship between the executive, parliament and the courts. There was a fear that the Supreme Court would challenge the sovereignty of parliament. In practice this has not occurred.

The most recent judicial statement on the relationship between the courts and the parliament in matters relating to the New Zealand Bill of Rights Act arose in *Boscawen v Attorney-General* ([2009]) where the Court of Appeal struck out an application to judicially review the Attorney General's decision not to issue a section 7 declaration of inconsistency report to the Electoral Finance Bill 2007. The court decided on the grounds of comity between the legislative and judicial branches not to review the decision of the Attorney General. This position of the New Zealand Court of Appeal accurately reflects the creative tension within the relationship.

The establishment of the New Zealand Supreme Court in 2004 as the final court of appeal thereby removing appeals to the Privy Council has enabled New Zealand to develop legal principles that reflect the needs of the New Zealand people and legal system. In the age of globalisation this can only be positive as it enforces the importance of the rule of law as an essential element of any New Zealand constitutional arrangements. Although this may be seen as obvious, Matthew Palmer (2007) noted that while the rule of law supported by judicial independence should be a cornerstone of New Zealand's constitution, he is not confident 'that New Zealanders currently understand the rule of law or, in a crunch, would necessarily stand by it as a fundamental constitutional norm' (2007, p. 589). He notes that the notions of representative democracy and parliamentary sovereignty attract much more public support as fundamental constitutional norms. For the rule of law to be an essential element of New Zealand's constitutional norms it must be seen to be relevant to the interests of New Zealand at a time when those interests may be threatened by the influence of globalisation.

## 2.7 ROLE OF THE PEOPLE

The importance of the institution of parliament in representing the views of the people in their decision-making was demonstrated in 1992 when the New Zealand people voted to replace the 'first past the post' electoral system with a mixed member proportional electoral system (MMP).

This electoral reform ensured that it was difficult for one political party to exercise power in parliament. As noted above, the neoliberal policy framework was implemented without a real informed mandate from the people. Although there was a willingness to trust the politicians to make the changes that were understood to be necessary given the reality of globalisation, there were limits to that trust. Therefore when in 1990 the new National government continued and extended the globalisation agenda, the people reacted by changing the electoral system to ensure there was greater representation in parliament and that there was a check on the power of the executive. The narrative about how this radical constitutional change was achieved gives an insight into the relationship between the people and the state institutions under globalisation. In also gives an understanding as to why flexibility, pragmatism and informality are defining characteristics of New Zealand's constitution. There is little respect for formality or tradition but an expectation that the will of the people will be heard and acted upon.

One of the failings of the neoliberal policy framework was to ignore the importance of the culture and the value system that lies within a community, however ill defined. The disjunction between the neoliberalism and the expectations of the people is seen in the most recent Public Values Survey. It reported that two-thirds of respondents followed politics in the news every day or several times a week; two-thirds reported they were very or fairly interested in politics; three-quarters had signed a petition and one in five had attended a demonstration (Perry and Howden-Chapman, 2005). This level of interest in politics may reflect the high expectations the people have of their governments to deliver services to them. The same survey reported that the vast majority considered that government should have a central role in: the provision of jobs; keeping prices under control; providing the elderly with a decent standard of living; providing decent housing; and that business should be subject to strict laws to prevent damage to the environment.

It can be seen that there are some obvious inconsistencies between the objectives of the globalisation agenda with the notion of the market governing public decision-making, and the people's expectation of their government to deliver the above services. There was also an underestimation of the people's engagement with the political system and their expectations of state institutions. The primary means for these expectations being fulfilled is through the general election that is held every three years. The vote is the only real check that the citizen has on the government and therefore the electors take the general election seriously. In the 1940s over 90 per cent took advantage of this right, but during the last three elections the percentage has fallen to around 80 per cent. Between elections

New Zealand citizens exercise their democratic right to participate in government decision-making formally through select committee hearings, or informally through direct contact with their member of parliament, organised interest groups, and direct action such as demonstrations. These tactics were all employed to effect electoral change. The road to MMP has also been described as 'a long and winding one' (James and Robie, 1993, pp. 121–135; Levine and Roberts, 1997).

Although there had been advocates for proportional representation in the 1920s, it was not until the 1970s that new trends began to emerge on the political landscape that ignited the campaign for electoral reform. Smaller political parties started to gain electoral support, but few seats in parliament; election campaigns focused on marginal seats; governments were elected with fewer votes than the opposition party; and the National government of the time exercised executive power in an arbitrary way that provoked public opposition. These developments raised questions of the legitimacy of the government and of the Representation Commission, an independent body with the responsibility for allocating electorate boundaries. It also started a debate on the whole nature of the electoral system.

Support for reform came from smaller political parties, community groups and the opposition Labour Party, which included in its election manifestos of 1981 and 1984 a promise to establish a Royal Commission to inquire into and report on (amongst other things) whether proportional representation or some other variant from the existing, 'first past the post' system should be introduced. Much of the activism of this period was driven by a post-war generation that challenged the traditional social and political institutions that no longer reflected their needs and interests.

When the Labour Party was elected in 1984 it established a Royal Commission on the Electoral System with comprehensive terms of reference to review all aspects of the electoral system (Royal Commission Report on the Electoral System, 1986). The commission report found that the electoral system was unfair in many respects, in particular to minor parties and Maori. Amongst its many recommendations was the adoption of an MMP electoral system similar to that in Germany.

Although the recommendation encouraged the electoral reform movement, there was resistance in Cabinet to change, so little happened until the 1987 election when David Lange misread his notes for a television interview during the election campaign and promised a referendum on electoral reform. Although this surprised most Labour supporters it was quickly affirmed as party policy for the election. Labour won the election and started to have second thoughts on a referendum. The prospect of sharing power was not appealing to many and it was difficult to envisage how any arrangements could work with political opponents.

The 1990 election campaign provided another of those electoral reform surprises when Jim Bolger, the then leader of the National Party, committed his party to a referendum on electoral reform before the end of 1992 (Thompson, 2008). There was little support in the National Party for electoral reform but bound by the election promise the decision was made for an indicative referendum on whether a change was supported, and if the majority voted yes, then the referendum offered a choice of four different electoral systems, including MMP. The expectation was that there would be little support for change. The policies of globalisation by 1992 had however, lost substantial public support. Public opinion polls recorded in 1992, the year of the referendum, that confidence in politicians and parliament had fallen to 4 per cent (McRobie, 1993).

Although only 55.2 per cent voters voted in the 1992 indicative referendum, 84.7 per cent supported a change in the system and 84 per cent of those who voted for change voted for MMP. The result was too great to ignore by any political party, so preparations were made for a second referendum to be held in conjunction with the next general election in 1993. A bill was prepared to put in place the legislative framework for an MMP electoral system if the referendum delivered that result. The campaign around the referendum was vigorous, with several politicians and the business community providing an opposing argument for reform. The referendum attracted votes from 82.2 per cent of the voters, of whom 53.9 per cent voted for MMP. The provisions of the new Electoral Act 1993 then came into force, including the Representation Commission promulgating new electoral boundaries with the 95 general electorates being reduced to 60, including five Maori seats, and for 60 party list seats. New Zealand had radically changed its electoral system in a way that could not have been envisaged by politicians or commentators at the time.

As can be seen the road to electoral reform was long and tortuous but ultimately successful. The reform of the electoral system was achieved through a combination of political action from within and outside parliament, and political accident in the form of two political leaders unexpectedly committing their parties to electoral reform. The grassroots community campaigns combined with the political advocacy from parliamentarians such as Sir Geoffrey Palmer enabled the campaign to be sustained and take advantage of the opportunities presented by David Lange and Jim Bolger.

The question has been asked whether the new electoral system has in fact achieved greater representation from across the community. The statistics would indicate that this objective has been partially achieved, with an increase in the number of women, Maori, Pacific peoples and people of Asian descent in the current parliament (NZ General Election

Results, 2008). The question of whether the new electoral arrangements have provided a check on the power of the executive is more difficult to access. However there is evidence that it takes longer to enact legislation, the coalition government requires more consultation and negotiation of policy, and the select committee process provides transparency of executive decision-making (Malone, 2008).

Transparency is the lifeblood of democracy and it is obvious that it remains a constant struggle to know what decisions are being made when the cloak of secrecy is invoked in the name of commercial sensitivity, or the need to maintain confidentiality in trade negotiations that could fundamentally change access to goods and services for New Zealanders (Kelsey, 2010). The two major current challenges to New Zealanders from globalisation are the various international trade agreements that bind New Zealand to obligations that threaten its autonomy, and the reconstruction of the social welfare state to reflect both the realities of globalisation and the wish of the New Zealand people to provide a level of social protection for people in need and provide equal opportunities for all through the public provision of health and education services, and adequate housing, clean water and a safe environment. The two issues are interrelated as international obligations constrain domestic decision-making which may be characterised as anti-competitive.

## 2.8 CONCLUSION

I have argued that New Zealand has faced various challenges from globalisation since colonisation. The latest wave that hit New Zealand in 1984 in the wake of the introduction of the radical neoliberal policy framework by the Fourth Labour government has been the most comprehensive because of the impact of technology. The impact through the initial economic and social policies and the restructuring of the public sector in accordance with the new public management ideology was considerable. The effect on the democratic process was also radical with the people voting through two referenda to replace the 'first past the post' electoral system with the German model of a mixed membership proportional electoral system. The effect of this electoral reform was to change the nature of the parliament to make it more representative of the people, and to curb the power of the executive in its decision-making. The purpose of the reforms was to enable a more transparent political system in which the community could participate through contributing to policy-making.

A more subtle change has also taken place within the court system and its relationship to the executive and parliament. While the comity principle still prevails there is a greater expectation that the courts will protect the rights of the individual against the executive if it does not comply with its own laws. While the normal legal challenge is through administrative law remedies, the incorporation of international obligations into domestic law has raised potential areas of conflict. The recognition of international obligations can be a double-edged sword however. Those who applaud the recognition of human rights obligations may be less comfortable with the legal enforcement of obligations under the international trade agreements. It is likely that in the future the courts will face major challenges as they navigate through the realities of international obligations and individual citizens' and institutions' rights.

While New Zealand appeared to enthusiastically embrace the rhetoric and policies of globalisation from 1984 to 1993, since that time there has been a more contested questioning of globalisation. This process has been conducted through the democratic institutions of governance and is still ongoing as New Zealand struggles to find a balance between the reality of globalisation and the desire to maintain control over its own affairs. The jury is out over whether it will succeed in finding that balance, and history would advise that it is a struggle that has been forever with New Zealand and will remain so.

New Zealanders have always had a strong sense of their own identity while embracing that of others. They have also had a strong belief and confidence in their ability to influence events that affect them and exercised that confidence through the political system. Whether that belief and confidence will be enough in the future, time will tell.

## REFERENCES

Arthurs, H.W. (2009), 'Law and Learning in an Era of Globalization', *German Law Journal*, **10**, 629–640.

*Attorney-General v New Zealand Maori Council* [1987] 1 NZLR 641 (CA).

Bertram, G. (2009), 'The New Zealand Economy, 1900–2000', in G. Byrnes (ed.), *The New Oxford History of New Zealand*, Melbourne, Australia and Auckland, New Zealand: Oxford University Press, pp. 537–572.

Bollard, A. (1994), 'New Zealand', in J. Williamson (ed.), *The Political Economy of Policy Reform*, Washington, DC: Institute for International Economics, pp. 73–110.

*Boscawen v Attorney-General* [2009] 2 NZLR 299 (CA).

Boston, J. and C. Eichbaum (2007), 'State Sector Reform and Renewal in New Zealand: Lessons for Governance' in Gerald E. Caiden and Tsai-Tsu Su (eds), *The Repositioning of Public Governance: Global Experience and Challenges*, Taipei: Best-Wise Publishing Co., pp. 127–179.

Boston, J., P. Dalziel and S. St John (eds) (1999), *Redesigning the Welfare State in*

*New Zealand: Problems, Policies, Prospects*, Auckland, New Zealand: Oxford University Press.

Boston, J., J. Martin, J. Pallot, and P. Walsh (1991), *Reshaping the State: New Zealand's Bureaucratic Revolution*, Auckland, New Zealand: Oxford University Press.

Chapman, J. and G. Duncan (2007), 'Is There Now a New "New Zealand Model"?' *Public Management Review*, **9**(1), 1–25.

Clark, M. (ed.) (1992), *The Labour Party after 75 Years*, Victoria University of Wellington, New Zealand: Occasional Publication No 4 Department of Politics.

Clark, M. (ed.) (2005), *For the Record: Lange and the Fourth Labour Government*, Wellington, New Zealand: Dunmore Press.

Clark, M. (ed.) (2008), *The Bolger Years 1990–1997*, Wellington, New Zealand: Dunmore Press.

Cooke, Sir R. (1987), 'The New Zealand National Legal Identity', *Canterbury Law Review*, **3**, 171.

Easton, B. (2008), 'The Globalisation of a Welfare State', in N. Lunt, M. O'Brien and R. Stephens (eds), *New Zealand, New Welfare*, Melbourne, Australia: Cengage Learning.

English, Hon B. (2011), '2011 Budget: Minister's Executive Summary', accessed 10 November 2011 at www.treasury.govt.nz/budget/2011/execsumm.

Farrar, J.H., L. Parsons and P.I. Joubert (2009), 'The Development of an Appropriate Regulatory Response to the Global Financial Crisis', *Bond Law Review*, **21**(3), 1–41.

Geiringer, C. (2004), 'Tavita and All That: Confronting the Confusion Surrounding Unincorporated Treaties and Administrative Law', *NZULR*, **21**, 66.

Hay, C. (2006), 'Globalisation and Public Policy', in M. Moran, M. Rein and R.E. Goodin (eds), *The Oxford Handbook of Public Policy*, Oxford: Oxford University Press, pp. 587–604.

International Labour Organization (2011), 'Social Protection Floor for a Fair and Inclusive Globalisation', Report of the Advisory Group chaired by Michelle Bachelet, accessed 10 November 2011 at www.ilo.org/global/publications.

James, C. and A. Robie (1993), *Turning Point: The 1993 Election and Beyond*, Wellington, New Zealand: Bridget Williams Books.

Jessop, C. (2006), 'The State and State Building', in R.A.W. Rhodes, S.A. Binder and B.A. Rockman (eds), *The Oxford Handbook of Political Institutions*, Oxford: Oxford University Press, pp. 111–130.

Keith, Sir Kenneth, *New Zealand Air Line Pilots Association Inc v Attorney-General* [1997] 3 NZLR 269, 293 (CA).

Kelsey, J. (1993), *Rolling Back the State*, Wellington, New Zealand: Bridget Williams Books.

Kelsey, J. (1994), *The New Zealand Experiment: A World Model for Structural Adjustment?* Auckland, New Zealand: Auckland University Press and Bridget Williams Books.

Kelsey, J. (1996), *Economic Fundamentalism: The New Zealand Experiment, A World Model for Structural Adjustment*, London: Pluto Press.

Kelsey, J. (1999), *Reclaiming the Future: New Zealand and the Global Economy*, Wellington, New Zealand: Bridget Williams Books.

Kelsey, J. (2010), *No Ordinary Deal: Unmasking Free Trade and the Trans-Pacific Partnership Agreement*, Wellington, New Zealand: Bridget Williams Books.

Kingsbury, B. (2008), 'Global Administrative Law: Implications for National Courts', in C. Geiringer and D.R. Knight (eds), *Seeing the Whole World: Essays in Honour of Sir Kenneth Keith*, Wellington, New Zealand: Victoria University Press in association with New Zealand Centre for Public Law, pp. 101–125.
Levine, S. and N.S. Roberts (1997), 'MMP: The Decision' in R. Miller (ed.), *New Zealand Politics in Transition*, Auckland, New Zealand: Oxford University Press, pp. 25–48.
Malone, R. (2008), *Rebalancing the Constitution: The Challenge of Government Law-Making Under MMP*, Wellington, New Zealand: Institute of Policy Studies, Victoria University of Wellington.
Mandelson, P. (2011), 'The World is Not Flat', Speech to the London Stock Exchange, accessed 10 November 2011 at http://www.ippr.org/press-release/111/2465/mandelson-the-world-is-not-flat.
Martin, J. (1990), 'Remaking the State Services', in M. Holland and J. Boston (eds), *The Fourth Labour Government: Politics and Policy in New Zealand*, 2nd edn, Auckland, New Zealand: Oxford University Press, pp. 123–139.
McAloon, J. (2009), 'The New Zealand Economy, 1792–1914', in G. Byrnes (ed.), *The New Oxford History of New Zealand*, Melbourne, Australia and Auckland, New Zealand: Oxford University Press, pp. 197–218.
McLean, J. (2008), 'Crown Him with Many Crowns: The Crown and the Treaty of Waitangi', *NZJPIL*, **6**(1), 35–58.
McRobie, A. (1993), 'A Question of Fairness', in C. James and A. McRobie (eds), *Turning Point: The 1993 Election and Beyond*, Wellington, New Zealand: Bridget Williams Books, pp. 123–127.
Ministers of State Services and Finance (2001), *Report of the Advisory Group on the Review of the Centre*, accessed 10 November 2011 at http://www.ssc.govt.nz/sites/all/files/review_of_centre.
New Zealand General Election Results (2008), accessed 10 November 2011 at http://www.parliament.nz/FinalResults2008Election1.pdf.
Nolan, M. (2007), 'The Reality and Myth of New Zealand Egalitarianism: Explaining the Pattern of Labour Historiography at the Edge of the Empire', *Labour History Review*, **72**(2), 113–134.
Palmer, Rt Hon. G. (2006), 'The Cabinet, the Prime Minister and the Constitution', *NZJPIL*, **4**(1), 1–36.
Palmer, M.S.R. (2007), 'New Zealand Constitutional Culture', *NZULR*, **22**(4), 565–597.
Perry, P. and P. Howden-Chapman (2005), *Public Life Values: A Report from New Zealand Values Study*, Wellington, New Zealand: Centre for Social and Health Outcomes Research and Evaluation, Wellington School of Medicine and Associate Professor P. Howden-Chapman.
Royal Commission Report on the Electoral System (1986), 'Towards a Better Democracy', *AJHR*, **H**(3), 28, 302.
Schick, A. (1996), *The Spirit of Reform: Managing the New Zealand State Sector in a Time of Change*, Wellington, New Zealand: State Services Commission.
Slaughter, A.M. (1996), *A New World Order*, Princeton, NJ: Princeton University Press.
Strange, S. (1996), *The Retreat of the State: the Diffusion of Power on the World Economy*, Cambridge: Cambridge University Press.
*Tavita v Minister of Immigration* [1994] 2 NZLR 257 (CA) Lord Cooke.
Thompson, G. (2008), 'Preparing the Party for MMP', in M. Clark (ed.),

*The Bolger Years:1990–1997*, Auckland, New Zealand: Dunmore Publishing, pp. 15–19.
Treasury (1987), 'Government Management: Brief to the Incoming Government', Wellington, New Zealand: The Treasury.
UN System Chief Executives Board for Coordination (2009), 'The Global Financial Crisis and Its Impact on the Work of the UN System', accessed 10 November 2011 at www.ilo.org/gimi/gess/RessShowResource.do?resourceld=12603.
Wilkinson, R. and K. Pickett (2010), *The Spirit Level: Why Equality is Better for Everyone*, London: Penguin Books.
Wilson, M. (1989), *Labour Party in Government 1984–1987*, Wellington, New Zealand: Allen & Unwin.

# 3. Rebuilding state systems post-GFC: the South African case

**Laurence Boulle***

## 3.1 INTRODUCTION

Economic globalisation has occasioned several paradoxes for contemporary state systems. On the one hand it has deprived them of domestic policy space, a result both of legal instruments having delegated to international institutions significant areas of national sovereignty and of market pressures having necessitated state compliance with global economic norms. On the other hand the gaps and inconsistencies in the governance of globalisation have required the retention, and in some areas the strengthening, of state systems to fill the spaces in the legal infrastructure on which it depends (Boulle, 2010). All state systems are affected by these contradictory impulses, but in different ways and in varying degrees. In some countries there has been virtual surrender by a state of the levers of economic, monetary and fiscal policy, while in others the state has retained relatively strong supervision over these mechanisms.

The global financial crisis (GFC) has contributed to the contradictory tendencies of the globalisation project in respect of state systems. This chapter examines some implications of the GFC for the South African state system. Given the nascent nature of the state system in its current iteration it is, however, relevant to refer initially to its background and genesis, before investigating the implications of the GFC for its current 'rebuilding'. This is necessarily a contingent examination, given the reality that while the GFC commenced in 2008 it is continuing in different manifestations to times and destinations unknown. Moreover while the repercussions of 'GFC-past' have not been as pronounced for the South African state as they have been for some state systems, it remains a matter of speculation as to what the repercussions of 'GFC-present' will be.

The theoretical framework for this chapter is found in the tensions among three contrasting types of forces operating on the South African state system. The first are the pervasive universal forces of economic globalisation, within which the GFC has introduced a particular set of demands and pressures. The second are the domestic political forces operating endogenously in a country with an apartheid legacy, high social expectations and pressing economic challenges. The third is a constitutional system which, beyond its normal governance enabling and constraining functions, enjoins the state to promote specific policies designed to liberate the country from past injustices. While there may at times be coincidence of direction between two of the different forces, the coalescence of all three is an unlikely eventuality, a theme considered in relation to specific topics raised in the chapter.

In the context of the above framework, five predominant themes are explored in the chapter:

1. The nature of South Africa's current state system in the context of the endemic political economy of the country and the relatively recent transition to constitutional democracy.
2. The relationships among the state, government and the ruling party, which in the developing world are of greater significance than in most advanced economies.
3. The nature of both the inherited and the constitutionalised legal systems in the country and their implications for the operations and responsiveness of state organs.
4. The state's mandated responsibilities towards socio-economic rights in a context of high social expectations of, and ubiquitous international pressures on, the domestic political economy.
5. The relationship between the state and the global economy and the impact of the GFC on the state system, as illustrated through selected issues of current significance.

The themes are brought together in the final section of the chapter, revolving around the tensions inherent in the tripartite framework referred to above. This includes the pressures on contemporary states to bring domestic policies and practices into alignment with the policies and principles of the market economy and globalisation, and the contradictory propensity for electoral priorities to prevail over judgement of the market in countries in which the state is obliged to provide extensive social services or is confronted with serious economic problems.[1] Here it is inevitable that in the social wreckage of the GFC the democratic pulse in many nation states beats more strongly than the pulse of the market and globalisation, but the relative precedence of the market and politics is usually a factor of ambiguity and indeterminacy.

## 3.2 THE ECONOMIC AND CONSTITUTIONAL CONTEXT

Given the recent major restructuring of the state system in South Africa it is necessary to provide some institutional background to GFC-related issues. In 1994 a sophisticated Constitution was introduced into post-apartheid South Africa in a country which has the following contemporary economic and social profile.

South Africa has a population of over 50 million people and the gross domestic product (GDP) was US$527.5 billion in 2010, the 26th largest in the world and the biggest in Africa, accounting for over 30 per cent of combined pan-African GDP.[2] The country has a diversified economy dominated by the services sector (65 per cent), followed by manufacturing, mining and agriculture. It has no oil but extensive coal reserves and has been a world pioneer in producing oil from coal. It is the world's largest producer of platinum, manganese and chrome but has dropped from first to fifth-largest producer of gold in the last two decades. It has traditionally exported food and agricultural products but in recent years has for the first time become a net importer of food, a significant concern in a world facing food insecurity. Inward foreign direct investment (FDI) is relatively low by emerging market standards and in some years South Africa is a net exporter of investment capital. In relation to trade its major export markets are China (its main trading partner), the United States (US), Japan, Germany, the United Kingdom (UK) and sub-Saharan Africa, and its imports derive mainly from China, Germany, the US, Saudi Arabia and Japan. South Africa currently has a relatively low level of economic growth (latest International Monetary Fund estimates are 3.9 per cent pa for 2011) and significant inequality (it competes for top spot on the Gini coefficient table).[3] This is not a society in which a 'demographic dividend' has brought economic benefits,[4] the official level of unemployment being nearly 30 per cent and the unofficial level considerably higher. In terms of business regulation South Africa ranks 21st out of 48 countries in the Organisation for Economic Co-operation and Development's (OECD) Regulatory Restrictiveness Index.[5] The 2010 Global Integrity Report, covering 36 countries, accorded South Africa a moderate overall score of 79 out of 100, with an implementation score of 70 (which is considered weak) but with strengths in the legal framework which scored 88. The country has a relatively low national debt of approximately 40 per cent of annual GDP.

Subsequent to the initial democratic elections in 1994, held in terms of an interim Constitution developed by a multi-party convention, the current South African Constitution was enacted in 1996 by the first democratic parliament. It was subsequently reviewed and approved by the Constitutional Court in terms of principles contained in the interim Constitution and reflecting its political genesis.[6] The outcome was a sophisticated constitutional system incorporating liberal features, such as the separation of powers doctrine, independent courts and a bill of rights; progressive features, such as enforceable socio-economic rights and transformation imperatives; and globalist features, such as the prospective incorporation of international law principles by domestic courts. Parliamentary sovereignty in the old regime was replaced by constitutional supremacy, with the legislative, executive and administrative branches of government now subject to constitutional norms enforced by the courts; while constitutional supremacy has deep roots in other state systems, it was an innovation in the South African context where parliamentary sovereignty had provided few checks and balances on the apartheid regime. The new constitutional order further diffused authority among national, provincial and local governments,[7] and a strong participatory principle informed all levels of government. The liberal and progressive tendencies were destined sometimes to come into conflict with each other, as were the federalist and centralising impulses in the system, the equality and transformation objectives, and the majoritarian and consociational principles also built into the constitutional framework. These tensions have tended to be reinforced by the pressures for rapid and exact executive action required by the vicissitudes of economic globalisation and the GFC.

The South Africa Constitution and electoral arrangements support a multi-party proportional representation system, though one ruling party has tended to be dominant during the democratic era. There is an independent central bank and a highly efficient revenue service. Apart from traditional governmental ministries and departments, Chapter 9 of the Constitution, headed 'State Institutions Supporting Constitutional Democracy', establishes a group of institutions designed to strengthen constitutional democracy in the country.[8] These include the offices of Public Protector, the Human Rights Commission, the Auditor-General and the Independent Electoral Commission. In each case the institutions are structurally and financially independent of the executive arm of government and are mandated to operate impartially; moreover other organs of state are required to assist these institutions to ensure their independence and effectiveness. Inevitably the Chapter 9 institutions create tensions within the state system as their monitoring, investigative and reporting activities are not always welcomed by government. There is provision for conventional departments of state under the political leadership of ministers responsible to the legislature and in respect of at least one department, the police service, which is not a Chapter 9 institution, the independence from government of its corruption-related functions has come before the Constitutional Court in a controversial recent case, dealt with below.

At the apex of the political-legal system is a Constitutional Court of 11 judges which can adjudicate on all matters with a constitutional element.[9] In the South African context this entails a broad jurisdiction over matters ranging from separation of powers restraints to citizens' rights to water, housing and anti-retroviral drugs, on which case illustrations are provided below. Since the advent of democracy South African courts, and in particular the Constitutional Court, have ranged far and wide in accessing relevant comparative jurisprudence from other legal systems, and have in turn been cited by courts in those jurisdictions. This feature of the legal system is considered in more detail below.

Of major significance in the new constitutional-legal regime was not only the constitutionalisation of citizens' socio-economic rights, referred to shortly, but also the capacity for parliament to legislate for norms of social behaviour, or at least to attempt to create a new moral order free from the discriminatory and exploitative practices of the past. Societal engineering is thus a constitutional imperative for the South Africa state. This is referred to in the Constitution as 'transformation', a more nuanced version of 'affirmative action', but in the local context it is aimed at the overwhelming majority of the population and not at minority groups.[10] The transformation dictate affects not only state agencies but also, in varying degrees, entities in the private sector. It finds expression in the policy of Broad-Based Black Economic Empowerment (B-BBEE) which is designed to empower black citizens economically and lead to a distribution of wealth in society as a whole. B-BBEE has a general legislative basis[11] and specific charters, developed by government, industry, unions and civil society, in different economic sectors.[12] In broad terms it envisages direct empowerment through black equity ownership and management, and indirect empowerment through employment equity, skills development, preferential procurement and socio-economic development. It entails potential conflicts with other constitutional norms and with international economic law principles.

Despite the sophistication of the constitutional system the new state, from its inception, had problems in developing capacity in different institutions and agencies, a problem exacerbated by its rapid accession to the global community after decades of political and economic isolation.[13] The need for developing human capital was affected by negative legacies at all levels of the educational system, by the absence of meritocracy in some public appointments and by rent-seeking behaviour in different institutions, exacerbated by periodic losses of human capital through emigration. The capacity shortfalls had inevitable implications for the functioning of state institutions and the long-term performance of the national economy.

At the same time unemployment, inequality and high social expectations imposed considerable pressures on the stability of the state because of difficulties in delivering basic social services. Effective interaction with the international community, including transnational corporations, was also necessarily affected by a lack of capacity and experience in key state bodies operating at this level. Inherent tensions within the constitutional system and the realities of strident political expression contributed to the challenges for the state system.

In comparative terms the current South African state system displays some ironic differences from that under the apartheid regime. The old order suffered from a major democratic deficit but there was no shortage of governance, the regime proscribing all manner of activities, including love and lust across the colour line. Under the new order the democratic deficit has been replaced with a highly participatory polity but there is a governance deficit in terms of state organs' capacity for ensuring service delivery in areas such as health, education and housing, and in providing compliance with sophisticated legislation and constitutional obligations, including in the provision of socio-economic rights. There is evidence that even where state resources are available, lack of experience and capacity leads to shortcomings in expending budgetary allocations.[14] This provides challenges for the state under conditions of globalisation as the contemporary state is not only about constitutional governance, in the traditional sense of the term, but also about economic governance. Capacity needs are more conspicuous where the South African state is required to engage on advantageous terms with advanced and other emerging economies. Against the background of a historically poor educational system and increasing social demands on the administrative state, economic growth strategies, industrial policies and capacity-building measures are major imperatives, as is shown below, despite their potential conflict with market principles.

This section's outline of the social and constitutional context of the South African state indicates the structural basis of the tensions referred to in the opening paragraphs. A modernising polity is required to respond to immanent pressures for state-provided social reforms while simultaneously accommodating globalisation norms and complying with sophisticated constitutional principles. The interaction among state, government and party is a significant factor within this crucible.

## 3.3 THE STATE AND THE LEGAL SYSTEM

Legal systems are significant in terms of how states respond and adapt to globalisation imperatives and how the state and private economic power are held to account. The heterogeneous South African legal system has an important constitutional significance, drawing as it does on Dutch jurists of the seventeenth century, and occasionally on Justinian's Corpus Iuris, as well as on varied modern sources of law (Rajak, 2011).[15] While this legal regime was not an effective bulwark against governmental excesses of the apartheid state it is, as an uncodified civil law system, open to growth and comparative influences. Historically the legal system was able to accommodate the intrusions of English law, and in parts to be subsumed by the invasive species, leaving a regime broadly supportive of the market, trade and commerce. There is a legacy of a legal system remarkably open to comparative and international influences. Its pluralistic tendencies have been reinforced by new constitutional principles, such as a requirement that the common law be developed in accordance with the spirit, purpose and objects of the Bill of Rights, referred to further below,[16] and that the legal system be open to African customary law[17] and to relevant international law influences.

Whereas parliamentary sovereignty in pre-1994 South Africa could override common law principles, including basic human liberties and the balance between law-making and law-application, the primacy of the democratic Constitution affords a dominant status to key elements of the legal system. There is now an overlay of constitutionalism on virtually all questions coming before the courts for determination. The openness of the legal system to international norms[18] is epitomised by the fact that customary international law is binding in the courts unless contrary to the Constitution or an Act of Parliament. There is also an injunction to courts when interpreting legislation to prefer any reasonable interpretation that is consistent with international law over an interpretation inconsistent with that regime. In overall terms the South African Constitution can be said to explicitly 'internationalise' the legal system,[19] part of the Constitution's globalisation tendency referred to above.

While even in its isolated phase South African case law exploited relevant jurisprudence from both European and common law countries, it now ranges globally in its selection of persuasive judgments, and is in turn cited by other jurisdictions.[20] This is particularly the case in relation to the universal constitutional and human rights issues of the day. These tendencies are accentuated by the recent emergence of a global 'community of courts' and increased globalised judicial thinking effectuated through both the ready accessibility of comparative legal precedents and extensive professional interactions among judges of the world (Slaughter, 2003). The internationalisation of legal practice has also reached South African shores, *inter alia* with the take-over of one of the largest national legal practices by a global mega-firm,[21] a reflection of the globalisation tendencies in other parts of the legal system (Hiscock and Caenegem, 2010).

As regards the requirement for the (Roman Dutch) common law to be developed in light of the Bill of Rights, this has potential implications for the traditional common law disciplines of contract, delict (tort) and property law. In the South African context it also invites prospective actions against the state and in one such situation the Constitutional Court was required to interpret the constitutional obligation under discussion. In the case of *Carmichele v Minister of Safety and Security*[22] the specific issue for determination was whether the concept of 'wrongfulness' in the law of delict should be broadened in accordance with the state's constitutional duty to safeguard the rights of women.[23] The applicant sued the state for damages resulting from a brutal attack on her from a person awaiting trial for attempted rape, the authorities having recommended to court his release on bail. At trial and on appeal the courts held that the applicant had not established that the police and prosecution had a duty of care towards her, despite the state's constitutional obligations in respect of rights to life, equality, freedom and security.[24]

The actual constitutional issue was first raised on appeal to the Constitutional Court which upheld the appeal, holding that while law reform was mainly the province of the legislature, courts had a subsidiary role to develop the common law when it deviated from the Bill of Rights. The court held that the state's constitutional responsibilities extended to both the police and the prosecution who could be found to have negligently failed in their duty to the claimant by omitting to produce before the court relevant evidence relating to the bail decision. This approach hinged very much on the constitutional and international law obligation to protect the freedom and security of women and prevent gender-based discrimination. The appellant having established a cause of action against the authorities, the matter was referred back to the High Court where the state could lead evidence as to whether on the facts it should be held liable for damages.

While this case involves what might be regarded as a healthy ingress of international norms into domestic law, the Constitutional Court has also shown more controversial deference to this influence. The case of *Glenister v President of the Republic of South Africa and Others*[25] raised issues surrounding public corruption and its investigation by independent authorities. Glenister, a prominent businessman, challenged a decision of the President to abolish an independent investigative unit, the Directorate of Special Operations, which was empowered[26] to investigate and institute criminal proceedings relating to organised crimes and other specified offences. In its stead the President signed into law a new section of the legislation regulating the police service,[27] creating a Directorate of Priority

Crime Investigation. The constitutional issue hinged around the extent to which the new unit within the police service was able to accommodate the need for an independent anti-corruption agency.

Both majority and minority judgments in a narrowly divided court emphasised the importance of the state fighting official corruption and the need for a body sufficiently protected from political interference to do so. The minority held that the new unit was sufficiently protected from such interference, the legislation providing adequate checks and balances to ensure it would not be 'subject to undue influence' by politicians. A more controversial majority judgment relied extensively on international law principles, finding that the legislative provision was unconstitutional inasmuch as it contravened the requirement of autonomy from the political branches of government. In explicating s. 39 of the Constitution, namely that 'when interpreting the Bill of Rights, a court must consider international law', the judgment relied on international covenants such as the 2004 United Nations Convention against Corruption, the 2001 United Nations Convention against Transnational Organized Crime and the 2003 African Union Convention on Preventing and Combating Corruption.[28] The *Glenister* decision signals the Constitutional Court's willingness to be 'bound' by these international instruments though none is reflected in constitutional provisions; it shows a high point in the internalisation of international legal norms. Needless to say judgments such as these are not well received in government and other state institutions responsible for policy development.[29]

In one important respect the legal system has avoided the impulse to internationalise, namely in its procedural dimensions. In the paradox encountered in other post-colonial situations, aspects of the legal system have been frozen in some areas in which the former colonial power has since introduced progressive reforms. This includes legal procedures in civil courts where the litigation management arrangements introduced in many jurisdictions around the world have largely bypassed the local court systems. In areas such as case flow management, e-filing, pre-trial settlement procedures and the incorporation of alternative dispute resolution (ADR) into the litigation system there has been little progressive modernisation. South Africa has also been slow to follow many comparative precedents in legislating to update and expedite its arbitration procedures, to incorporate domestically the UNCITRAL Model Laws on Arbitration and Conciliation,[30] or otherwise to make its legal system attractive for choice of law, choice of forum and enforceable dispute resolution purposes.[31] This can be seen as detrimental to a state's need to provide both substantive and procedural laws conducive to trade, business and investment. There would be no constitutional impediment to these reforms and they would be compatible with relevant global norms but have not proved to be a priority in a judicial system inundated with endemic legal issues, as shown in the following section.

## 3.4 THE STATE AND SOCIO-ECONOMIC RIGHTS

A major innovation for the South African political and legal systems relates to the democratic state's new-found obligations towards its citizens, and others, in respect of the socio-economic rights enumerated in the Constitution. Here the constitutional Bill of Rights includes provisions on enforceable socio-economic rights relating to education, health care, food, water, the environment and access to housing. This is an example of the progressive tendencies referred to earlier. During the pre-1994 negotiations it was resolved that under the new regime socio-economic rights would be entrenched to counteract the negative legacies of the apartheid system. This was a major responsibility for the new state, involving a category of rights not similarly entrenched in jurisdictions with liberal constitutions based on social contract principles. Whereas Bills of Rights have traditionally comprised negative charters of liberties based on civil and political rights,[32] the South African Constitution incorporated, alongside the traditional liberal rights, a range of socio-economic rights of a positive nature involving an active role for state instrumentalities.

The new rights posed challenges to the separation of powers doctrine, at least to the extent that courts could direct governments to provide specific social services. As state functions are multi-variable and interconnected with one another, the court-mandated provision of social services in one area would, under conditions of resource scarcity, necessarily have implications in other areas – the predicament of polycentricity in decision-making. In anticipation of these difficulties the socio-economic rights prescribed in the Constitution were infused with qualifications relating to their enforceability. The rights to housing, health care, food, water and social security were qualified by the provision that the state should:

1. take reasonable legislative and other measures;
2. within its available resources;
3. to achieve the progressive realisation of these rights.[33]

The qualifications were designed to mitigate the factor of polycentricity referred to above, and to reduce the danger of the separation of powers principle being breached. However the question of what constitutes 'reasonable legislative and other measures' was predictive of uncertainty, equivocation and disputation – the latter inevitably materialising.[34] The meaning of the 'reasonableness' standard was discussed and established in the groundbreaking judgment of the Constitutional Court in the case of *Grootboom*.[35]

Irene Grootboom and others had been evicted from their informal homes, situated on private land earmarked for formal low-cost housing by the Cape Town local council. They applied for orders requiring government to provide them with adequate basic shelter or housing until they obtained permanent accommodation. The case revolved around the state's obligations in relation to the universal right of access to adequate housing and children's rights to shelter, as prescribed in the Constitution.[36] The court noted that the Constitution obliges the state to act positively to ameliorate the plight of thousands of people living in deplorable conditions throughout the country, including the provision of housing and shelter, to those unable to support themselves and their dependants. The court stressed that all rights in the Bill of Rights are interrelated and mutually supportive, holding for example that human dignity, freedom and equality are denied to those without food, clothing or shelter. This was to give potential substance to rights often accorded only nominal significance in other state systems.

As regards the qualifying conditions relating to socio-economic rights, referred to above, the court indicated that the state must foster conditions that enable citizens to gain access to land on an equitable basis, but this does not oblige government to go beyond available resources or to realise the rights immediately. The state must nevertheless give effect to the rights and, in appropriate circumstances, courts can and must enforce these obligations. The question is always whether measures taken by the state to realise these rights are reasonable in the circumstances. Yacoob J held, in this regard, that reasonableness must:

1. Be more than legislation – legislative measures must be supported by appropriate, well-directed policies and programmes implemented by the executive.
2. The policies and programmes must be reasonable, both in their conception and in their implementation.
3. They must be comprehensive.
4. They must address the powers of different levels of government.
5. They must be directed at the progressive realisation of the rights concerned.
6. In order to test socio-economic rights it must be questioned whether:
   a. there are people in dire need;
   b. they have been left out.

If both questions are answered in the affirmative, there has been a breach of a socio-economic right enshrined in the Constitution.

In its *Grootboom* judgment the Court emphasised that neither constitutional provision under consideration gave any respondent the right to claim shelter immediately. Instead it issued a declaratory order requiring the state to devise and implement a programme that included measures to provide relief for desperate people who had not been catered for in terms of their housing needs.

The *Grootboom* case can be viewed as one of the more progressive judgments of the Constitutional Court as it made socio-economic rights legally enforceable within the limits of the enumerated qualifications.[37] Given the inevitable resource and capacity constraints facing the new state system, the Constitutional Court was required to determine the practical implications of different socio-economic rights in different areas, and in this case the relevant provisions were given teeth (Pieterse, 2004). It was followed in *Treatment Action Campaign*[38] in which the court actually prescribed provision of a particular anti-HIV drug for sufferers, while in the case of *Khosa*[39] the court effectively rewrote a social welfare budget. These judgments, all delivered in the first eight years of the new dispensation, provided significant challenges for the state system.

However in the case of *Mazibuko*[40] the Constitutional Court became more deferential and formalistic in its approach to the state's obligations regarding socio-economic rights. Under consideration here was the constitutional provision that everyone has the right to 'sufficient water'.[41] A local authority had, in improving supply and reducing water losses, installed pre-paid meters to charge consumers who used water in excess of the 6 kilolitres a month allowed for each household at no charge. The applicants challenged both aspects of the scheme and were successful at trial, the court finding the pre-paid meters to be unlawful and prescribing that the city should provide each person with 50 litres of free water a day. On appeal the Supreme Court of Appeal held that 42 litres of daily water was sufficient and directed the council to amend its by-laws accordingly, and it also held the metering system to be unlawful. On further appeal to the Constitutional Court the council conceded that it was under a continuing obligation to take progressive measures to achieve the right of access to sufficient water and it indicated how it had allocated additional free water allowances for the lowest-income groups and assisted them financially with levied charges.

While the Constitutional Court recognised the state's obligation to take reasonable measures to seek progressive realisation of rights to water, it had to resolve whether the actual policy was a reasonable one, given the fact that full access for all would take time. In contrast to the previous decisions it found it inappropriate for the court to give a quantified content, in litres per day, as to what constitutes 'sufficient' water, a matter best addressed by government. It found that the council's existing policy was not unreasonable and that the use of meters was neither unfair nor discriminatory in nature. While this case reinforces government's responsibility to account for its policies and administrative practices, it found that the city had done enough in reviewing and revising its systems to ensure the progressive realisation of the right to water and there was no interference with its administrative policies or practices.

While at one level this case was a confirmation of the court's role in supervising socio-economic rights, it involves something of a retreat by the Constitutional Court in upholding government discretion. While it did not detract from the state's obligations in respect of socio-economic constitutional rights it rendered their enforceability more remote. In many other African states, such as Ghana and Tanzania, the privatisation of water, often at the direction of international institutions or overseas development agencies, has had serious consequences for both consumers and the state.[42] It seems that a privatisation policy in relation to water rights is less likely to ensue in the South African context, because of both the poor precedents elsewhere in Africa and the constitutional obligation on the state in respect of water provision.

Both the enumeration of socio-economic rights and their inevitable qualifications in the Constitution had significant implications for the state system in South Africa. In the first place they created legitimate expectations in the citizenry that the most basic requirements for a decent and dignified life would be provided by the state. Secondly, they imposed resource strains on the state system in terms of meeting these social expectations and constitutional obligations. Thirdly, they inevitably entailed disputations between citizens and the state and dilemmas for courts required to develop a complex and balanced jurisprudence on the appropriate contours of socio-economic rights. Fourthly, this in turn has led to friction between the executive and the judiciary and in a recent keynote conference presentation the President expressed concern over judicial intervention in the proper realm of the executive government.[43]

These tensions are not likely to be resolved in the short term. There has arguably been an over-judicialisation of policy and administrative decision-making within the state system, initiated by individuals, ratepayers, minority groups and non-governmental organisations (NGOs). While some of the initiatives result in matters entirely appropriate for judicial determination, others are a function of applicants' frustration with aspects of government service delivery, often at the local authority level.[44] This raises the counter-majoritarian dilemma which is encountered in all jurisdictions in which the rule of law is established and courts can review state decisions and activities.

The counter-majoritarian problem arises where government policy which has both popular and political support is invalidated by courts through their powers of judicial review, legal legitimacy trumping democratic legitimacy as part of the checks and balances encountered in constitutional democracies. An essential tension exists between majoritarian democracy, implying that both electoral systems and parliamentary decisions operate on the basis of majority preferences; and constitutionalism, which denotes the maintenance of various rights and liberties for minorities and, by implication, restrictions on governance in accordance with the majority will. Constitutions both enable and constrain and they typically designate a non-political branch, the judiciary, to resolve differences in the tension between majoritarian democracy and constitutional democracy. In essence the review function of the courts serves to enhance constitutional democracy, provided courts themselves do not stray beyond their legitimate mandate into the realm of 'judicial activism'. In the unchartered aspects of the South African political constitution these boundaries are by no means self-evident, nor do different stakeholders agree on them.

This dilemma is traditionally encountered in state systems where constitutional rights act as a negative check on executive action, whereas in the South African context they extend to being a positive obligation in relation to executive inaction to basic service provision. One area in which the Constitutional Court has acted in explicit awareness of its being contrary to the popular will in South African society is in relation to the death penalty, which it declared unconstitutional despite apparent majority support for the penalty.[45] Here the Court emphasised not only its independence from the executive but also the fact that strong public opinion would not deflect it from its constitutional responsibilities. Given the 'political' role thrust on judges in this context, their method of appointment is a critical issue, but is beyond the scope of this contribution. However the exigencies of the times, both nationally and globally, will ensure further conflicts between the executive and principles of the constitution, with constitutional supremacy frustrating government attempts to address socio-economic issues in the country. Restrictions on reformist state policies are, indirectly, supportive of globalisation norms.

## 3.5 THE STATE AND THE GLOBAL ECONOMY

In this section consideration is given to four specific aspects of the South African state's interaction with global economic norms, processes and institutions, against the background of the country's relatively quick accession to the global economic order.

### 3.5.1 Tensions between State Policies and the International Economy

The first theme relates to the tensions between the market state and the developmental state. Prior to democracy in South Africa state capitalism had been prevalent in the economic system, accompanied by extensive monopoly capitalism despite rhetorical commitments to the market system. During the liberation period extensive state involvement in the economy was advocated in terms of developmental and socialist economic objectives but in reality constitutional democracy soon witnessed significant state endorsement of neoliberal principles associated with the Washington Consensus, despite their tendency to restrict domestic policy space and the economic role of the state. While 1994 heralded internal democracy in South Africa it was subject to the constraints commensurate with membership of the global community which often frustrate the democratic impulse.

Globalisation's neoliberal pressures resulted in state commitments to national treatment for foreign capital, the privatisation of state enterprises, significant elements of deregulation, the floating of the national currency and reductions in restrictions on cross-border capital mobility. Conversely, however, the South African state did not nationalise the mines, banks or other significant parts of the private sector economy, despite political pressure for these interventions, and it became in many ways a conformist member of the global economy. This included compliance with trade and investment obligations and with the prescriptions of international bodies such as the Basel Committee on Banking Supervision[46] and the International Monetary Fund.

The question of national treatment for foreign investors raises a specific tension in relation to the retention of domestic policy space. As indicated above, South Africa in the mid-1990s rapidly ratified a series of bilateral investment treaties (BITs) which followed the template of such agreements developed by advanced capital-exporting economies in previous decades. Of particular relevance was their provision for financial compensation for expropriation, including 'regulatory takings', of investor assets. There is in fact mixed evidence on the effectiveness of these instruments in attracting FDI (UNCTAD, 2009). Moreover the tendency of BITs to 'constitutionalise' (Schneiderman, 2008)[47] the rights of foreign investors, with few reciprocal rights for host countries, has led to concerns that their effect is to freeze domestic policy-making, either directly or indirectly. A recent ICSID arbitration (*Foresti v Republic of South Africa*),[48] brought this issue to the fore when a foreign investor in South Africa contended that B-BBEE policies in the mining sector designed to redress disadvantages from the apartheid past amounted to expropriation of their assets, entitling the investor to financial compensation. While this matter settled before adjudication and the arbitration was discontinued, an arbitral decision on damages provided some support for the South African position – implicitly finding that state policy could trump international treaty norms. However there is a hidden factor at work in this regard: it is impossible to estimate the extent to which apprehended or threatened investor claims along these lines restrain developing countries such as South Africa from flexing their regulatory muscles.

A further dimension of the domestic policy space conundrum concerns the fact that non-state entities are increasingly involved in governance activities that were formerly the preserve of state organs. Much of this activity occurs at the global level in an increasingly wide range of international financial and economic institutions. These include the World Bank, the International Monetary Fund, the Basel Committee and, since the GFC, the Financial Stability Board.[49] While the activities of these bodies are nominally subject to the discipline of 'global administrative law', their governance functions lack the accountability and transparency mechanisms provided by the South African constitutional system (Bradlow and Hunter, 2011).[50] Notwithstanding a 'democratic deficit' at the global level, economic policies emanating from these institutions can effectively trump those emanating internally from domestic democratic processes.

### 3.5.2 Engagement in International Institutions

The second theme in the South African state's interaction with the global political economy concerns its relationship with regional and international institutions. Since shedding its pariah status and diplomatic isolation in 1994 South Africa has become, for its size, a prominent member of the international community and institutions of global governance.

In a sense the international relationships involve a 'reconstruction' of the state as South Africa in the post-apartheid era becomes more integrated into international institutions and the global economy. Given the impact of global institutions and processes on state systems, referred to above, changes in the powers and functions of the former have necessary implications for the latter. When a state such as South Africa participates in an international body it has a dualistic impact. On one hand it hollows out areas of domestic policy space in relation to the levers of the economy, while on the other it provides part of the foundations for the globalisation superstructure and the policies globalisation propagates. In regard to the latter factor, the involvements with regional and international organisations involve 'extensions' of a state system as it becomes part of the authority, policy-making and dispute resolution activities exercised by international and non-state institutions. While some of its authority is reduced, it operates, in conjunction with other states, in new transnational areas of jurisdiction.

Regionally South Africa is an active member of the Southern African Customs Union, the Southern African Development Community and the African Union (and its off-shoot NEPAD),[51] in all of which it is the dominant political and economic force. Internationally South Africa is a long-standing member of the United Nations (UN), the Global Agreement on Tariffs and Trade (GATT) and the World Trade Organization (WTO), and of the World Bank and the International Monetary Fund (IMF), and it participates in the Financial Stability Board and the Bank for International Settlements. South Africa is currently a rotating member of the UN Security Council, but is not a member of the OECD. It is a member of the G-20 group of countries, a member with India and Brazil of the development-oriented group of countries known as IBSA (India–Brazil–South Africa), and since 2011 it has been a member of the BRICS grouping together with China, India, Russia and Brazil. An indication of South Africa's activity internationally is that the country has entered more than 50 international investment treaties,[52] predominantly in the immediate post-apartheid era, and many other economic-related agreements in ensuing years. In the political domain South Africa has had some prominence in continental peace initiatives in Cote d'Ivoire, Sudan, Libya, Zimbabwe and Madagascar.

The 'first in Africa' syndrome[53] has raised two factors in relation to South Africa's international involvements. The first is the state's putative 'representative' role on behalf of Africa in its involvement in bodies such as the G-20, a characterisation not entirely disowned by its representatives. The second is the 'gateway into Africa' notion, raised particularly in respect of the country's membership of BRICS. There are limits to both these characterisations as South Africa has no formal mandate to represent any other African state, or group of states, and the gateway notion is a simplistic representation of complex and sometimes disguised trade and investment networks.[54] Nonetheless this is not an entirely self-assumed identity and there is a perception among some African countries and regions that South Africa has a responsibility, albeit not a representative one, to advance the continent's interests not otherwise given voice in international bodies.

As a relatively minor player in the global political economy South African necessarily has a modest impact on international institutions and economic policies and it is too soon to estimate the implications of its membership of the BRICS grouping. However some noteworthy dynamics have emerged within the G-20 group of countries. In the build-up to the June 2011 appointment of the new IMF chair, South Africa and Australia, as joint chairs of the G-20 Working Group on Development,[55] issued a statement calling for greater transparency in a merit-based selection process (Manuel, 2011, p. 33).[56] More significant has been the country's co-chairing role in this group in relation to the Seoul Development Consensus for Shared Growth.[57] The Seoul Consensus is a set of principles and guidelines[58] developed to assist G-20 nations and other global actors to work collaboratively with less developed countries to boost economic growth and to achieve the UN's Millennium Development Goals. The Consensus was endorsed by the leaders of G-20 nations at the 2010 Seoul summit, with a multi-year action plan drafted for the delivery of tangible results. In contrast to the Washington Consensus, the Seoul Consensus entertains a more interventionist role for state organs in national economies; rather than seeking to impose a uniform 'top-down' solution through structural adjustment programmes and other conditionalities it postulates that solutions should be tailored to requirements of individual developing nations, the countries themselves taking the lead in designing reforms and policies best suited to their needs.

Given their limited influence on substantive outcomes, one function for South Africa and other emerging states in their international economic engagements is to attempt to influence the agenda of the G-20 and like institutions (Boulle, 2011). It has, for example, been largely at the insistence of emerging countries such as South Africa that 'financial inclusion' has become a prominent feature of both the G-20 and broader international agendas. Needless to say while agendas do affect the normative discourse of international economic policy and reform they have no necessary impact on outcomes, in respect of which dominant power, exercised by individual states or groups of states, tends to prevail over less powerful entities. However there remains a monitoring function for emerging countries against the background of the often dismal compliance by advanced economies with international policy resolutions. Here they could establish procedures to monitor compliance with G-20 policy recommendations, which are usually directed to individual nation states and to other international institutions such as the IMF. As has been the case with many of the NGOs' activities, monitoring and publicity by such countries could, over the long term, have effects on policy development.

Also of significance to the South African state system is the extent to which the country's membership of regional and international organisations contributes to a regrouping of emerging countries in the fluid geo-political circumstances of the current era. This phenomenon predates the GFC and since the late 1990s various regional organisations have emerged in Africa, commensurate with other regional political and economic institutions throughout the world – though not always compatible with the more prominent globalisation norm of multilateralism. At the regional level the contours of state authority have been both extended and retracted by membership of the Southern African Customs Union (SACU) and Southern African Development Community (SADC), referred to above. Thus in relation to the negotiation of Economic Partnership Agreements with the European Union, South Africa has resolved for the future not to undertake these activities on its own but only on a regional basis. Membership of groups such as the G-20 and BRICS entails association with, and potential influence over, collective actions in these and other groupings within the fluidity of the policy space in the post-GFC world. These engagements also involve challenges for emerging state systems as global economic rules intrude into their domestic regimes.

### 3.5.3 Domestic Intrusion of Global Trade Rules

The third theme relates to the intrusion of global trade rules into domestic jurisprudence such that principles and policies enunciated in supranational bodies assume primacy in domestic law and politics. Here the Constitutional Court has had occasion to pronounce on South Africa's interaction with the global economy in a case where the domestic issues in dispute revolved around separation of powers principles but the consequences of the decision involved the intrusion of international trade principles. In *International Trade Administration Commission v SCAW South Africa (Pty) Ltd*[59] issues arose in relation to local procedures for reviewing anti-dumping duties. By virtue of its WTO membership South Africa has the standard obligations under Art. VI of the General Agreement on Tariffs and Trade and the Anti-Dumping Agreement in terms of how it deals with alleged dumping of goods by foreign exporters. South Africa duly enacted domestic legislation to regulate the setting of anti-dumping duties in accordance with the WTO obligations. In terms of the legislation the responsible minister decided to impose anti-dumping duties on various imported steel products, including those from a UK exporter. This decision was based on the recommendation of the predecessor to the International Trade Administration Commission (ITAC), the state agency responsible for the administration of trade rules.[60]

The respondent, SCAW, was a local enterprise producing the same products as those in respect of which the duties were imposed. Prior to the lapsing of the stipulated duty period affecting the UK exporter, SCAW sought a statutorily prescribed review with the intention of having the duties maintained beyond the five-year period. On the basis that the removal of tariffs would not lead to product dumping injurious to local industry, ITAC recommended to the minister that they be terminated. SCAW sought urgent orders, *inter alia* to prevent the minister from acting on the recommendations, and these were granted, effectively extending the period of the duties for longer than the five-year period countenanced by WTO rules. Interim relief having been granted to SCAW, ITAC appealed to the Constitutional Court, contending that the original order effectively extending the anti-dumping duties was contrary not only to domestic law but also to the WTO rules limiting the lifespan of duties; it contended, moreover, that in terms of separation of powers principles the court should not encroach on the executive's domain in this regard. The Constitutional Court granted leave to appeal on the basis, *inter alia*, of the separation of powers principle and South Africa's international trade obligations. Judgment was ordered against SCAW, definitely terminating the anti-dumping duties.

The Constitutional Court is not a trade tribunal, and no such body exists in South Africa as is the case in some state systems. This leaves trade-related issues to be determined domestically by administrative organs of state and thereafter through judicial review. The Constitutional Court was able to exercise review powers in the ITAC case because of the separation of powers principle enshrined in the constitution. Whereas dumping disputes are routinely managed through the WTO Dispute Settlement Understanding these disputes are nominally state-to-state matters in that only WTO member states can formally engage in the dispute resolution system, though they might do so on the complaint of a local corporation or industry body. However in this case SCAW, a South African company, was affected by a decision of the South African state and not by that of the UK government where the exporter was based and there was no interstate dispute susceptible to WTO adjudication. Nevertheless the Constitutional Court, while basing its decision on constitutional and administrative law principles, was clearly influenced in its reasoning by South African's international trade obligations (*Progress Office Machines CC v South African Revenue Services and Others*),[61] implying the domestic internalisation of international economic law norms. The court also deferred to the pre-eminence of the executive in relation to this aspect of the international economy. While the decision does not constitute a strong precedent in relation to the application of global economic norms in domestic jurisprudence, it does illustrate the reach of these norms into the domestic law and constitutional system of a developing state.

### 3.5.4 Transnational Corporate Acquisitions: A Case Study

The fourth example of the South African state's interaction with economic globalisation involves the 2011 attempt by the largest global corporation to acquire a majority holding in one of South Africa's biggest retailers. Generally speaking South Africa, as a low-savings economy, is very much open to cross-border investors, subject to foreign exchange requirements and compliance with local regulations, and there is no equivalent investigative and determinative process to that conducted by the Foreign Investment Review Board in Australia.[62] In the case of *Walmart Stores Inc v Massmart Holdings Ltd*, unions, government, suppliers and commercial rivals expressed extensive opposition to the proposed acquisition which resulted in the case coming before the Competition Tribunal for resolution.[63] Among the concerns of the unions were the likely implications of the merged corporation for employment levels, and the possibility of a loss of collective bargaining rights in the light of Walmart's labour practices in other jurisdictions. There were also concerns that local suppliers would lose market share if their procurement contracts were replaced by contracts with overseas suppliers, and that other local contractors, such as small transport operators, would be crushed under the weight of the retail giant. The state was faced with a predicament typical of those facing other developing economies. On the one hand it required foreign investment and the employment it could generate, as well as the international perception that the country was an attractive business option. On the other hand it was concerned about the prospective loss of jobs, perceptions of it being inattentive to its political constituents, and the potential implications for industrial and social instability.

While the South African Competition Tribunal is essentially concerned with economic competition factors, such as monopolistic conditions and market domination, a 'public interest' test allows it to canvass a broad range of considerations in relation to the benefits and drawbacks of a proposed acquisition. Its role relates to both domestic and foreign acquisitions and it has no particular responsibilities in relation to the latter. However this contest was also played out in the media as retailers, suppliers, unions and state organs promoted their views in the court of public opinion, which included concerns over loss of local economic autonomy. Apart from the competition issues, concerns were also expressed over the fact that, as with all mergers and acquisitions, there was no firm expectation of a contribution to economic growth, nor even of increased employment.[64]

After protracted public hearings the Competition Tribunal approved the merger, subject to various conditions, some effectively conceded by the mega-corporation in the closing stages of the proceedings. They included a ban on employee retrenchments for a period of two years; preference in future employment vacancies to 500 employees retrenched six months previously by the local company; no challenge to the current unions' position within the enterprise; the establishment of a programme aimed at the development of South African suppliers, including small, medium-sized and micro enterprises (SMMEs), with R100 million to be expended on the programme within a three-year period;[65] and the establishment of a training system for local suppliers on how to do business with the merged entity and with Walmart itself.

While the lodgement of a notice of appeal against the Tribunal's decision entails that the last word has yet to be spoken on this episode, the events show the interaction between state authority, private power and the public interest in the dynamic conditions of globalisation. As indicated above, the state was confronted with the dilemma of having to balance conflicting economic, political and social considerations. The public interest is always an elastic concept, which can be pulled in various directions in terms of the short-, medium- or long-term precedence of political pressures, employment figures, global reputation, and the like. Private corporate power, backed by free trade ideologies, can often overcome the authority of developing states, sometimes with the backroom diplomatic assistance of home countries. In these circumstances of conflicting objectives and policies, state systems are required to provide forums and procedures for processing the resultant disputes. In the Walmart case the availability of a sophisticated set of competition laws and independent adjudicative institutions allowed government to avoid some of the political fallout of any final decision.[66] However the long-term benefits and costs for the different stakeholders remain to be assessed.

The four instances of the South African state's interaction with the realities of economic globalisation illustrate the shifting supremacy of domestic political pressures, constitutional principles and international economic policies. These tensions have been accentuated by the GFC, referred to in the following section.

## 3.6 THE SOUTH AFRICAN STATE AND THE GFC

In the above sections references were made to various modalities of interaction between the South African state and the global economy and its governance institutions. In this section an attempt is made to provide an analysis of some contradictory impulses in the post-GFC state system.

The GFC's main impact on the South African political economy was in relation to unemployment, it being estimated that about half a million jobs were lost in 2009 alone, and more in subsequent years.[67] This was a function of a slow-down in economic growth and in FDI, resulting from inertia in global trade, which had serious implications for social stability and hence for the state system. However the country was not faced with some of the systemic problems encountered in the advanced economies. Sound fiscal policies entailed that there was no sovereign debt problem, prudential regulation contributed to an absence of bank failures, and the emerging world's demand for resources ensured that the extractive industries continued to export commodities abroad. While industrial growth and development policies were formulated in the years after the GFC these would have ensued in any event and the state did not introduce any significant bail-out or nationalisation measures, nor were 'financial necessity' or trade protectionist interventions required. While inward FDI fell during the height of the crisis it was no more serious than in equivalent countries elsewhere, and the resumption of investment occurred thereafter, albeit less impressively than in competitor markets in Africa (UNCTAD, 2011, pp. 40–42).

Nevertheless the GFC accentuated the significance of a topical issue in the South African political economy. This concerns the state's involvement in the profitable mining sector and the question as to whether financial returns to the state from mining should derive solely from licensing fees, taxation and royalties, as at present, or through increased state ownership within the sector. The issue is sometimes presented in reductionist terms in a debate over 'nationalisation of the mines', though it is in reality a more nuanced subject than these words suggest. In terms of current legislation all mining rights are vested in the state, which confers prospecting and extractive concessions through licensing arrangements.[68] While increased state 'ownership' is premised on potential benefits for economic growth, employment and financial returns to the fiscus, concern is expressed over capacity issues and potential corruption in mines under state control. Moreover the requirement of redistribution, which is a prerequisite for addressing serious wealth inequalities in the country, is not a necessary consequence of either private or public sector control as even economic growth does not necessarily entail distributive equity. In this regard, although there are already some state enterprises involved in the mining sector, South Africa is unlikely to follow the precedent of those nation states in which nationalisation of energy and minerals has provided some overall benefits. Whatever the strengths and shortcomings of precedents in this area, the constitutional protection of property rights and trade obligations towards foreign enterprises preclude the state from nationalising the mining sector in any serious respect. However the dilemma remains a pressing issue for the state: on one hand, there is a need to be responsive to redistributive demands in the face of massive unemployment and grotesque disparities in wealth and, on the other, there is a need to retain the confidence of existing and prospective investors in the mining sector.

Another GFC-related tension concerns the institutional design and operation of the state system. This includes the question of whether the finely tuned constitutional balance in terms of the separation of powers and the quasi-federal division of powers can hold in an age of executive ascendancy. Global governance and financial crises have increased the power of executive branches of government, and within the executive branch the roles of Departments of Finance, Treasury, Foreign Affairs, Trade and Investment and the Presidency, or their equivalents in other countries. In general terms economic treaty-making is dominated by state officials with limited involvement by legislatures, and institutions such as the Financial Stability Board and Basel Committee allow the development of international standards which are de facto policy, and often become law, in many countries. In this context there is an inevitable centralising tendency in respect of state policy and the 'democratic deficit' encountered in global institutions could creep incrementally into state systems despite democratic local credentials.

Some indication of the future of the South African state system had been provided by the government's policy paper of 2010, the New Growth Path (NGP), which developed in the context of the GFC. The NGP was essentially a response to the unemployment problems exacerbated by preceding financial and economic crises. It placed employment at the centre of government policy and posited six priorities for job creation, involving a target of 5 million jobs in ten years: infrastructure development, enhancing the agricultural value chain, mining and metal beneficiation, the expansion of manufacturing, growth of the green economy, and further development of the key service sectors of tourism and business services.[69] The NGP was also predicated on the exploitation of new economic opportunities on the African continent, particularly in the services sector.[70] In furtherance of the NGP the Industrial Development Council will make available R102 billion over five years in NGP priority areas[71] and a Jobs Fund will provide financing, at prime less 3 per cent, to local firms in areas with high employment potential impact. There is also provision for mandatory localisation practices in designated procurement sectors.

A further elaboration of state policy was provided in July 2011 when the Minister of Planning released a diagnostic report from the National Planning Commission (NPC).[72] It identified eight key challenges facing the state system and broader society: that too few South Africans are working, that the quality of black education is substandard, that infrastructure is inadequate for the country's social and economic needs,[73] that the spatial legacy of apartheid limits social inclusion and economic growth, that the development path is too resource-intensive and unsustainable, that the public health system is overburdened and service performance uneven, that corruption levels are high, and that South Africa remains a socially divided society. While some of these issues had been self-evident earlier, the report was based on both research and consultation and, as a diagnosis initiated by the ruling party, it carried considerable challenges for the state system. The diagnosis was followed by the NPC's Development Plan – Vision for 2030, which was published in November 2011. In depicting a pathway for the republic's future development this comprehensive economic and social plan attempts to reconcile many of the tensions facing the state system referred to above (NPC, 2011).

It is inevitable that the state's NGP and industrial policy framework, and the reports of the NPC, are and will involve inconsistencies with global economic dictates. They do not, for example, fit easily with theories of 'comparative advantage' on which economic globalisation is predicated in that industrial policy is designed precisely to grow the economy in areas lacking current strength.[74] Comparative advantage is also at odds with aspects of the NGP which aim to restructure the country's economy through diversification beyond traditional economic sectors and by moving into non-traditional tradeable goods and services. There are also protectionist tendencies in local content requirements, the alignment of procurement with B-BBEE and financing of local industry through the Industrial Development Council. Here specific claims could potentially be brought against the domestic measures before the WTO's dispute resolution system or before arbitral tribunals in terms of international investment agreements.

There are also constitutional challenges awaiting the state policies referred to above as government attempts to implement them through regulatory frameworks and administrative actions. The tight strictures on all levels of government introduced in the democratic Constitution in 1996 will have particular impacts on economic reforms championed by the current government, and to a lesser extent on the social policies advanced by the NPC. As has been the case in the past, their legitimacy will be determined through the judicial process but a range of other resource and capacity issues will affect the practical viability of these policies, and the restructuring of the state itself.

## 3.7 CONCLUSION

It has been suggested in the preceding analysis that state formation, functioning and rebuilding in South Africa is susceptible to ad hoc

GFC pressures, as well as to the more enduring forces of economic globalisation. While the ideology of the Washington Consensus may have been weakened by the GFC and the reactive protectionist and nationalisation measures it provoked in the advanced economies, neoliberal economic theory has been a great survivor of the crisis, legitimising the market-driven and speculative aspects of the global economy ahead of distributive and equity objectives. In this context the rebuilding of the South Africa state, occasioned in part by the GFC, is potentially at odds with the dominant paradigm of the global political economy insofar as it focuses on the very issues of distribution and equity subordinated in dominant ideology. Here references have been made to tensions between transformation injunctions in the South African constitution and pressures to comply with international norms such as national treatment and treaty compliance.

These tensions in the normative terrain are reflected in inconsistent practices on the ground, the earlier sections having identified aspects of South Africa's emerging domestic policy framework which require a significant level of state intervention, some of it preferential and protectionist in nature and designed to respond to the pervasive social and economic challenges facing the state. It is true that in other respects the South African state has acted as a compliant global citizen even in the face of strong political, business and popular resistance locally. It has, for example, not interfered with the high value of the currency despite industry and union concerns over its implications for export-related jobs.[75] However the immediacy of political pressures constitutes an extensive challenge for the South Africa state as volatility, uncertainty and unpredictability continue to characterise the global economy.

As the international centre of economic gravity moves gradually towards the global South and the East, it brushes parts of Africa. Recent decades have witnessed the increasing integration of Africa into the global economy, evidenced in relation to both trade and investment. The South African economy is a major beneficiary of the new global economic and investment forces and trends. This creates tensions for its political processes and constitutional values, setting the scene for a dynamic interplay of economic forces in the decade ahead.

## NOTES

* Thanks are extended to Michael Power and Mary-Rose Nthabiseng, interns at the Mandela Institute, for research assistance.

1. There are many manifestations of this tension, epitomised by citizen resistance to 'market disciplines' imposed on Greece during the first eight months of 2011.

2. Combined African GDP grew by 4.9 per cent in 2010, up from 3.1 per cent in 2009 and is expected to grow by 5.8 per cent in 2012. While South Africa has the continent's dominant economy, its growth rate is well below the average: 3.6 per cent in 2010 (see African Economic Outlook, 2011).
3. League competitors are Brazil, in the past, and Equatorial Guinea, at present (see World Bank, n.d.).
4. The demographic dividend involves a rise in the rate of economic growth due to a rising share of working-age people in a population. This usually occurs late in the demographic transition when the fertility rate falls and the youth dependency rate declines. In Africa countries continue to have high fertility and youth dependency rates, which contribute to economic stagnation (see Ross, 2004).
5. China, Iceland and Russia are the most restrictive and the Netherlands, Portugal and Luxembourg the least restrictive.
6. In the *First Certification Case* 1996 (4) SA 774 (CC). Unusually, parts of the Constitution from which the Constitutional Court derived its authority were declared unconstitutional; they were subsequently brought into compliance by the national parliament.
7. The Constitution establishes a quasi-federal system in that, while the status of provincial and local governments are entrenched, their powers and responsibilities are not.
8. These are known colloquially as the 'Chapter 9 institutions', after the Chapter which established them.
9. There have been proposals to make the Constitutional Court the highest court on all legal matters, not just those with a constitutional element, but these have proved to be controversial.
10. In terms of still deployed racial categories, 'whites' in South Africa constitute about 9 per cent of the total population, and 'blacks', 'coloureds' and 'Indians' all have some claim to remedial treatment for past discriminatory practices.
11. The Broad-Based Black Economic Empowerment Act 53 of 2003, supplemented by Codes of Good Practice on Black Economic Empowerment, gazetted on 9 February 2007. An Interpretive Guide to the regulatory scheme was added in June 2007.
12. For example, a Mining Charter for the prospecting and mining sectors of the economy.
13. There are many examples of the global acceleration, for instance most of the over 45 bilateral investment treaties in South Africa were signed shortly before and after 1994 in a 'mad scramble' by developed countries. By 2011 there were serious concerns about the implications of these treaties.
14. *Business Day* of 14 June 2011 reported that only 45 per cent of capital funding allocated to local authorities for infrastructural development had been spent in the preceding year.
15. While referred to as 'Roman-Dutch' common law it was in reality based on the common law of Western Europe (see Rajak, 2011).
16. Constitution Act 1996, s 39(2).
17. Constitution Act 1996, ss 211 and 233. A notable decision of the Constitutional Court in this regard is *Bhe and Others v Khayelitsha Magistrate and Others* 2005 (1) SA 580 (CC). The case effectively outlawed the notion of customary succession through male primogeniture, ruling it unconstitutional as it infringed on the equality of women. The case highlighted the fact that even African customary law is subject to constitutional norms.
18. Constitution Act 1996, ss 232 and 233.
19. The negotiation of treaties is the prerogative of the national executive and, as in other dualistic systems, treaties in most instances require approval by the legislature in order to be effective in domestic law; Constitution Act 1996, s 231.
20. South African constitutional law has been referred to by the Supreme Court of Canada, the US Supreme Court and the UK House of Lords. The SA Constitutional Court has referred to decisions of the Supreme Court of Canada in its application of the Canadian

Charter of Rights and Freedoms, of the Supreme Court of India, of the Federal Constitutional Court of Germany and in certain instances of the US Supreme Court.

21. A long-established Johannesburg firm, Deneys Reitz, 'merged' with the transnational firm Norton Rose on 1 June 2011.
22. 2001 (4) SA 938 (CC).
23. Constitution Act 1996, ss 9, 10, 11 and 12 – the right can be inferred from the rights to equality, human dignity, life and security of person.
24. Constitutional Act 1996, s 12(1).
25. *Glenister v President of the Republic of South Africa and Others* 2011 (3) SA 347 (CC).
26. Under the National Prosecuting Authority Act 32 of 1998, s 7(1).
27. South African Police Services Act 57 of 2008.
28. The majority further referred to statements on corruption made by Kofi Annan preceding the text of the UN Convention against Corruption 2004, and to interpretations of the South African Bill of Rights (see Constitution Act 1996, Chapter 2).
29. The Constitutional Court afforded government a two-year grace period to bring relevant legislation into compliance with the principles contained in the judgment.
30. See http://www.uncitral.org/, accessed 12 July 2011.
31. That revision of the domestic Arbitration Act 42 of 1965 is long overdue, as was recognised some time ago; see SA Law Commission (1997).
32. For example in India, Germany, the United States and Canada.
33. Constitution Act 1996, s 27(2). The right to emergency medical treatment is absolute – s 27(3). For the more general limitation of rights see s 36.
34. This condition now goes under the title of the 'reasonableness' standard, as opposed to the Constitutional Court's initial use of the 'rationality' standard.
35. *Government of RSA and Others v Grootboom & Others* 2001 (1) SA 46 (CC).
36. Constitution Act 1996, ss 26 and 28(1)(c), respectively.
37. The judgment is bitter-sweet one in that Irene Grootboom died in 2008 without receiving a house, seeing out her days in a temporary shelter.
38. 2002 (5) SA 721 (CC).
39. 2004 (6) SA 505 (CC).
40. *Mazibuko and Others v City of Johannesburg and Others* [2009] ZACC 28.
41. Constitution Act 1996, s 27.
42. For some of these difficulties see the decision of the International Centre for the Settlement of Investment Disputes Tribunal in *Biwater Gauff (Tanzania) Ltd v United Republic of Tanzania*, ICSID Case No Arb/05/22. See also International Committee of the Fourth International (ICFI) (2002).
43. President Jacob Zuma (2011).
44. In mid-2011 a High Court judgment ordered a local government authority to repair potholes in the town's main roads within a specified period; *Society for the Protection of our Constitution v Victor Khanye Municipality* (North Gauteng High Court, 2011, unreported).
45. See *Makwanyane* 1995 (3) SA 391 (CC). In this 'right to life' case the court abolished the death penalty on the basis that it was inconsistent with the Constitution, despite evidence of widespread popular support for the punishment.
46. See www.bis.org/bcbs, accessed 12 July 2011.
47. This is the term of David Schneiderman.
48. Case No ADR (AF) 07/01, ICSID.
49. See www.financialstabilityboard.org, accessed 12 July 2011.
50. For a full analysis of the governance of the international financial institutions see Bradlow and Hunter (2011).
51. The New Partnership for Africa's Development, see www.nepad.org, accessed 12 July 2011.
52. It is also a signatory to the New York Convention on the Enforcement of Foreign Arbitral Awards but is not a member of the International Convention on the Settlement of Investment Disputes.

53. This was strongly evident during the 2010 Soccer World Cup held in Africa for the first time.
54. For example Mauritius is a major source and target of South African investment but is a country of convenience for other sources and destinations because of its tax regime. China's biggest cross-border investment in 2008 (US$5.5 billion) bought it a 20 per cent stake in South Africa's Standard Bank which had, and continues to grow, involvement in Africa.
55. 'IMF Boss Should Be Chosen On Merit Say Australia and SA' BBC (London, 22 May 2011) www.bbc.co.uk/news/business-13490145, accessed 12 July 2011.
56. Neither South Africa nor the BRICS grouping nominated Trevor Manuel for the position despite his extensive experience as a national Treasurer, his standing in the international economic community and his role in IMF reform.
57. See the Seoul Development Consensus for Shared Growth, http://www.G-20.org/Documents2010/11/seoulsummit_annexes.pdf, accessed 12 July 2011.
58. The six core principles are a focus on economic growth, a global development partnership, global or regional systemic issues, private sector participation, complementarity, and outcome orientation
59. 2010 (5) BCLR 457 (CC).
60. The Board on Trade and Tariffs. Its replacement, ITAC, was established through the International Trade Administration Act 71 of 2002.
61. 2008 (2) SA 13 (SCA).
62. See www.firb.gov.au/content/default.asp, accessed 12 July 2011.
63. Case No 73/LM/Dec10, Competition Tribunal.
64. Whether through causation or coincidence, a long-term rival of the company acquired by Walmart retrenched over 3000 employees shortly after the Tribunal's decision; see 'Pick n Pay Retrenchments as a Result of Walmart Invasion' *Mail & Guardian* (South Africa, 7 July 2011) http://mg.co.za/article/2011-07-07-pick-n-pay-retrenchments-a-result-of-walmart-invasion, accessed 12 July 2011.
65. The programme is to be administered by a committee established by the merged entity and including government and unions, and it has to report annually to the Competition Commission.
66. While government had joined the unions in opposing the merger it was not party to the notice of appeal.
67. Even where there has been economic growth in South Africa it has not necessarily been accompanied by an increase in employment – the now not uncommon phenomenon of 'jobless growth' encountered in economies dominated by the services sector; see '267000 Jobs Lost In Last Quarter – Stats SA' *Politics Web* (South Africa, 28 July 2009) http://www.politicsweb.co.za, accessed 20 July 2011.
68. See the Mineral and Petroleum Resources Development Act 28 of 2002.
69. On the funding of the NGP see Minister Ebrahim Patel (2011).
70. Nearly half of the Economic Development Department budget is allocated to small, medium-sized and micro businesses, while 10 per cent is committed to trade administration, mainly in relation to tariff investigations and trade remedies.
71. Of this sum 50 per cent is allocated to venture capital and other significant amounts to funding distressed companies, green industries and mining and beneficiation.
72. See Minister Trevor Manuel's Address to the National Planning Commission, http://www.thepresidency.gove.za/pebble.asp?relid+4320, accessed 13 July 2011.
73. Infrastructure bottlenecks are experienced in electricity, transportation, water, communications and other areas of state activity.
74. The National Industrial Policy Framework was adopted by Cabinet in 2007. It is fleshed out by the 2012–13 Industrial Policy Action Plan (IPAP 2) (2011).
75. In September 2011 the Swiss central bank indicated that it would not allow the Swiss franc to rise above US$1.20 and China has long stood accused of keeping its currency sufficiently low to benefit exports.

## REFERENCES


2012/13 Industrial Policy Action Plan (IPAP 2) (2011), Department of Trade and Industry, Tshwane.

African Economic Outlook (2011), accessed 13 July 2011 at www.africaneconomicoutlook.org/en/outlook.

Boulle, Laurence (2010), *The Law of Globalisation,* Kluwer Law: The Netherlands.

Boulle, Laurence (2011), 'Why Developing States Wish to be Represented in the G-20', Konrad Adenauer Stiftung Conference, Seoul, South Korea, May.

Bradlow, Daniel and David Hunter (eds) (2011), *International Financial Institutions and International Law*, The Hague: Wolters Kluwer.

Foreign Review Investment Board, accessed 12 July 2011 at www.firb.gov.au/content/default.asp.

Global Integrity Report (2010), accessed 12 July 2011 at www.globalintegrity.org/information/downloads.

Hiscock, M. and W. van Caenegem (eds) (2010), *The Internationalisation of Law – Legislating, Decision-making, Practice and Education*, Cheltenham, UK and Northampton, MA, USA: Edward Elgar.

International Committee of the Fourth International (ICFI) (2002), 'What Water Privatisation Means for Africa', accessed 12 July 2011 at www.wsws.org/articles/2002/sep2002/wate-s07.shtml.

Manuel, Trevor (2011), 'Global Economic Governance: The Search for Economic Justice in a Globalised World', in Laurence Boulle (ed.), *Globalisation and Governance*, Cape Town: Siber Ink, pp. 33–42.

NPC (2011), 'National Development Plan – Vision for 2030', accessed 12 July 2011 at http://www.npconline.co.za/medialib/downloads/home/NPC%20National%20Development%20Plan%20Vision%202030%20-lo-res.pdf.

Patel, Minister Ebrahim (2011), 'How the New Growth Path Will be Funded', 12 April, accessed 13 July 2011 at www.proudlysa.co.za/area/media_room/2011/april/HOWIPAP.pdf.

Pieterse, Marius (2004), 'Coming to terms with the enforcement of socio-economic rights,' *South African Journal on Human Rights*, **20**, 383.

Rajak, H. (2011), 'A Virile Living System of Law: An Exploration of the South African Legal System', *Focus*, **61**, 44.

Ross, John (2004), 'Understanding the Demographic Dividend', accessed 12 July 2011 at www.policyproject.com/pubs/generalreport/Demo_Div.pdf.

SA Law Commission (1997), 'Arbitration: A Draft International Arbitration Act for South Africa', Discussion Paper 69.

Schneiderman, David (2008), *Constitutionalising Economic Globalisation: Investment Rules and Democracy's Promise*, Cambridge: Cambridge University Press.

Slaughter, Anne Marie (2003), 'A Global Community of Courts', *Harvard International Law Journal*, **44**, 191.

UNCTAD (2009), 'The Role of International Investment Agreements in Attracting Foreign Direct Investment to Developing Countries', UNCTAD Series on International Investment Policies for Development.

UNCTAD (2011), *World Investment Report 2011*, Geneva: UNCTAD.

World Bank (n.d.), 'Measuring Inequality', accessed 12 July 2011 at http://go.worldbank.org/3SLYUTVY00.

Zuma, President Jacob (2011), Key-note Address, Access to Justice Conference, Johannesburg, 8–10 July.

# 4. Chinese multinationals and the state: an institutional perspective

**Xiaohua Yang and Clyde D. Stoltenberg**

## 4.1 INTRODUCTION

Chinese outbound foreign direct investment (OFDI) remained largely insignificant until 2004, and Chinese multinationals were rarely heard about in the news. Yet, China's OFDI flow in 2010 amounted to more than \$60 billion (see Figure 4.1). By 2010, about 17 000 Chinese companies had invested abroad, reaching virtually every country in the world. China's shopping spree continues in defiance of the current global economic crisis. High-profile acquisitions include Sinopec's \$7.2 billion purchase of Addax, a Swiss oil company with extensive holdings in Iraq, in 2009. More recently, Sichuan Tengzhong Heavy Industrial Machinery Co., a Chinese heavy construction equipment maker, acquired General Motors' Hummer brand for US\$150 million, and Geely acquired the Volvo brand from Ford for US\$1.8 billion in 2010.

Chinese OFDI has been characterised by a number of unique features: (1) Chinese multinational firms are backed by strong government support, unlike their counterparts from other countries; (2) large state-owned enterprises are the key investors among all those going global; (3) Chinese firms invest with lightning speed, primarily through acquisitions; (4) Chinese firms have invested in a large spectrum of industries, ranging from natural resources to high-technology sectors; and (5) most Chinese firms do not normally possess advanced technologies.

What explains the rapid growth of Chinese OFDI? What is the role of the state in this picture? This chapter attempts to address these questions from an institutional perspective. We will first discuss the historical contexts for the rise of Chinese multinationals and explore the role of the state by examining its economic policies, innovation policies, and its responses to two recent financial crises. We will then probe the future path of China and Chinese multinationals before we make our conclusions.

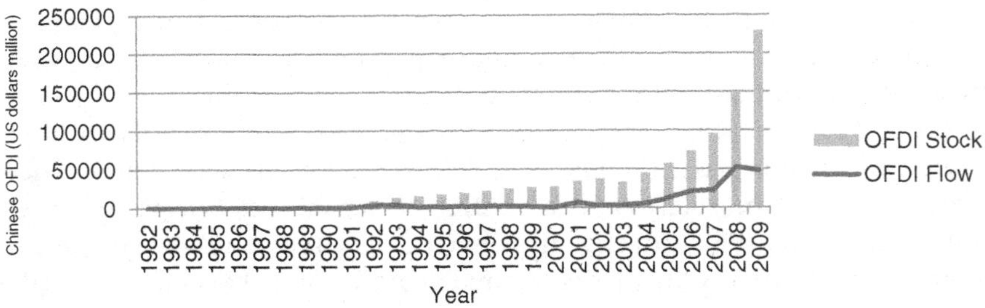


*Source:* UNCTAD and Chinese Statistical Yearbooks, various years.

*Figure 4.1 China OFDI flow and stock (US dollars million)*

## 4.2 GROWTH OF CHINESE MULTINATIONALS

### 4.2.1 The Early Development of Institutions and the Rise of Chinese Multinationals

We argue that the case of China demonstrates the profound impact of institutions on business. While 'going out' policy was envisioned by Deng Xiaoping, it was developed by Jiang Zemin as early as 1992, when he encouraged Chinese firms to go abroad to build world-class corporations to compete successfully in the global marketplace. Since then, the development of OFDI policies and growth stages of made-in-China multinationals have been going hand in hand, as illustrated below.

**1979–95**

The Chinese government established 'go abroad' economic policies on 13 August 1979. This was the first time that China had included outward foreign direct investment in the national economic development programme, aiming at paving the way for large-scale overseas expansion activities. During this phase, the Chinese government issued permits to large state and provincial trading houses to set up overseas operations. As a result, many of the OFDI projects were set up in Southeast Asia and developing countries to facilitate exports from Chinese petrochemical and machinery companies. These firms experimented with Japan's *keiretsu* operations through networks of subcontractors. While the Chinese government played a pivotal role in promoting OFDI as part of its economic and foreign policy, many of the OFDI projects were poorly managed and underperformed. As Hong and Sun (2006) observe, the key decisions on overseas investments during this period, including choices of location and sector, 'were mainly determined by the consideration of enhancing China's political and economic influence and expanding its international trade relationships rather than that of maximizing market profit'.

After 1991, the Chinese government began to grant permits to large state-owned enterprises (hereafter these production-oriented state-owned enterprises will be referred to as SOEs) to allow these firms to access international markets directly, thus bypassing large state-owned trading companies in order to further economic liberalisation. This move contributed to competitive growth of these SOEs in international markets (Luo et al., 2005). During this phase, the government's motivation to promote OFDI was associated with the desire to address natural resource constraints to further development (Hong and Sun, 2006) as well as the desire to shift mature technologies and industries to other developing countries to maximise profits by using some comparative advantages. However, at the beginning of 1993, the government undertook rigorous screening of OFDI projects due to the overheating of the economy, and the level of investment and number of projects fell over the previous years, which led to slowdown of OFDI growth.

**1996–2003**

Starting in 1996, a large group of enterprises established after the 1978 economic reforms began trying to internationalise their business. Many of these firms concentrated on home appliances and vehicles because the domestic markets in these sectors were becoming saturated around that time.

A significant development during this period affecting the form in which Chinese companies could pursue outward investment lay in the increasing numbers of firms listed on developed-country stock exchanges with the goal of raising equity capital directly in hard currency and establishing international image and reputation (Hong and Sun, 2006). Capital raised in this manner by highly publicised initial public offerings (IPOs) has gradually allowed transnational merger and acquisition (M&A) to become the main form of China's direct investment abroad and, in the process, led to further privatisation of SOEs. 'The major explanations for this increased M&A by Chinese companies include[d] the need for direct access to natural resources, overcoming the low brand value of Chinese products, and obtaining as quickly as possible advanced marketing and distribution networks and R&D operations' (Hong and Sun, 2006).

During this stage, the government's key efforts focused on building banking, foreign exchange programmes, evaluation systems and other infrastructures to facilitate international expansion of Chinese firms. New regulations including the 'Rules on Foreign Exchange Administration of the People's Republic of China', the 'Circular on Relevant Issues Regarding Perfecting Foreign Exchange Administration Relating to Capital Account' and the 'Circular on Relevant Issues Concerning Return of Guaranty for Profit of Overseas Investment Being Transferred to China' were put in place.

**2004–present**

This stage has seen acceleration of overseas expansion activities by way of mergers and acquisitions, such as Lenovo acquiring IBM's personal computer (PC) business in December 2004. This acceleration followed up China's 2001 accession to the World Trade Organization (WTO) (Kwan, 2006).

To further facilitate the growth, China's State Administration of Foreign Exchange issued new regulations in October 2005 in its 'Notice on Issues Relating to the Administration of Foreign Exchange in Fundraising and Reversed Investment Activities of Domestic Residents Conducted via Offshore Special Purpose Vehicles [Notice 75]'. Where prior regulation had created hurdles for Chinese firms seeking to restructure their domestic businesses under an offshore holding company as a prelude to overseas fundraising, Notice 75 established a consistent foreign exchange registration system to facilitate offshore restructurings (Foo, 2006).

At the same time, regulation of M&A within China has also continued to evolve, with the 2003 M&A Rules replaced by the 2006 M&A Rules. The 2006 M&A Rules expressly allow (for the first time) the use of a foreign publicly listed company's shares as consideration for the exchange of Chinese equity securities in connection with an M&A transaction (Hsia et al., 2006). Concurrently, the Ministry of Finance issued a series of new and revised Accounting Standards for Business Enterprises (effective beginning in 2007) which largely reflect the approaches and principles of the International Financial Reporting Standards, and the China Securities Regulatory Commission has been promoting since April 2005 a share liquidity reform programme under which listed companies are being restructured to convert almost all non-tradable legal person shares into freely tradable A shares within two years (Hsia et al., 2006). Along with promulgation of the new Company Law effective 1 January 2006, all of these developments reflect continued Chinese government policy in moving business enterprise decision-making toward economically motivated goals and policies rather than the pursuit of state-imposed mandates.

### 4.2.2 The Changing Patterns of Chinese OFDI

As illustrated above, the internationalisation process in Chinese firms is intertwined with the unique Chinese institutional environment in which

*Table 4.1 Phases of China's OFDI policy*

| Year | China's OFDI policy |
|---|---|
| Phase 1: 1979–1983 | Tight controls |
| Phase 2: 1984–1991 | Cautious encouragement |
| Phase 3: 1992–1996 | Active encouragement |
| Phase 4: 1997–1999 | Stepping back |
| Phase 5: 2000–2006 | Formulation & implementation of the 'going global' policy |
| Phase 6: 2007–present | Growing political support for transnational corporations and a new push for liberalisation. |
| 1 May 2009 | Ministry of Commerce (MOFCOM)<br>Administrative measures on regulation of outbound investment Effective |
| May, 2009 | State Administration of Foreign Exchange (SAFE)<br>Draft regulations of foreign exchange administration for domestic enterprises' overseas direct investments<br>Draft rules published for comment |
| 1 August 2009 | State Administration of Foreign Exchange (SAFE)<br>Notice on the administration of cross-border loans by domestic enterprises Effective |

*Sources:* UNCTAD, various years; Buckley et al. (2007); Yang and Stoltenberg (2008).

it has taken place. During the three stages, government involvement remained prevalent, and state-owned enterprises continued to dominate the whole scene. Table 4.1 summarises these stages.

While Chinese firms have chosen to invest in locations that enable firms to minimise costs of their operations for their constituent activities – that is, developing economies – Chinese firms have shifted FDI to Organisation for Economic Co-operation and Development (OECD) countries recently because of new government policies, a new profit-maximising initiative and the rapidly changing goals of Chinese firms. Chinese firms are now looking to use their large cash reserves to compete in the international market place to become global players (Sauvant, 2005). Because many assets in Western countries have become far more affordable during the global economic crisis, many Chinese firms have expanded their international business through mergers and acquisitions and leveraged their low-cost position to gain a foothold in the developed countries. This new investment behaviour was enabled by the timely relaxation of foreign exchange restrictions by the State Administration of Foreign Exchange (SAFE) in May 2009 and further facilitated by SAFE's new policies on loans to Chinese firms investing abroad in August 2009.

These 'made-in-China' multinational enterprises have also begun pursuing aggressive strategies in attaining technological capability and human capital (Yang and Stoltenberg, 2008). In a study conducted on over 100 publicly listed Chinese firms investing overseas from 2001to 2009, over 30 per cent of them invested in developed countries (Yang et al., 2011). This is in line with what the national economic policy called for in a statement from Bai Rongchun, Director General, Industrial Planning Department, State Economic and Trade Commission, in July 2001:

> The state will encourage big state-owned businesses to become internationally competitive corporations by listing on domestic and overseas stock markets, increasing research and development expenditure, and acquiring other businesses. The country will develop thirty to fifty large SOEs in the next five years through public offerings, mergers and acquisitions, restructuring and co-operation.

The Chinese government not only actively facilitates and encourages OFDI, but also specifically encourages investment in research and development to enhance innovative capability (UNCTAD, 2005). For instance, in October 2004, the National Development and Restructuring Committee and Export–Import Bank of China issued a circular to promote overseas investment via M&A to enhance the global competitiveness of Chinese firms and to accelerate their expansion into Western markets (Deng, 2009).

Expansion into the United States (US), Europe and Australia allowed Chinese firms to strengthen their competiveness in the global marketplace. For instance, the specialised nature of companies and industries in the US allows China to diversify its business at a relatively low cost in comparison with developing its own technology. This is seen in a database developed at the University of San Francisco's Globalization of Chinese Business Facility in the US, where we observe that the number of Chinese firms investing in OECD countries is larger than that in non-OECD countries between 2009 and 2010, as compared with the 2002–08 period (Figure 4.2).

China has directed its OFDI goals toward advanced proprietary, strategic technologies that are immobile, such as distribution networks and specific branding already in place by US firms, and other capabilities that US firms have (Buckley et al., 2007). For instance, China is determined to become a major global player in the global information and communications technology (ICT) industry, already a $23 billion industry in 2008. The goal is to develop leading worldwide brands across the entire ICT spectrum: hardware, software, telecommunications, semiconductors and sourcing. China's ICT industry is predicted to grow 30 per cent per year during the 12th Five Year Plan (2011–15). Today, all major Chinese ITC

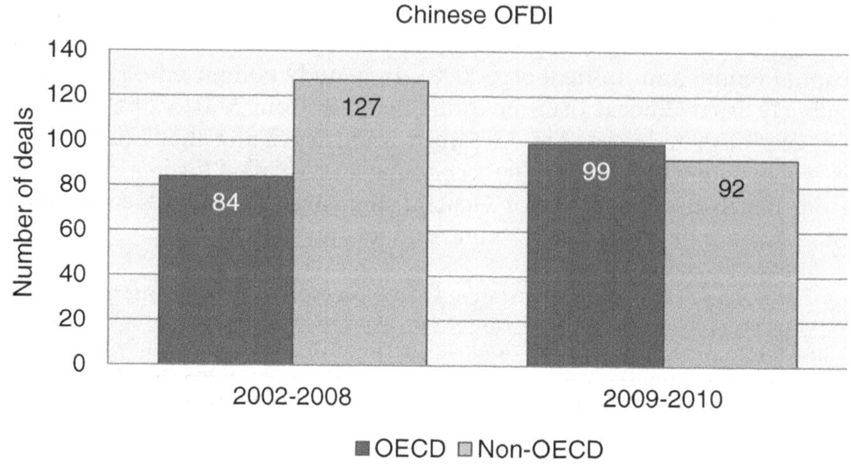


*Source:* Authors' own database.

*Figure 4.2 Number of Chinese firms investing in OECD and non-OECD countries*

firms have a presence in the US, including China Mobile, China Telecom, China Unicom and Huawei.

While China has been busy building domestic and export markets over the last 30 years, it has not built a globally recognizable slate of name brands, nor has it developed many world-class manufacturing capabilities including human resources with global operating talents (Rosen and Hanemann, 2009), comparable to OECD countries. Acquiring these strategic assets will be critical for Chinese firms to better integrate into the world market and overcome their competitive disadvantages (UNCTAD, 2006). With the global financial crisis leading to many cheap assets being available on the market, the Chinese government has adjusted its policies in time to enable more Chinese firms to acquire foreign firms and global brands.

## 4.3 THE ROLE OF THE STATE IN CHINA

### 4.3.1 The Role of Institutions and Emerging Economic Growth

The institutional theorists argue that firms are not agents of free choice, but rather, their strategic choices are influenced by both formal rules and informal cultural norms and values from home and host countries (North, 1990). However, voluntary compliance with institutional norms could bring legitimacy and favorable access to resources (Oliver, 1991). It is generally understood that the institutional environment rewards firms which align themselves with the opportunities and resources in the environment.

North (1990) suggests that 'the agent of change is the individual entrepreneur responding to the incentives embodied in the institutional framework'. In China, however, the state itself is a player alongside the individual entrepreneur and enterprises (in which government units tend to continue to hold significant ownership interests even after their shareholding reforms) (Deng et al., 2010); this is consistent with broader global trends. In the case of emerging economies transitioning from a centralised planning process toward more market-oriented practices, it was widely assumed by the late 1990s that private markets had triumphed over the state and that countries wanting to succeed had to embrace the policies favoured by private capital (Setser, 2008). However, more recent developments involving emerging economies such as China challenge the notion that private markets have completely triumphed over the interventionist state. Two key developments have emerged: 'First, large states are again key actors in financial markets and second, national governments have more financial firepower than do the multilateral institutions' (Setser, 2008). '[T]he west can no longer assume the global order will be remade in its own image' (Spencer, 2009).

At the micro level, however, the state cannot operate SOEs by itself; it needs to delegate their control to the enterprises' managers (Lin et al., 1998). China's gradualist approach to piecemeal privatisation of SOEs has allowed existing enterprises to evolve toward forms consistent with China's comparative advantage, with a feedback effect driving continued change of the institutional environment. Institutionalists typically attribute evolutionary change to a process known as path dependence, 'whereby contingent events or decisions result in the establishment of institutions that persist over long periods of time and constrain the range of actors' future options, including those that may be more efficient or effective in the long run' (Campbell, 2004).

Alongside such path-dependent constraints impacting upon the firm, the reforms continue to evolve, however. Changes in reform objectives reflect, 'first, the increasing knowledge in China about the merits of different resource allocation mechanisms'; and 'second, and more fundamentally, the changes in the social balance between various interest groups and the changes of economic structure resulting from the process of reform and development itself' (Fan, 1994). As stakeholders embrace more market system-type efficiencies, they may tend to offer less resistance to more profound changes, producing a continuing feedback effect between firms' evolution and the institutional environment in which they function. As one commentator has described it, the reforms have inserted 'one by one new institutional elements into the existing framework, thus changing the dynamic of the institutional matrix' (Liu, 1997).

Doug Guthrie (1999) has argued that the emergence of formal rational bureaucracies at the firm level in China had an impact on the Chinese transitional economy, especially with regard to the use of *guanxi*. He challenged the notion that social networks or their use to accomplish economic and procedural tasks were becoming increasingly important in China's economic transition. Based on his interviews of managers and government officials, he demonstrated how the reforms transformed the role of *guanxi*. Guthrie (1999) based his argument on such statements as the following:

> In the old system, if you wanted to get procedures done, you had to make sure you knew people in the right places; you had to try to get procedures passed by relying on people you knew. You had to talk to many people, and the process always took a long time. It wasn't always certain that you would know the right people to take care of the procedures. But now, it's all very clear. You just follow the laws and make sure that you follow them closely. Things happen much more quickly today.

While such observations should not be exaggerated, they do reflect changing practices that have a direct bearing on institutional evolution.

### 4.3.2 Markets, State Intervention and Firm Strategy

The main goal of the Chinese state via its reform path has been to achieve social stability by maintaining growth. In terms of the relationship between state and enterprise, the impact has been to create some space between firm management and bureaucratic state control. Reducing the strictures of central planning and allowing for the development of markets was designed to increase efficiency by enhancing enterprise accountability. Ultimately, to achieve efficiency in capital allocation and management, institutions had to emerge that would dilute state ownership by injecting non-state property into it, thereby highlighting the risk of property use in market competition (You, 1998). Robert Reich (2007) has summarised the phenomenon as follows:

> China's market freedom does seem essential to its capitalist success; unless people there can own their property and exchange it without worrying that the central authority will confiscate their goods, they have no incentive to save and invest. And only if they're confident the capitalist game isn't rigged against them are they willing to play it to the best of their abilities.

How big the space between firm management and bureaucratic state control can become, of course, depends on the sector and its relationship to perceived national security interests and resource needs for innovation to achieve higher value-added competitiveness in global markets. But even where SOEs are involved in areas of essential technology, there is evidence that market mechanisms have acquired independent significance. Witness, for example, the investigation recently launched by the National Development and Reform Commission to determine whether China Telecom and China Unicom, two of the country's biggest state-run telecom companies, may be engaging in monopolistic behaviour and overcharging consumers for broadband Internet under China's three-year-old anti-monopoly law. While such a proceeding is unusual in China, commentators have suggested that the government's state planning agency may be striking a more consumer-friendly tone over concern about the public's impatience with hugely profitable state-backed entities amid rising inflation (Barboza, 2011a).

In this evolving institutional environment, commentators have described Chinese enterprises as occupying a complex and unique situation in which 'they have to adapt their strategy to a new environment and improve their capabilities before participating effectively in global economic integration' (Jin, 2009). Three strategies for growth by Chinese enterprises have been identified (Jin, 2009). Firstly, because the level of concentration is quite low in most sectors of Chinese industry, 'it is imperative for Chinese enterprises to carry out integration strategies in order to create economies of scale, enlarge the scope of their activities, and achieve a better control of key elements of the value chain'. This has led to both vertical and horizontal integration. Secondly, firms seek to redeploy their assets, capabilities and resources to achieve diversification. Now, firms focus on diversifying 'around their core business or capabilities in order to improve their management efficiency, technology, sales and clientele . . . with a greater emphasis on related products or services'. Thirdly, Chinese firms embrace a strategy of globalisation to take part in the international division of labour and expand from the domestic to the international market; 'at the corporate level this means increased integration and interaction with the world economy in terms of production factors, capital, technology and human resources, as well as in terms of business functions such as R&D [research and development], supply, production and marketing.' The principal motivations for Chinese firms to go global are 'to protect and expand export markets, ensure the availability of essential resources, acquire advanced technology and management skills, and export increased overseas opportunities' (Zhang, 2009).

## 4.4 FINANCIAL CRISES AND REINVENTING OF THE ROLE OF THE STATE IN CHINA

### 4.4.1 1997–98 Asian Financial Crisis

Inasmuch as this chapter is part of a book examining the reinvention of the state in light of globalisation and the global financial crisis, it may make sense at this point to assess China's response to external financial crises. Before addressing the most recent global financial crisis, the impact of the 1997–98 Asian financial crisis on China should first be noted. Western and East Asian views of the Asian financial crisis seem to agree on: '(1) the speculative excesses in Asian economies that led to the meltdown, (2) the value of the substantial reforms implemented in the banking and financial services sectors, and (3) the need to end the most extreme forms of government-business collaboration' (Hellmann, 2007). However, the market-supporting institutional reforms established by the International Monetary Fund (IMF) as a condition for emergency loans to several East and Southeast Asian countries were implemented unevenly, and the region's return to substantial growth levels has meant that Asia is participating in the global financial and trading systems without fully embracing the Washington Consensus norms (Hellmann, 2007).

The most visible legacy of the 1997–98 Asian financial crisis appears to have been the creation of new multilateral institutions and bilateral free trade agreements to build on a market-driven and China-centred regionalism. China now has ten free trade agreements with 31 countries, with the China–Association of Southeast Asian Nations FTA the most prominent (Yong, 2011). This development of Asian regionalism has reduced dependence on the IMF and the global economic institutions, at the same time as the importance of Asia in the global economy has grown (Hellmann, 2007). Indeed, it has been claimed that 'a redistribution of geoeconomic and geopolitical power of the magnitude now unfolding in a China-led Asia has led to a basic recasting of the framework for managing the international system' (Yong, 2011). The institutional impact is momentous:

> [T]he continuing success of Asian nations with their various forms of state-led growth, with no comparable established legal traditions and with highly developed cultures in which the individual is not the ethical and legal core, assures that true convergence will need time . . . nurtured by skillful leadership, and an appropriate multilateral framework. (Yong, 2011)

The impact of regional institutional integration resulting from the 1997–98 financial crisis is seen in the growth of Chinese OFDI in Southeast Asia.

For many Chinese multinationals, Southeast Asia became a preferred location. For instance, for Haier, Southeast Asian countries provide a training base for its managers so that they can learn the complexities of international expansion at lower cost. Today, Haier trains its international managers in the Philippines before they are sent to the North American market (Yang and Stoltenberg, 2008).

### 4.4.2 2008–09 Global Financial Crisis

The most fundamental impact of the Global financial crisis on China has been to change its perception of the costs and benefits of an increased role in the global economy (Yong, 2011). This recognition has been manifested in several significant ways. Most fundamentally, decreased export demand resulted in a shift from an export-led growth model to a more domestic demand-driven economy. This led to the government's adoption of a stimulus package of 4 trillion RMB ($626 billion) over three years to maintain economic growth of 9.2 per cent in 2009 and 10.4 per cent in 2010 (Yong, 2011). Government control over the financial system allowed China to keep the fiscal cost of intervention down. Banks' reserve requirements steadily increased from 7 per cent in 2003 to 17.5 per cent in 2008, and banks came to hold over 80 per cent of central bank securities issued for that purpose, with their share in total bank assets exceeding 20 per cent (Akyuz, 2010).

The government also fortified state businesses to fuel growth. While private sector production had been growing faster than the state sector, World Bank data showed that the proportion of industrial production by companies controlled by the Chinese state edged up in 2009 (Wines, 2010). It is noteworthy that the central organisation department of the Communist Party appointed more than half the chairpersons and more than one-third of the chief executive officers (CEOs) of the 129 major state companies, and local governments set up 8000 state-owned investment companies to channel government dollars into business and industrial ventures (Wines, 2010). Some analysts suggested that the state-owned conglomerates became political power centres in their own right, able to resist Beijing's efforts to rein them in (Wines, 2010). These developments had important ramifications for the development of institutions.

### 4.4.3 Institutional Evolution in China and Impact of International and Regional Organisations

Zhu Rongji's dogged efforts to lead China into the WTO were founded upon his notion that China's increased integration into the global economy would force internal change leading to greater economic efficiency and competitiveness. His objective appears to have been attained. Although China's opening to world trade has not been seamless, the overall gains from WTO membership have certainly exceeded the losses (Yong, 2011). Greater integration into the global economy, however, has coincided with 'fragmentation of economic policy into multiple competing agendas' (Frazier, 2010) complicating the fit between domestic economic goals and pursuit of foreign policy.

The growth of China's role in regional organisations since the 1997–98 Asian financial crisis has already been noted. While China continued to focus on its commitment to regional cooperation, it also joined other developing countries in pressing for more balance in international institutions to rectify the disproportionate influence of developed countries in the international economic governance system (Yong, 2011). For example, China played a significant role in the emergence of the Group of Twenty (G-20) as the primary forum for considering changes to the global monetary and financial regulatory regime (Frazier, 2010). It has also been much more assertive on the agenda for trade liberalisation in the WTO's Doha Round. From an institutional perspective, it is interesting to note that China's shift to a 'role as a shaper in international regimes coincides with internal debates . . . over a new growth model and with a pluralization of decision making in foreign policy' (Frazier, 2010). Yet, China's increased role will likely not promote radical departures from past practices of international policy organisations. Even as it 'pursues incremental reforms to international economic institutions, China's foreign policy will remain focused on the imperative of preserving the core framework of those institutions, which have brought greater benefits to China than to any other developing country' (Frazier, 2010).

At the same time, international organisations will continue to attempt to impact upon China's behaviour to achieve broader global goals. In a November 2011 report on China's financial system, the IMF observed that state controls over the economy contributed to soaring property prices, excessive bank lending and mounting local government debt, and that these were among the growing risks threatening to undermine China's economic growth (Barboza, 2011b). The report continued the IMF's efforts:

> to pressure Beijing to quicken the pace of its economic reforms and adopt a more market-oriented approach to banking and finance . . . by strengthening regulatory oversight of the financial system, liberalizing interest rates, giving banks more control over lending and risk management and expanding the authority of the nation's central bank. (Barboza, 2011b)

Similarly, the government's attempt to establish a distinctly Chinese mobile phone standard after a de facto standard had already been established through market-based mechanisms, appears unlikely to succeed (Buthe and Mattli, 2011). China's relationship to international organisations thus functions as a two-way street, both expanding its role and level of participation in global decision-making but at the same time opening its internal processes to greater external scrutiny.

A key component of China's quest for increased competitiveness in global markets has been its innovation policy. Like other aspects of Chinese society impacted by the last 30 years of reform, 'the Chinese Innovation System has evolved over time, aiming at different priorities and implemented through various programs and regulations' (Larcon and Wang, 2009). At this stage in their internationalisation process, the priority for Chinese firms is to learn from other countries' technology and experience (Li, 2009). Initially, such learning focused on foreign direct investment into China; Chinese companies:

> had to compete and cooperate with foreign MNCs actively operating in the country, and had the opportunity to learn from their experience. They . . . improved their technology, accumulated management experience, cultivated management talent, and enhanced their capacity thanks to joint ventures, collaborative agreements and joint projects with foreign multinationals. (Li, 2009a)

More recently, OFDI policy has sought to contribute to the development of top-quality enterprises through various forms of cooperation with foreign companies, and Chinese companies have begun to grow and expand their core business through acquisitions of foreign assets in China and abroad (Li, 2009).

Concurrently, Chinese research and development intensity (research and development expenditure as a percentage of gross domestic product, GDP) has increased rapidly (from 0.6 per cent of GDP in 1995 to 1.34 per cent in 2005). While China's research and development intensity is still lower than that in Japan (3.12 per cent), the US (2.76 per cent) and the EU-25 (1.93 per cent), in absolute terms, China has been catching up very rapidly during the past decade (Larcon and Wang, 2009). Along with substantial investment in research and development has come development of intellectual property (IP) laws and institutions. China's substantive IP laws and institutions are in accord with international expectations. However, China's problems of domestic governance already noted (fragmented central government authority and disjunctions between central government intent and local government implementation and enforcement) 'have ensured that social values more often than not trump formal objectives, including enforcement of the IP regime' (Suttmeier and Yao, 2011).

China's innovation policy is now documented in a 15-year Medium- to Long-Term Plan for Scientific and Technological Development (MLP) that sets objectives for IP creation and commercialisation for the year 2020 in areas such as patents and technical standards. Further emphasis on the importance of IP for the goals of the MLP came with the announcement of the National Intellectual Property Strategy in 2008 and, more recently, the National Patent Development Strategy (2011–20) in November 2010 (Suttmeier and Yao, 2011). A core component of the MLP is an:

> R&D programme built around sixteen 'megaprojects' intended to accelerate the catch-up process by introducing advanced technologies from abroad and developing focused R&D programmes to assimilate and improve on these technologies, thereby producing indigenously developed IP and technical standards. China has implemented a series of industrial policies to reinforce the objectives of the MLP . . . [and] has launched national strategies to support the MLP, including education and human resource development. (Suttmeier and Yao, 2011)

Suttmeier and Yao, (2011) have concluded that:

> while it is fair to continue to characterize China as a Communist-controlled developmental state, one should recognize that the role of the state is becoming increasingly contested by Chinese and foreign stakeholders in China's technological development, and the interactions of state initiatives and market forces involving non-state actors are producing a complex, *sui generis* political economy that defies easy categorization . . . Thus, in considering whether China's IP transition is moving toward harmonization with the international system or diverging from it, the evidence is mixed.

### 4.4.4 The Future Path of China and Chinese Multinationals

#### The 12th Five-Year Plan

The National People's Congress approved the 12th Five-Year Plan in March 2011. It emphasises higher quality, more inclusive growth and sets some important goals: (1) developing Western China; (2) energy efficiency and environmental protection; (3) reducing reliance on exports and increasing domestic consumption; (4) improving citizens' lives; and (5) developing seven priority industries: (a) new energy; (b) energy conservation and environmental protection; (c) biotechnology; (d) new materials; (e) new IT; (f) high-end equipment manufacturing; and (g) clean energy vehicles.

The new Five-Year Plan has significant implications for the MLP as it seeks to develop 'emerging strategic industries', some of which are intended to attain positions of global scientific and technological leadership. The Plan commits to producing more knowledge-intensive development and to creating IP and standards in China, along with an expanded community of stakeholders in a strong IP regime. The strategic industries programme calls special attention to the importance of intellectual property rights (IPR) in stimulating 'patent alliances' among enterprises and in facilitating the transfer of IP from universities and research institutions to industry. The new policy commitments of the Plan are calculated to produce an increasingly IP-intensive pattern of industrial development in China (Suttmeier and Yao, 2011).

The new Plan's national strategic goals will require continued institutional development to address the two major weaknesses of Chinese companies in both domestic and international markets: technology and management. Chinese firms will have to develop processes for the flow of knowledge from headquarters to subsidiary and vice versa. Organising knowledge processes in the multinational corporation is a subject undergoing intense scrutiny, even in more mature, developed-country firms. While it is common to address MNC organisation in knowledge terms, current research reflects a lack of adequate understanding of many of the causal mechanisms and contextual factors in relations between knowledge processes and organisational factors (Foss and Pedersen, 2004). Among the issues Chinese multinationals will have to address are: (1) knowledge flows, subsidiary power and rent-seeking within MNCs (Mudambi and Navarra, 2004); (2) processes of knowledge transfer in international strategic alliances (Simonin, 2004); (3) how relational embeddedness between a foreign parent and international joint venture managers influences transfer of tacit and explicit knowledge (Dhanaraj et al., 2004); and (4) the impact of headquarters control mechanisms on managing knowledge transfer in MNCs (Bjorkman et al., 2004). These issues will challenge institutional processes of many Chinese firms in view of their current organisational capabilities, property rights and corporate culture (Wang, 2009).

**The rise of civil organisations in China**

Frazier (2010) has pointed out that 'the coherence of China's economic goals and the coordination needed to achieve them are eroding as multiple competing interests within the Chinese polity emerge to pursue and protect power and resources'. This situation constitutes a major source of tension for Chinese institutions, suggesting that increased scrutiny be given to associations and their relationship to the Chinese State. 'Under Mao or even during the early years of Deng Xiaoping's rule, few associations existed beyond the so-called mass organisations that are officially extensions of the Party-state' (Unger, 2008). Since then:

> China has witnessed a veritable explosion in the number of associations at both national and local levels . . . ranging from charities to scientific associations, trade and business associations, cultural groups, professional societies, youth groups, environmental associations, women's advocacy groups – the types that have emerged are too lengthy to list in full. (Unger 2008)

The government has referred to these new associations as 'bridges' between the state and China's various social and economic constituencies (Unger, 2008).

Whether they function as bridges, and if so, the types of functions they fulfil and for whose interests, has been the subject of considerable study:

> By the mid-1990s a debate was developing between those who believed that Chinese associations should be studied in terms of *civil society* [the capacity of an organized society to create a zone that stands apart from the state and that serves potentially as a bulwark against expansions of state power] and those whose investigations instead led them to believe that almost all associational life in China was state corporatist in nature . . . Under one variant of corporatism – state corporatism – the state dominates the associations and sometimes even plays a major role in establishing them. (Unger 2008)

The debate continues. As Scott Kennedy (2008) has suggested:

> The mixed success of associations in coordinating their members' activities suggests that no one label – civil society, corporatism, or any other – adequately reflects the nature of government-business relations in China . . . The existence of rival norms and interests in China and different levels of influence over public policy ensures the continuation of a complex struggle to define China's economic system and the role of associations in it.

What is clear is that China's political economy is in a state of flux and government participants are not the only players in the policy process (Kennedy, 2008).

## 4.5 CONCLUSION

We suggested several years ago that Chinese multinationals' OFDI was motivated by both economic and non-economic objectives, but that as China's economic reforms deepened, the relationship between government institutions and SOE behaviour shifted, with market forces playing an ever-increasing role (Yang and Stoltenberg, 2008). The question now is the extent to which the financial crisis may have impacted upon this dynamic. This, in turn, requires an examination of how both domestic and international institutions were affected by the crisis, and the role they play in Chinese OFDI. While the financial crisis reduced the volume of global trade and foreign investment growth for a time, the emerging economies, exemplified by the BRICS (Brazil, Russia, India, China, South Africa) countries, have been quicker to recover and are now in the somewhat unaccustomed role of driving global economic growth through not only strengthening of domestic industries, but also by global expansion of Chinese firms. This represents a major change in the dynamic by which in recent times it has fallen to developed economies, and especially their consumers, to lead the global economy out of recession. While we now know that the emerging markets have not become decoupled from the global economy to the extent some had suggested (Bollen, 2008), they have become stronger players in the game.

In terms of China's post-crisis domestic institutional evolution, the government's movement of resources into SOEs increased their role in the economy generally, at the same time that economic stimulus focused on enhancing infrastructure development to increase China's competitiveness. This investment will assist all Chinese enterprises, not just the SOEs, in their striving for global competitiveness. Along with physical infrastructure, the other great need Chinese multinationals have is enhanced levels of knowledge as they move up the ladder from more basic manufacturing to higher technology production and services; that is, value chain migration. The emphasis of the 12th Five-Year plan on reducing reliance on exports, increasing domestic consumption and developing seven priority sectors points in the direction of greater focus on more knowledge-intensive development. Both IP policy and the rise of non-government associations have created a more complex interaction between state initiatives and market forces involving both SOEs and non-state actors. The knowledge focus of China's development plan puts a premium on the OFDI being undertaken by the country's multinationals. When assets of foreign firms are available at depressed prices resulting from the crisis, the opportunity to acquire them, along with the explicit and tacit knowledge embedded in them, is fully consistent with both firm and larger national goals.

When it comes to international institutional impact, one must first recognise the tension in times of global financial stress between national interest and appeal to international institutions to tackle problems that are global in nature. The increased profile of the G-20 (and China's role in it) in the wake of the financial crisis reflects the need for more harmonised responses to problems affecting all counties in a more interconnected world. At the same time, national political leaders have to balance what they know might be globally desirable and possibly in their countries' interest over the longer term with the very immediate and direct demands of their constituents, without whose support they may well be turned out of office. China has been able to straddle these competing demands and opportunities since the crisis by simultaneously raising its profile in international institutions and pursuing market-driven, China-centred regionalism in that part of the world being looked to for driving global economic growth.

The post-crisis growth of global regulatory governance 'has posed sharp challenges to traditional international law, to standard approaches to the law of international organisations, and to some elements of national legal systems that struggle to grapple with external sources of regulations and regulatory decision making' (Kingsbury, 2012). Given China's experience with its own reforms and Chinese firms' responses to evolving institutional change, they have become adept at seeing their way through thickets of conflicting signals. China's national goal of enhancing competitiveness via knowledge acquisition and development seems a good fit for the OFDI initiatives and strategies its multinationals are now undertaking.

We expect that the future landscape for China and Chinese firms will be far from dull and unimaginative. While the role of the state will by no means recede and Chinese multinationals will become ever more active and visible on the global scene, other actors, such as civil organisations and associations, will inject new energy and visibility into the landscape.

## REFERENCES

Akyuz, Y. (2010), 'The Management of Capital Flows and Financial Vulnerability in Asia', in S. Griffith-Jones, J. Ocampo and J. Stiglitz (eds), *Time For a Visible Hand: Lessons from the 2008 World Financial Crisis*, Oxford: Oxford University Press, pp. 219–241.

Barboza, D. (2011a), 'China Investigates Pricing by 2 Broadband Companies', *New York Times*, 10 November, p. B4.

Barboza, D. (2011b), 'Monetary Fund Urges China to Ease State Controls on Banking', *New York Times*, 16 November, p. B6.

Bjorkman, I., W. Barner-Rasmussen and L. Li (2004), 'Managing Knowledge Transfer in MNCs: The Impact of Headquarters Control Mechanisms', *Journal of International Business Studies*, **35**(5), 443–455.

Bollen, J. (2008), 'Emerging Markets Fail to Decouple from Downturn in US', accessed 17 November 2011 at www.efinancialnews.com/usedition/content/3352501729/24622.

Buckley, P.J., L.J. Clegg, A.R. Cross, X. Liu, H. Voss and P. Zheng (2007), 'The Determinants of Chinese Outward Foreign Direct Investment', *Journal of International Business Studies*, **38**(4), 499–518.

Buthe, T. and W. Mattli (2011), *The New Global Rulers–The Privatization of Regulation in the World Economy*, Princeton, NJ: Princeton University Press.

Campbell, J. (2004), *Institutional Change and Globalization*, Princeton, NJ: Princeton University Press.

Deng, J., Y. Zeng and J. He (2010), 'Shareholding Reform of State-Owned Enterprises and Control', *Frontiers of Business Research in China*, **4**(2), 185–208.
Deng, P. (2009), 'Why Do Chinese Firms Tend to Acquire Strategic Assets in International Expansion?', *Journal of World Business*, **44**, 74–84.
Dhanaraj, C., M. Lyles, H. Steensma and L.Tihanyi (2004), 'Managing Tacit and Explicit Knowledge Transfer in JVs: The Role of Relational Embeddedness and the Impact on Performance', *Journal of International Business Studies*, **35**(5), 428–442.
Fan, G. (1994), 'Dual-Track Transition in China', *Economic Policy*, **19**, 100–122.
Foo, T. (2006), 'Investors Cheer Reversal of Chinese Offshore Controls', *International Financial Law Review*, **25**(2), 33.
Foss, N. and T. Pedersen (2004), 'Organizing Knowledge Processes in the Multinational Corporation: An Introduction', *Journal of International Business Studies*, **35**(5), 340–349.
Frazier, M. (2010), 'China's Domestic Policy Fragmentation and "Grand" Strategy in Global Politics', *Asia Policy*, **10**, 87–101.
Guthrie, D. (1999), *Dragon in a Three-Piece Suit: The Emergence of Capitalism in China*, Princeton, NJ: Princeton University Press.
Hellmann, D. (2007), 'A Decade After the Asian Financial Crisis-Regionalism and International Architecture in a Globalized World', *Asian Survey*, **47**(6), 834–849.
Hong, E. and L. Sun (2006), 'Dynamics of Internationalization and Outward Investment: Chinese Corporations' Strategies', *China Quarterly*, **187**, 610–634.
Hsia, T., C. Li and D.P. Eich (2006), 'Moving Target: A Guide to Recent Chinese M&A and Private Equity Reform', *International Financial Law Review*, **25**(10), 42.
Jin, Z. (2009), 'Corporate Strategies of Chinese Multinationals', in J. Larcon (ed.), *Chinese Multinationals*, Singapore: World Scientific Publishing, pp. 1–29.
Kennedy, S. (2008), 'The Price of Competition: The Failed Government Effort to Use Associations to Organize China's Market Economy', in J. Unger (ed.), *Associations and the Chinese State-Contested Spaces*, Armonk, NY: M.E. Sharpe, pp. 149–174.
Kingsbury, B. (2012), 'Global Administrative Law in the Institutional Practice of Global Regulatory Governance', *World Bank Legal Review*, **3**, 3–33.
Kwan, C.H. (2006), 'An Ever-Expanding Asset Bubble – Why China Has Failed to Take Lessons from the Japanese Experience', accessed 28 June 2006 at www.rieti.go.jp/en/china/06062801.html.
Larcon, J. and G. Wang (2009), 'Technology-Based Competition and Chinese Multinationals', in J. Larcon (ed.), *Chinese Multinationals*, Singapore: World Scientific Publishing, pp. 127–149.
Li, D. (2009), 'Innovation and Knowledge Transfer', in J. Larcon (ed.), *Chinese Multinationals*, Singapore: World Scientific Publishing, pp. 151–166.
Li, Z. (2009), 'China's Outward Foreign Direct Investment', in J. Larcon (ed.), *Chinese Multinationals*, Singapore: World Scientific Publishing, pp. 49–75.
Lin, Y., F. Cai and Z. Li (1998), 'Competition, Policy Burdens, and State-owned Enterprise Reforms', *American Economic Review*, **88**(2), 422–427.
Liu, L. (1997), 'China's Gradual Approach to Reforming Its State-Owned Enterprises', in K. Lieberthal, S. Lin and E.Young (eds), *Constructing China:*

*The Interaction of Culture and Economics*, Ann Arbour, MI: University of Michigan, pp. 265–295.
Luo, X., L. Zhou and S. Liu (2005), 'Entrepreneurial Firms in the Context of China's Transition Economy: An Integrative Framework and Empirical Examination', *Journal of Business Research*, **58**, 277–284.
Mudambi, R. and P. Navarra (2004), 'Is Knowledge Power? Knowledge Flows, Subsidiary Power and Rent-Seeking within MNCs', *Journal of International Business Studies*, **35**(5), 385–406.
North, D. (1990), *Institutions, Institutional Change and Economic Performance*, Cambridge: Cambridge University Press.
Oliver, C. (1991), 'Strategic Responses to Institutional Processes', *Academy of Management Review*, **16**(1), 145–179.
Reich, R. (2007), *Supercapitalism: The Transformation of Business, Democracy and Everyday Life*, New York: Alfred A. Knopf.
Rosen, D.H. and T. Hanemann (2009), 'China's Changing Outbound Foreign Direct Investment Profile: Drivers and Policy Implications', *Peterson Institute for International Economics: Policy Brief*, **9**(14), 1–21.
Sauvant, K. (2005), 'New Sources of FDI: The BRICs Outward FDI from Brazil, Russia, India and China', *Journal of World Investment and Trade*, **6**(5), 639–709.
Setser, B. (2008), 'A Neo-Westphalian International Financial System?' *Journal of International Affairs*, **62**(1), 17–34.
Simonin, B. (2004), 'An Empirical Investigation of the Process of Knowledge Transfer in International Strategic Alliances', *Journal of International Business Studies*, **35**(5), 407–427.
Spencer, D. (2009), 'Watch for Emerging Nations', *International Financial Law Review*, **28**(6), 45.
Suttmeier, R. and X. Yao (2011), 'China's IP Transition: Rethinking Intellectual Property Rights in a Rising China', National Bureau of Asian Research NBR Special Report, 29.
UNCTAD (2005), *World Investment Report: Transnational Corporations and the Internationalization of R&D*, New York and Geneva: United Nations Publications.
UNCTAD (2006), *World Investment Report: FDI from Developing and Transition Economies: Implications for Development*, New York and Geneva: United Nations Publications.
UNCTAD (2009), *World Investment Report: Transnational Corporations, Agricultural Production and Development*, New York and Geneva: United Nations Publications.
UNCTAD (2010), *World Investment Report: Investing in a Low Carbon Economy*, New York and Geneva: United Nations Publications.
Unger, J. (2008), 'Chinese Associations, Civil Society, and State Corporatism: Disputed Terrain', in J. Unger (ed.), *Associations and the Chinese State-Contested Spaces*, Armonk, NY: M.E. Sharpe, pp. 1–13.
Wang, Y. (2009), 'Corporate Culture and Organization of Chinese Multinationals', in J. Larcon (ed.), *Chinese Multinationals*, Singapore: World Scientific Publishing, pp. 167–191.
Wines, M. (2010), 'China Fortifies State Businesses to Fuel Growth', *New York Times*, 30 August, pp. A1, 6.
Yang, X. and C. Stoltenberg (2008), 'Growth of Made-in-China Multinationals: An Institutional and Historical Perspective', in I. Alon and J. McIntyre (eds),

*Globalization of Chinese Enterprises*, Basingstoke, UK: Palgrave Macmillan, pp. 61–76.

Yang, Y., X. Yang and B. Doyle (2011), 'Location Strategy and Firm Value Creation: The Case of Chinese MNEs', *Proceedings of Harvard Conference on China Goes Global*, Boston, MA, 2–4 October.

Yong, W. (2011), 'WTO Accession, Globalization, and a Changing China', *China Business Review*, **38**(4), 31–33.

You, J. (1998), *China's Enterprise Reform: Changing State/Society Relations after Mao*, London: Routledge.

Zhang, K. (2009), 'Rise of Chinese Multinational Firms', *Chinese Economy*, **42**(6), 87–96.

# 5. The EU and the member states: Germany and supranationalism in times of financial crisis

**Jürgen Bröhmer**

## 5.1 INTRODUCTION

The European sovereign debt crisis is bringing to the fore imminent questions on constitutionalism and democracy and the ability of international and, in this case, supranational institutions to deal with a crisis with potentially major repercussions on the national and international level. The debt crisis highlights once again what the global financial crises had already demonstrated, that is, that the management of international affairs, especially international economic affairs, has long left the realm of the nation state. The nations are still major players, but institutions such as the European Union (EU), the G-20, the International Monetary Fund (IMF) or intergovernmental specialised instruments such as the ESM (European Stability Mechanism) in the future and currently the EFSF (European Financial Stability Facility) have entered the playing field. Recently unimaginable amounts of money have been committed and guaranteed. Wide-ranging policy decisions of whole countries are heavily influenced by outside forces.

The executive branches of government are at the core of all this decision-making. National parliamentary oversight is severely hampered by time and information constraints and supranational parliamentary control is also largely absent. In contrast to the international executive management of such crises stand largely domestic, national systems of democratic accountability. The German Constitutional Court has tried to define the role of the democratic principle in this context in a number of decisions dealing with the sovereign debt crisis and Germany's participation in attempts to control this crisis.

Three decisions of the Court stand out in this respect. The general framework was developed by the Court in its decision on the constitutionality of the Lisbon Treaty,[1] where the Court included decisions with major budgetary ramifications as part of the canon of matters where the

German Parliament must retain the final word as part of maintaining constitutional identity.[2]

The second and third decisions specifically deal with the constitutionality of concrete steps taken by Germany in the context of measures taken by member states of the EU and especially those that are part of the euro as a common currency ('the Euro-Group') to support Greece in the sovereign debt crisis in the light of the conditions and requirements set by the Court for the democratic legitimisation of these measures in the Lisbon decision.[3] The third decision applies these principles to the very concrete question of whether and to what degree the German Parliament can delegate such decisions to a nine-member subcommittee of the Budget Committee in cases of urgency, and whether secrecy is required.[4]

The problem is, of course, not just a German problem. It is a general one and can be abstractly described as an inherent conflict between democracy and democratic legitimisation on the one hand, and the growing need for international cooperation and decision-making on the other hand. Protests in the past decade or so concerning primarily international trade and finance on the occasion of World Trade Organization (WTO) meetings, summits and various economic forums and movements such as ATTAC (the Association for the Taxation of Financial Transactions and Aid to Citizens) or the more recent Occupy Wall Street movement are largely driven by concerns about important decisions being reached without any democratic legitimisation by anonymous organisations and faceless men and women accountable to no one. In July 2011, Vaclav Klaus, the President of the Czech Republic, wrote in the *Australian* and summarised the problem quite clearly:

> The accelerating move towards global governance and even more dramatically towards European governance is weakening the traditional pillar of democracy, the nation state . . . The solution to the pressing problems of our era doesn't lie in creating new governmental and supranational agencies. It is also not about the technicalities of these solutions. It is about democracy, and democracy needs demos: citizens and citizenship. Without them democracy cannot be constituted. We can't have democracy at the level of the EU, with 27 different nation-states. Similarly, there can't be democracy at the level of the world. It is possible to have an efficient intergovernmentalism but not a democratic worldwide supranationalism. Recent attempts to start organising global governance on the basis of organisations such as G-20 are unacceptable. (Klaus, 2011)

## 5.2 BACKGROUND

The European sovereign debt crisis has been, is and will continue to be on the top of the agenda of European policy-makers for some time to come.

The measures that have been taken were at times forced by market reactions and have the markings of emergency responses. They are complex and even experts find them difficult to understand. The issue here is not to give a detailed account of the reaction of the European Union and its member states to the sovereign debt crisis. The scope of the problem at issue here can be demonstrated by looking at the main instruments now in place, which are designed to become effective as soon as possible.

### 5.2.1 EFSF – The European Financial Stability Facility

The EFSF is a private company incorporated in Luxembourg under Luxembourg law on 9 May 2010 and is owned by those member states of the EU which have introduced the euro as their common currency.[5] The objective of the EFSF is to safeguard financial stability in Europe by providing – or preventively being able to provide – financial assistance to member states of the euro area. To this end the EFSF can use a number of instruments, especially conditional loans to countries in financial difficulties. To fund these loans and other instruments the EFSF can issue bonds or other debt instruments on the capital markets. The activities of the EFSF are backed by guarantees by its owner states. The total volume of guarantees by the euro area states currently amount to €780 billion, equivalent to just under AUS$1 trillion.[6] The share per contributing state as of October 2011 is relative to the economic weight of the respective state and its ability to contribute. For Germany the contribution key is set at 29.07 per cent which amounts to just over €211 billion. The EFSF is part of a wider safety net to preserve financial stability within Europe. The EU has its own European Financial Stabilisation Mechanism (EFSM), which allows the Commission to borrow up to €60 billion from financial markets under an implicit guarantee of the EU's budget.[7]

A further important factor is the International Monetary Fund (IMF), which has provided just under €80 billion in loans in conjunction with the EFSF.[8] The IMF's resources are provided by its member states in the form of quotas and special drawing rights which means that the IMF's activities are partially underwritten by Germany as one member state, but also by all the other 187 member states of the IMF.[9]

### 5.2.2 European Stability Mechanism

The EFSF started out as an emergency undertaking to stabilise Greece, Portugal and Ireland in the wake of the debt crisis. However, the unfolding of the crisis, especially the risk of what is being referred to as the danger of 'contagion', has led to the creation of a permanent financial safety institution, the European Stability Mechanism (ESM). As such the ESM will not raise any additional funding or provide additional guarantees. Rather it will take over from the EFSF its task of acting with a stabilising effect in the capital markets to secure EU member states from financial instability.[10] The ESM is to be something like the International Monetary Fund for Europe.

In order to achieve this, the Treaty on the Functioning of the European Union (TFEU) had to be amended. The new Article 136 TFEU provides:

> The Member States whose currency is the euro may establish a stability mechanism to be activated if indispensable to safeguard the stability of the euro area as a whole. The granting of any required financial assistance under the mechanism will be made subject to strict conditionality.

The separate treaty establishing the European Stability Mechanism was signed on 11 July 2011 but was quickly amended and the new version was signed on 2 February 2012.[11] It was originally envisaged that the ratification processes in the member states would be finished in time for an entry into force on 1 July 2013.[12] As a result of the European Council meeting in December 2011, member states agreed to speed up this process for the ESM to be operational mid-year 2012. To this end the threshold for the coming into effect of the ESM Treaty was lowered from ratification in countries whose aggregate signed capital amounted to 95 per cent, to an aggregate capital of 90 per cent.

According to Article 8 of the ESM Treaty the ESM will have an authorised capital stock of €700 billion with an initial maximum lending capacity of €500 billion. At the March 2012 European Council meeting the member states agreed to review these numbers within one month.[13]

## 5.3 (NATIONAL) DEMOCRACY AS ONE IDENTITY PILLAR OF GERMAN CONSTITUTIONALISM: THE CONSTITUTIONAL COURT'S LISBON DECISION

The German Constitutional Court has closely monitored the involvement of Germany in the European integration process from the very beginning. The German Constitution prominently warrants in its preamble[14] and more importantly in Article 23[15] that Germany play an active and positive role in this process. However, participation in this process is not the only fundamental objective of the German Constitution. Another one is the principle of democracy.[16] The Court has consistently deduced from Article 38 of the Basic Law[17] that this provision not only guarantees free elections but also that the body to be elected, the Federal Parliament, has something of significance left to decide and does not deteriorate to a meaningless assembly of powerless deputies. In its judgment on the constitutionality of the Treaty of Lisbon,[18] the Court formulated:

> [246] The election of the Members of the German Bundestag by the people fulfils its central role in the system of the federal and supranational intertwining of power only if the German Bundestag, which represents the people, and the Federal Government sustained by it, retain a formative influence on the political development in Germany. This is the case if the German Bundestag retains its own responsibilities and competences of substantial political importance or if the Federal Government, which is answerable to it politically, is in a position to exert a decisive influence on European decision-making procedures.[19]

For this purpose the Court attempted to define what is part of German constitutional identity and confirmed that it will safeguard this identity core and that this core cannot – without principal constitutional reform – be sacrificed to further steps of European integration:

> [240] Furthermore, the Federal Constitutional Court reviews whether the inviolable core content of the constitutional identity of the Basic Law pursuant to Article 23.1 third sentence in conjunction with Article 79.3 of the Basic Law is respected . . . The exercise of this review power, which is rooted in constitutional law, follows the principle of the Basic Law's openness towards European Law (Europarechtsfreundlichkeit), and it therefore also does not contradict the principle of sincere cooperation (Article 4.3 Lisbon TEU); otherwise, with progressing integration, the fundamental political and constitutional structures of sovereign Member States, which are recognised by Article 4.2 first sentence Lisbon TEU, cannot be safeguarded in any other way. In this respect, the guarantee of national constitutional identity under constitutional and under Union law go hand in hand in the European legal area.[20]

The various areas to which the Court afforded special significance in this respect were described as follows:

> [249] European unification on the basis of a treaty union of sovereign states may, however, not be achieved in such a way that not sufficient space is left to the Member States for the political formation of the economic, cultural and social living conditions . . . Essential areas of democratic formative action comprise, inter alia, citizenship, the civil and the military monopoly on the use of force, revenue and expenditure including external financing and all elements of encroachment that are decisive for the realisation of fundamental rights, above all in major encroachments on fundamental rights such as deprivation of liberty in the administration of criminal law or placement in an institution. These important areas also include cultural issues such as the disposition of language, the shaping of circumstances concerning the family and education, the ordering of the freedom of opinion, press and of association and the dealing with the profession of faith or ideology.[21]

The Court thus regards as one essential area of democratic formative action 'revenue and expenditure including external financing'.

## 5.4 THE CONSTITUTIONAL COURT'S DECISION REGARDING THE CONSTITUTIONALITY OF THE MEASURES TAKEN WITH REGARD TO GREECE

The Greek crisis gave the Constitutional Court an opportunity to explain further the meaning of its constitutional identity doctrine and its ramifications for the budget process respectively for financial measures undertaken by the government with potentially huge budgetary consequences.[22]

The decision also amply illustrates a new quality of globalisation if one is willing to speculate about the potential consequences that a negative verdict stipulating the unconstitutionality of the German participation in the Greek and euro rescue measures might have had. Speculation though it is, it is not implausible that such a negative decision could have caused major turmoil in the financial markets with grave consequences around the globe. It is very possible that the decision by this German court rendered on that Wednesday in Karlsruhe could have had a profound impact on the superannuation balances of millions of Australians.

## 5.5 THE COURT'S JURISDICTION

The Court's decision illustrates another aspect of the German legal system relevant in this context: that is, the rather strict definition of the jurisdiction of the various courts in general and the German Constitutional Court in particular. The Court again upheld its view that the constitutional complaint procedure, by which the citizens have access to the Constitutional Court for review of government action infringing on their fundamental rights as protected in the Basic Law's, catalogue and similar rights such as the voting rights contained in Article 38 of the Basic Law, must be available as a last resort of judicial review.

The key to the constitutional complaint procedure is the Court's consistently broad interpretation of Article 38 of the Basic Law as reaffirmed by its Lisbon decision and again expressly confirmed in this decision concerning the Greek measures. Financial aid packages do not as such impact on individual rights, and the mere fact that some day there might be repercussions in the form of increased state debt, higher taxes or inflation would otherwise not be sufficient grounds for individuals to challenge such government action. In the Greek measures case the Court specifically justified its broad approach with the need for judicial review in favour of the fundamental democratic principle. By linking the principle of democracy to human dignity,[23] the ultra-fundamental clause of the German Basic Law (Article 1),[24] a norm which appears to increasingly evolve into a trans-legal quasi-religious sphere, the Court reaffirmed its own safeguarding role. The citizen is enlisted as the Basic Law's foot soldier defending democracy in general and the rights of the Parliament in particular, which the Parliament itself, notwithstanding its and its members' privileged access to the Constitutional Court, is unwilling to assert because of broad majorities backing the governmental action.

Another special feature of the Basic Law is that it contains absolute limits as to its own amendment. Article 79.3 of the Basic Law makes it legally impossible to amend the Basic Law with regard to the core contents of the state fundamental principles set out in Articles 1 and 20: human dignity, republican structure, rule of law, federal organisation, a social or welfare state, and democracy.[25] Amendment affecting these principles is possible, for example a change of the electoral system from a proportional to a majority system, but not when that change goes to the core of the principle, with the Constitutional Court defining where the periphery ends and the core begins. Reference to Article 79.3 and its absolute limits is also made in Article 23.1[26] which deals specifically with the scope of Germany's participation in the project of European integration; and such participation of Germany in the European Union and hence the structure of the European Union itself must adhere to these core principles if Germany is to continue to be a part of this Union. It is interesting to note that the Court felt compelled to explain that the application of Article 79.3 of the Basic Law is not restricted to a *coup d'état* and the overthrow of the democratically elected government, but rather sets in much earlier.[27]

Whereas one should carefully resist the danger of over interpreting such dicta, the fact remains that by choice of language what is at issue in the case is being looked upon in a suggestive context of a perceived danger of the usurpation of powers by some extra-national entity. In the final analysis the Court – unsurprisingly – came to the conclusion that all is in constitutional order. But it confirms a tendency of the Court, much more visible in its Lisbon judgment, to speak of European integration as a constitutional risk and threat that needs to be contained, before concluding its risk assessment with a verdict that the dangers are still manageable.[28]

### 5.5.1 The Court's Decision on the Merits

The Court's decision on the merits is interesting in its general approach. It appears to be raising the bar by emphasising the role and autonomy of the national parliament in matters with significant budget implications, and thus strengthens the Parliament's procedural involvement in these matters and its role vis-à-vis the executive branch. At the same time the Court acknowledges the wide margins of appreciation in the risk assessment of such rescue measures and in the assessment of to what degree they actually influence the domestic budget autonomy.

The Court commences by formulating high standards for parliamentary participation – at least that is what the language used wants to communicate. Parliamentary responsibility for the budget prohibits the current and subsequent parliaments from taking decisions that would make it impossible for this or subsequent parliaments to exercise the budget right autonomously.[29] This budget autonomy must be secured even within systems of 'intergovernmental governing',[30] and would be violated if the determination of the extent and the type and scope of taxation and other levies on the citizens were 'supranationalised' and no longer to be decided by the Bundestag.[31] Never mind that the supranationalisation of taxation decisions was not at issue in the case. The Court uses this fictive constellation merely as an example.

The more interesting question – to what extent decisions today will invariably have consequences on decisions tomorrow – is only indirectly touched upon by the Court. This question points far beyond the concrete debt crisis. Germany too has amassed too much public debt[32] and debt servicing has been and is the second-largest item of the federal budget after 'work and welfare', expenditures but ahead of defence.[33] The temporal aspect of democracy raises the question to what degree today's decision makers are legitimised to make decisions that cannot be undone by future legislators who will have to bear the consequences of these decisions.[34] Environmental decision-making (or avoiding such decisions) is one example and it is no coincidence that the concept of sustainability which tries to capture this temporal problem figures most prominently in this field. However, the problem arises in regard to any longer-term policy-making where certain choices narrow the decision-making scope of future legislators. Amassing structural financial deficits that will have to be serviced by future generations of taxpayers is a very illustrative example because depending on how and why such debts were incurred will determine to what degree future generations will not only bear the burdens of the debt but also enjoy the benefits created.[35] In both cases, however, the fact remains that those affected by the decisions had no input into the making of those decisions and that is inherently true in the context of this – and other – financial crises.[36] There is of course no blanket solution. Whereas one must have recurring elections in a democracy, limiting the decision-making to activities the consequences of which could be contained to the term of one parliament is not only impossible but also logically not maintainable, because even inaction will have effects into the future and that is true for budgets as well. Not incurring debts can determine the future as much as incurring debts.

Fiscal sustainability is the only qualitative measurement that could address this problem and without using the term as such, the Constitutional Court took recourse to sustainability criteria when assessing the constitutionality of Germany's participation in the rescue measures. The Court emphasised that it could only address evident violations of the democratic rights of the Bundestag and that the Bundestag enjoys a large margin of appreciation in the assessment of the risk of the guarantees taken on by Germany actually materialising and becoming real liabilities.[37] The Court expressly states that it is 'questionable' whether the Constitution and the principle of democracy provide a justiciable limit for the possible extent of such guarantees.[38] The Court assessed the overall risk if all guarantees became liabilities at about €170 billion and stated that it is irrelevant that the potential risk of the rescue measures exceeds the largest single item of the federal budget (which it does) or even exceeds half of the total budget (which it also does)[39] because the Constitution contains no such formal limits. Thus the government's assertions that in a worst-case scenario these liabilities could be dealt with by tax increases, spending cuts and longer-term debt instruments was regarded as sufficient to pass the constitutional threshold.[40]

When the substantive law cannot provide sufficient answers, procedural rules are what is left. Given the inherent difficulties with determining whether rescue measures will be effective and what further measures might be required in the future, and given the inherent difficulties in assessing what the price of not acting would be, insisting on the decisive procedural involvement of the Bundestag in the decision-making process as far as Germany is concerned, must be regarded as the cornerstone of the Court's approach. Core decisions must be legitimised by direct involvement of the Parliament – one is inclined to speak of leveraged democratic legitimisation. The notion that Parliament must take all fundamental decisions is not new at all and has dominated the discourse in the context of the rule of law and fundamental rights protection from the beginning of the Basic Law in 1949.

### 5.5.2 The Parliament's Role and Responsibilities: What Does It Mean in Practice?

**Background**

About five months after laying the general groundwork for Germany's participation in such rescue efforts, the meaning of the democratic principle in general and the participation and principal responsibility of the Parliament (Bundestag) in this process, the Constitutional Court had an opportunity to specify how these obligations must be discharged by the Parliament. The dispute arose because the – amended – German statutory implementation of the rescue measures[41] provided in Section 3.3 that in cases of urgency the participation rights of the Bundestag were to be exercised by a special subcommittee of the budget committee comprising of the minimum number of members necessary to proportionally represent each political 'fraction'.[42] The members of this 'Committee of Nine' had been unanimously elected by the Bundestag in plenary on 26 October 2011. This notwithstanding, two representatives instituted an 'organ dispute'[43] to challenge the constitutionality of the delegation of such far-reaching powers from the 620 deputies of the plenary to a nine-member subcommittee of the Budget Committee (41 members).

**The court's decision**

The Court decided that the broad empowerment of the 'Committee of Nine' was unconstitutional and violated Article 38 of the Basic Law.[44] As a matter of principle, the participation rights of the Parliament must be exercised by the Bundestag as a whole. Exceptions to this principle – that is, delegation to committees and subcommittees – are only possible if necessitated by a requirement to defend other constitutionally recognised interests and on the basis of a strict application of the principle of proportionality.[45] For the Court this follows from the democratic principle and its concrete manifestations in the context of the budget, the determination of which is a core function of Parliament. The Court also referred to the specific requirement of the Basic Law that the giving of guarantees requires statutory authority.[46] The Court weighed this against the established practice that the Bundestag conducts much of its work through committees.[47] The Bundestag's procedure is part of its procedural autonomy and governed by Rules of Procedure passed by each newly constituted Bundestag in statutory form.[48] Generally these committees prepare decisions of the plenary, for example as part of the legislative procedure, when after assignment of a bill to one or more committees in the first reading, the bill undergoes fine tuning or even major overhaul in the assigned committees in preparation for the second reading.[49] In some cases the Basic Law contains specific language empowering certain committees with decision-making power.[50] In the absence of similar special constitutional exceptions, such delegation of the plenary's decision-making power is only possible if it can be justified by overarching mandatory requirements representing legal interests that are constitutionally protected just like the status of the individual representative and the institution of the Bundestag as a whole, and that its rights are protected and under strict observance of the principle of proportionality. The ability of Parliament to function effectively is one such interest.[51] The need for confidentiality is another possible reason and the Court had no problem accepting that confidentiality could be required for some forms of intervention on the capital markets, namely in the secondary bond market. But even for this case the Court demanded the subsequent informing of and explanation to the plenary for the action authorised by the small subcommittee.[52]

In summary, while the Court had issues with the concrete procedure and the broadness of the powers of the 'Committee of Nine', it did not deny the Bundestag the possibility to maintain such a procedure if the rights of the plenary and thus the vast majority of individual members are adequately protected.

## 5.6 NATIONAL DEMOCRACY IN A GLOBALISED WORLD

The German Constitutional Court's approach in European matters has consistently been one strongly emphasising the role of the domestic Parliament as the prime institution when it comes to democratic legitimisation. Former US House of Representatives Speaker Thomas 'Tip' O'Neill's famous phrase that 'all politics is local' has been adapted by the German Constitutional Court to read: 'almost all democracy is national'. Whereas there can be no doubt that the proximity between those governing and those governed, spatial and otherwise, cannot be underestimated as one important parameter for the functioning of democratic governance, it begs the question how that proximity can be maintained in today's world. Or, to formulate the question differently, is the mandated democratic proximity merely a formal criterion that can be ticked off if only some form of constituent authority is given by the national Parliament or is it a more substantive principle that requires choice, that is, a realistic possibility of the Parliament choosing between two alternative options? Did the Bundestag really have a choice in the matter or were the decisions reached 'without alternative' as was so often stipulated, because any negative decision would have created havoc on the financial markets? The question has an international and a domestic aspect.

### 5.6.1 International Perspective: Trail Smelter and Financial Meltdown

Internationally the question gets an additional twist if one assumes that a negative decision could have caused significant financial damage in other countries. In the famous *Trail Smelter* arbitration,[53] a case which is widely held to be one of the foundation statements of international environmental law, the Tribunal held that:

> no state has the right to use or permit the use of its territory in such a manner as to cause injury by fumes in or to the territory of another or to the property or persons therein, when the case is of serious consequence and the injury is established by clear and convincing evidence.[54]

The International Court of Justice confirmed the underlying idea in its decision on the *Corfu Channel* case, holding that every state has an obligation 'not to allow knowingly its territory to be used for acts contrary to the rights of other States'.[55]

It is an interesting question to what degree this now accepted principle of state responsibility in environmental law could be transferred to the behaviour of states in areas other than the environment when that activity has direct negative effects on other states.[56] To put the question more concretely, could Germany decide against a rescue package if that negative decision were to lead to significant turmoil on the financial markets and cause major harm, for example to the superannuation balances of Australians, to the welfare of ordinary Greek citizens or to the pensions of Portuguese retirees?

According to the criteria established in *Trail Smelter* the answer to the question could rest on whether the consequences of rejecting the rescue package were sufficiently serious and whether a clear causative nexus between the rejection of the rescue package and the effects on the financial markets and the subsequent consequences in other states could be established. And even if that could be established one would still have to address the question of any contributory factors for which the affected states would have to take responsibility. Evidently, reckless budgetary behaviour is the root cause of the problem. That said, the reckless behaviour of one person does not per se negate another's obligation to engage in reasonable rescue measures when the damage is done.

However, *Trail Smelter* implicitly recognises that the damages caused and the price to be paid for avoiding the damages are reasonably similar in quality and quantity. If the cessation or adaption of the smelter operation in Canada could have been considered to cost lives in Canada, the people in the state of Washington might have had to bear the fumes. Conversely, if Germany's participation could be said to cause similar financial damage, or respective risks, to Germany as its non-participation in the rescue efforts could cause elsewhere, one would have to conclude for that reason alone, that any international liability is out of the question.

To argue in this way implies that there is at least a possibility for international liability under the *Trail Smelter* principles with regard to a country's economic and financial policy, even if the concrete factual situation might preclude the liability. That alone would be a far-reaching conclusion. The property based principle of *sic utere tuo ut alienum non laedas*[57] would in effect be adapted in international law and the present context to prohibit the use of a state's sovereign budget rights in such a way as to inflict serious harm on another state's capability to fulfil its sovereign functions.

Here is not the place to conclusively answer the question of the applicability of *Trail Smelter* in the context of financial rescue packages. Clearly the factual assessment, if nothing else, would make application of these principles and the argument for liability rather difficult. But in a financially globalised world this is a question the international legal community must engage with.

### 5.6.2 The Rights of the Bundestag from a Domestic Perspective

Strictly from a domestic and legal perspective the Bundestag could of course have voted no to the rescue package.[58] The fact that this might have had negative effects for Germany as well does not reduce the discretion of the Parliament. Risk assessment is the very nature of the job in any decision-making of the Parliament and the notion of democratic decision-making rests on the recognition that we do not know what exactly the consequences of various alternative decisions are, and which are better or worse. We may all have our own opinion but we do not have the knowledge. Regardless of the controversy around the benefits or harm of the rescue measures for Greece, it appears to be a still plausible risk assessment that the potential cost for Germany outweighs the potential risk of rejection for Germany, at least if one does not operate on the basis of worst-case scenarios. From a German perspective the question therefore is little different from the question whether the Lehman Brothers investment bank should have been bailed out or not, or whether other investment banks or insurers should have been allowed to go bankrupt.

## 5.7 QUESTIONS – BUT NO ANSWERS

As has been shown, everything is in order with the German participation in the Greek rescue package and the Federal Constitutional Court has made clear that for this to remain so, the Bundestag must be, and remain, the decider. One could leave it at that, and perhaps one must leave it at that for the time being. But it begs the question whether this is an approach that sets form over substance. Is it not fictitious to assume that 'national democracies' are indeed in a position to master crises like this in an insular fashion – the German Bundestag for Germany, the United States (US) Congress for the US and the Commonwealth Parliament for Australia? If that were so, would not in effect the 'powerful' national parliaments dictate the agenda? For if the German Bundestag or the US Congress says no in this context of triple-billion commitments, the opinion even of the Commonwealth Parliament or, as it were, the Greek Parliament might not be that important any more.

If one were to proceed from the assumption that these matters are really beyond the scope of the national democracies (and the sovereign state for that matter), what does this mean for the definition of democracy?[59] Is the 'national democracy' view espoused by the German Constitutional Court obsolete? And if it is, what should replace the national stream of democratic legitimisation? When speaking about democratic legitimisation one also speaks of the acceptability of decisions by those affected. It is not just a theoretical debate by constitutional scholars – it has tangible effects. A solution of the sovereign debt crisis can only be achieved if the populations affected accept the necessary measures. Sacrificing democracy on the altar of utility because of the difficulties or even the impossibility of reconciling the globalised reality with national democratic legitimisation is therefore not an option, because it will precisely remove the utility one might hope to gain from a disconnected international regime. Elements of this disconnect are already visible. Publicly espoused views in Greece about German dominance and similar views in Germany about being taken advantage of as the paymaster in essence reflect in part a feeling that important decisions are made not at home but elsewhere.

However, there is no silver bullet to solve this global governance crisis.[60] There is a mix of approaches to minimise the problem but the problem will persist. Insofar as transnational decision-making is needed, the national democratic process is weakened. If the reaction to this inherent process is the nationalisation or renationalisation of political decision-making it will necessarily result in governance deficits. Hence, and this would have to be a major element of a solution, a balancing of domestic and transnational decision-making is required, as trivial as that may sound. The principle of subsidiarity will go some way in this respect, albeit it is only able to allocate political issues to the right level of government and therefore does not and cannot solve the problem of the democratic legitimisation of those problems attributed to the higher level. Multilevel forms of democratic legitimisation are another element.[61] In the European Union this would be afforded by the European Parliament and the national parliaments in interwoven decision-making processes. However, whereas this solution has some potential for superstructures like the EU it is equally obvious that it is already under stress even within the EU's relatively homogeneous context, and it is hard to see whether it could be stretched much further to even larger or more heterogeneous superstructures. The current phenomenon of trying to compensate deficits in democratic legitimisation by technocratic, expert-based decision-making can only reach as far as the credibility of the experts extends, and hence not very far. If indeed the essence of democracy is that we do not know, then the capacity of legitimisation by expert knowledge is inherently limited.[62]

In the economic world it is often said that the free market reaches its limits if the players become too big to fail. If that is the case, these big players will inevitably amend their risk management strategies and incorporate into these strategies the possibility that governments will come to the rescue when things go bad in order to protect the system and the overriding public interest. Conversely one could say that international governance would also function much better if all states were much smaller and there were many more of them. Individual states could then not be perceived as dominating the decision-making process, and mistakes of individual states such as excessive deficits could not affect other states. However, in the world of states 'too small to matter' is obviously even less a possible part of a solution than it is in the economic arena as an antidote for 'too big to fail'. To some extent we can organise the market in such a way by effective competition and merger rules. But states cannot be organised in this way. States are created and organised ethnically, historically, sociologically, culturally or religiously, to name perhaps the most important factors. Optimising governance is not one of those important factors.

## NOTES

1. Treaty of Lisbon amending the Treaty on Europ ean Union and the Treaty establishing the European Community, signed at Lisbon, 13 December 2007, OJ C 306/1 (2007), http://eur-lex.europa.eu/JOHtml.do?uri=OJ:C:2007:306:SOM:EN:HTML (6/4/2012).
2. The decision of the German Constitutional Court of 30 June 2009 was published in English at the same time it was released in German: BVerfG, 2 BvE 2/08, 30 June 2009, http://www.bverfg.de/entscheidungen/es20090630_2bve000208en.html (6/4/2012).

3. BVerfG, 2 BvR 987/10, 7 September 2011, http://www.bverfg.de/entscheidungen/rs20110907_2bvr098710.html (6/4/2012); see also press release of 7 August 2011 in English, http://www.bverfg.de/pressemitteilungen/bvg11-055en.html (6/4/2012).
4. BVerfG, 2 BvE 8/11, 28 February 2012, http://www.bverfg.de/entscheidungen/es20120228_2bve000811.html (6/4/2012).
5. See EFSF Framework Agreement, http://www.efsf.europa.eu/attachments/20111019_efsf_framework_agreement_en.pdf (6/4/2012); Terms of Reference of the Eurogroup European Financial Stability Facility, 7 June 2010 http://www.consilium.europa.eu/uedocs/cms_Data/docs/pressdata/en/misc/114977.pdf (6/4/2012); Terms of Reference Maximising the Capacity of the EFSF, Terms and Conditions – 29 November 2011, http://www.efsf.europa.eu/attachments/efsf_terms_of_reference_maximising_the_capacity.pdf (6/4/2012). See also European Financial Stability Facility, 'About EFSF', http://www.efsf.europa.eu/about/index.htm (6/4/2012).
6. Greece, Portugal and Ireland are so-called 'stepping-out guarantors', i.e. they are unable to contribute to the guarantee pool. The total guarantee commitment is therefore reduced to €726 billion, see Annex 1 of the Framework Agreement.
7. Council Regulation (EU) No 407/2010 of 11 May 2010 establishing a European Financial Stabilisation Mechanism, OJ L 118/1 (2010), http://eur-lex.europa.eu/LexUriServ/LexUriServ.do?uri=OJ:L:2010:118:0001:0001:EN:PDF (6/4/2012).
8. See International Monetary Fund, 'Factsheet: the IMF and Europe', http://www.imf.org/external/np/exr/facts/europe.htm (6/4/2012).
9. See International Monetary Fund, 'About the IMF', http://www.imf.org/external/about.htm (6/4/2012) and International Monetary Fund, 'IMF members' quotas and voting power, and IMF board of governors', http://www.imf.org/external/np/sec/memdir/members.aspx (6/4/2012).
10. In a statement of the Eurogroup of 30 March 2012 the Eurogroup Finance Ministers declared that they reassessed the adequacy of the overall EFSF/ESM lending ceiling of €500 billion and came to the conclusion that whereas there would be no nominal increase the programs already initiated by the EFSF would not be counted towards the ESM ceiling as was previously planned and hence be added to that €500 billion ceiling creating an aggregate firewall of approx. €800 billion. For details see http://www.consilium.europa.eu/uedocs/cms_data/docs/pressdata/en/ecofin/129381.pdf (6/4/2012).
11. Text of ESM-Treaty available at http://www.european-council.europa.eu/media/582311/05-tesm2.en12.pdf (6/4/2012).
12. See European Council 24/25 March 2011, Conclusion 16, http://www.consilium.europa.eu/uedocs/cms_data/docs/pressdata/en/ec/120296.pdf (6/4/2012).
13. The possible financial extent of the problems and the complexity surrounding them is illustrated by a dispute among leading economists and finance experts on the significance, if any, of balances in the Trans-European Automated Real-time Gross Settlement Express Transfer system (Target 2), http://www.ecb.int/paym/t2/html/index.en.html (6/4/2012), relevant legal documents at http://www.ecb.int/ecb/legal/1003/1349/html/index.en.html (6/4/2012). As of 29 February 2012, the German Central Bank (Bundesbank) held Target-2 claims totalling just over €547 billion; http://www.bundesbank.de/target2/target2_saldo.en.php (6/4/2012). The ECB indirectly addressed the criticism and concerns raised especially by German economist Hans-Werner Sinn with regard to these balances and their growth since 2007 in its October 2011 Monthly Bulletin, p. 35 et seq., http://www.ecb.int/pub/pdf/mobu/mb201110en.pdf (6/4/2012). For Sinn's contributions to the debate see http://www.cesifo-group.de/portal/page/portal/ifoHome/B-politik/90spezial/Target (6/4/2012). Another leading economist, Peter Bofinger, largely rejected the concerns raised in the media, see, for example, Bofinger (n.d.).
14. The Preamble of the Basic Law states: 'Conscious of their responsibility before God and man, Inspired by the determination to promote world peace as an equal partner in a united Europe, the German people, in the exercise of their constituent power, have adopted this Basic Law.'

15. Article 23.1 of the Basic Law states: '(1) With a view to establishing a united Europe, the Federal Republic of Germany shall participate in the development of the European Union that is committed to democratic, social and federal principles, to the rule of law, and to the principle of subsidiarity, and that guarantees a level of protection of basic rights essentially comparable to that afforded by this Basic Law. To this end the Federation may transfer sovereign powers by a law with the consent of the *Bundesrat*. The establishment of the European Union, as well as changes in its treaty foundations and comparable regulations that amend or supplement this Basic Law, or make such amendments or supplements possible, shall be subject to paragraphs (2) and (3) of Article 79.'
16. The so-called fundamental principles of state are contained in Article 20 of the Basic Law and summarised in Article 20.1: '(1) The Federal Republic of Germany is a democratic and social federal state.'
17. Article 38.1 of the Basic Law states: '(1) Members of the German *Bundestag* shall be elected in general, direct, free, equal and secret elections. They shall be representatives of the whole people, not bound by orders or instructions, and responsible only to their conscience.'
18. BVerfG, 2 BvE 2/08, 30 June 2009; several case notes and critical commentaries are available online in the special edition of the 2009 *German Law Journal* **10** (8) 1201–1308, http://www.germanlawjournal.com/pdfs/FullIssues/Vol_10_No_08.pdf (6/4/2012).
19. Id (n 188) para. 246.
20. Id (n 188) para. 240.
21. Id (n 188) para. 249.
22. BVerfG, 2 BvR 987/10, 7 September 2011 (decision available in German language only). A relatively comprehensive press release by the Court in English is available at http://www.bverfg.de/pressemitteilungen/bvg11-055en.html (6/4/2012).
23. BVerfG, 2 BvR 987/10, 7 September 2011, para. 101.
24. Article 1.1 of the Basic Law states: '(1) Human dignity shall be inviolable. To respect and protect it shall be the duty of all state authority.'
25. Article 79.3 of the Basic Law states: '(3) Amendments to this Basic Law affecting the division of the Federation into *Länder*, their participation on principle in the legislative process, or the principles laid down in Articles 1 and 20 shall be inadmissible.'
26. See supra n 155 for text of Art. 23.1 of the Basic Law.
27. BVerfG, 2 BvR 987/10, 7 September 2011, para. 101.
28. On that tendency see Bröhmer (2009); for a selection of other comments on that judgment see supra n 188.
29. BVerfG, 2 BvR 987/10, 7 September 2011, para. 121 et seq.
30. Id at para. 124.
31. Id at para. 126.
32. For 2010 Eurostat quotes the German debt to GDP ratio at 83.2 per cent (Data of 8 March 2012), http://epp.eurostat.ec.europa.eu/portal/page/portal/government_finance_statistics/data/main_tables (6/4/2012).
33. Germany's 2012 Federal Budget contains aggregate expenditures of €306.2 billion. The budget position 'work and welfare' is by far the largest with €126.5 billion. Servicing the federal debt is the second largest item with €38.3 billion followed by defence with €31.9 billion. See http://www.bundesfinanzministerium.de/nn_124500/DE/BMF__Startseite/Multimedia/Infografiken-Bundeshaushalt/20111206Ausgabenstruktur-BHH-2012.html?__nnn=true (6/4/2012). About 64 per cent of the debt is federal debt. About 30 per cent lies with the 16 states and around 6 per cent with the municipalities.
34. See, for example, Henseler (1983, p. 489) and Glaser (2006). See also Holmes (1988, p. 195 et seq.). The opening quotation presented there from Rousseau's *Social Contract* (full context at http://fr.wikisource.org/wiki/Du_contrat_social/Livre_II (6/4/2012), *Du contract social*, Chapitre 2.1 Que la souveraineté est inaliénable) that it is absurd to restrain today's will by the chains of the future ('Il est absurd que la volonté se donne des chaines pour l'avenir') addressed the concept of sovereignty and could only

indirectly be linked to the problem here at issue but it nonetheless presents an interesting hypothesis in today's European sovereign debt crisis with regard to the durability and reliability of the activities promised by the various states to henceforth engage in fiscal responsibility.

35. Before the latest reforms of the German Basic Law and the introduction of more determinative constitutional debt control obligations the German Basic Law tried to address fiscal sustainability by limiting the amount of debt in the federal budget to the amount of investment spending contained in the budget thus in effect disallowing deficits for consumptive spending. The old Article 115 of the Basic Law read: '(1) The borrowing of funds and the assumption of surety obligations, guarantees, or other commitments that may lead to expenditures in future fiscal years shall require authorisation by a federal law specifying or permitting computation of the amounts involved. Revenue obtained by borrowing shall not exceed the total of investment expenditures provided for in the budget; exceptions shall be permissible only to avert a disturbance of the overall economic equilibrium. Details shall be regulated by a federal law.' The new Article 115.2 of the Basic Law abandoned this distinction between investment and consumption spending in favour of more concrete debt ceilings and an emphasis on the other side of the Keynesian equation, namely that debt incurred to combat recession must be separately accounted for and repaid when the economy returns to growth.
36. Thomas Jefferson's attempt at a solution may at least in principle not be that far off the mark, see Letter to James Madison of 6 September 1789, reproduced at http://classic-liberal.tripod.com/jefferson/mad02.html (6/4/2012): 'What is true of every member of the society, individually, is true of them all collectively; since the rights of the whole can be no more than the sum of the rights of the individuals. To keep our ideas clear when applying them to a multitude, let us suppose a whole generation of men to be born on the same day, to attain mature age on the same day, and to die on the same day, leaving a succeeding generation in the moment of attaining their mature age, all together. Let the ripe age be supposed of twenty-one years, and their period of life thirty-four years more, that being the average term given by the bills of mortality to persons of twenty-one years of age. Each successive generation would, in this way, come and go of the stage at a fixed moment, as individuals do now. Then I say, the earth belongs to each of these generations during its course, fully and in its own right. The second generation receives it clear of the debts and incumbrances of the first, the third of the second, and so on. For if the first could charge it with a debt, then the earth would belong to the dead and not to the living generation. Then, no generation can contract debts greater than may be paid during the course of its own existence. At twenty-one years of age, they may bind themselves and their lands for thirty-four years to come; at twenty-two, for thirty-three; at twenty-three, for thirty-two; and at fifty-four, for one year only; because these are the terms of life which remain to them at the respective epochs.'
37. BVerfG, 2 BvR 987/10, 7 September 2011, para 130.
38. Id at para. 131.
39. For both of these budget items see supra n 333.
40. BVerfG, 2 BvR 987/10, 7 September 2011, para. 135.
41. Article 1 of the Amendment Statute to the Act Concerning the Giving of Guarantees in the Framework of a European Stabilisation Mechanism of 9 October 2011, BGBl. I 1992 (2011) [Art. 1 des Gesetzes zur Änderung des Gesetzes zur Übernahme von Gewährleistungen im Rahmen eines europäischen Stabilisierungsmechanismus vom 9. Oktober 2011]. The original version of the Act was from 22 May 2010, BGBl. I 627 (2010).
42. A 'fraction' of parliament, to use the literal translation, is an organisational entity of the Bundestag which is afforded special rights under the Rules and Procedures of the German Bundestag. According to Section 10 of these rules a 'fraction' is a political group comprising of at least 5 per cent of the representatives of the same or similar political persuasion so that they do not compete against each other in any state. See http://www.bundestag.de/dokumente/rechtsgrundlagen/go_btg/index.html (6/4/2012).

That minimum number came out to nine members for the five political groups currently organised in the Bundestag, see http://www.bundestag.de/bundestag/ausschuesse17/a08/a08_sta/mitglieder.html (6/4/2012).
43. 'Organ disputes' are institutional disputes between constitutional organs of the German state, i.e. the Federal President, the Bundestag, the Bundesrat or the Federal Government. They are also admissible for intra-organ disputes such as this one where one or more representatives allege a curtailment of their rights as deputies or a curtailment of the right of the whole organ which indirectly affects their rights as well. See Article 93.1 No. 1 of the Basic Law in conjunction with Sections 13 No. 5, 63-67 Federal Constitutional Court Act [Bundesverfassunsggerichtsgesetz], http://www.gesetze-im-internet.de/bverfgg/BJNR002430951.html (6/4/2012).
44. See supra n 177.
45. BVerfG, 2 BvE 8/11 of 28 February 2012, Headnote 3 and para. 102 et seq., 110 et seq.
46. Art. 115.1 first sentence, see supra n 355 (text of first sentence has remained unchanged); BVerfG, 2 BvE 8/11 of 28 February 2012, paras 111–12.
47. For general information on the Bundestag's committees see http://www.bundestag.de/htdocs_e/bundestag/committees/index.html (6/4/2012).
48. Rules of procedure of the German Bundestag, available in English at https://www.btg-bestellservice.de/pdf/80060000.pdf (6/4/2012).
49. For general information see http://www.bundestag.de/htdocs_e/bundestag/function/legislation/passage.html (6/4/2012).
50. That is the case in Article 45 of the Basic Law for the Committee on the European Union which is empowered to exercise the rights of the Bundestag under Article 23 of the Basic Law vis-à-vis the Government. See also the Petitions Committee under Article 45c and the Parliamentary Control Panel under Article 45d which oversees the intelligence activities of the Federal Republic and the Joint Committee under Article 53a of the Basic Law which will hopefully never convene as it will only operate when a 'state of defence' has been determined, i.e. 'a determination has been made that the federal territory is under attack or imminently threatened with such an attack' (Article 115a of the Basic Law).
51. BVerfG, 2 BvE 8/11 of 28 February 2012, para. 141 et seq.
52. Id at para. 132.
53. See Miller (2008).
54. Trail Smelter Arbitration, in: 3 UNRIAA, 1905, p. 1965, http://untreaty.un.org/cod/riaa/cases/vol_III/1905-1982.pdf (6/4/2012).
55. Corfu Channel (*UK v Albania*) (Merits), 1949 ICJ 4, 21, http://www.icj-cij.org/docket/files/1/1645.pdf (6/4/2012).
56. See for example Bratspies and Miller (2006), and the contribution of Hoss and Dupuy (2006, p. 225 et seq).
57. See in the context of constitutional law and takings Lunney (1991–92, pp. 1906, 1916) with reference to the fact that this principle has, albeit domestically, been expanded from property (do not use your property to inflict harm on another's property) to rights as in do not use your rights to inflict harm on another's rights.
58. Leaving aside the question to what degree the international and the domestic can even be separated in this manner. Article 25 of the Basic Law stipulates that '[T]he general rules of international law shall be an integral part of federal law. They shall take precedence over the laws and directly create rights and duties for the inhabitants of the federal territory.' The general rules referred to are the rules of customary international law.
59. Interestingly R. Domingo's development of a 'global human community' appears to be largely free of democratic constraints, despite the fact that it operates under the principle of 'quod omnes tangit, ab omnibus approbetur' [what affects everyone must be approved by everyone], Domingo (2012, pp. 563 et seq., 581).
60. For an overview on the attempts to redefine governance on the EU level see Shore (2011, p. 287 et seq.) with further references.

61. Weber (2010), p. 694 speaks of the democratic deficit of multilayered governance.
62. See the critique by Weiler (2001), at para. 19 et seq.

## REFERENCES


Bofinger, Peter (n.d.), 'Bofinger attackiert Sinns "Jammer-Diskussion"', accessed 6/4/2012 at http://www.spiegel.de/wirtschaft/soziales/0,1518,818022,00.html.

Bratspies, R.M. and R.A. Miller (eds) (2006), *Transboundary Harm in International Law: Lessons from the Trail Smelter Arbitration*, Cambridge: Cambridge University Press.

Bröhmer, Jürgen (2009), '"Containment eines Leviathans" – Anmerkungen zur Entscheidung des Bundesverfassungsgerichts zum Vertrag von Lissabon' [Containment of a Leviathan – Some remarks on the decision of the Federal Constitutional Court in regard to the Lisbon Treaty], *ZEuS*, 543.

Domingo, R. (2012), 'The new global human community', *Chicago Journal of International Law*, **12**(2), 563.

European Central Bank (ECB), October 2011 Monthly Bulletin, accessed 6/04/2012 at http://www.ecb.int/pub/pdf/mobu/mb201110en.pdf.

Glaser, A. (2006), *Nachhaltige Entwicklung und Demokratie*, Tűbingen: Mohr Siebeck.

Henseler, P. (1983), Verfassungsrechtliche Aspekte zukunftsbelastender Parlamentsentscheidungen, 108 *AöR* 489.

Holmes, S. (1988), 'Precommitment and the Paradox of Democracy', in J. Elster and R. Slagstad (eds), *Constitutionalism and Democracy*, Cambridge: Cambridge University Press, pp. 195–240.

Hoss, C. and P.M. Dupuy (2006), '*Trail Smelter* and Terrorism: International Mechanisms to Combat Transboundary Harm', in R.M. Bratspies and R.A. Miller (eds), *Transboundary Harm in International Law: Lessons from the Trail Smelter Arbitration*, Cambridge: Cambridge University Press, pp. 225 et seq.

Klaus, Vaclav (2011), 'Eurocrats Steamroller Democracy', *Australian*, 25 July, accessed 6/4/2012 at http://www.theaustralian.com.au/news/opinion/eurocrats-steamroller-democracy/story-e6frg6zo-1226100894685.

Lunney, G.S. (1991–1992), 'A Critical Examination of the Takings Jurisprudence', *Michigan Law Review*, **90**, 1892.

Miller, R.A. (2008), '*Trail Smelter* Arbitration', in R. Wolfrum (ed.), *The Max Planck Encyclopaedia of Public International Law*, Oxford University Press, online edition, accessed 20/3/2012 at www.mpepil.com.

Shore, C. (2011), '"European Governance" or Governmentality? The European Commission and the Future of Democratic Government', *European Law Journal*, **17**, 287.

Weber, R.H. (2010), 'Multilayered Governance in International Financial Regulation and Supervision', *Journal of International Economic Law*, **13**(3), 683.

Weiler, J.H.H. (2001), 'The Commission as Euro-Skeptic: A Task Oriented Commission for a Project-Based Union – a Comment on the First Version of the White Paper "Memorandum to the Commission: Approaches to European Governance for Democratic European Governance"', 10 March, accessed 6/4/2012 at http://centers.law.nyu.edu/jeanmonnet/archive/papers/01/013401.html.

# PART II

# Commercial perspectives

# 6. Corporatisation in Australia: a Queensland perspective*

**Tahnee Booth and Adrian Noon**[1]

## 6.1 CORPORATISATION OF GOVERNMENT BUSINESSES IN QUEENSLAND

Why does the government own businesses? Many government-owned businesses were originally established to overcome perceived shortcomings in the market, for example, to provide strategic infrastructure services that commercial businesses would not provide, deal with natural monopoly situations, support state economic development and achieve a more socially desirable outcome (Queensland Treasury, 1992, p. 6).

In the early 1990s the Queensland Government commenced a micro-economic reform process to enhance the efficiency of Queensland's industries, particularly government trading activities. There was an acknowledgement that to achieve the maximum efficiency gains, government trading activities needed to be placed as far as possible on a commercial basis in a competitive environment. The government moved to commercialise its trading enterprises under a policy of corporatisation (Queensland Treasury, 1990, p. 1).

This policy direction was given further impetus following agreement by Australian governments on the need for a national competition policy. With the outcome of the Hilmer review recommending a national competition policy (Commonwealth of Australia, 1993), implementation of this policy further pushed structural reform and the compliance of government businesses with competitive neutrality requirements.

In some cases, the historical policy drivers which resulted in the creation of these government businesses no longer exist but the competitive neutrality drivers remain. Now, the government's goal from ownership of its existing government-owned corporations (GOCs) is to create value through a long-term approach, economic and financial efficiency, profitability, development capacity and social responsibility (Queensland Treasury, 2011, pp. 3–4).

Corporatisation as a structural reform process aims to provide a private sector environment and governance regime for all GOCs, so that they operate, as far as practicable, on a commercial basis and in a competitive environment. Corporatisation provides for continued public ownership – it is not a step towards privatisation, although certainly the government has divested itself of some businesses which will be discussed later. It allows the state as owner to provide strategic direction through performance targets and community service obligations (Queensland Treasury, 1992, pp. 5–9).

The objectives of corporatisation as outlined in Section 14 of the Government Owned Corporations Act 1993 (GOC Act) are to improve Queensland's overall economic performance, and the government's ability to achieve its social objectives by improving the efficiency and effectiveness of GOCs; and improving the accountability of GOCs.

The government's corporatisation framework is characterised by four key principles as outlined in Section 16 of the GOC Act:

- clear and non-conflicting objectives and specific performance targets;
- management autonomy, authority and responsibility;
- strict accountability for performance; and
- competitive neutrality with the private sector and any special advantages or disadvantages because of public ownership being removed, minimised or made apparent.

## 6.2 OVERVIEW OF THE GOC MODEL

### 6.2.1 The Corporatisation Spectrum

Historically Queensland's GOC model consisted of statutory GOCs and company GOCs, with statutory GOCs providing a staged transition to a company GOC (Queensland Government, 2006). All GOCs were subject to the state's GOC Act and company GOCs were also subject to the company law.

Following the introduction of the Corporations Act 2001 (Corporations Act), differences resulted in the governance regime for statutory GOCs and company GOCs. Following significant legislative change in 2007, all statutory GOCs converted to company GOCs, subject to the Corporations Act and its governance regime including independent regulation by the Australian Securities and Investments Commission.

### 6.2.2 Legislative and Policy Framework

In addition to the Corporations Act and the GOC Act, the state's GOCs are subject to other specific legislation, for example the Right to Information Act 2009, the Electricity Act 1994 (energy GOCs) and Competition and Consumer Act 2010 (Cth) (formerly Trade Practices Act 1974) to name a few.

GOCs also comply with a range of policies which can be GOC-specific policies such as the Corporate Governance Guidelines for Government Owned Corporations and the Investment Guidelines for Government Owned Corporations; or broader public sector policies such as State Procurement Policy and Local Industry Policy.

### 6.2.3 GOC Board of Directors

Each GOC has an independent board of directors whose role, as outlined in Section 88 of the GOC Act, includes:

- responsibility for the GOC's commercial policy and management;
- ensuring the GOC acts in accordance with its Statement of Corporate Intent (SCI) and carries out the objectives outlined in its SCI;
- accounting to shareholders for its performance; and
- ensuring the GOC performs its functions in a proper, effective and efficient way.

Section 89 of the GOC Act outlines that a GOC's board is to consist of the number of directors appointed by the Governor in Council, and Section 90 outlines that public servants and GOC executives cannot be on GOC boards.

### 6.2.4 GOC Ownership and Shareholding Ministers

Section 78 of the GOC Act prescribes that GOCs have two shareholding ministers, the GOC Minister and the Portfolio Minister, who make decisions in accordance with statutory responsibilities in the GOC Act. Section 80 outlines that shareholding ministers hold shares in the GOCs on behalf of the state.

The GOC Act provides powers to shareholding ministers to deliver notifications or give directions to GOCs. In most (but not all) cases, these powers require shareholding ministers to consult with the GOC before giving the notification or direction. GOCs can advise if the notification or direction is not in their commercial interests. Notifications or directions must be published in the gazette.

The threshold for shareholding ministers giving a direction in the public interest is high. Under Section 115 of the GOC Act, shareholding ministers must be satisfied that the direction is necessary because of exceptional circumstances. Shareholding ministers provided public interest directions to one of the state's GOCs during the drought, which effectively prevented the GOC from sourcing water from Wivenhoe Dam, Brisbane's main water supply.

Shareholding ministers are supported in their decision-making by the Office of Government Owned Corporations (OGOC) and portfolio departments. OGOC administers the GOC Act, develops and reviews GOC-specific policies and procedures, and oversees GOC performance (Office of Government Owned Corporations, http://www.ogoc.qld.gov.au/about-ogoc.shtml).

### 6.2.5 Financial Arrangements and Balance Sheet Management

To ensure that GOCs' borrowing rates reflect their cost of capital and not the creditworthiness of the state, a Competitive Neutrality Fee is applied to all borrowings and financial arrangements in the nature of debt obligations (Office of Government Owned Corporations, 2009, p. 7).

The government is mindful of the commercial environment that GOCs operate in and aims to maintain appropriate capital structures to ensure optimal utilisation of capital resources and that GOCs are adequately funded to undertake approved projects.

GOCs have their capital structure reviewed annually by Queensland Treasury Corporation. An optimal capital structure is recommended for each GOC with the aim of an appropriate investment grade credit rating. As a result of the review, government may provide or repatriate equity to maintain credit ratings appropriate to each GOC. Government also provides equity for major projects that generate a strong commercial return.

### 6.2.6 Community Service Obligations

Some GOCs perform community service obligations (CSOs) which arise because of a direction, notification or duty given to the GOC by shareholding ministers. Section 112 of the GOC Act outlines that CSOs are obligations to perform activities that the GOC's board establishes, to the satisfaction of the shareholding ministers, are not in the GOC's commercial interests to perform.

The CSOs are specified in the GOC's Statement of Corporate Intent, along with how the GOC is to be compensated by the government for performing those CSOs. For example, under its Uniform Tariff Policy that provides for parity of pricing for all non-market electricity customers, the government pays a CSO to Ergon Energy Corporation Limited for the supply of electricity to remote customers.

### 6.2.7 Returns to Government

The government earns returns from GOCs in the form of dividends and tax equivalent payments (TEPs). Table 6.1 provides a summary of returns to government from GOCs in the form of dividends and current TEPs and a budget for the 2011–12 financial year.

In terms of dividends, GOCs have an obligation to satisfy the three-part solvency test under Section 254T of the Corporations Act which restricts the payment of a dividend unless:

*Table 6.1 Returns to government*

| Dividends and Current TEPs | 2009–10 Actual $M | 2010–11 Actual $M | 2011–12 Budget $M |
|---|---|---|---|
| Energy sector | 657 | 763 | 709 |
| Transport sector (rail and ports) | 212 | 455 | 268 |
| Other | 44 | 77 | 53 |

*Notes:*

1. Numbers for 2009–10 and 2011–12 drawn from Queensland Government (2011b), Table 8.2 and Table 8.3. Numbers include QIC Limited but exclude Non-GOCs. Numbers for 2010–11 drawn from GOC 2010–11 Annual Reports.
2. The increase in energy sector dividends from 2009–10 to 2011–12 can be mainly attributed to ENERGEX and Ergon, reflecting the impact of the Australian Energy Regulator (AER) Final Determination 2010–11 to 2014–15 on regulated revenue.
3. The increase in 2010–11 energy sector dividends and TEPs is largely the result of one-off increases from Stanwell following the sale of a surplus mining development lease.
4. The increase in transport sector dividends for 2010–11 largely represents the receipt of a dividend from Queensland Rail Limited. In 2009–10 no dividend was paid by the former QR Limited.
5. The transport sector 2009–10 TEPs reflects the adjustments made to QR Limited's accounts in preparation for the separation of Queensland Rail. Subsequently the 2010–11 increase of transport sector TEPs is reflective of Queensland Rail's profitability as a separated business, offset by financial results for North Queensland Bulk Ports Corporation Limited (NQBP) and Port of Brisbane Corporation Limited.
6. SunWater Limited's dividends for 2010–11 (in the 'other' category) relate only to financial performance of 2010–11 and do not include dividends provided for in 2010–11 that relate to prior financial years.

- the company's assets exceed its liabilities immediately before the dividend is declared and the excess is sufficient to pay the dividend;
- the payment of the dividend is fair and reasonable to the company's shareholders as a whole; and
- the payment of the dividend does not materially prejudice the company's ability to pay its creditors.

In accordance with Section 131 of the GOC Act, dividend payments are approved by shareholding ministers on the recommendation of GOC boards.

To ensure competitive neutrality with the private sector, GOCs are subject to the National Tax Equivalent Regime which is an administrative arrangement under which the relevant taxation laws are applied notionally to the GOCs as if they were subject to those laws. The primary objective of the National Tax Equivalent Regime is to promote competitive neutrality, through a uniform application of income tax laws, between GOCs in all states and their private counterparts (Australian Taxation Office, 2008, p. 6).

The Australian Taxation Office assesses the GOCs' income tax equivalent liability annually which is paid by the GOCs into the State Government's Consolidated Fund.

### 6.2.8 Pros and Cons of the Corporatisation Model

The Queensland Government has continued with its corporatisation model. Key strengths of the model include:

- continued public ownership enabling government to receive returns which can be used for broader service provision, for example education, health and law enforcement;
- the government can provide broader strategic direction by agreeing key financial and non-financial performance targets and community service obligations;
- the independent GOC boards are clearly accountable for the GOCs' performance; and
- the governance framework which sets out the relationship between management autonomy and shareholder oversight is strong.

It can, at times, be difficult to balance GOC autonomy with the expectations of government. For example, GOCs are required to seek shareholding ministers' approval of investments where the investment value exceeds specific thresholds. GOCs would probably prefer to not have to obtain such approval.

The government faces significant barriers to exit for its investments and the government cannot diversify its investments to the degree private sector investors are able. These factors and the implications of GOC investment activities for the state's credit rating means the shareholder becomes involved in significant investment matters, similar to the governance arrangements that apply to unlisted public companies where the owners become more directly involved in investment decisions that can significantly influence their risk-return exposure (Office of Government Owned Corporations, 2009, p. 1).

While shareholding ministers' approval of significant investment decisions may be perceived as slowing the investment process, the government, as a risk-averse investor, wants to ensure a prudent oversight of potential investments. This oversight, in conjunction with the GOC boards' management of the GOCs, has proven to be beneficial, with the state's GOCs generally managing well during the recent global financial crisis.

## 6.3 GOC GOVERNANCE AND ACCOUNTABILITY FRAMEWORK

Queensland GOCs are subject to a rigorous performance management and reporting framework which establishes a clear line of sight from the Queensland public, the ultimate owners of the GOCs, through to the performance management and reporting process (Queensland Treasury, 2011, pp. 7–8). Key aspects of the framework include:

- Shareholding ministers' strategic expectations letters – outline high-level expectations of the following financial year and guidance for the next five years.
- Corporate Plans – prepared annually by GOCs and consider the medium- to long-term outlook for the business, focussing on the next five years.
- Statements of Corporate Intent (SCIs) – prepared annually by GOCs and represent a performance agreement between a GOC's board and shareholding ministers for the following financial year.
- Forecast report – prepared annually by GOCs after the SCI and outline high-level objectives and forecasts of the GOCs for the coming financial year, for publication on their websites.

- Quarterly report – prepared by GOCs and reports on their operations for the relevant quarter and progress in meeting financial and non-financial performance targets established in their SCIs.
- Interim Report – prepared by GOCs in February and provides a summary of performance for the first half of the financial year for publication on their websites.
- Annual Report – prepared by GOCs following the financial year end. Contains a comprehensive review of the GOC's operations, governance and performance including annual financial statements. Annual Reports are lodged with the Australian Securities and Investments Commission (ASIC), tabled in Parliament and published on GOC websites. For tabling, GOCs include their SCI for the same year with commercially sensitive material deleted.

### 6.3.1 GOC performance

The government currently has 12 GOCs.

Energy GOCs:

- CS Energy Limited;
- Stanwell Corporation Limited;
- ENERGEX Limited;
- Ergon Energy Corporation Limited; and
- Queensland Electricity Transmission Corporation Limited (Powerlink Queensland).

Funds management:

- QIC Limited.

Natural resources:

- SunWater Limited.

Transport:

- Far North Queensland Ports Corporation Limited;
- Gladstone Ports Corporation Limited;
- North Queensland Bulk Ports Corporation Limited;
- Port of Townsville Limited; and
- Queensland Rail Limited.

*Table 6.2 GOC financial information and financial performance*

| Total GOC Sector (excluding entities affected by asset sales) | 2009–10 Actual | 2010–11 Actual | 2011–12 Budget |
|---|---|---|---|
| Total assets ($M) | 34 513 | 35 643 | 38 260 |
| Total equity ($M) | 11 717 | 12 259 | 12 453 |
| Earnings before interest and tax ($M) | 2 066 | 1 377 | 2 218 |
| Return on assets (%) | 6.27 | 3.94 | 5.99 |
| Return on equity (%) | 6.11 | 4.31 | 5.71 |
| Gearing (debt/debt+equity) (%) | 56.39 | 55.74 | 59.67 |

*Notes:*
1. Numbers for 2009–10 and 2011–12 based on Queensland Government (2011b), Table 8.1 and include QIC Limited but exclude Non-GOCs. Numbers for 2010–11 drawn from GOC 2010–11 Annual Reports.
2. For the purposes of this table and to enable valid comparisons, the following entities are excluded: Port of Brisbane Corporation Limited (sold as part of the Queensland Government's Asset Sales Program in 2010–11), NQBP (due to the lease of Abbot Point Coal Terminal No. 1), Queensland Rail Limited (a new entity formed in 2010–11), QR Limited (no longer a GOC as at 21 September 2010).

GOC sector financial information and financial performance against a selection of key performance indicators is provided in Table 6.2.

## 6.4 GOVERNMENT'S ROLE IN SECTORAL AND INDUSTRIAL DEVELOPMENT

The 1970s and early 1980s saw the development of very significant infrastructure to support the export coal industry, which has now effectively stepped in as the major economic force in several of Australia's major regional areas, particularly central Queensland and the Northern Bowen Basin. The Queensland Government oversaw the establishment of four deep-water ports and an extensive rail network, much of which was subsequently electrified in the late 1980s. A series of bilateral commercial agreements between Queensland Rail (as it was then) and the port authorities underpinned the ongoing development of these facilities.

Queensland further diversified its economic base with the construction of the State Gas Pipeline from Roma to Gladstone in the late 1980s. This pipeline was subsequently sold to the private sector which also played a significant part in new gas pipeline developments from South West Queensland to both Mt Isa and Roma (Wallumbilla). Government thereby took on a facilitation role, preferring to harness the capital and risk appetite of the private sector in developing those facilities.

The government's Cleaner Energy Strategy 2000 introduced the Queensland Gas Scheme to progressively raise the contribution of gas, as a low greenhouse gas emissions fuel, to 15 per cent of electricity marketed via the electricity retailers (Department of Employment, Economic Development and Innovation, http://www.energyfutures.qld.gov.au/gas/qld-gas-scheme.htm). This policy was instrumental in encouraging some 2700 megawatt capacity of gas-fired electricity generation, through private sector investment. Swanbank E and Mica Creek power stations owned by the state's electricity generator GOCs are accredited generators under the gas scheme.

## 6.5 REFORM OF THE GOC SECTOR: SOME CASE STUDIES

### 6.5.1 Retail Sales of ENERGEX Limited and Ergon Energy Corporation Limited

The government recognised that the retail aspect of the electricity business was mature and with the introduction of full retail contestability into the domestic electricity market in 2007, this business would be better operated by the private sector (Boston Consulting Group, 2006). Through the retail sales, government removed the contestable retail side of ENERGEX Limited and Ergon Energy Corporation Limited, allowing them to focus on their distribution networks. The retail businesses had been a significant distraction to both entities as they tried to compete in the national market.

The retail sales involved:

- ENERGEX's retail electricity business consisting of approximately 1.2 million non-contestable customers in South East Queensland;
- ENERGEX's and Ergon Energy's contestable electricity customers;
- Allgas Limited (ENERGEX's gas distribution business); and
- ENERGEX's retail gas business.

To ensure the success of retail contestability, government saw the need for new entrants to have sufficient retail mass to be competitive. For this reason, ENERGEX's non-contestable retail customers were broken into two tranches. Ergon's non-contestable customers were not sold as they were supported by CSOs and were unlikely to ever be contestable. The two separate packages sold were:

- Tranche one: approximately 800 000 non-contestable ENERGEX retail customers, ENERGEX's contestable customers (Australia-wide), together with various sites for future power stations.
- Tranche two: approximately 400 000 non-contestable ENERGEX retail customers, Ergon Energy's contestable customers (Australia-wide), retail customers of Powerdirect (a retailer purchased by Ergon at the end of 2005).

Tranche one was sold to Origin Energy in November 2006 for $1.202 billion (Bligh and Beattie, 2006) and Tranche two was sold to AGL in February 2007 for $1.203 billion (Bligh and Wilson, 2007). Additionally, Allgas Limited was sold in late 2006 for just over $500 million (Bligh, 2006) and ENERGEX's retail gas business was sold in November 2006 for under $100 million (Bligh and Beattie, 2006).

### 6.5.2 Cairns, Mackay and Brisbane Airports Sale

In April 2008, shortly before the effects of the global financial crisis became apparent, the government announced the sale of its interests in Cairns, Mackay and Brisbane airports. Cairns and Mackay airports were owned and operated by the local port authorities – Cairns Ports Limited and Mackay Ports Limited – both GOCs, while the Brisbane Airport interest was held through another GOC, the Port of Brisbane Corporation Limited, as a 12.4 per cent stake in BAC Holdings.

As the aviation markets at all three airports were well developed, the government decided there was no longer a justification for government ownership of airports which were generating commercial returns. Brisbane Airport had experienced high growth rates since its privatisation by the Australian Government in the late 1990s. At the time of the sale, Cairns Airport was the country's seventh-largest airport (the largest government owned) with a well-developed domestic and international route network catering primarily for the tourism market. Passenger numbers at Mackay Airport were growing strongly as a result of the resources boom – primarily Bowen Basin coal mining – with mining fly-in/fly-out passengers and business travel accounting for a significant portion of this growth.

The state received gross proceeds of $1.028 billion (Fraser, 2008; Bligh and Boyle, 2008) from the disposal of its airport interests which allowed the repayment of Cairns Ports' debt and avoided future capital requirements, and the government publicly committed the remaining proceeds towards hospital redevelopments in Cairns, Mackay and Mt Isa.

The stake in Brisbane Airport was sold to a number of existing shareholders through a pre-emptive rights process under provisions of the Shareholder Agreement. Cairns and Mackay airports were disposed of by long-term leases following competitive bid processes. The state is now the owner and lessor of the land and infrastructure at both airports, but has no day-to-day operational role.

## 6.6 THE GLOBAL FINANCIAL CRISIS AND GOC REFORM

In the 2009–10 Budget, the Queensland Government estimated that the global economic downturn had stripped \$15 billion off the forward estimates of the state's key revenue streams of royalties, taxes and Goods and Services Tax (GST) (Queensland Government, 2009, p. 87). As at the 2011–12 Budget, this figure had been revised to a \$9.2 billion reduction over the period 2008–09 to 2011–12 (Queensland Government, 2011b, p. 71). While the government's response was to maintain infrastructure investment in the short term, it also recognised the importance of the Budget's fiscal sustainability in ensuring the health of the Queensland economy in the medium to longer term. As a result, a number of key initiatives were implemented in the 2009–10 Budget, including revised fiscal principles, the abolition of the Queensland Fuel Subsidy Scheme, public sector efficiency measures, a revision to the government's wages policy and a comprehensive programme of asset sales.

On 2 June 2009, the government announced a significant infrastructure assets reform and sale programme over the following three to five years, including the sale of the following government-owned assets (Bligh and Fraser, 2009):

- Queensland Rail's above-rail freight and below-rail coal network businesses;
- The Port of Brisbane;
- Forestry Plantations Queensland;
- Queensland Motorways Limited; and
- Abbot Point Coal Terminal No. 1.

The asset sales programme has been crucial in ensuring the sustainability of the state's balance sheet through both a reduction in the state's borrowings and also a reduction in the state's commitment to fund capital investment in these businesses.

This asset sales programme generated a net realisable value of \$15.1 billion and has allowed the state to hand responsibility for significant capital investment to the private sector – $2.8 billion of this capital requirement had been factored into the 2010–11 Budget (Queensland Government, 2011b, p. 15). Primarily as a result of the asset sales programme, total state borrowings at 30 June 2011 are estimated to be $17.5 billion lower than projected in the 2009–10 Budget (Queensland Government, 2011a, p. 3). Each of the asset sales is discussed below.

### 6.6.1 Forestry Plantations Queensland

The Queensland Government established a plantation-based timber resource throughout the last century. During the last 20 years, management of this resource transitioned from a government agency to a fully fledged commercial timber business and Forestry Plantations Queensland (FPQ) was established as a commercial corporation on 1 May 2006.

FPQ was included in the asset sales programme as it was a mature plantation business supporting a well-established and competitive timber processing sector. Inclusion of FPQ in the proposed restructure programme signalled the government's intention to transfer ownership of this business to the private sector and provide the private sector with an opportunity to further invest in the future of the forestry plantation sector in Queensland.

On 26 November 2009, the State Government announced the commencement of a two-stage competitive bid process for interested parties to bid for the assets and business of FPQ. The State Government received a strong response from credible and reputable domestic and international plantation forestry investors. On 18 May 2010, the Treasurer announced in Parliament the government's sale of FPQ Pty Ltd to Hancock Queensland Plantations (HQP) Pty Ltd, a company associated with the Hancock Timber Resource Group, for $603 million (Fraser, 2010b). This consideration, together with a post-sale purchase price adjustment of approximately $10 million in favour of the state, takes the total sale proceeds to $613 million. A 99-year licence to use government-owned state plantation forests for the purposes of managing, harvesting and regrowing plantation timber was granted.

### 6.6.2 Sale of Queensland Rail National Limited (QRN)

The government saw the need to sell QRN due to the increasing infrastructure requirements of the company. This was particularly relevant in the booming coal mining sector of the Queensland economy, but also in New South Wales and Western Australia where QRN had a significant presence. QRN had infrastructure costs of nearly $10 billion in the short term and the government saw this constant demand for funding conflicting with its requirement to provide capital expenditure for social infrastructure.

The government's objectives in the sale were to:

- maximise sale proceeds;
- minimise ongoing risks;
- ensure a competitive market; and
- ensure sufficient funding available for future infrastructure requirements.

Government noted the options of selling QRN as separate below-rail and above-rail businesses but determined that a vertically integrated company would provide a sufficient mass to guarantee that QRN remained a significant company. The coal companies raised significant opposition to this model and launched a separate bid for QRN's below-rail assets which was later withdrawn.

Due to the size of QRN (valued at approximately $7 billion), an initial public offering (IPO) was seen as the only way to sell the asset. The IPO was the largest in Australia since Telstra. The state sold a 66 per cent interest in QRN at $2.55 per share ($2.45 retail element) and the price has increased on the market from day one (listing date 22 November 2010). As at 21 October 2011 it was trading at $3.16. The state received proceeds of $4.6 billion (Fraser, 2010d), after taking into account retail incentives and employee free shares.

The government has retained a stake of 34 per cent which it is required to hold until the release of QRN's 2012 annual report (around September 2012). At the 21 October 2011 share price of $3.16, these shares are valued at approximately $2.62 billion. The government has stated that it is not a long-term holder of the shares.

### 6.6.3 Sale of the Port of Brisbane

Similar to the other asset sales, the rationale behind the sale of the Port of Brisbane was threefold: to improve the state's financial position through an injection of sale proceeds; to remove future capital expenditure commitments; and to unlock the growth potential of the port through private sector investment which is expected to result in an increase in Queensland's economic growth.

The sale of the 99-year lease for the Port of Brisbane in late 2010 delivered $2.1 billion in cash proceeds to the state with a further estimated $200 million being committed to upgrading surrounding road infrastructure.

The sale also avoided the state incurring up to $1 billion in expected future infrastructure expansion costs (Fraser, 2010c).

The new owner, Q Port Holdings, will continue to expand the capacity of the port through investing private sector funds in the development of additional facilities. The growth potential of the port as a multi-user facility is further supported by the 20 per cent port user ownership cap imposed by the state. This ownership cap will be enforced by the state to provide fair and equitable access which will ensure competition and growth of the port is not impeded. The sale has seen the state retain ownership of the port land and key infrastructure but transfer the expense and risk of operating a commercial shipping port to the private sector.

### 6.6.4 Queensland Motorways Limited

In late 2010, the State Government decided that Queensland Motorways Limited (QML) would be transferred to the defined benefit superannuation scheme of QIC Limited (QIC) (Bligh and Fraser, 2010). It is anticipated that the transfer of QML to QIC will assist the state's defined benefit superannuation scheme to remain fully funded.

In preparation for the sale, a new tolling structure, including toll prices, was introduced along with supporting legislation that protects against above-inflation toll increases. This occurred to ensure that users of the motorways were not subjected to unfair price increases.

Commercial negotiations with QIC for the transfer of the 40-year leases of the QML motorways were finalised in May 2011 with a price of $3.088 billion paid to the state (Fraser, 2011). Under the arrangements, the state continues to own the land, roads and bridges and QIC has the right to operate the road and bridge infrastructure and collect tolls, and the obligation to maintain and upgrade the motorways.

### 6.6.5 Abbot Point Coal Terminal No. 1.

Prior to the completion of the long-term lease, the Abbot Point Coal Terminal No. 1 was owned by North Queensland Bulk Ports Corporation Limited (NQBP). At the time of the announcement of the asset sale programme by the government, NQBP had already commenced a significant expansion of the terminal from 21 million tonnes per annum to 50 million tonnes per annum – the X50 Project (Fraser, 2010a). This expansion was driven by expected strong demand for increased coal export capacity and coordinated with the planned connection of the Newlands and Goonyella coal rail systems – known as the GAPE Project.

As the terminal is a commercial asset generating a commercial return, with no demonstrable market or policy failure requiring continued government ownership, government considered it a suitable candidate for divestment. Similar to previous asset disposals, the transaction was structured by way of a 99-year lease over the relevant onshore and offshore areas, with an associated sale of shares in a special-purpose company which holds the relevant assets and contracts.

On 3 May 2011, the state reached agreement with Mundra Port and Special Economic Zone Limited and its Australian subsidiaries regarding the lease and share sale for the total amount of $1.829 billion (Bligh and Nolan, 2011). Following the January 2011 floods and cyclone Yasi, the government has announced that proceeds from this transaction will directly fund Queensland's share of the recovery effort.

## 6.7 RECENT REFORM OF THE GOC SECTOR

In its December 2008 Major Economic Statement (Queensland Government, 2008, p. 36), the government announced a shareholder review to:

- consider the GOC generators' position as dominant providers of electricity; and
- foreshadowed target of reduction to 50 per cent of aggregate capacity owned or operated by the state.

The shareholder review commenced in February 2009 and examined 'the structure and preparedness of the GOC generators to meet the new challenges facing those businesses' (Queensland Government, 2008, p. 36).

The key driver for the review being undertaken (Queensland Government, 2010, p. 6) was underperformance of the government's investment in its generation assets, primarily as a result of:

- the emergence of vertically integrated retailers;
- Australian Government proposals associated with carbon pollution reduction and other climate change policies;
- development of a liquefied natural gas (LNG) industry in Queensland;
- substantial private sector investment in generation capacity;
- an oversupply of generation capacity; and
- low electricity pool prices and increased input costs since the 2006 to 2008 drought.

The review recommendations announced on 25 November 2010 were:

- Change focus to one of cost and performance of the existing asset base, rather than new business development. New assets to be predominantly driven by the private sector.
- Manage the portfolio under a two-generator structure: Stanwell Corporation Limited/Tarong Energy Corporation Limited and CS Energy Limited.
- Redistribute the portfolio across the two-generator structure to achieve maximum sustainability.
- Target date for commencement of 1 July 2011. The aggressive implementation timetable was due to commercial considerations and to minimise change impact on employees.

The benefits of a two-generator business structure include:

- creates synergies by allowing lowest-cost plants to be dispatched, with higher-cost plants to be operating in an intermediate role, improving overall returns;
- facilitates improved management of asset maintenance schedules;
- allows existing intermediate and peaking assets to be allocated to both portfolios which will facilitate improved contract and trading strategies; and
- two-portfolio structure would increase the capacity available for contracting.

As at 1 July 2011, the state had two generator GOCs: Stanwell Corporation Limited and CS Energy Limited.

## 6.8 THE FUTURE OF CORPORATISATION IN QUEENSLAND

So where to from here? What are shareholding ministers' expectations of the state's GOCs in the future? Shareholding ministers expect that GOCs will focus on:

- their core business;
- managing costs and finding new ways to fund major new projects sought by customers with the private sector; and
- enhancing efficiency and productivity to leverage good shareholder returns;

whilst at the same time ensuring they maintain:

- high ethical standards and corporate governance practices;
- good workplace health and safety practices; and
- appropriate employment conditions and industrial relations practices.

GOCs will continue to be involved in the further development of projects in existing industries and the development of new industries. Commercial partnerships with the private sector are also expected to occur.

### 6.8.1 Facilitation of Mining and Coal Seam Gas Projects

SunWater Limited is involved in a number of large commercial water projects and proposals that will support mining and coal seam gas projects in the Bowen, Galilee and Surat Basins. The total capital cost of identified projects is estimated to be $3.9 billion over the next ten years. Major projects include construction of a new dam to supply water for mining customers in the Bowen Basin, construction of a pipeline to supply water for the development of coal mines in the Galilee Basin and construction of pipelines to transport treated water by-product from coal seam gas production for use by coal mining, residential, commercial and agricultural customers (Queensland Government, 2011b, pp. 169–170).

In addition to providing commercial returns on investment, SunWater's projects will also underpin projects that support other developments such as Surat Basin Rail, Wiggins Island Coal Terminal, Abbot Point Coal Terminals and Multi Cargo Facility, LNG at Gladstone and Galilee Basin rail projects.

### 6.8.2 Involvement in Commercial Partnerships with the Private Sector

#### Development of LNG in Queensland

Six LNG projects using coal seam gas from the Surat Basin (South West Queensland) and Bowen Basin (Central Queensland) as feedstock have been proposed for the Port of Gladstone. These projects vary in size and are at various stages within Commonwealth and State Government approval processes.

The Gladstone Ports Corporation Limited (GPC) is facilitating the LNG industry's development by project managing the dredging associated with the deepening and widening of existing channels and swing basins, and the creation of new channels, swing basins and berth pockets in the Western Basin that support the LNG proponents (Queensland Government, 2011b,

p. 166). The total project cost is currently estimated at up to $1.474 billion. It is estimated that a local LNG industry exporting at 28 million tonnes per annum could add more than $3 billion – or around 1 per cent – to gross state product and offer around $850 million a year in royalties.

**Wiggins Island Coal Export Terminal**

The proposed Wiggins Island Coal Terminal is to be located on Golding Point at the Port of Gladstone (Queensland Government, 2011b, p. 166).

Wiggins Island Coal Export Terminal Pty Ltd and WICET Holdings Pty Ltd (collectively the WICET Group) will own and finance the new terminal with Gladstone Ports Corporation Limited (GPC) as operator. The terminal will be a common-user facility under agreed open access and terminal expansion arrangements.

Initial capacity is planned to be 27 million tonnes per annum, with total terminal capacity of approximately 80 million tonnes per annum to be delivered in stages.

Financial close for stage one of the $2.5 billion project occurred on 30 September 2011 (Nolan, 2011). The WICET Group expects first shipments through the terminal in 2014–15. A range of preparatory activities for construction are under way.

**Abbot Point**

Beyond the long-term lease of the Abbot Point Coal Terminal No. 1, the state is facilitating broader private sector-funded development of new coal terminals within the Port of Abbot Point to meet the ongoing strong demand from coal mining companies for additional export capacity (Queensland Government, 2011b, pp. 164–165). This includes appointing BHP Billiton Ltd (BHP Billiton) and Hancock Coal Pty Ltd (Hancock) as preferred proponents for the new Terminals 2 and 3 at the Port of Abbot Point (Taylor, 2010). BHP Billiton anticipates that exports from its terminal will commence in 2015, while Hancock anticipates exports from its terminal will commence in 2013–14.

North Queensland Bulk Ports Corporation Limited (NQBP) has been working with BHP Billiton and Hancock to develop framework agreements for Terminal 2 and Terminal 3. Both BHP Billiton and NQBP have indicated they will utilise NQBP's proposed Multi Cargo Facility (MCF), provided they are not financially disadvantaged. The MCF is proposed as a sheltered harbour at the Port of Abbot Point designed to accommodate multiple trades. NQBP is currently in the planning stages of the project. Stage one will involve up to four berths and a common user tug facility to accommodate Terminals 2 and 3.

NQBP is also considering further expansions at Abbot Point. Terminals

4–9 could involve up to an additional six coal terminals with a nominal capacity of 180 million tonnes per annum in aggregate, and NQBP sought expressions of interest in May 2011 from potential private sector proponents for which it has received a very strong response.

**Dudgeon Point**

Dudgeon Point is located at the Port of Hay Point approximately 5 kilometres northwest of the Hay Point Services Coal Terminal and Dalrymple Bay Coal Terminal. Dudgeon Point is a potential location for the export of coal from mines in the Galilee and Bowen Basins.

Following an Expressions of Interest process in mid-2010, NQBP selected two companies as preferred proponents for the development of Dudgeon Point – the Adani Group (an Indian conglomerate) and Dudgeon Point Project Management Pty Ltd, a wholly owned subsidiary of the Brookfield Infrastructure Group and sister company to Dalrymple Bay Coal Terminal Management Pty Ltd (DBCTM) (Queensland Government, 2011b, p. 165). The preferred proponents will work with NQBP to prepare a Master Plan for the development of coal terminals at Dudgeon Point.

**North West Queensland energy review**

The final report of an independent review of energy delivery in the North West Queensland Minerals Province (NWQ Minerals Province) recommended a customer-led competitive process during which proponents would negotiate with customers to confirm a long-term energy solution for the North West and its growing resources sector (Queensland Government, 2011b, pp. 161–162). The customer-led competitive process engaged with energy supply proponents of local gas-fired generation or transmission line connection to the national electricity market.

On 6 October 2011, Xstrata publicly announced that it had entered into a 17-year contract with the Diamantina Power Station consortium (Xstrata, 2011), comprised of the APA Group and AGL Energy Limited, effectively concluding the process. The Xstrata load would have underwritten a significant level of alternative transmission provider for Copperstring's load and, as a result, Copperstring has announced that it is reviewing its transmission project.

## 6.9 CONCLUSION

This chapter discusses why Queensland has the corporatisation model, the reform that Queensland has undertaken in the GOC sector both before and after the global financial crisis, and the role that GOCs are having in the further development of existing industries and the development of new industries. Currently the state has 12 GOCs. It is expected that these GOCs will continue to be subject to shareholding ministers' oversight in terms of their performance, governance and accountability, given the state's significant investment in GOCs.

As discussed in the chapter, GOCs are likely to undertake more commercial partnerships with the private sector. Private sector-funded development of new coal terminals at some of the ports to meet customer demand is already occurring and further development is expected. Some of the state's GOCs will undertake projects that will support other projects, such as those proposed for the Surat and Galilee Basins, or facilitate the development of industries such as liquefied natural gas.

It is the integrated response to infrastructure development by GOCs, which is possible with a GOC model, that is expected to help facilitate Queensland's economic growth and maximise the benefits of development for Queenslanders.

## NOTES

* This paper was prepared for a conference at the University of Auckland in October 2011, it reflected current government policy and project outlook as things stood at that time. Since that date there has been a change of government.

1. The authors would like to acknowledge the contributions from other officers in the Queensland Treasury and Queensland Treasury Corporation who provided material that assisted in the development of this chapter.
The chapter is not Queensland Government policy.



## REFERENCES

Australian Taxation Office (2008), *National Tax Equivalent Regime Manual*, Australian Government, accessed 6 December 2011 at http://www.ato.gov.au/content/00166836.htm.

Bligh, A. (2006), 'Qld Govt Announces Win–Win Sale of Allgas', Queensland Government.
Bligh, A. and P. Beattie (2006), 'State's Future Growth Fund Gets a $1.3B Kick', Queensland Government.
Bligh, A. and D. Boyle (2008), 'Cairns Hospital Redevelopment is Full Steam Ahead', Queensland Government.
Bligh, A. and A. Fraser (2009), 'Renewing Queensland: Future Investment Plan', Queensland Government.
Bligh, A. and A. Fraser (2010), 'Toll Roads Stay in Public Hands as Qld Moves Further along the Path to AAA', Queensland Government.
Bligh, A. and R. Nolan (2011), 'Premium Price for Abbot Point Coal Terminal Boosts Disaster Recovery', Queensland Government.
Bligh, A. and G. Wilson (2007), 'Qld Future Fund Tops $3B with AGL Sale', Queensland Government.
Boston Consulting Group (2006), *Queensland Energy Structure Review*, Queensland Treasury, accessed 6 December 2011 at http://www.treasury.qld.gov.au/pdf/bcg_final.pdf.
Commonwealth of Australia (1993), *National Competition Policy*, Canberra: Australian Government Publishing Service.
Fraser, A. (2008), 'Treasurer Announces Successful Sale of Mackay Airport', Queensland Government.
Fraser, A. (2010a), 'Abbot Point Coal Terminal Sale Process Begins', Queensland Government.
Fraser, A. (2010b), 'Forestry Sale Exceeds Expectations', Queensland Government.
Fraser, A. (2010c), 'Government Announces Successful Port of Brisbane Transaction', Queensland Government.
Fraser, A. (2010d), 'QR National', Queensland Government.
Fraser, A. (2011), 'QML Transfer Finalised', Queensland Government.
Nolan, R. (2011), 'Major Coup for Qld Economy as WICET Reaches Financial Close', Queensland Government.
Office of Government Owned Corporations (2009), *Code of Practice for Government Owned Corporations' Financial Arrangements*, Queensland Treasury.
Queensland Government (2006), Government Owned Corporations Amendment Bill 2006 (Qld) Explanatory Note, accessed 29 November 2011 at http://www.legislation.qld.gov.au/Bill_Pages/Bill_52_06.htm.
Queensland Government (2008), *Major Economic Statement 2008–09*, Queensland Government.
Queensland Government (2009), *State Budget 2009–10, Budget Strategy and Outlook, Budget Paper No. 2*, Queensland Government.
Queensland Government (2010), *Shareholder Review of Queensland Government Owned Corporation Generators*, Queensland Government, accessed 6 December 2011 at http://www.ogoc.qld.gov.au/current-issues/review-goc-generators.shtml.
Queensland Government (2011a), *State Budget 2011–12, Budget Speech, Budget Paper No. 1*, Queensland Government.
Queensland Government (2011b), *State Budget 2011–12, Budget Strategy and Outlook, Budget Paper No. 2*, Queensland Government.
Queensland Treasury (1990), *A Green Paper on Government Owned Enterprises*, Queensland Treasury.
Queensland Treasury (1992), *Corporatisation in Queensland Policy Guidelines*, Queensland Treasury.

Queensland Treasury (2011), 'Government Owned Corporations Guide to the Performance Management Framework' (unpublished), Queensland Treasury.
Taylor, L. (2010), 'Two New Coal Terminals for Port of Abbot Point', North Queensland Bulk Ports Corporation Limited, accessed 6 December 2011 at http://www.nqbp.com.au/index.cfm?newsID=8.
Xstrata (2011), 'Long-Term Energy Supplies Secured for North West Queensland Operations', Xstrata, accessed 20 April 2012 at http://www.xstrata.com/media/news/2011/10/06/0800CET.

# 7. Putting 'why' before 'how': evaluating the rationales for partial privatisation of state-owned enterprises in New Zealand

**Chye-Ching Huang, Susan Watson and Jenny Chen***

## 7.1 INTRODUCTION

Some of New Zealand's state-owned enterprises (SOEs) will almost certainly be partially privatised from 2012 onwards. The government intends to partially privatise power companies; Mighty River Power Limited, Meridian Energy Limited, Genesis Power Limited and Solid Energy New Zealand Limited, and to further reduce the Crown's 74.32 per cent share in Air New Zealand Limited (Secretary of the Cabinet, 2011, para. 5). The government has stated that it intends to retain at least 51 per cent of each entity, initial public offerings are the preferred mode of sale, and that proceeds from SOE sales would be used through a Future Investment Fund to finance as yet unspecified capital expenditure (Secretary of the Cabinet, 2011, para. 28). Expected proceeds are between NZ$5 billion and NZ$7 billion (Secretary of the Cabinet, 2011, para. 27). The government has signalled the potential use of incentives (e.g. bonus shares) to encourage broad participation.

In undertaking a privatisation programme of this sort, it is crucial that policy-makers know what they are trying to achieve in order to make rational design choices, and to be held accountable for those choices. Different policy goals can indicate radically different design choices for implementing a privatisation (or partial privatisation) programme. For example, a focus solely on short-term fiscal deleveraging would indicate structuring the sale to achieve the maximum possible sale proceeds, net of sale costs. This may mean selling shares without restrictions on ownership and transfer. By contrast, a goal of encouraging wider participation in domestic capital markets has led other countries to accept a lower financial return in order to structure the sale in a way that is attractive to many subscribers. For that reason, why privatisation is being pursued should drive how it is carried out.

The international experience bears this out: the reasons for privatisation (in particular, the economic and fiscal conditions that may give rise to particular policy goals) are closely related to privatisation methods. Further, if policy-makers do not make their rationales for privatisation clear, it becomes all too easy for any privatisation experience to be painted as a 'success' on one measure or another, regardless of the intended objective.

This chapter examines the rationales, identified by the New Zealand Treasury in its initial advice on the 'mixed ownership model', as possible reasons for New Zealand to undertake partial privatisation of some of its SOEs (Crown Ownership Monitoring Unit, 2010a). We find that some rationales are more compelling than others, and that in sum, while we agree with the bulk of the Treasury's analysis, the Treasury may understate the case for partial privatisation, yet also understate the case for the Crown continuing to hold some (or even a majority) stake in the privatised entities.

As discussed in the conclusion, we are also concerned that rather than choosing to focus on one or two of the most compelling reasons for partial privatisation put forward by the Treasury, the government instead has affirmed no less than ten goals of partial privatisation, and not given any upfront prioritisation of those objectives. This will make it extremely difficult for policy-makers to make consistent and rational design choices when implementing the partial privatisation programme. The lack of clear priorities may also make it difficult to evaluate the outcomes of the programme, and for the public to hold government to account over those outcomes.

## 7.2 EVALUATION OF RATIONALES

The Treasury, in its initial advice on the 'mixed ownership model', attempted to clarify what it considered to be the convincing and unconvincing rationales for partial privatisation (Crown Ownership Monitoring Unit, 2010a). Below we set out and assess these rationales under the headings of fiscal, static and dynamic efficiency, capital market development, public good and policy stability.

### 7.2.1 Fiscal

The Treasury concluded that fiscal drivers should be considered, at best, a 'moderate' driver for partial privatisation in the current environment.

The Treasury notes that: 'the commercial value of an asset represents the future income stream from that asset. Therefore, selling part or all of that asset would be swapping cash now for the equivalent discounted stream of cash into the future (assuming the price is fair)' (Crown Ownership Monitoring Unit, 2010a, para. 56). The price might be more or less than these cash flows, for example where the residual Crown ownership is perceived as some type of guarantee reducing risk to other investors, or where an investor perceives improved performance in a privatised entity (Crown Ownership Monitoring Unit, 2010a, para. 56). But in the absence of a sale premium or discount on the current value of cash flows, public sector net worth is unchanged, and 'selling public sector assets is equivalent to selling fixed interest debt' (Yarrow, 1986, p. 360). In that circumstance, Yarrow bluntly notes that 'it would be surprising if asset sales represent a free lunch through which current government deficits can be financed without upward pressure on interest rates and consequent crowding out of private sector expenditure' (Yarrow, 1986, p. 360). That is:

> for a developed country with a stable financial and political system, the risk of default on bonds is likely to be low, and it is hard to make the case for privatisation purely on revenue grounds. But for a less developed country prone to bouts of rapid inflation, bond sales may be constrained in such a way that there is a pure revenue motive for the privatisation of firms in sectors where the default risk on equity is not too great. (Vickers and Yarrow, 1988, p. 119)

It is for these reasons that, in the absence of any large expected premiums on net present value of cash flows from sale, while SOE privatisations could facilitate capital reallocation or reduce gross debt, the argument for this is 'moderate' in New Zealand's current fiscal climate (Crown Ownership Monitoring Unit, 2010a, paras 56–64). A fiscal driver would be more persuasive in situations of extreme fiscal pressure and, if it were an overriding consideration, it would support full rather than partial privatisation to the extent that it would maximise the sale price.

The Treasury's analysis appears to assume that the government, retaining some implied responsibility to guarantee the financial viability of the partially privatised business, will bring about a low risk of potential fiscal downside. Of course, such risks may exist with the Crown as 100 per cent shareholder, but the assumption the Treasury appears to make is that the Crown does not retain any implied liability greater than its proportionate share in partially privatised enterprise, post-privatisation. This assumption may be inappropriate. The Crown may be required to assume liabilities well beyond proportion to its stake in the partially privatised entity, either due to political pressure or where it is seen that doing so produces a public good.

The Treasury considered only direct fiscal impacts from sale price. The Treasury did not, however, consider the long-run fiscal impacts from economic growth differentials under various ownership structures, likely because although these long-run economic growth impacts may be significant, identifying their direction and magnitude involves much more uncertainty. To the extent, however, that any design option is asserted to have large economic growth benefits or detriments, this flow on fiscal impact could be a consideration, although it would need to be weighted to take account of the uncertainty around the actual impact it would in fact have.

Costs connected with privatisation are likely to be significant. The Organisation for Economic Co-operation and Development (OECD) documents that the typical privatisation requires the services of:

- legal advisors to structure and implement the sale;
- financial advisers to review the SOE's business and finances, its accounting practices and to advise on matters such as preparation of the company books, valuation and financial restructuring;
- management consultants and industry experts to advise on firm-specific restructuring and sector restructuring, particularly for large enterprises and those operating in non-competitive sectors of the economy;
- strategic advisers who advise on the privatisation programme in general and the privatisation strategy; and
- sale advisers, such as investment bankers, to advise on transaction-specific details, and to deal with matters such as the preparation of the offer and general management and execution of the sale. (OECD, 2003, p. 64)

In sum we agree with the Treasury that the fiscal driver for a partial privatisation programme is modest. Proceeds from partial privatisation are, as Yarrow notes, no free lunch from a net debt perspective. The deleveraging motivation for privatisation does not appear pressing, nor has privatisation been argued as superior to other methods of deleveraging (such as management of revenues and expenditures). Long-term revenue benefits and expenditure risks from partial privatisation should also be considered, as should the cost of sale, but neither of these factors significantly strengthens nor weakens the Treasury's evaluation of the fiscal rationale.

### 7.2.2 Static Efficiency Gains

The international literature seems clear that significant efficiency gains can be achieved from full privatisation of SOEs in situations where the

SOEs are performing inefficiently relative to private sector benchmarks and where other policy settings (for example regulation of market power) are supportive. In the New Zealand situation, when determining whether static efficiency gains present a strong rationale for partial or full privatisation of some or all of the commercial SOE portfolio, two specific questions must be considered: (1) the extent of the efficiency gains possible, given the current performance of the commercial portfolio; and (2) whether partial privatisation short of relinquishing state control would realise any such gains.

**Scope for static efficiency gains**

The Treasury concludes that there is scope for modest efficiency gains from privatisation or partial privatisation of the commercial portfolio given that the commercial portfolio does not appear to be performing demonstrably poorly. However, the Treasury's analyses are subject to limitations in measuring SOE capital growth because of the lack of a market valuation for SOE assets (Crown Ownership Monitoring Unit, 2010b). Large differences in the valuations of a number of SOEs illustrate the difficulty of measuring performance where there is no market for capital in the portfolio (Crown Ownership Monitoring Unit, 2010b, p. 25). Nevertheless, there is no evidence that current board valuations of SOEs are systematically optimistic (Crown Ownership Monitoring Unit, 2010b, p. 25). Thus, it does not seem sensible to assume that there is significant scope for static efficiency improvements.

**Extracting static efficiency gains without relinquishing Crown control**

In addition to the question of whether efficiency gains are in fact possible, there is the issue of whether privatisation, short of relinquishing state control, would realise any static efficiency gains. It has been argued that partial privatisation, where the Crown holds a controlling stake in the privatised SOE, would not in fact generate any efficiency gains. This is because the market for corporate control has not been opened, thus preventing the threat or reality of a takeover, inducing efficient management practice (Vining and Boardman, 1992, pp. 209–216).

If the lack of a market for corporate control explains public enterprise inefficiencies, then partial privatisation that does not open the market for corporate control will not increase enterprise efficiency (Gupta, 2005, pp. 988–991). This is the traditional explanation for the existence of large private corporations.

However in theory there is a reasonable basis for concluding that partial privatisation short of vesting control can in some contexts deliver efficiency gains, although granted not to the extent that may be realised by full privatisation. Eckel and Vining explain that, even if control is not divested, some private ownership in an SOE could improve efficiency because that private ownership would reduce monitoring and bonding costs:

> Partial private ownership provides an alternative source of pressure for efficiency, lessening the need for efficiency monitoring by government. Private shareholders care about the profitability and riskiness of the firm, and managers of the firm recognize the need to maintain share price to facilitate the raising of capital, etc. So managers have an incentive to improve efficiency, since share price provides a signal to government and private investors of perceived efficiency. (Eckel and Vining, 1985, p. 92)

As noted by Sam (2007, pp. 65–67), the empirical evidence on whether partial privatisation and in particular privatisation where the state retains control, delivers efficiency or other performance gains, is limited and mixed:

- Boardman and Vining's (1989) empirical study of the profitability of mixed enterprises found that they performed no better than 100 per cent state owned enterprises and worse than comparable private sector enterprises. Their sample comprised the 500 largest non-US manufacturing and mining corporations, of which 23 were Mixed Enterprises, defined as a company where the stock was partially in private hands and partially in public hands.
- Megginson et al. examined 61 companies across 18 countries and 32 industries, but included only share issue privatisations. Tracking the performance of companies before and after privatisation, the study found that:

  > for our full sample, we document significant increases in profitability, output per employee (adjusted for inflation), capital spending, and total employment . . . our results are generally robust when we partition our data into various subsamples . . . our results are also unchanged when we . . . examine privatisations where the government surrenders control and contrast these with 'revenue' privatisations where the purpose of share sales is primarily to raise cash. (Megginson et al., 1994, p. 448)

- Mok and Chau studied a sample of Chinese corporations listed on the Hong Kong stock exchange. The study found that privatised firms were more profitable than their partially privatised counterparts, but that the partially privatised firms were more efficient than fully privatised firms for three of the four years in the study (Mok and Chau, 2003, p. 534). They hypothesise that this was due to the effects of the Asian financial crisis and the fact that business location was not controlled for (Mok and Chau, 2003, p. 534).

- Oum et al. concluded that airports that are in majority public ownership are less profitable than those that are either fully state owned or fully private (Oum et al., 2006, p. 119). It should be noted however that their findings are likely to be sensitive to the specification. The sample was a cross-sectional, time series dataset over 2001–03 for 116 Asia-Pacific, European and North American airports. Oum et al. note previous contrasting findings that airlines with mixed ownership tend to perform better than government-owned airlines (Oum et al., 2006, p. 111 citing Backx et al., 2002).
- Gupta (2005) examined the pre- and post- (partial) privatisation performance of Indian firms over 1990–2000, and found positive impacts from partial privatisation on profitability, productivity and investment spending following privatisation. The sample was 339 manufacturing and service sector firms.
- Li and Xu found no significant impact from partial privatisation in the telecommunications sector (Li and Xu, 2004, pp. 426–427).
- Zinnes et al. found that economic performance gains come only from 'deep' privatisation, that is, when ownership changes occur once key institutional and agency-related reforms have exceeded certain threshold levels. (Zinnes et al., 2001, p. 166)

Thus the studies of the effects of partial privatisation are mixed. In addition they are subject to three key limitations.

Firstly, the use of private rather than fully public benchmarks in some studies (e.g. Mok and Chau, 2003) may limit the ability to draw conclusions about the efficiency gains of partial privatisation over enterprises fully owned by the state. However to the extent that the literature generally shows efficiency gains from full privatisation over full state ownership, convergence between partially privatised and private benchmarks may indicate a superior performance of partial over full state ownership.

Secondly, some of the studies do not distinguish between privatisation in which control has been divested and privatisation in which the state has retained control (e.g. Boardman and Vining, 1989). Even though a study of 384 share issue privatisations between 1977 and 1997 in 59 countries found that less than 30 per cent of those privatisations involved (initially) the sale of more than 50 per cent of an SOE (Jones et al., 1999, p. 230), Gupta notes that '[s]urprisingly, little is known about the effect of partial privatisation where the government remains the controlling owner' (Gupta, 2005, p. 987).

Thirdly, these studies are subject to the same data limitations and potential biases that affect studies of full privatisation, and privatisation more generally. The empirical findings are also often constrained by a specific context. For example sector-specific findings (e.g. Boardman and Vining, 1989) or country-specific findings (e.g. Gupta, 2005; Mok and Chau, 2003) should be treated with caution in the New Zealand context. Further as the Treasury notes, things other than control and ownership may matter, including regulatory contexts and the state of capital markets in the privatising jurisdiction; factors that are often not controlled for in these studies (Crown Ownership Monitoring Unit, 2010a, para. 22). Megginson and Netter discuss in detail the many other potential weaknesses of empirical studies on privatisation, including data limitations, lack of consideration of welfare effects on consumers, and lack of controls for market power of privatised firms (Megginson and Netter, 2001, pp. 334–337).

Notwithstanding these limitations, it nevertheless appears that in some circumstances efficiency gains can be extracted under conditions of partial privatisation. Further, a 2006 study indicates that partial privatisations in which the state retains control may be more common than earlier studies have recognised and therefore, some of the efficiency benefits identified in earlier studies as accruing to full privatisations, may in fact, accrue to partial privatisations.

In sum, although the empirical and theoretical evidence is far from comprehensive or conclusive, it does provide solid reasons to conclude that efficiency gains may accrue from partial privatisation even where the Crown retains a controlling interest. However, as the Treasury cautions, the scope of any such benefits is still likely to be small given the lack of evidence of severe underperformance by companies in the commercial portfolio, and limited further by the reasonable assumption that some of the potential efficiency benefits are relinquished if the Crown retains control.

Even if static efficiency gains are modest in scope relative to the current efficiency performance of the SOE portfolio, this does not mean that the gains would not be economically significant. Booth and Noon (2011) note that static efficiency gains are not only enjoyed by the privatised company, but these gains may have upstream and downstream effects on both suppliers and customers. The turnover of the commercial portfolio constitutes approximately 8 per cent of gross domestic product (GDP) currently (Crown Ownership Monitoring Unit, 2010b, p. 4). Thus even modest static efficiency gains could have a significant economic impact. In sum, static efficiency gains should be considered a moderate driver of any partial privatisation policy and perhaps given a little more weight than the Treasury places on them.

### 7.2.3 Dynamic Efficiency Gains

The Treasury concludes that there is more scope for dynamic efficiency gains from privatisation 'through different investment decisions, for example, as opposed to static efficiency gains from closing the performance gap at a point in time'. This may include the enterprises developing a stronger risk appetite, including a willingness to invest overseas and to innovate. Such gains can be potentially significant compared to static efficiency gains, as quite small growth gains from moving into different operational activities can rapidly outweigh any static gains, through the more efficient use of resources within existing businesses. However while static efficiency gains can be relatively easy to estimate by examining comparable private sector enterprises, potential dynamic gains are inherently more difficult to quantify, being highly firm- and industry-specific, and requiring a longer-term view of returns.

Empirical literature has to date paid little attention to estimating the impact of privatisation on dynamic efficiency gains, particularly those arising from innovation (Carreira and Deza, 2009). While a number of studies show reduced research and development (R&D) spend associated with privatisation, many of these studies are country- or industry-specific in contexts where the SOEs have strong public-good rationales pre-privatisation rather than a commercial focus, as with New Zealand's portfolio (Munari, 2003, p. 141). Further, studies indicate that R&D performance and efficiency improve post-privatisation, although those improvements are neither immediate nor simple (Munari, 2002, pp. 230–231).

The existing literature does not consider in depth whether dynamic efficiency gains would necessarily accrue to a partially privatised entity in which the state retains control. It may be however, that the same theoretical basis exists for believing that some dynamic efficiency gains may be realised (if not to the same degree as for full privatisation) as for static efficiency gains. That is, improved monitoring and access to external capital may improve management willingness and ability to generate dynamic efficiency gains.

In the New Zealand situation, there appears to be greater scope for dynamic efficiency gains than there is for static efficiency gains from altered management of the current commercial portfolio. In particular Treasury notes that 'total offshore investment by the SOE portfolio is currently about 1 per cent of assets, probably much lower than it would be in private ownership' (Crown Ownership Monitoring Unit, 2010a, para. 51). Further, the portfolio is generally regarded as underleveraged (Skilling and Weldon, 2008, pp. 16–17). The initial listing targets announced by the government (in particular the three 'gentailers') are also particularly capital intensive, potentially allowing significant dynamic efficiency gains from decisions around capital deployment. We have been unable to locate any studies that isolate the R&D investment of New Zealand's SOEs, or evaluate the R&D performance of those entities.

Again as with static efficiency gains, even small gains may have a significant economic impact, given the significance of the existing commercial portfolio in the economy. Thus the theoretical ability to generate dynamic efficiency gains, coupled with the apparently significant scope for such gains in the commercial portfolio, mean that dynamic efficiency gains may be a fairly strong rationale for considering full or partial privatisation.

We caution however that the scope of potential dynamic efficiency gains depends on the structure and type of underlying business being privatised, and should not be assumed in the abstract. For example, Heatley and Schwass highlight the flawed assumption that changing the ownership model would fix the underlying economics of NZ Rail (despite rail's history; Heatley and Schwass, 2011, p. 236). Thus from a cautious perspective, it would seem sensible to undertake further study in an attempt to identify potential sources of dynamic efficiency, even at a high level, for the 'gentailers' and for Air New Zealand, the current targets for partial privatisation. Such a study would need to take into account industry- and firm-level characteristics. We are not aware of any detailed work of this nature to date.

### 7.2.4 Capital Market Development

The scope for economic gains from improving New Zealand's capital markets is high given their current state of underdevelopment. New Zealand's economic performance is poor relative to other developed countries. Skilling and Boven identify New Zealand's poor export and foreign direct investment performance relative to other developed countries as one of the causes of its economic underperformance (Skilling and Boven, 2006, pp. 5–10). Skilling and Boven argue that reversing these trends requires the creation and growth of larger, more internationally engaged companies with significant overseas direct investment activities (Skilling and Boven, 2006, p. 21). This in turn requires expanding the domestic pool of capital because, to cite Rajan and Zingales:

> capital market strength and firm growth are strongly related, particularly for firms that have a heavy reliance on external financing. This will be the case for many New Zealand firms that are seeking to expand into international markets, given that they will frequently be small and will need to scale up their activities substantially to operate in much larger offshore markets. (Skilling and Boven, 2006, p. 21 citing Rajan and Zingales, 1998)

The Capital Market Development Taskforce Secretariat also concluded that 'capital market development leads to more investment, higher labor productivity and faster economic growth', and that there are a number of reasons for thinking that local financial market development is important for local growth (Capital Market Development Taskforce Secretariat, 2009, pp. 2, 11–15). Thus according to the Taskforce, a number of considerations 'argue for a focus on domestic capital market development as an integral part of our economic growth strategy' (Capital Market Development Taskforce, 2009, p. 9). The Treasury also recognises that there is reason to believe that the development of domestic capital markets is important for economic growth, and that 'retaining a local stock market could be important for firms seeking access to finance especially new and emerging firms' (Crown Ownership Monitoring Unit, 2010a, para. 70).

Some of these economic benefits of capital market development could be extracted from the listing or partial listing of SOEs. We attempt to consider those benefits by examining each of five dimensions of capital market development along which privatisation of SOEs might have some impact. For some but not all of these dimensions, full listing would likely deliver greater benefits than partial listings.

**Market size, capitalisation and depth**

Evans in 2009 noted that New Zealand's share market capitalisation of domestic companies relative to GDP is small relative to comparator countries (Switzerland, Singapore, Ireland, Australia and Norway) and that it declined between 1997 and 2000. A potential rationale for full or partial privatisations is to increase market size. The Taskforce recommended that central and local government partially list some of their commercial assets on the NZX because it would 'materially improve the depth of our capital market, particularly in some of the areas in which central and local government is a key holder of assets' (Capital Market Development Taskforce, 2009, p. 47). While agreeing with the Taskforce that listing SOEs would increase market depth (and liquidity, discussed below), the Treasury is less sanguine about the materiality of listing parts of the commercial portfolio. It notes that:

> The commercial portfolio is equivalent to 30% of the NZX's market capitalization. However, listing a small subset of the portfolio would have much smaller impact. For example, 25% of all three electricity SOEs would increase the NZX's capitalization by around 5%. (Crown Ownership Monitoring Unit, 2010a, para. 74)

We think that the impact on stock market size of listings may however, be material. If capital market size development is a strong rationale for considering privatisation, then there is no reason that over time listings above 25 per cent, and listings in more than the three electricity SOEs, should not be considered (to the extent that the market capitalisation rationale is a driver of any privatisation, full may therefore be preferred to partial privatisation.) Further, an immediate 5 per cent increase in capitalisation could be material in light of the lack of other options, and the ability for immediate improvements to lead to cumulative benefits over time. As the Taskforce notes, partially floating some state-owned assets 'is the only way in which our share market can markedly increase in size in the near term' (Capital Market Development Taskforce, 2009, p. 47).

The Treasury also argues that there would be only modest economic gains from capital market development (including increasing capitalisation) due to SOE listings, as 'the more important drivers of capital market development are domestic savings and the broader tax and regulatory environment' and that 'listing some SOEs without other complementary measures would limit the benefits' (Crown Ownership Monitoring Unit, 2010a, para. 75). This argument cuts both ways: implementing other measures to improve domestic savings would have limited benefits if the size and diversity of investments on offer remain restricted. Further, many of these other policy levers may take a longer time to shift and, as the Taskforce noted, the net present value of immediate improvements may be greater due to the spillover benefits generated, including 'making it more attractive to other companies considering listing on the market, by increasing activity and investor interest' (Capital Market Development Taskforce, 2009, p. 47).

**Market composition**

The Taskforce argues that partial listing of some SOEs would 'materially increase investors' choices of domestic assets' (Capital Market Development Taskforce, 2009, p. 47). The Treasury notes however that 'the SOE portfolio is dominated by the electricity sector, but "electric" is the single largest sector currently listed on the NZX (including Contact, Infratil, Trustpower, and Vector)' (Crown Ownership Monitoring Unit, 2010a, para. 74). But even within the broad electricity sector, the commercial portfolio may offer a distinctive mix of underlying assets. For example Skilling and Weldon note that the renewable energy generation capabilities of the existing commercial SOEs may present a distinct offering to the market (they propose considering the creation and floating of one large renewable energy generator from the existing portfolio assets; Skilling and Weldon, 2008, p. 16).

Even if not introducing diversity in terms of underlying asset types, the introduction of investment options in the large SOEs would improve capital market diversity along other dimensions. In particular some of the SOEs in the commercial portfolio would be among the larger firms listed on the NZX by a number of measures and would be relatively low-geared. As the Treasury notes, 'the ability to invest in relatively low risk large companies may be appealing to many New Zealanders' (Crown Ownership Monitoring Unit, 2010a, para. 72). Further, Skilling and Boven argue that due to their low gearing and other factors, some of the large SOEs would be in a good position to undertake significant international expansion (Skilling and Boven, 2006, p. 28). If this were to eventuate, it would also add an important diversity dimension to current capital offerings, given the poor current outward direct investment (ODI) performance of existing New Zealand firms.

Partial privatisation would increase the diversity of offerings less than full privatisation would, in that partial privatisations would not contribute to the market control stakes in the large SOEs (it would however offer diversity of ownership structures in creating a unique mixed ownership model, which may be attractive if investors perceive benefits of government shareholding in the partially privatised entities, for reasons of implicit financial guarantee or for other reasons).

**Participation**

Listing of SOEs may lead – at least temporarily – to a broader-based participation in the capital market in New Zealand, particularly if the listing is designed specifically for that purpose. The government, by expressing a preference for IPOs and that 'Mum and Dad' investors be first in line, indicates that this is considered a key rationale for partial privatisation and a key driver of decisions about how to privatise. Other countries, in order to encourage broad domestic participation, have commonly used mechanisms such as offering domestic investors first access to shares, discount rates and limiting parcel sizes (Keloharju et al., 2008, pp. 2068–2070). Mechanisms designed to prevent initial investors from 'flipping' shares quickly (to realise the benefit of any initial discount on fair value), such as restrictions on transfer or bonuses for holding shares for a certain period, are also common (Keloharju et al., 2008, pp. 2068–2070). Such mechanisms have a fiscal cost.

Nevertheless as the Treasury notes, the positive effects of SOE floats on financial literacy and savings culture, while perhaps speculative, may well prove complementary to other measures relating to domestic saving preferences (Crown Ownership Monitoring Unit, 2010a, paras 72–73). While not sufficient to rebalance saving rates, the increased and more attractive investment choices offered by SOE floats may be a necessary part of a broader package. Thus the speculative nature of the benefits of SOE floats on 'saving culture' may be reduced by ensuring that it is part of a package of mechanisms to improve saving rates.

Other jurisdictions have commonly used SOE floats in an attempt to encourage broader capital market participation. Keloharju et al. examined 360 privatisations from 24 countries (including 55 from the UK, 43 from France, 43 from Portugal and 34 from Italy) and found the common use of incentives, designed to attract retail investors to participate in privatisations and to discourage them from flipping[1] their shares (Keloharju et al., 2008, pp. 2068–2072). At least one type of incentive was used in 50 per cent of the sample (181 privatisations), with bonus shares for investors who kept their original shares for a minimum period the most frequently used incentive (Keloharju et al., 2008, p. 2066). Retail discounts on the institutional price were also popular. Instalment plans allowing for payment over several instalments were used most frequently in the UK (in 39 privatisations). In some instances, incentives were combined such as bonuses and discounts, or bonuses and instalments (Keloharju et al., 2008, pp. 2075–2076). Four New Zealand privatisations were included in the study; interestingly no incentives were used in any of those four offerings. This can be compared with Australia, where in ten privatisations, four used discounts and three used instalments. The study found that larger offerings tend to rely more heavily on retail incentive schemes than smaller offerings, that the use of retail incentives has increased over time, and that the use of retail incentives was not significantly related to right- or left-leaning government (Keloharju et al., 2008, p. 2072).

The evidence is that such measures do on average tend to increase the breadth of participation in the initial offering. Keloharju et al. found that retail incentives did influence the numbers of shareholders participating in privatisations and subsequent holding periods. Discounts were found to have a greater effect on the number of investors than underpricing. Keloharju et al. suggest that this may be due to the fact that terms of retail incentives are known in advance but underpricing terms are not. Discounts were found to have a slightly stronger effect on the number of investors than bonus shares. The study also found that countries with more social inequality require more costly incentives to attract middle-class voters. This may be a particular consideration in New Zealand given its relatively high income inequality relative to the OECD median (Ministry of Social Development, 2010, pp. 64–65).

However Abromeit's (1988) case study of UK privatisations suggests that even if participation incentives may increase participation in the initial listing of an SOE, diversity of ownership in the privatised entity is not sustainable in long term. In the UK, a series of sales of public assets, designed to encourage wide participation, was undertaken with the stated goal of creating a 'people's capital market' (Abromeit, 1988, p. 78). Although the number of shareholders doubled between 1980 and 1985, many shareholders did not retain their shares (Abromeit, 1988, p. 78). Abromeit documents that:

- Amersham International had approximately 65 000 shareholders at the first date of trading (25 February 1982). Four months later (14 June 1982), this had fallen to 8600, and at 1 June 1984 there were only 8129.
- By 1985 only 1.6 million of the original 2.3 million British Telecom shareholders held onto their shares with only 12 per cent of shares owned by individual shareholders.
- In Aerospace, the total number of shareholders sank by 83 per cent and the total number of small shareholders decreased by 93 per cent post float.
- Cable and Wireless's number of shareholders dropped from 157 000 to 26 000 within a year, and Jaguar's dropped from 120 000 to 50 000 within six months of issue. Abromeit argues that shares are a means of saving for the small investor but even more a means to realise the easy and quick gains that can be safely expected from a low initial share price. (Abromeit, 1988, pp. 78–79)

Such sales were considered a success by HM Treasury on the basis of the initial offerings being oversubscribed (Abromeit, 1988, p. 79). *The Economist* (1986) however argued that it was 'theft disguised as generosity', for 'this is not a gift from the government but a transfer from non share buying taxpayers to the minority of taxpayers lucky or smart enough to buy the shares'. The Public Accounts Committee of the House of Commons similarly criticised the underselling of Amersham and British Telecom and believed that that the government was in the practice of creating windfall gains for the investor at the public's expense (*The Economist*, 1986, p. 77).

Both perspectives miss the mark somewhat. Wide participation in initial offerings, or even sustained wide participation in the privatised entity, is not a good measure of whether such floats improve capital market participation in the long run. And a wealth transfer in the form of a discounted price may be a deliberately incurred cost of encouraging capital market participation; the question is not whether such a transfer occurs, but whether it purchases – and at good cost – the desired benefit of significant improvement in capital market participation. If ineffective, or disproportionate to the capital market participation improvement secured, such a wealth transfer may be appropriately characterised as wasteful, or as

Abromeit argues, simply a tactic to secure votes (Abromeit, 1988, p. 79). Neither Abromeit nor other authors however offer empirical evidence about whether divestments in the floated assets were followed by reinvestments in the capital markets, or how the structure of participation in the capital markets as a whole changed, post float.

The empirical literature as a whole is frustratingly silent on the crucial issue of whether investments in shares of privatised SOEs leads to broader and continued participation in capital markets in the long term. Shares divested may be used to fund further capital market investments. Equally, even if shareholders retain a long-term stake in the privatised entities, that stake may not be part of a diversified portfolio and may simply substitute for, rather than be held in addition to, other saving instruments. The observation of Keloharju et al. that retail incentives can on average increase the breadth of participation (and in the case of bonus issues, the length of participation) in privatised entities, is only informative if considered alongside the fiscal cost of the sale price forgone.

In sum, the theory and evidence is mixed on whether partial privatisation can be designed to deliver significant improvements in capital market participation that justify the likely significant fiscal cost of designing a float to appeal to a large number of small shareholders. Other dimensions of capital market improvement appear to offer a stronger motivation for pursuing partial privatisation.

**Liquidity**

Treasury finds that the international evidence is that privatisations of SOEs can improve capital market liquidity. There is some scope for such gains in New Zealand. Evans finds that, controlling for the size of the market, liquidity is similar in New Zealand to other countries but that New Zealand has a relatively low number of traded equity transactions per head of population and that there is some evidence that liquidity or transactions on a value basis are generally less in New Zealand than comparator countries (Evans, 2009, pp. 15–16). The Treasury notes that market liquidity appears currently to be concentrated in large companies, and that listing larger companies may not have an impact on the liquidity of smaller companies. This conclusion is based on the observation that the lower liquidity in smaller companies is due to the lack of equity research in those companies (Crown Ownership Monitoring Unit, 2011a). Even if the lack of equity research is the main reason for the lower liquidity in smaller companies, improving liquidity in larger companies may have some modest flow on impact on liquidity in smaller companies.

Floats of Crown assets have contributed significantly to capital market liquidity in the past. Kerr et al. found that nine privatisations in New

Zealand from 1990 to 1999 increased the total market capitalisation by four times, and that liquidity improved between 1991 and 2001, with privatisations contributing an estimated 6.61 per cent of the 21.15 per cent improvement in market liquidity over that time (Kerr et al., 2007, pp. 46–48). However the scale of privatisation currently under consideration would contribute a maximum of about a 10 per cent increase to market capitalisation (if government retains a controlling share in all privatised entities), so the incremental contribution to liquidity is likely to be much smaller than from the privatisations in the 1990s.

**Efficiency**

The above rationales might indicate that full privatisation may be preferable to partial privatisation for capital market development reasons. But Eckel and Vining suggest that partial privatisation can be superior to full state ownership or full private ownership from an efficiency perspective where capital market imperfections prevent efficient risk-sharing, because 'partial government ownership provides a means of absorbing risks unacceptable to private shareholders' (Enderwick, 1997, p. 143, citing Eckel and Vining, 1985).

That is, it could be argued that our capital markets are underdeveloped to the extent that they are operating inefficiently. It has been argued that this is the case in New Zealand, in particular around the availability of risk capital, and investment at the private equity and venture capital stage (Capital Market Development Taskforce, 2009, pp. 56–57). Further, direct government investment has been proposed around investment in particular strategic infrastructure projects to correct perceived market failures; for example in broadband. Thus it has been suggested that a potential benefit of partial, as opposed to full privatisation, is that the privatised entities or a holding company responsible for the portfolio mix and proceeds from partial privatisation, could 'have a mandate to invest in New Zealand infrastructure assets (such as the proposed broadband funds) and other strategic investment opportunities' (Skilling and Weldon, 2008, p. 17). The potential for such efficiency gains in light of possible existing market failures is not considered explicitly by Treasury.

**Summary of capital market strengthening rationales**

Overall the Treasury concludes that capital market development improvements from SOE privatisations might only bring about modest economic gains. We suggest that the capital market development rationale for full or partial privatisation may be stronger than the Treasury suggests, on the basis that even a modest improvement to stock market size could be significant, and that divestment of some part of the portfolio offers more diversity benefits than those considered by the Treasury. Further, capital market underdevelopment may provide an efficiency rationale for partial privatisations. We do agree that the evidence and theory about the use of privatisations to broaden capital market participation and improve saving rates over the long term is fairly inconclusive. For that reason it would seem unwise to incur large fiscal costs in order to design privatisations for the sole purpose of securing broad domestic participation by holders of small share parcels.

## 7.3 PUBLIC GOOD RATIONALES

While full privatisation tends to be superior to partial privatisation as against most or all of the above rationales (fiscal, static and dynamic efficiency, capital market development), Enderwick notes that Eckel and Vining theorise two cases in which partial privatisation may be the preferred form rather than full public ownership:

> The first is where dual goals (profitability and social objectives) are pursued . . . it may be more efficient to combine market and political monitoring within a mixed ownership model. The monitoring of profitability but residual shareholders and political monitoring of social goals by state employees can coexist. The second arises where capital market imperfection prevent efficient risk-sharing. (Enderwick, 1997, pp. 142–143)

The capital market concern has been discussed above. Below we discuss four other (overlapping) potential market failure and social objective rationales for preferring partial to full privatisation: monopoly, strategic objectives and hollowing out, social responsibility, and Treaty of Waitangi principles.

### 7.3.1 Competition

As Hodge notes, '[t]he success of privatisation is intimately tied to notions of strong regulation to protect the interests of citizens and consumers as well as requiring governance with integrity' (Hodge, 2011, p. 8). Where enterprises are natural monopolies, public ownership is an alternative to regulation of the market to ensure competition. Where they are not, privatisation or partial privatisation may lead to additional competitive pressures in the relevant industry (Barry, 2002). The Treasury notes that there are natural monopolies in the portfolio. The Treasury finds the competition rationale a limited reason for Crown participation in SOEs and prefers a regulatory approach to solving problems arising from market dominance, including reliance on existing competition law structures and industry-specific regulation. The Treasury's assessment is that current regulatory regimes in force, offer adequate consumer protection (Crown Ownership Monitoring Unit, 2011a, paras 36–40).

By contrast, Queensland offers an example of a 'belts and braces' approach to competition issues on privatisation. In privatising some infrastructure assets, Queensland imposed directly on the (fully) privatised entity a 15 per cent cap on individual shareholdings due to the fear of takeovers undermining competition, rather than relying solely on existing competition law regimes. This was a response to a particular perceived risk of vertical integration in the relevant industry. Another potential approach to the problem of any perceived market immaturity may be 'partial privatisation' by splitting out and divesting only business units and assets that operate within mature and well regulated markets, sidestepping the need for significant regulatory reform on privatisation of those elements. This was the approach favoured in Queensland, where the government recognised that the retail aspect of the electricity business was mature and would be better operated by the private sector (Booth and Noon, 2011, p. 9). The divestment was further broken into two tranches to ensure that the new entrants had sufficient retail mass to be competitive (Booth and Noon, 2011, p. 9). A cautious approach to competition issues suggest that such non-regulatory approaches be considered in addition to reliance on existing competition law and industry specific regulation.

### 7.3.2 Strategic and Economic Development

Treasury concludes that there are few, if any, circumstances where Crown ownership (presumably participation at any level) would be required to achieve strategic objectives such as the ability to deploy assets in response to a crisis, or national security. The Treasury also gives economic spillover benefits of Crown control little weight, stating that:

> another common argument is that in air transport, for example, there may be a spillover benefit from having a national flag carrier for national brand, tourism, and so on. We would be sceptical of the size of such spillovers, and there are alternative ways of achieving national branding through contracting (e.g. tourism promotion).

The Treasury did not however engage in detail with the literature on these spillover benefits, which indicates the potential for such benefits. For example, Skilling and Boven argue that national airlines provide significant spillover benefits particularly for small or remote countries (Skilling and Boven, 2007, p. 23). For example national airlines tend to provide more direct provision of commercial passenger flights to the home market, which increases freight carrying capacity. The availability of such linkages in a global supply chain can be strategically important for a small remote economy, particularly given New Zealand's poor export performance. While beyond the scope of this chapter, we suggest that the identification and evaluation of such benefits should be given further specific consideration rather than dismissed in principle.

Further the Treasury's concern may have been focused on specific, static market failures, whereas some of the arguments for partial privatisation (as opposed to full privatisation) are based on concerns that may be more readily perceived as 'economic development' concerns. For example, Skilling and Boven, and Skilling and Weldon make a case for strategic investment as part of a range of complementary policy initiatives designed to promote economic growth by strengthening international linkages, ODI, and exporting performance at the firm level. This, they argue, would grow large New Zealand firms in order to generate agglomeration benefits, secure global supply chains in both the heavy and weightless export sectors, and thus facilitate a move of New Zealand's comparative advantage towards high-value-added products consumed in international markets. Again, while other policy measures may be complementary to this approach, we argue that a cohesive approach using a variety of policy levers would be the best way to alter New Zealand's economic performance.

An objective of shifting the composition of the economy towards higher-value-added production, rather than addressing traditional market failures, seems to be the rationale for state participation in commercial enterprises in many other jurisdictions. For example, Queensland's participation in infrastructure assets has the intended goal of developing the supply chain infrastructure needed to expand and support Queensland's extractive industries (Booth and Noon, 2011). As we discuss in a forthcoming paper, Singapore's approach to partially privatising its government-linked corporations through the holding company Temasek was driven primarily by economic development goals. Such concerns may also be described in terms of market failure (Huang and Watson, 2012). For example, Temasek's investment themes are directed to allocating additional capital to industries and investments that perceived failures in the (previously small) domestic capital markets were argued to have stunted. This strategy was not driven simply by the desire to correct all market inefficiencies, but by the expectation that correcting this particular capital market failure would encourage high-value-added activity and therefore particularly support Singapore's economic growth aspirations.

Thus we consider that the strategic benefits of retaining at least some part of the commercial portfolio in Crown ownership should be given greater consideration and that in the absence of such consideration these benefits may have been underestimated. We do however accept and reinforce the Treasury's caution that strategic and spillover benefits can be ill-defined and may in some cases serve as a rhetorical cloak for nationalistic or other unarticulated concerns. Thus if public participation in commercial assets is to be retained on a strategic basis, it is imperative that the strategic rationale be made clear, and that design choices are consistent with that objective. A benefit of any full or partial privatisation activity may be that it forces policy-makers to consider and to articulate the compelling strategic reasons, if any, for Crown participation in different parts of the commercial portfolio, either individually or in aggregate.

## 7.4 SOCIAL RESPONSIBILITY AND OTHER SOCIAL GOALS

In Section 4 of the State Owned Enterprises Act 1986, the principal objective of an SOE is made clear: it is to be a successful business. To that end, it is charged with being: as profitable and efficient as comparable businesses that are not owned by the Crown; a good employer; and an organisation that exhibits a sense of social responsibility by having regard to the interests of the community in which it operates and by endeavouring to accommodate or encourage these when able to do so (State Owned Enterprises Act 1986, ss. 4(1)(a)–4(1)(c)).

This sits alongside the Section 7 provision that '[w]here the Crown wishes a State enterprise to provide goods or services to any persons, the Crown and the State enterprise shall enter into an agreement under which the State enterprise will provide the goods or services in return for the payment by the Crown of the whole or part of the price thereof'. The government has to date not stated whether it intends to retain Sections 4 and 7 or the equivalent, for the partially privatised entities. The government can thus direct an SOE to undertake a particular social or non-commercial activity. If such a direction is given, the Crown and the SOE will enter into an agreement whereby the Crown agrees to compensate the SOE for a portion or the whole of the extra cost incurred in carrying out the activity (State Owned Enterprises Act 1986, s. 7). The purpose of this provision is to prevent the ad hoc subsidisation of certain goods or services which someone decides are for the social good. Such subsidisation was a characteristic of government departments. Because the costs of the social activities are clearly defined, non-commercial obligations cannot be used to mask poor management. When used, the subsidies have been quite specific. For example the government provided a subsidy to New Zealand Post Limited which was later withdrawn (New Zealand Treasury, 1996, pp. 41–42). New Zealand Post Limited then closed its non-commercial, previously subsidised outlets. However Section 7 does not now appear to be in common use. The 2011 Annual Portfolio Report of the Crown does not mention any specific instances of contracting under Section 7. This may be because when contracts are entered into between the Crown and an SOE (for example MetsService's six-year contract with the Ministry of Transport; Crown Ownership Monitoring Unit, 2011b, p. 85), it is not clear in practice whether that contract is made pursuant to Section 7 or as an 'ordinary' arm's-length contract. This may stem from the fact that it is not clear from the face of Section 7 whether it simply restates the ability at contract law of the Crown and SOEs to contract with each other, or whether it alternatively allows the government to require an SOE to agree to provide goods and services (New Zealand Treasury, 1996, pp. 38–42). There has been no judicial examination of Section 7. This means that in considering whether or not Section 7 or equivalent should be retained for the partially privatised companies, it is critical that policy-makers consider what Section 7 does that is different from default contract rules. It is beyond the scope of this chapter to undertake that analysis.

At first blush, regulation or a contracting framework is a more attractive way of securing any appropriate public goods than a generic requirement that the partially privatised corporation act in a 'socially responsible' manner. A regulatory or contracting approach would encourage the careful identification of a specific market failure, the crafting of specific regulation or purchase contract to secure that good (if appropriate) and in doing so may provide more certainty about the legal obligations of the corporation than a generic social responsibility requirement.

A generic social responsibility requirement may however be attractive as a backstop for regulation when regulation is in flux or particularly uncertain. The Treasury does not find any alarming regulatory uncertainty in the areas in which the target SOEs operate, but does note that there is some regulatory uncertainty around electricity regulation and carbon pricing (Crown Ownership Monitoring Unit, 2011c, p. 4). It might be argued that a generic social responsibility requirement might encourage – or require – a partially privatised entity to adopt corporate best-practice norms even when regulatory requirements are unclear or have not adjusted to new norms. In such circumstances, Section 4 can also be seen as the backstop rule for an incomplete contract, implying that even the Crown's ability to enter into future transactional contracts for the provision of specific public goods is considered insufficient in some way.

Whether or not this is a convincing argument for the retention of Section 4 or some equivalent, is beyond the scope of this chapter.

In weighing these options, experience of other jurisdictions may be instructive. For example Queensland's framework appears to reflect a view that a separate social responsibility requirement is unnecessary when the government can contract for the delivery of social goods, including for the fulfilment of specific 'social responsibilities'. Section 13 of the Government Owned Corporations Act 1993 (Qld), (the 'GOC Act'), allows corporatised government entities to change the conditions and structure under which they operate so that they are managed on a commercial basis and in a competitive environment, but does not require those entities to be as profitable and efficient as comparable businesses in the private sector. The GOC Act (s. 14) further provides that the objectives of corporatisation are to 'improve Queensland's overall economic performance and the ability of the Government to achieve social objectives' and requires a corporatised GOC to:

- have clear, non-conflicting objectives;
- set specific financial and non-financial targets for its commercial activities;
- transfer any activities of a governmental policy formulation or regulatory nature from the GOC to a department, separate regulatory authority or other agency;
- be appropriately compensated for its community service obligations;
- set performance targets for its community service obligations. (Government Owned Corporations Act, s. 16)

Under the Queensland model, the contracting framework and a Section 4 equivalent appear to be viewed as substitutes. The Crown in New Zealand currently also has the ability under Section 7 of the SOE Act to require an SOE to provide goods or services, but must contract and compensate for that provision. The Queensland model indicates that if a Section 7 equivalent is retained in the mixed ownership model, a Section 4 equivalent may be unnecessary, but by contrast, if no provision for the contracting of social goods (other than on a purely private law basis) is retained a Section 4 equivalent may be more attractive (if it is decided that such responsibilities should be recognised, and in some generic way rather than by specific regulation).

Thirdly, it will need to be considered whether the retention by the Crown of partial ownership will leave public law remedies available against partially privatised SOEs. In *Te Heu Heu* it seemed that SOEs were considered separate entities at law from the Crown (*Te Heu Heu v Attorney-General* [1999] 1 NZLR 98 (HC)). In that case the plaintiffs quoted a statement of Lord Woolf in *New Zealand Maori Council v Attorney General* that 'although, under the Act, a state enterprise is structured so that it is separate from the Crown, as its title indicates it remains very much the Crown's creature' as supporting their assertion that the Crown includes SOEs and their subsidiaries (*New Zealand Maori Council v Attorney General* [1994] 1 NZLR 513 (PC), p. 520). Robertson did not accept this argument, stating that the purpose behind the move to a state-owned enterprise scheme was to distance the Crown from activities perceived as better carried out on a commercial basis. Partial privatisation would of course increase that distance.

In sum, it is extremely hard to evaluate whether 'social responsibility' is a compelling rationale for retained Crown ownership in the partially privatised SOEs. The uncertain legal meaning of the term is a key reason.

### 7.4.1 Treaty of Waitangi Principles

Section 9 of the SOE Act states that nothing in the Act permits the Crown to act in a manner inconsistent with the principles of the Treaty of Waitangi. This provides scope for iwi (extended family groups) to challenge sales.

In early 1995 the government decided to sell Radio New Zealand's commercial arm. To make this possible, its SOE status had to be removed. The New Zealand Maori Council brought an action under the Judicature Act 1972, attempting to prevent steps towards the sale (*New Zealand Maori Council v Attorney General* HC, Wellington, 29 March 1996). McGechan said the proposed sale was not in breach of Section 9 of the SOE Act since retaining commercial radio stations in public ownership would not assist in broadcasting the Maori language. The action also failed on other grounds. The New Zealand Maori Council appealed. The Full Court of Appeal struck out the sale challenge (6 to 1), stating the Cabinet decision was not subject to judicial review (*New Zealand Maori Council v Attorney General* [1996] 3 NZLR 140 (CA)).

*Te Heu Heu v Attorney General* concerned the Taupo District Council's acquisition of 253 hectares of land from Landcorp (*Te Heu Heu v Attorney General* [1999] 1 NZLR 98 (HC)). The land was subject to a Waitangi Tribunal claim, but this was not disclosed until after the agreement for sale and purchase had been signed. The plaintiffs sought to stop the sale, arguing that the Crown and shareholding ministers had acted in a manner inconsistent with Section 9 of the SOE Act. In particular, they argued that the obligations in Section 9 imposed additional obligations on the Crown when transferring land to those set out in the Treaty of Waitangi

(State Enterprises) Act 1988 (the 'TOWSE Act'). Robertson considered the history of the legislation and prior case law at length, concluding that there may be room to argue that TOWSE Act may not always be sufficient to discharge the Crown's obligations but:

> where those provisions do apply there will usually be very little room to argue that Section 9 demands something more. Such circumstances will be rare. It will need to be demonstrated, for example, that the Crown was acting in bad faith or contrary to the terms of the settlement which is encapsulated in the TOWSE Act. (*Te Heu Heu v Attorney General* [1999] 1 NZLR 98 (HC), p. 107)

The cumulative effect of this litigation in the past was to block the intended privatisation of selected SOEs. The value of an SOE is reduced if there is uncertainty about SOE asset values. It was considered imprudent to proceed with the sale of SOEs with large landholdings because the sale of such land to a private owner can be revoked with the Waitangi Tribunal. Recent suggestions by the Maori Party that it might support partial privatisations post-election if shares were first offered to iwi interests may mean that Section 9 may again be invoked to halt partial privatisations that are not considered to be on terms commensurate with Section 9 and Treaty obligations.

Similar to 'social responsibility' considerations, a programme of partial privatisation will require considering: what meaning judges are likely to ascribe to Section 9 in a contemporary setting; what public goods Section 9 therefore attempts to secure; whether Crown participation is required to secure those goods; and if so, whether Section 9 (or equivalent) is the best way to continue to secure those goods.

### 7.4.2 Policy Stability and Quality

There is mixed theory and evidence about how Crown participation in commercial enterprises affects the stability and quality of regulatory settings. There is a substantial body of literature considering whether privatisation leads to greater demand for, and enactment of, stable and sound regimes to regulate capital markets, and the incidence of private and public sector corruption. However much of this work focuses on privatisation programmes in economies that were, prior to the programme, heavily centralised and developing. It is not clear that the lessons from this literature are applicable to the New Zealand situation in which regulation of capital markets and property rights is already well developed (Capital Market Development Taskforce, 2009, p. 10).

Some studies suggest that full divestment of state assets can too often be coupled with hasty and ill-designed deregulation that destroys capital value. The Californian energy crisis of 2003, for example, has often been attributed to profiteering incentives arising from poorly staged deregulation of the electricity industry (Brand and Scheffran, 2005, pp. 66–71). On the other hand partial privatisations may come with other incentives that may lead to suboptimal regulatory regimes. Pargendler (2011) surveys historical government ownership in the United States, Brazil, China and Europe, and argues that conflicts of interest (stemming from the state's dual role as shareholder and regulator) can influence the content of corporate laws to the detriment of outside investor protection and efficiency, and that such conflicts of interest are most evident in cases of partial privatisation. For example controlling corporate shareholdings incentivised the Brazilian government to revise Brazil's Corporations Law and remove minority shareholder rights in order to sell its holdings in return for a significant premium (Pargendler, 2011, pp. 14–23). Although retention of control may be more politically acceptable than partial privatisation where the state becomes a minority shareholder, ceding control removes the conflict-of-interest problem.

Short of full state ownership or divestment, Pargendler suggests that these conflicts may be overcome by dual regulatory regimes where separate corporate laws applicable to only the state as a shareholder are adopted. Pargendler notes dual approaches in Germany and the United States (US), and considers the use of golden shares to be a form of dual regulatory regime because the state is able to exercise certain special rights granted by the shares and is able to influence the governance of the particular firm through its holding of the golden share. This addresses the government's interests while keeping intact the legal regime applicable to private firms. Another approach may be dual regulatory authorities, in which foreign or non-state regulatory authorities are given the power to design and enforce corporate and securities regulations.

## 7.5 CONCLUSION

This chapter reaches four main conclusions. Firstly, considered in isolation, many of the rationales for privatising SOEs indicate that full rather than partial privatisation may be superior in many contexts. There is therefore no reason why full (rather than partial) privatisation should not be considered for some SOEs in the current commercial portfolio on a case-by-case basis, other than political reasons.

Secondly, full privatisation is not necessarily superior to partial privatisation on every policy basis. While it seems reasonably clear that full privatisation is, on average, over time superior to partial privatisation on a static efficiency basis, as against other policy rationales, partial privatisation may deliver benefits as opposed to full privatisation. The room for strategic benefits from some Crown involvement in the commercial portfolio appears to be wider than the Treasury currently accepts, including in areas such as addressing capital market imperfections and for economic development purposes.

Thirdly, it appears that as a whole and on average, for partial privatisation:

- The short- to medium-term fiscal rationale seems reasonably weak. But if done in a way that induces economic growth, partial privatisation may have significant long-run fiscal impacts.
- The static efficiency rationale is modest, but perhaps greater than the Treasury concludes, for the reason that even small efficiency gains in a significant part of the economy may be material.
- The dynamic efficiency rationale for partial privatisation is stronger than the static efficiency rationale and may be significant.
- Capital market development rationales on the whole appear somewhat stronger than the Treasury concludes (in particular given that diversity benefits can be realised in ways other than adding new industry classifications to the market). However we are somewhat sceptical about the capital market participation dimension of capital market development. Increasing market size and asset diversity are stronger rationales.
- Strategic (including capital market efficiency improvement) reasons for holding (and better managing) retained shares in SOEs may be much more significant than the Treasury indicates, given potential economic development considerations that have not yet been fully explored.
- Policy stability rationales for fully divesting, or retaining some Crown ownership in SOEs, are in tension.

That is, we suggest that the strongest rationales for partial privatisation appear to be the realisation of dynamic efficiency gains, the development of capital markets (particularly along the dimensions of size and asset diversity), and the fulfilment of strategic (and perhaps most significantly, economic development) aims. We consider that these are the most compelling 'whys'. It is sensible that in designing 'how' partial privatisation should proceed, policy-makers should focus on maximising those benefits while minimising costs against the other rationales.

Fourthly, the public should demand that policy-makers explain clearly which rationales they consider to be the most important reasons for partial privatisation. Lack of clarity about the primary goal of partial privatisation would make it impossible for policy-makers to choose rationally from among the many ways that partial privatisation can be carried out, and would make it all too easy for any outcome to be spun as a 'success' against some goal or other, irrespective of the initial reason for privatisation.

The risk of lack of clarity in policy rationales for partial privatisation appears to be materialising. Despite initial Treasury analysis that sought to crystallise the drivers for partial privatisation (and which this chapter has sought to further sharpen and evaluate), subsequent Treasury advice to Cabinet recommended that Cabinet agree that the government has no fewer than ten objectives for the mixed ownership model:

- Fiscal (static) – optimise the value for the Crown and free up capital.
- Fiscal (dynamic) – allow the companies to obtain growth capital without depending entirely on the government.
- Capital market development – broaden the pool of investments available to New Zealand savers, and increase the depth of New Zealand capital markets.
- New Zealand participation – place New Zealand investors at the front of the queue and achieve widespread and substantial New Zealand share ownership.
- Commercial disciplines – ensure that these large and important companies reap the benefits of sharper commercial disciplines, more transparency and greater external oversight to allow them to make the strongest possible contribution to New Zealand's economic growth.
- Majority Crown ownership – ensure that the government has a controlling stake.
- Good investment opportunities – ensure that the companies involved present good opportunities for investors;
- Protect consumers – ensure that industry-specific regulations adequately protect New Zealand consumers.
- Low execution risk – successful implementation is achieved (such as good demand for shares, and the shares perform well after listing).
- Timing – the programme will be well advanced by 2014 to allow capital to be released over the next few years to finance other capital priorities. (Crown Ownership Monitoring Unit, 2011a, para. 55)

Cabinet so agreed. These objectives appear to map more closely to a series of government statements (some made in requesting advice from the Treasury) than to the Treasury's analysis of the objectives of privatisation. The Treasury also recommended that Cabinet 'note that it is not possible for all ten objectives to be maximized simultaneously, and that objectives will need to be balanced throughout the process'. This recommendation is based on the Treasury's advice that:

> Some of these objectives have the potential to pull in different directions, particularly between fiscal and other objectives. It will not be possible for all ten objectives to be maximised simultaneously, and as a result trade offs between different objectives will need to be balanced to achieve a successful outcome. Maintaining maximum flexibility as long as possible into the process will be critical to ensure that Ministers have adequate policy space to balance competing objectives. (Crown Ownership Monitoring Unit, 2011a, para. 14)

Ten objectives is a very large number to affirm, particularly when no clear indication about which objectives are considered most important or convincing is given upfront. The proposed process – leaving that prioritisation of objectives open as long as possible and trading off between those objectives in an ad hoc way as privatisation proceeds – appears to be a recipe for both a lack of coherent balancing and also for opacity about the key drivers of privatisation. The public will be required to wait to see how competing objectives are balanced when specific design choices are made, before they can infer which objectives policy-makers consider most important. With no upfront prioritisation of objectives, there is no guarantee that design choices and the balancing of competing objectives will be carried out in a way that is consistent or rational.

## NOTES

* The authors thank David Mayes, Stephen Franks, Phil Barry, and the participants of the 28 October 2011 New Zealand Governance Centre Conference for helpful discussions and comments.

1. Purchasing shares at a discount and immediately selling them, usually for a profit.

## REFERENCES

Abromeit, Heidrun (1988), 'British Privatisation Policy', *Parliamentary Affairs*, **41**(1), 68–85.

Backx, Mattijs, Michael Carney and Eric Gedajlovic (2002), 'Public, Private and Mixed Ownership and the Performance of International Airlines', *Journal of Air Transport Management*, **8**(4), 213–220.

Barry, Phil (2002), 'The Changing Balance Between the Public and Private Sectors', New Zealand Business Roundtable, http://www.nzbr.org.nz/site/nzbr/files/publications/publications-2002/changing_balance.pdf, accessed 28 January 2012.

Boardman, Anthony and Aidan Vining (1989), 'Ownership and Performance in Competitive Environments: A Comparison of the Performance of Private, Mixed, and State-Owned Enterprises', *Journal of Law and Economics*, **32**(1), 1–33.

Booth, Tahnee and Adrian Noon (2011), 'Corporatisation in Australia: A Queensland perspective', paper presented to Revisiting the State and Market conference, University of Auckland, Auckland, 28 October.

Brand, Ruth and Jurgen Scheffran (2005), 'The Price to Pay for Deregulation of Electricity Supply in California', in Ernst Ulrich von Weizsacker, Oran R. Young and Matthias Finger (eds), *Limits to Privatisation: How to Avoid Too Much of a Good Thing*, London: Earthscan, pp. 66–71.

Capital Market Development Taskforce (2009), 'Capital Markets Matter: Report of the Capital Market Development Taskforce', http://www.med.govt.nz/business/economic-development/pdf-docs-library/cmd-capital-markets-matter-exec-summary.pdf, accessed 16 March 2012.

Capital Market Development Taskforce Secretariat (2009), 'Why Capital Markets Matter for New Zealand: Report prepared for the Capital Market Development Taskforce', http://www.med.govt.nz/business/economic-development/pdf-docs-library/cmd-taskforce-research/why-capital-markets-matter.pdf, accessed 16 March 2012.

Carreira, María Del Sánchez and Xavier Vence Deza (2009), 'Effects of Privatisation on Innovation: Evidence of the Spanish Case', Paper presented at the Summer Conference, Copenhagen Business School, Frederiskberg, Denmark, July, http://www2.druid.dk/conferences/viewpaper.php?id=6031&cf=32, accessed 28 January 2012.

Crown Ownership Monitoring Unit (2010a), 'Crown Ownership of Commercial Entities – New Zealand Treasury: 1959696v1', paper attached as annexe to Crown Ownership Monitoring Unit (2010), *Treasury Report: Crown Asset Portfolio – Issues and Implications Arising from the Investment Statement*, T2010/2513, http://www.comu.govt.nz/resources/pdfs/mixed-ownership-model/mom-coce-dec10.pdf, accessed 30 January 2012.

Crown Ownership Monitoring Unit (2010b), '2010 Annual Portfolio Report', http://purl.oclc.org/nzt/apr-1340, accessed 27 January 2012.

Crown Ownership Monitoring Unit (2011a), 'Budget 2011 Information Release: Aide Memoire: Cost of IPOs: Domestic and International Comparisons – Treasury 2082400v1', http://www.comu.govt.nz/resources/pdfs/mixed-ownership-model/b11-2095670.pdf, accessed 25 January 2012.

Crown Ownership Monitoring Unit (2011b), 'Annual Portfolio Report 2011', http://purl.oclc.org/nzt/apr-1426, accessed 28 January 2012.

Crown Ownership Monitoring Unit (2011c), 'Extending the Mixed Ownership Model T2011/336', http://www.comu.govt.nz/resources/pdfs/mixed-ownership-model/t2011-336.pdf, accessed 30 January 2012.

Eckel, Catherine and Aidan Vining (1985), 'Elements of a Theory of Mixed Enterprise', *Scottish Journal of Political Economy*, **32**(1), 82–94.

*The Economist* (1986), 'Go for the Money: Privatising Britain Can Learn from Japan', 22 November, p. 17.

Enderwick, Peter (1997), *Foreign Investment: The New Zealand* Experience, Palmerston North, New Zealand: Dunmore Press.

Evans, Lewis (2009), 'Capital Market Integration: The Structure of the New Zealand Economy and its Capital Markets', report prepared for the Ministry of Economic Development and the Capital Market Development Taskforce, http://www.iscr.org.nz/f523,15233/15233_Capital_Markets_Report_LE_final.pdf, accessed 28 January 2012.

Gupta, Nandini (2005), 'Partial Privatisation and Firm Performance', *Journal of Finance*, **60**(2), 987–1015.

Heatley, Dave and Margot Schwass (2011), 'Rail Transport in New Zealand', in Christopher Findlay (ed.), *The Impacts and Benefits of Structural Reforms in Transport, Energy and Telecommunications Sectors*, Adelaide, Australia: University of Adelaide, pp. 230–253.

Hodge, Graham (2011), 'Revisiting State and Market through Regulatory Governance: Observations of Privatisations, Partnerships, Politics and Performance', paper presented to Revisiting the State and Market conference, University of Auckland, New Zealand, 28 October.

Huang, Chye-Ching and Susan Watson (2012), 'Options for Partial Privatisation: The Holding Company Structure', forthcoming.

Jones, Steven, William Megginson, Robert Nash and Jeffry Netter (1999), 'Share Issue Privatisations as a Means to Political and Economic Ends', *Journal of Financial Economics*, **53**(2), 217–253.

Keloharju, Matti, Samuli Knüpfer and Sami Torstila (2008), 'Do Retail Incentives Work in Privatisations?' *Review of Financial Studies*, **21**(5), 2061–2095.

Kerr, J., M. Qiu and L. Rose (2007), 'Privatisation in New Zealand and Australia: An Empirical Analysis', *Managerial Finance*, **34**(1), 41–52.

Li, Wei and Lixin Xu (2004), 'The Impact of Privatisation and Competition in the Telecommunications Sector around the World', *Journal of Law and Economics*, **47**(2), 395–430.

Megginson, William, Robert Nash, Matthias Van Randenborgh (1994), 'The Financial and Operating Performance of Newly Privatised Firms: An International Empirical Analysis', *Journal of Finance*, **49**(2), 403–452.

Megginson, William and Jeffry Netter (2001), 'From State to Market: A Survey of Empirical Studies on Privatisation', *Journal of Economic Literature*, **39**, 321.

Ministry of Social Development (2010), '2010 The Social Report', http://social-report.msd.govt.nz/documents/the-social-report-2010.pdf, accessed 28 January 2012.

Mok, Henry and Sandy Chau (2003), 'Corporate Performance of Mixed Enterprises', *Journal of Business Finance and Accounting*, **30**(3), 513–538.

Munari, Federico (2002), 'The Effects of Privatisation on Corporate R&D Units: Evidence from Italy and France', *R&D Management*, **32**(3), 223–232.

Munari, Federico (2003), 'The Organization of R&D Activities in Privatised Companies', in M. Calderini, P. Garrone and M. Sobrero (eds), *Corporate Governance, Market Structure and Innovation*, Cheltenham, UK and Northampton, MA, USA: Edward Elgar Publishing.

New Zealand Treasury (1996), 'Internal Paper: State Owned Enterprises: History of Policy Development and Implementation', released under the Official Information Act 1982, http://www.comu.govt.nz/resources/pdfs/soe-pol-dev.pdf, accessed 1 February 2012.

Organisation for Economic Co-operation and Development (OECD) (2003), *Privatising State-Owned Enterprises: An Overview of Policies and Practices in OECD Countries*, Paris: OECD Publications.

Oum, Tae, Nicole Adler and Chunyan Yu (2006), 'Privatisation, Corporatization,

Ownership Forms and their Effects on the Performance of the World's Major Airports', *Journal of Air Transport Management*, **12**, 109–121.
Pargendler, Mariana (2011), 'State Ownership and Corporate Governance', http://papers.ssrn.com/sol3/papers.cfm?abstract_id=1854452, accessed 29 January 2012.
Rajan, R. and L. Zingales (1998), 'Which Capitalism? Lessons from the East Asian Crisis', *Journal of Applied Corporate Finance*, **11**, 40–48.
Sam, Choon-Yin (2007), 'Partial Privatisation, Corporate Governance, and the Role of State-Owned Holding Companies', *Journal of the Asia Pacific Economy*, **13**(1), 63–88.
Secretary of the Cabinet (2011), 'Extending the Mixed Ownership Model – Cabinet Minute, CAB Min (11) 18/6', http://www.comu.govt.nz/resources/pdfs/mixed-ownership-model/b11-2076970.pdf, accessed 23 January 2012.
Skilling, David and Danielle Boven (2006), 'Developing Kiwi Global Champions: Growing Successful New Zealand Multi-National Companies', New Zealand Institute, Discussion Paper 2006/2.
Skilling, David and Danielle Boven (2007), 'So Far Yet So Close: Connecting New Zealand to the Global Economy', New Zealand Institute, Discussion Paper 2007/1.
Skilling, David and Mark Weldon (2008), 'Economy on the Edge: Swan Dive or Belly Flop? A Draft Strategy For Coming out of the Crisis Stronger (Version 2)', *The New Zealand Institute*, http://blog.nzx.com/wp-content/uploads/2008/11/swan-dive-or-belly-flop-versiontwo1.pdf, accessed 28 January 2012.
Stiglitz, Joseph (1999), 'Promoting Competition in Telecommunications', Centro de Estudios Económicos de la Regulación, Instituto de Eonomía, Universidad Argetina de la Empresa, Working Paper No. 2, http://cdi.mecon.gov.ar/biblio/docelec/uade/WP02.pdf, accessed 29 January 2012.
Vining, Aidan and Anthony Boardman (1992), 'Ownership versus Competition: Efficiency in Public Enterprise', *Public Choice*, **73**(2), 205–239.
Yarrow, George (1986), 'Privatisation in Theory and Practice', *Economic Policy*, **1**(2), 323–377.
Zinnes, Clifford, Yair Eilat, and Jeffrey Sachs (2001), 'The Gains from Privatisation in Transition Economies: Is "Change of Ownership" Enough?' *IMF Staff Papers*, **48**, 146–170.

# 8. Public project procurement and the case for public–private partnerships

**Michael Regan**

## 8.1 INTRODUCTION

Historically, theoretical explanations of the state were developed around two perspectives. First, the organic view which draws an analogy between the state and natural organisms in which all members of the governed community are part.[1] In this construct, the state is viewed as a continuum with an independence from, and authority over, its individual members. It was argued by many of the early political philosophers that an understanding of the state suggests a dichotomy in the way the state serves its own interests on the one hand, and as a separate and distinct action, acts in the interests of all members of the community. The organic view is frequently cited as an explanation for the emergence of absolute monarchies and totalitarian states throughout history.[2] A second explanation is the mechanistic approach in which members of the community form a state to undertake collective decision-making on behalf of its members (Hobbes, 1651 [1996]). The mechanistic state has as its object the maximisation of the welfare of all members of the community (Abelson, 2003) and provides a basis from which to understand the core functions of government including the creation of institutions to regulate social and economic behaviour such as a legal system and the provision of public goods (Heilbroner, 1999, p. 69). The mechanistic view regards the provision of public goods in the public interest as a primary responsibility of a state, provided by the state for the benefit of the community and financed from taxation or debt. In the nineteenth and early twentieth centuries, public goods were delivered by public ownership of the assets delivering the service. In the last 20 years, systemic failure in state delivery of public goods, especially in construction, led to calls for a new approach (Egan, 1998). This relied, in part, on the state reconsidering its role as the owner of the means of production to that of a buyer of services to specification at the best price. The Project Finance Initiative announced in the United Kingdom (UK) in 2001 proposed greater private sector provision of public goods and services through a variety of procurement methods, including joint ventures, public private partnerships and concession arrangements.

This approach was not new. Since the time of the Roman Emperor Augustus a variation of the traditional public good was evident with the franchising of some state services financed from a user-pays approach with tolls and tariffs. These came to be described as quasi-public goods and were fairly common throughout the Early and Late Middle Ages and are no less evident today with privately financed toll roads and local government waste management services.

In contemporary society, an important public good is the provision of economic and social infrastructure. Economic infrastructure refers to the networks and assets that facilitate trade and commerce in the form of roads, tunnels, bridges, ports, railway systems, airports, energy generation and distribution and the conservation and management of water resources. Economic infrastructure contributes to an economy's productive capacity, output and growth. It also drives reduction in private transaction costs, multi-factor productivity, employment and incomes especially in regional economies where these benefits are more readily measurable (Regan, 2007). These variables have an important association with an economy's competitiveness and terms of trade. Social infrastructure is an important driver of a community's social development in the form of public hospitals and disease eradication programmes, facilities for regional public administration, primary and secondary schools.

Public investment in Australia accounts for around 6 per cent of gross domestic product (GDP) (AUS$71 billion in 2010) of which around 70 per cent is applied to economic and social infrastructures (Australian Bureau of Statistics (ABS), 2011). The Australian data are not representative for members of the Organisation for Economic Co-operation and Development (OECD) with the country's physical, economic and human geography presenting specific infrastructure challenges that include long-distance transport networks on the one hand, and high levels of urbanisation on the other. On average, infrastructure investment in developed countries accounts for around 4 per cent of GDP of which around 2.2 per cent is absorbed by depreciation of existing capital stocks (Regan, 2010).

Around 64 per cent of public infrastructure in Australia is procured using short-term construction contracts, a further 17 per cent using alliance contracting methods and around 14 per cent is outsourced. Nearly all public procurement is delivered by private contractors using traditional practices based on a comprehensive input specification, a competitive tender or pre-qualification and negotiation process, and selection criteria heavily weighted in favour of lowest cost. Around 65 per cent of economic and social infrastructure in Australia is owned and operated by government.

In the years immediately following the global recession of 1989–90, Western countries were facing a number of systemic economic problems. Inflation and unemployment rates were rising, the oil shocks of the 1980s were fuelling inflation and high interest rates, public debt and deficits were at their highest for 50 years and Keynesian fiscal interventions were not having the desired effect of stimulating private investment, improving productivity or output growth (OECD, 1985). The response in many developed economies was for government to undertake programmes of microeconomic reform which included deregulation of sectors such as banking and finance, the privatisation of government business enterprises in competitive markets, reduction in barriers to trade and greater economic openness. In Australia, these reforms included an accord between labour unions, government and employers to limit wage increases above productivity gains and removal of exchange controls over currency.

In the early 1990s, there was also recognition of the relative performance differences between government agencies delivering public goods and services and private companies (New South Wales Government, 1991). At this time, a number of OECD countries including the United Kingdom and Australia commenced wider use of outsourcing arrangements including concessions, the long-term leasing of ports and airports and build–own–transfer (BOT) contractual arrangements to narrow the performance gap. At the same time, a growing body of evidence was pointing to the inefficiency of traditional public procurement practices (Latham, 1994; Egan, 1998). As recently as 2007, most public projects were delivered late and over budget (Allen Consulting Group, 2007) and land transport projects, in particular, attracted a high level of optimism bias leading to financial outcomes well below expectations (Mott McDonald, 2002). Reports by the United Kingdom National Audit Office (NAO) in 2001 and 2003 (NAO, 2001, 2003) identified late delivery and over-budget performance in around 70 per cent of public projects.

Evidence suggests the poor performance of traditional procurement is a consequence of government agency failure in the preparation of the business case, inter-agency friction, separation of the design and construction components, and an input specification that is either incomplete at the time of tender or is subject to ongoing change during the early stages of the project (Mott McDonald, 2002; Flyvbjerg et al., 2003; NAO, 2003). It is not unusual for a combination of an incomplete design and the lowest-price tender for a project to end up the more costly form of procurement. Bidders may bid low in competitive markets in the expectation of boosting margins during construction by cutting corners and adopting an aggressive approach to negotiation about the scope of work and change in specification. Poor procurement outcomes are evident from a long list of traditionally procured infrastructure projects including the Scottish Parliament building in Edinburgh, the Southampton Oceanographic Laboratory, Guy's Hospital Stage III, the New British Library and Quarry House in the United Kingdom (NAO, 2003, 2005) and the higher rate paid by state governments for construction work at schools (Australian Government, 2011).

Public–private partnerships (PPPs) were identified in the mid-1990s as one of several procurement initiatives to be introduced by the United Kingdom Government to address an infrastructure shortfall in that country and commence the procurement reform process identified in *Constructing the Team* in 1994 (Latham, 1994) and the Report of the Construction Task Force in 1998 (Egan, 1998).[3] PPPs were the first significant policy-based procurement reform to be introduced in developed economies. They built on the historical precedent of government outsourcing evident in Sumeria around 2500 BCE, in the Greek city-states around 550 BCE and privately financed and operated postal, water and transport services in the Roman Empire in the time of Augustus. British colonial administration was managed by private companies in the seventeenth and eighteenth centuries, and the industrial revolution in the nineteenth century was largely the result of private capital and ownership of the new economic infrastructure services. Several hybrid forms of private participation in local service provision were employed by local government in France during the second half of the twentieth century; and in the 1990s, BOT contracts based on long-term outsourcing arrangements were widely employed by cash-strapped governments in both developing and developed economies to supply essential government services.

In Australia, PPPs were introduced to Victoria in 2001 and progressively adopted in the other states and territories. A uniform national policy was put in place in 2009. Around 59 PPPs have been delivered in Australia under various state and national PPP policies and antecedent policy principles (Infrastructure Australia, 2010). It is estimated that a further 107 BOT projects employing PPP policy principles were delivered by public agencies, universities and local government bodies between 1997 and 2009. Collectively, these projects accounted for 6 per cent of public capital investment in this period.

## 8.2 WHAT ARE PPPS?

As a policy-based procurement framework, PPPs are implemented with either a statutory or policy framework. The latter approach was adopted

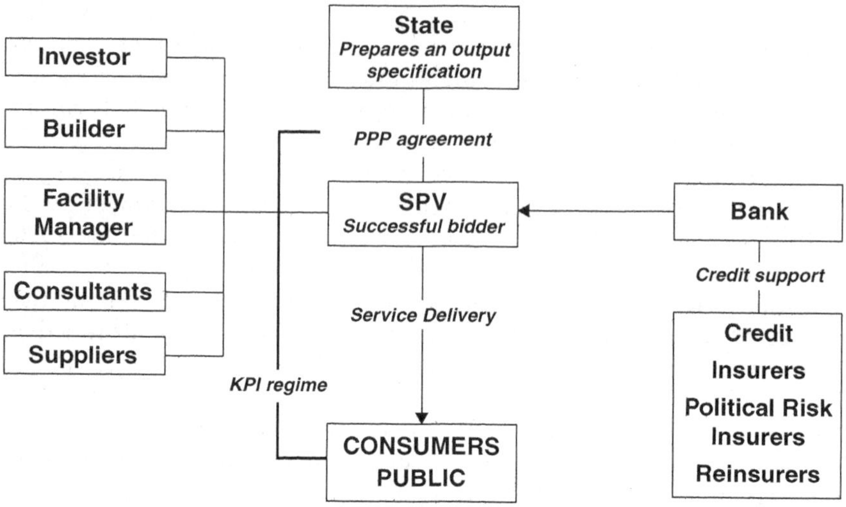


*Figure 8.1 A typical PPP contractual arrangement*

in Australia and is typical of OECD countries. Most nations possess a PPP policy and this method of procurement is currently employed in more than 100 nations around the world.

PPPs permit a standardised approach to large and complex procurements that incorporates rigorous project selection and evaluation and best practice performance benchmarking. PPPs in Australia are excluded from state procurement policy frameworks and differ from traditional procurement processes in several respects (see Figure 8.1).

Firstly, projects are identified and developed by national and state agencies and proposals are advanced through a series of qualifying stages or gateways in the approval process. The gateways are based on the following criteria:

1. Project selection – an analysis of the business case for each proposal.
2. Project affordability – projects should have an existing capital budget allocation.
3. Procurement strategy – an evaluation of different procurement options.
4. Selection of a successful proponent and negotiation of contract terms over an exclusive dealing period. This process includes negotiation about the regulatory and contract management arrangements.
5. Contract finalisation and financial close.[4]

Secondly, the project is put to competitive tender with an output specification which transfers ownership of design and decision-making to the contractor and compares with the input specification commonly employed with traditional procurement whereby the owner retains decision-making and specifies the exact work to be undertaken by the contractor.

Thirdly, the agency constructs a public sector comparator. This is a risk-weighted measure of traditional procurement over the project life cycle and is used to compare the optimal method of state procurement against bids submitted in a competitive market. The transfer of project and operational risk to the contractor underpins the economics of PPP projects.

Fourthly, the PPP approach uses a value-for-money test based on asset life cycle rather than lowest *ex ante* procurement cost. Value for money takes into account both quantitative and qualitative dimensions of the procurement and the service to be delivered.

The major challenge for governments using PPP procurement is to achieve changes in culture in its dealings with the private sector and undertake the extensive retraining necessary in line agencies to equip them with skills in advanced project evaluation and measurement methods, including:

- discounted cash flow analysis;
- risk identification, measurement and valuation;
- life-cycle costing;
- project management;
- incentive-based regulation;
- real options.

PPPs differ from traditional contracting in two important ways. Firstly, traditional construction contracts are generally short-term complete contracts that are adversarial in nature. The incentives that guide the conduct of the client are short-term and cost-centric and directed at achieving the completed works on time, within budget and with least additional cost for variations and changes to the contract or scope of works. These are essentially *ex ante* components of the service delivery process. Contractors will perform services under the contract, many of which are either non-contractible or non-observable, and seek to profit from ambiguity or incompleteness in the contract and variations and changes to specification or scope of works. If the contractor can cut corners to reduce costs it will do so without regard to life-cycle costing or the quality of long-term service delivery. The tension resulting from the adversarial nature of the contractual relationship manifests itself in renegotiation during the contract term or post-contractual disputes that absorb management time and can add significantly to transaction costs.

A PPP contract is not collaborative in nature although both client and contractor invest heavily in a satisfactory contract management relationship. As a long-term contract incorporating both *ex ante* and *ex post* service delivery components, the contractor carries life-cycle cost risk and has the incentive to ensure well-designed and sustainable works that feature low energy, maintenance and replacement costs over the term of the contract. The incentive for the contractor is to design and construct an efficient building or works that delivers services to specification. If the contractor's remuneration arrangement includes abatement of payment for outages or poor service performance, and incentive payments for performance that exceeds specification, the contractor has a favourable marginal return on investment by investing further when the economics warrant.

Secondly, a traditional contract is owned by the client who develops the specification and scope of works. The client is also responsible for life-cycle costs and *ex post* service delivery. The contractor has no interest in service delivery outcomes and all risk, with the exception of construction, is borne by the client. In this context, ownership refers to a residual control right (Grossman and Hart, 1986), and is central to the conduct of the parties (Besley and Ghatak, 2003, p. 246). In long-term service contracts, ownership has value (Selanie, 2005, p. 198). In a PPP contract, the contractor controls service production and management, which is important with incomplete contracts in which mediation and arbitration provisions compensate for the uncertainties that cannot be written into the contract (Hart, 2001, pp. 1083–1084). PPPs are moving state procurement away from ownership of assets and issues of residual control to the purchase of services and the contractual and informational aspects of long-term service delivery.

The PPP procurement method underwent development in Britain and Australia in the period 2003–08 as reviews and transactional experience informed policy changes (Fitzgerald, 2004; Allen Consulting Group, 2007); transactional information became more common, and various government audit authorities published project performance reviews (Auditor-General of Victoria, 2005, 2006, 2007, 2008; Mott McDonald, 2002; NAO, 2003, 2005, 2006). Further development of the PPP model is necessary to ensure that project performance and policy governance are observed at best practice standards.

Poor procurement performance may involve significant financial loss of monies, and when the problems are systemic, are a form of public failure which occurs when governments are unsuccessful in allocating resources efficiently or the social cost of market intervention exceeds its benefit (Winston, 2006). Additional contributing factors include optimism bias (the overestimation of benefits and underestimation of costs), low levels of design and construction innovation, and little regard to whole-life costing and the risks associated with the long-term management of complex assets such as hospitals, corrective service institutions and public utilities.

## 8.3 VALUE FOR MONEY (VfM)

Most traditional procurement is based on an input specification for the assets and/or services being acquired with separate contracts for design, construction and asset management. Government departments and agencies directly tender most traditional contracts pursuant to prevailing procurement policy, and in all but the largest of projects, without Treasury, public accounts or works committee oversight. The bidding criteria for traditional procurement are primarily lowest procurement or *ex ante* cost. Whole-life costing of assets during the *ex post* service period of the asset are not always taken into account.

In recent years, state procurement policy in Australia and the UK has moved away from strict lowest-tender selection criteria to VfM. In this instance, VfM is used to examine the direct and indirect impacts of procurement. The Northern Territory Government's procurement directions policy, for example, employs the following VfM tender assessment criteria:

- past performance;
- whole-of-life costs;
- local development and value-adding;
- timeliness;
- capacity; and
- innovation.

For PPPs, comprehensive qualitative and quantitative criteria are employed which may include (NAO, 2003; Government of Victoria, 2001b, 2003a; Grimsey and Lewis, 2004):

- lower procurement cost or user charges using a comparative evaluation against a risk-weighted traditional procurement method;
- early project delivery or minimum community disruption during construction;
- variations to specification that create additional utility or value for the state;

- improved state resource allocation or utilisation;
- the transfer of additional project risks;
- service delivery outcomes that exceed specification or improve service standards, consumer utility or enhancements to the public interest;
- improvements in the quality, scope and scale of service delivery;
- the use of processes and inputs which are likely to produce more reliable and better quality services; and
- sustainability and environmental protection.

The key quantitative measure of value for money with PPP projects is the public sector comparator (PSC). The PSC is based on a reference case built around the best traditional procurement option. The general rule adopted in many countries is for a PSC to be prepared when traditional procurement is an option. When the state does not have the capital to undertake the project, a PSC may be prepared as a benchmark although it is expected that, in these circumstances, a competitive market will deliver better service outcomes, lowest procurement cost and VfM (Sturgess, 2003).

Preparing a financial forecast for an infrastructure project is a complex exercise that is arguably more art than science and relies on the estimates, advice and judgement of the project management group. The qualitative measure of value for money involves an analysis of each bid on the basis of (NAO, 1999; Government of Victoria, 2001b, 2003b):

- a public interest test;
- the prospects for the quality and reliability of service delivery;
- design amenity; and
- The sustainability of the bidder's proposal.

The drivers of VfM in PPP projects include:

- risk transfer;
- innovation in design and construction;
- price certainty including life-cycle costing of refurbishment, repair and maintenance obligations;
- timeliness of delivery; and
- the use of new and more effective technologies (Fitzgerald, 2004).

Matters that affect VfM outcomes include the size of the project, the complexity of the construction and operational tasks, the scope for innovation and technology, and bid criteria. Another source of difference is qualitative outcomes such as landmark design (e.g., Southern Cross Station project in Melbourne); e-tolling (e.g., Transurban City link in Melbourne); construction methods that do not impose congestion on existing roads (e.g., Heathrow Terminal 5 in London; EastLink in Melbourne); upfront payments to the state (e.g., Cross-City Tunnel, Sydney); new filtration technology (e.g., Enviro Altona); early commissioning (e.g., Albury Wodonga Treatment Plant); public security, technology services and user amenity (e.g., County Court Building in Melbourne); lower consumer charges (e.g., EastLink in Melbourne); and improved asset management (e.g., NSW Schools Project; Darent Valley Hospital). The VfM evaluation process is a more comprehensive method for evaluating proposal attributes and offers a platform for comparing bidder proposals and the PSC. Value for money is acknowledged as a best-practice template for project procurement especially with one-off, large and complex projects offering scope for innovation and the deployment of new technology.

Nevertheless, a number of UK PPP project and audit reviews point to inaccuracies and systemic optimism bias in state agency evaluation of major projects (Mott McDonald, 2002; Flyvbjerg et al., 2006). The PSC can be difficult to price particularly when a government agency has a long history of underperformance using traditional procurement methods (NAO, 2004). Optimism bias is being addressed by a number of techniques at the early business case development stages of the project including forecasting methods (Flyvbjerg and COWI, 2004). [5] Life-cycle costs are also difficult to accurately predict over service intervals of 20–40 years and may account for up to five times the initial procurement cost, in nominal terms, for an average commercial building over a 20-year investment period. This suggests that the PSC is not definitive for large and complex projects and offers little more than a guide (NAO, 2004).

The identification, measurement and pricing of risk are a subjective exercise for long-term projects, and forecasts prepared on a risk-weighted basis are as sound as the quality of the thinking that is employed in their construction. The same problem exists for private sector bidders although the financial costs of error go straight to the bottom line. Possibly it is a question of incentive and the marginal utility of investment. The investor with more at stake is more likely to take greater care in measuring the risk profile of an undertaking than one with less.

A major driver of better VfM outcomes with PPP projects is the rigour imposed by the project management process. Although processes vary in each country and state, a PPP originates with a state department or agency and is evaluated against alternative procurement options with Treasury oversight. When the project is nominated as a PPP, the agency prepares the output specification and proceeds through a series of approval 'gateways'. Unless specifically mandated under procurement policy, most traditional procurement relies solely on market price responses as an indicator of fair value.[6]

## 8.4 PROCUREMENT PERFORMANCE

Evidence suggests that PPPs are reducing the cost of public procurement although there is significant variation between jurisdictions and applications. In the UK, for example, cost savings based on a comparison of the risk-weighted benchmark for traditional procurement (the public sector comparator) were within the range 10–20 per cent. In Australia, the results have been at the lower end of that range with the Fitzgerald Report (2004) identifying an average 9 per cent cost saving for a portfolio of diversified projects, Allen Consulting Group (2007) 11.4 per cent, and the State Government of New South Wales schools project revealing 7–10 per cent (Auditor-General of NSW, 2006a). The difference between Australia and the United Kingdom can be explained by the greater opportunity which existed with early Private Finance Initiative (PFI) projects to improve industry construction practices following the Latham and Egan Inquiries in 1994 and 1998 respectively.

Performance is also measured in terms of delivery cost and timeliness (see Table 8.1). The data indicate that PPP delivery performance is significantly better than traditional procurement although the difference is less over time as the spillovers of the rigorous PPP project evaluation process are applied to other forms of procurement.

## 8.5 VALUE FOR MONEY AND THE BID MARKET

A successful PPP bid programme requires a competitive bid market and firms with the financial resources and capacity to manage long-term contracts and both the operational and life-cycle risks involved. It is in the interests of the state to maintain a bid market with considerable depth, limit barriers to entry, create a regular pipeline of transactions to retain market experience and minimise bid costs.[7]

The value of the PSC will also depend on the bid criteria, which may include the PPP franchise term, user charges such as a toll, state charges such as an availability cost of a hospital bed, or upfront payments to the state. In the case of the EastLink project in Melbourne, for example, the project was awarded to the bidder with lower user charges and higher traffic forecasts than the PSC. This was considered in the interest of toll

*Table 8.1 Procurement performance, United Kingdom and Australia*

| | Survey of Procurement Outcomes | | |
|---|---|---|---|
| | On Budget | On Time | Outcomes |
| Traditional Contract | 25% | 34% | 27% |
| | 27% | 30% | 35% |
| | 55% | 63% | 55% |
| Gateway Programs | 69% | 73% | 65% |
| Alliance Contracting | 72% | 75% | *na* |
| PFI (UK) | 78% | 76% | 69% |
| PPP (Australia) | 79% | 82% | 73% |
| UK Defence Contracts | 17% (14%) | 8% (24%) | *na* |

*Notes:*
Indicative only. Variation in sample size and evaluation criteria.
Outcomes based on surveys of agencies, managers and users.
na indicates information not available.

*Source:* Regan 2010

users and met both the quantitative and qualitative VfM tests applied under the Partnerships Victoria model (Auditor-General of Victoria, 2005).

A difficulty often arises with multiple criteria for the PPP bid process. This has been particularly demonstrated with Sydney's Cross-City Tunnel (CCT), which invited bids on the basis of length of tenure, an upfront payment and user charges. The bid documentation recommended a franchise term and a recommended toll, which left the amount of any upfront payment to the discretion of the bidder (Auditor-General of NSW, 2006b).

Multiple bid evaluation criteria can create problems for government and generate consumer resistance. Upfront payments to the state contribute to higher user charges and consumers eventually reimburse any upfront payment that is made to government over the life of the project. The Audit Office of NSW reviewed the CCT project which proceeded as a PPP on a 'no cost to government' approach. The upfront fee was designed to meet all of the costs of the project incurred by the state and the surplus was unallocated. The Audit Office found that an upfront fee for PPP concession needs strong justification, if the cost is to be met by users of the service. A further matter raised in the CCT review was variations in the cost of the project requested by the state. These were paid for by raising tolls and changing escalation factors. The review found that the basis for changing the tolls was reasonable but the result was to significantly increase medium-term toll revenue (Auditor-General of NSW, 2006b).

The strategy for the CCT project aimed at reducing surface traffic volumes, easing road congestion and improving amenity within the Sydney Central Business District with partial road closures. Poor communication with stakeholders and a bid framework that used a 'no cost to government' approach led to the perception that partial road closures were designed to benefit the tunnel operators. Two recent state inquiries have revealed that this was not the case (Auditor-General of NSW, 2006b; New South Wales Parliament, 2006). Nevertheless, this was the perception and the outcome is a terrible one for Sydney: a tolled tunnel competing with free urban roads and only minor alleviation of the Central Business District congestion problem. However, the CCT project should not be viewed as a total failure, although this is the result for the project's equity investors. It is not the case for the project's secured lenders or the New South Wales Government. The state has secured the private investment that it needed for a strategic east–west by-pass for the city and it has not been required to provide additional capital nor ongoing revenue support for the project.

The CCT tunnel also demonstrated demand price elasticity for this group of assets. Patronage increased significantly during toll-free periods, suggesting that demand is quite sensitive to pricing in the presence of substitutes. The Transurban City Link tollway in Melbourne has met traffic forecasts and options within the contract having proved sufficiently robust to meet the cost of financing the recent Calder Interchange (Melbourne) upgrade suggesting that long-term contracts can retain flexibility to meet changes in future operating requirements. Flexibility was also achieved with the refranchising of Victoria's public transport PPPs with the withdrawal of National Express in 2002. The Victorian Government maintained uninterrupted service delivery and conducted bilateral negotiations with other franchisees for the transfer of the services preserving value for money outcomes in the process (Auditor-General of Victoria, 2005). Service continuity was also maintained with other failed PPP transactions including the Sydney Airport rail link and La Trobe Hospital in Melbourne.

## 8.6 *EX POST* MEASURES OF PERFORMANCE

Once commissioned, PPPs are generally measured against key performance indicators and compliance with the terms of the contract. It is often difficult to measure qualitative service outcomes particularly for long-term social infrastructure contracts, although recent case studies in Australia and UK suggest that PPPs are generating significant spillovers (Smith, 2007). In the County Court building in Victoria, for example, greater building flexibility, higher court utilisation and employee satisfaction with the operational performance of the new building are being favourably compared with conventional government buildings (Fitzgerald, 2004).[8] Of particular importance here is the role of certainty and life-cycle costs with the state only paying for the services it receives to specification.

## 8.7 INNOVATION

In the UK, recent case studies suggest that innovative design is improving the quantitative dimensions of public service delivery such as better educational results and reduced truancy, improved public housing, better health standards in juvenile detention centres, and reduced accidents and injuries in the operation of public transport systems (NAO, 2005; Mathias and Smith, 2007). Recent surveys also point to ameliorated relationship management with operational PPPs resulting in low abatement deductions for underperformance and average performance levels that exceed the contract specification (KPMG and Business Services Association, 2005; Mathias and Reddington, 2004). In the UK, the integration of design and construction elements of a project and incentive performance-based management techniques are particularly improving the effectiveness of service delivery in corrective services and local area health (Smith, 2007). In Australia, private innovation and new technology has been employed in motorways (the e-tolling system), the water sector (new water filtration technology), building design and optimal use of facilities (County Court Building; Southern Cross Station) and project delivery methods (EastLink).

## 8.8 TRANSACTIONAL EXPERIENCE

In Australia, several early BOT transactions were taken over by the state including Deer Park Women's Prison and La Trobe Hospital. The state has 'step-in' rights in the event of specified franchisee financial or operational failures, and the terms of the intervention may include full or partial compensation. However, rarely does the exercise of step-in rights impose extraordinary costs on the state. As with the Cross City Tunnel, the project is sold to new investors and the loss is carried by equity investors. The debt providers recovered their loan. The PPP failure rate is low with Standard & Poor's measuring defaults for international credit standard BBB-rated (investment grade) projects of less than 5 per cent in 2007–08, a lower rate than for other rated securities and significantly lower than the rate for business failures generally. This default rate reflects the wide use of credit insurance in the industry and credit 'wrapping' practices that boosted project credit ratings to AA or better. In 2007, Transurban's M7 motorway in western Sydney obtained a credit rating of A-, making it one of only a few private toll roads in the world to achieve such a high underlying rating. However, the market has changed since the global financial crisis and the demise of the credit insurance industry has meant that most consortium bids hoping to attract limited recourse project and corporate finance will increasingly rely on underlying transaction credit ratings which rarely exceed BBB grade in developed countries. This will increase the cost of debt and mitigate the value for money outcomes achieved in the past decade.

An important aspect of procurement performance is the rate of project failure. Australia has commissioned 59 PPP projects since 1998 including three BOT transactions which were implemented before the first PPP policy framework was introduced in 2001. The failure rate has been 12 per cent with three contracts placed in administration, two resumed by the state with compensation and two taken back without compensation. In each transaction, there was loss of investor equity but marginal losses to debt providers. Unless the result of a settlement was pursuant to subsequent litigation, there was little cost to the state as a result of these failures and service delivery was fully maintained. In each of the projects that were subject to resumption, traffic forecasting or case mix estimation was the primary cause of difficulty, and toll roads in urban areas accounted for the majority of projects in this group. The failure rate of 12 per cent compares favourably with attrition rates in overseas countries and the failure rate of both start-up and continuing businesses in the private sector. In the United Kingdom, a National Audit Office survey found 65 per cent of operational PFI projects were rated as having excellent or good relationships between the agency and project consortium with a further 24 per cent rated satisfactory (NAO, 2008).

## 8.9 MANAGING CHANGE

A criticism often levelled at PPPs is their long-term nature and concerns about the lack of flexibility this gives state agencies dealing with future uncertainty and change. PPPs are incomplete contracts and do not attempt to provide for all of the events and possibilities that may arise over the contract term. This is recognised in the regulatory framework, which provides alternative dispute resolution procedures and mechanisms for dealing with change in the form of embedded options and non-adversarial decision-making processes without recourse to contract cancellation or renegotiation (NAO, 2008). The PPP policy framework is an evolutionary model and has been subject to change in response to transactional experience and lessons learnt. The more significant changes in the past eight years include new guidance for change management in state agencies, sharing of refinancing gains, contract management practices and variation in operational arrangements that did not adversely affect the value for money proposition, the private sector risk profile or service quality (NAO, 2006, 2008).

## 8.10 LESSONS LEARNT

PPP policies and procedures are being frequently revised in both the United Kingdom and Australia with the benefit of lessons learnt. Recent changes include standardised commercial principles, the taxation of windfall gains and changes to the PSC (Department of Health, 2008; Government of Victoria, 2005). In early PPP projects, agencies transferred all risk to the bidder with little thought to the risk premium to be paid, or who was the better manager of the risks at the optimal price. This practice was reducing VfM and the procurement savings averaged less than 10 per cent compared with 10–20 per cent in the UK.

Progressively, the three eastern states invested more time in the risk analysis aspects of the business case and the preliminary PSC and began to model risk using a variety of stochastic and deterministic assessment techniques and commenced programmes to raise line agency skills in these practices. They were then able to revisit their business cases and identify and retain those risks that the state could manage at lower cost (e.g., pre-existing building and contamination risk). Risk transfer has become the major driver of VfM outcomes and the wholesale risk transfer of earlier years is being replaced by a systematic approach based on the capacity of the parties to best manage risk at the lowest cost. Reviews suggest that risk transfer can contribute to procurement cost savings in the range of 12–19 per cent (Fitzgerald, 2004). Risk transfer significantly outweighs the lower cost of state capital when measured under VfM criteria although this has not prevented critics of this procurement method from misrepresenting the cost of capital as the major determinant.

## 8.11 CERTAINTY

An important benefit of the PPP method of procurement is that new projects are being viewed from the perspective of whole life-cycle operation. Investment economics need to consider not only the project delivery costs but the maintenance, repair and refurbishment expenses likely to be incurred over operational life-cycles of up to 40 years. International evidence is pointing to large multipliers for life-cycle costs over these time frames. It is not unusual for conventional commercial buildings to incur life-cycle costs of up to five times the initial procurement cost in nominal terms and the multiplier increases with more complex applications such as power generation, water filtration and recycling, hospitals and public transport facilities.

Traditional procurement is subject to the stop-start budgetary volatility of governments elected for terms of three or four years. Short-termism and the mismatch of short-term fiscal cycles and long-term operational economics is mainly responsible for the poor condition of Australia's infrastructure assets and the frequent breakdown in service delivery of essential services such as urban transport. The life-cycle approach used with PPPs avoids this problem and assures long-term operational certainty. PPPs are also applied to a wide range of applications. In Victoria, this method of procurement has been successfully used for public buildings (e.g. Royal Agricultural Society Showground, Melbourne Convention Centre), corrective services, law courts, hospitals, communications services, water treatment and waste management, a film and television studio, and public transport facilities, and new projects are under way for schools and a desalination plant. The Partnerships Victoria model (Government of Victoria, 2001a) is considered a 'best-practice' benchmark and is being employed as a policy framework in transition economies.

## 8.12 INCENTIVE

The PPP procurement framework strikes a balance between penalties for underperformance and incentives to exceed minimum performance criteria. Identifying, correctly structuring and harnessing the incentive for managers to perform consistently to 'best-practice' standards is central to the performance of alternative project procurement methods. Public choice theory provides a framework for understanding incentives in the public sector and attempts to explain the drivers of public policy formation, implementation and management (Buchanan, 2003). The theory acknowledges public failures which arise when the state creates inefficiencies in the process of market interventions or when it could have solved a problem or furnished public goods more efficiently (Wolf, 1993; Winston, 2006).

In the private sector, incentive is generally linked to ownership in the form of residual control rights and financial return. However agency and privatisation theories (Boardman and Vining, 1989; Megginson, 2005) suggest that what motivates the private sector in long-term contracts is not always readily identifiable (Coase, 1960; Grossman and Hart, 1986; Besley and Ghatak, 1999). The procurement methods that create the strongest incentive for *ex ante* private investment and *ex post* operation are those where the private operator's remuneration is linked to key performance indicators that extend over the project life cycle. These methods include asset-based procurement such as BOT arrangements, long-term outsourcing contracts and output specification-based PPPs (Hodge, 2000; Megginson, 2005). The objective of infrastructure projects is to deliver sustainable services over long periods of time in industries whose economics are frequently determined by short-term impacts such as volatile energy prices, changes to networks and the introduction of legislation imposing limits on greenhouse gas emissions.

Public goods delivered by traditional procurement and services managed by government agencies or business units operate within a poor incentive framework. These units achieve rates of return equal to or less than the bond rate (Productivity Commission, 2007). There are several reasons for this – the institutions responsible for construction and management may be different, there are few rewards if management delivers ahead of time or earlier than planned, investment decisions may include social as well as economic objectives. At an enterprise level, government agencies and business units are also expected to meet community service obligations, output pricing is not always set by reference to production costs and there can be political interference in board and senior management appointments. This is reflected in the state's poor track record of project delivery and asset management using traditional practices (NAO, 2001).

PPPs based on availability payments generally contain a base charge calculated by reference to the goods or services supplied and a smaller incentive payment that is activated by performance against qualitative criteria or consistent achievement of key performance indicators. An abatement formula also applies to reduce payments in periods when the agreed quantity of goods or services is not supplied or performance falls below the required standard. PPPs involving full transfer of patronage risk also give the private operator a strong incentive to achieve forecast operating revenues and meet minimum debt servicing criteria.

Incomplete contracts with embedded real options also enter the incentive argument. Many PPPs contain maximum return on equity thresholds that cap investor returns, and revaluation gains attract profit-sharing arrangements with the state. These requirements limit windfall profits for the private sector without exposing the state to operating losses. The broad effect of these limitations on 'blue sky' returns is to preserve incentives for investors to maintain efficient life-cycle operation whilst avoiding the possibility that it is cheaper for them to walk away from a project than continue with a contract that offers insufficient return or worst case, involves future losses. This occurred with the original arrangements for the franchised management of Melbourne's public transport assets.

## 8.13 INTERGENERATIONAL EQUITY AND FISCAL SUSTAINABILITY

Intergenerational equity describes the economic, sociological and philosophical relationship between current and future generations and living standards. In the context of major project procurement, intergenerational equity refers to state debt or taxation that will need to be paid by future generations to meet the cost of current investment. This is also referred to as fiscal sustainability and favours a 'user pays' approach to public benefit – those who derive benefit from the asset should pay and those that do not should not (Thompson, 2002). Fiscal sustainability has greater relevance with state spending on current consumption than it does with current investment in economic and social infrastructure assets that continue to deliver benefits over several generations.

For traditional procurement, intergenerational equity favours the use of debt for capital investment amortising over the economic life of the asset (Coombs and Dollery, 2004). PPPs essentially come in two forms – the private sector assumes market risk and charges consumers for the service or the state pays an availability charge for the use of an asset. Both forms fit within user pays principles and neither pass inequitable taxation or debt burdens to future generations. However, the imposition of user charges does give rise to potential inequities (Auditor-General of NSW, 2006b, p. 3).

Under nearly all PPP arrangements in Australia, property in the asset passes to the state without cost at maturity. PPPs do not give rise to concerns in either intergenerational equity or fiscal sustainability terms.

## 8.14 NON-ADVERSARIAL CONTRACTING METHODS

Traditional procurement is based on adversarial contracting methods. Following negotiation of the building contract, the state agency, contractor and sub-contractors commence a process whereby omissions or incompleteness in the specification, variations to the contract and the settlement of claims is a source of ongoing friction against the backdrop of potential litigation if the intermediate steps of negotiation and alternative dispute resolution are unsuccessful. Adversarial contracting and staff time devoted to resolution of disputes is a major impediment to improved industry productivity with flow-on consequences for industry profitability and investment (Egan, 1998, p. 7). The adversarial foundations of traditional procurement are estimated to cost around 10 per cent of annual construction capital spending and 5 per cent of building operating costs (NAO, 2005, p. 6).

Alternative procurement methods including PPPs and relationship contracts are circumventing the numerous problems associated with adversarial contracts including its cost and adverse impact on productivity performance. Project collaboration enables real-time sharing of information, drawings, specifications, time-scales and budgets. From the state agency's perspective, the benefits of collaborative project management software are better communication, a reduction in mistakes and increased speed. A PPP assigns design, construction and operation risk to the consortium to be managed on an integrated basis with significant value improvement and cost reduction (Egan, 1998).

## 8.15 CONCLUSION

When viewed in context, PPPs are a new approach to social and economic infrastructure procurement that is reforming the costly inefficiencies associated with traditional government procurement methods. The changes that have been introduced include more rigorous project evaluation, the adoption of output specification to encourage innovation and technology, the use of risk-weighted models of public procurement, certainty created by life cycle costing, independent project reviews and government capacity building in the areas of project and contract management. The model is evolutionary and derivatives will continue to improve the science of social and economic infrastructure procurement. It is an evolving model that is being modified in the light of experience and new applications, and has led to major improvements in state procurement that will lead to significant cost savings and efficiencies in the 90 per cent of projects that are not procured in this way.

Do PPPs represent a contraction in the state's primary role as provider of public goods? As a long-term contract with full reversion of assets to the state, the PPP approach changes the state's role from the ownership of assets to the procurement of services. In the case of core state services such as health, education, public security and the judicial system, state agencies continue to be the primary provider and the role assumed by the private contractor is limited to non-core services and the provision of the service-producing assets. In PPPs, the state retains control of the decision-making architecture, the planning and prioritising of services and formulates the output specification, essential state responsibilities. The wider service benefits of PPPs and derivative procurement methods are beginning to be recognised (NAO, 2005) and PPPs are a feasible procurement alternative for specialised applications which offer scope for improved delivery of public assets and services. The PPP procurement option also remedies the systemic failings of traditional procurement – delivery time and cost overruns, poor life-cycle costing practices, lack of rigour in the asset allocation and project development processes and suboptimal service delivery outcomes. PPPs also deliver improved VfM outcomes (via lower procurement cost and capped life-cycle expenditures), incentivised management, design and construction innovation and new technology, improved sustainability at both the asset and service levels, and a rigorous project evaluation framework that is informing traditional procurement process. Issues remain, such as uniform methods for dealing with accountability and transparency, private sector capacity constraints and maintaining a competitive bid market, incomplete contracts, long service intervals and questions about the suitability of PPPs in some sectors of the economy. These are challenges for future improvement of the model and wider use of derivative forms for specialist procurement applications. Given the available evidence from more than ten years of applications, the question that no longer needs to be asked is whether PPPs are a good or a bad thing, but should be directed at how the model can be improved to achieve better public services in the future.

## NOTES

1. Aristotle (c. 350–346BCE) took this meaning of the state a step further when he depicted the *polis* or state as a natural community that meets the moral and material needs of those who inhabit it. Exiled or separated from the state, human beings lost their identity. In his view, members of society were defined by the organic relations existing between them and the whole of which individuals were mere parts (Adams and Dyson, 2003, pp. 15–16).
2. The rise of totalitarianism throughout history does not suggest that the organic view of society serves only that purpose. Adam Smith also viewed the state as a dynamic organism with its own life history (Heilbroner, 1999, pp. 54–55).
3. Recommendations were incorporated in the Green Book procurement guide for UK government departments and agencies (HM Treasury, 2003).
4. Government of Victoria (2001a). PPP policy and guidelines have been issued by Infrastructure Australia and each of the Australian states and territories. Australia has

adopted a uniform national policy approach although each state may vary the policy to meet regional differences in complementary procurement policies and preferences. Responsibility for PPP policy and approval processes remains with state agencies and ministers in each jurisdiction (Infrastructure Australia, 2008, p. 12). The Partnerships Victoria policy is widely regarded as international best PPP practice and provides the policy and guidance template for many developing economies.

5. Reference forecasting is a comparative process in which the forecasts and expectations for the subject project are reviewed against the performance of recent projects similar in scope, specification and application.
6. The United Kingdom introduced the gateway procurement method for traditional procurement in 2001 (2004 in Australia). The method requires the procurement agency to undertake a strategic assessment for the project, prepare a business case and procurement strategy, identify and manage stakeholder liaison and undertake an analysis of the best tender strategy. A review is conducted at each 'gateway' by a panel that includes agency officials, Treasury staff, industry advisers and practitioners (Government of Victoria, 2004). Reviews of the programme in 2003 show superior time and cost delivery performance compared with non-gateway procurement (NAO, 2003).
7. In Australia and the United Kingdom, bid costs typically average 1–2 per cent of the total development cost. A bidder unsuccessful after three or four losing bids is unlikely to participate in further bids. Recent moves to mitigate high bid costs include limits for the request for tender stage to two or three consortia, full or partial reimbursement of losing bidders in the request for tender stage and reimbursement pool funds where projects are complex or bidding occurs over an extended period of time (NAO, 2004, 2007).
8. A criticism of PPPs is that they are long-term contracts and should be subject to periodic review during the contract term. This may be difficult to achieve with a long-term contract entered into after a competitive bid process and extended negotiation period. The state's overriding concern with PPP contracts is to ensure compliance with the terms of the contract and standards specified for the quantity and quality of services. The contract may contain mechanisms to manage change, abate service payments for substandard performance and provide additional incentive payments for above-standard performance. Mechanisms may also exist to cap the consortium's return on investment, embed real options and require refinancing gains to be shared with the state (NAO, 2008), and a member of the consortium cannot dispose of its interest in the project without agency consent. These devices address the incompleteness of PPP contracts. Adjustment of financial terms to compensate for changes in demand, for example, is a residual risk borne by the state.

## REFERENCES

Abelson, P. (2003), *Public Economics, Principles and Practice*, Sydney and Canberra: Applied Economics.

Adams, I. and R.W. Dyson (2003), *Fifty Major Political Thinkers*, 2nd edn, London and New York: Routledge.

Allen Consulting Group (2007), 'Performance of PPPs and Traditional Procurement in Australia', report to Infrastructure Partnerships Australia, 30 November, www.allenconsult.com.au, accessed 13 March 2012.

Auditor-General of New South Wales (2006a), 'The New Schools Privately Financed Project', Performance Audit, March.

Auditor-General of New South Wales (2006b), 'The Cross City Tunnel Project', Performance Audit, May.

Auditor-General of Victoria (2005), *Refranchising Melbourne's Train and Tram System*, PP No. 154, Session 2003-05, Melbourne.
Auditor-General of Victoria (2006), *Results of Special Audits and Other Investigations*, PP No. 224, Session 2003-06, Melbourne.
Auditor-General of Victoria (2007), *Funding and Delivery of 2 Freeway Upgrade Projects*, PP No. 69, Session 2006-07, Melbourne.
Auditor-General of Victoria (2008), *The New Royal Women's Hospital – A Public Private Partnership*, PP No. 114, Session 2006-08, Melbourne.
Australian Bureau of Statistics (2011), 'Australian System of National Accounts, Expenditure on GDP at Current Prices', Table 5, p. 23, Canberra.
Australian Government (2011), 'Building the Education Revolution Implementation Taskforce', Final Report, July, Canberra.
Besley, T. and M. Ghatak (1999), 'Public Private Partnerships for the Provision of Public Goods: Theory and an Application to NGOs', Development Economics Discussion Paper Series no. 17, Suntory and Toyota International Centre for Economics and Related Disciplines, London School of Economics, August.
Besley, T. and M. Ghatak (2003), 'Incentives, Choice and Accountability in the Provision of Public Services', *Oxford Review of Economic Policy*, **19**(2), 235–249.
Boardman, A.E. and A.R. Vining (1989), 'Ownership and Performance in Competitive Environments: A Comparison of the Performance of Private, Mixed and State Owned Enterprises', *Journal of Law and Economics*, **32**(1), 1–33.
Buchanan, J.M. (2003), *Public Choice: The Origins and Development of a Research Program*, Fairfax, VA: Center for Study of Public Choice, George Mason University.
Coase, R. (1960), 'The Problem of Social Cost', *Journal of Law and Economics*, **3**(1), 1–44.
Coombs, G. and B. Dollery (2004), 'The Ageing of Australia: Fiscal Sustainability, Intergenerational Equity and Inter-Temporal Fiscal Balance', Working Paper no. 2004-1, University of New England, Armidale, Australia.
Department of Health (2008), 'Treasury's Value for Money Assessment for PFI: Guidance for NHS Build Schemes', London.
Egan, J. (1998), 'Rethinking Construction', report of the Construction Task Force to the Deputy Prime Minister, John Prescott, London.
Fitzgerald, P. (2004), *Review of Partnerships Victoria Provided Infrastructure*, Final Report to the Treasurer, Growth Solutions Group, Melbourne.
Flyvbjerg, B. and COWI (2004), 'Procedures for Dealing with Optimism Bias in Transport Planning', Guidance Document, Report for British Department of Transport, June.
Flyvbjerg, B., N. Bruzelius and W. Rothengatter (2003), *Megaprojects and Risk, an Anatomy of Ambition*, Cambridge: Cambridge University Press.
Flyvbjerg, B., M.K. Skamris and S.L. Buhl (2006), 'Accuracy in Traffic Forecasts', *Transport Reviews*, **26**(1), 1–24.
Government of Victoria (2001a), *Practitioners Guide*, Partnerships Victoria, Melbourne: Department of Treasury and Finance.
Government of Victoria (2001b), 'Public Sector Comparator, Technical Note', Melbourne: Department of Treasury and Finance.
Government of Victoria (2003a), 'Use of Discount Rates in the Partnerships Victoria Process', Technical Note, Melbourne: Department of Treasury and Finance.

Government of Victoria (2003b), 'Public Sector Comparator, Supplementary Technical Note', Melbourne: Department of Treasury and Finance.

Government of Victoria (2004), 'Gateway Review Process, Leadership Guide', Melbourne.

Government of Victoria (2005), 'Standard Commercial Principles', Department of Treasury and Finance, Melbourne.

Grimsey, D. and M.K. Lewis (2004), *Public Private Partnerships: The Worldwide Revolution in Infrastructure Provision and Project Finance*, Cheltenham, UK and Northampton, MA, USA: Edward Elgar.

Grossman, S. and O. Hart (1986), 'The Costs and Benefits of Ownership: A Theory of Vertical and Lateral Integration', *Journal of Political Economy*, **94**(4), 691–719.

Hart, O. (2001), 'Financial Contracting', *Journal of Economic Literature*, **39**, 1079–1100.

Heilbroner, R.L. (1999), *The Worldly Philosophers, The Lives, Times, the Ideas of the Great Economic Thinkers*, 7th edn, New York: Touchstone / Simon & Schuster.

HM Treasury (2003), *The Green Book: Appraisal and Evaluation in Central Government*, London: TSO.

Hobbes, T. (1651 [1996]), '*Leviathan*', in M. Cohen and N. Fermon (eds), *Princeton Readings in Political Thought*, Princeton, NJ, USA and Chichester, UK: Princeton University Press.

Hodge, G.A. (2000), *Privatization: An International Review of Performance*, Boulder, CO: Westview Press.

Infrastructure Australia (2008), 'National PPP Guidelines, Vol. 5, Discount Rate Methodology Guidance', Commonwealth of Australia, Canberra, www.infrastructureaustralia.gov.au, accessed 12 March 2009.

Infrastructure Australia (2010), 'PPP Projects Contracted as at November 2010', Canberra, www.infrastructureaustralia.gov.au/public_private/contracted.aspx, accessed 13 November 2011.

KPMG and Business Services Association (2005), 'Effectiveness of Operational Contracts in PFI', London.

Latham, M. (1994), *Constructing the Team: Joint Review of Procurement and Contractual Arrangements in the United Kingdom Construction Industry. Final Report*, London: HMSO.

Mathias, M. and E. Reddington (2004), *Good People, Good Systems, What Public Service Managers Say*, London: Serco Institute.

Mathias, M. and B. Smith (2007), 'HMYOI Ashfield – the Health Service Case Study', London: Serco Institute.

Megginson, W.L. (2005), *The Financial Economics of Privatisation*, Oxford, UK and New York, USA: Oxford University Press.

Mott McDonald (2002), 'Review of Large Project Procurement in the United Kingdom', report for HM Treasury, July, Croydon.

National Audit Office (NAO) (1999), 'Examining the Value For Money of Deals under the PFI', report by the Comptroller and Auditor General, HC739, Session 1998-99.

National Audit Office (NAO) (2001), 'Modernising Construction', report by the Comptroller and Auditor General, HC87, Session 2000-01.

National Audit Office (NAO) (2003), 'PFI: Construction Performance', report by the Comptroller and Auditor-General, HC371, Session 2002-03.

National Audit Office (NAO) (2004), 'London Underground PPP: Were they Good Deals?' report by the Comptroller and Auditor General, HC645, Session 2003-04.
National Audit Office (NAO) (2005), 'Improving Public Services Through Better Construction', report by the Comptroller and Auditor General, Volumes 1 and 2, HC 354-1, Session 2004-05.
National Audit Office (NAO) (2006), 'PFI/PPP in Focus, NAO Good Practice Briefing for PFI/PPP', London: Working in Partnership.
National Audit Office (NAO) (2008), 'Making Changes in Operational PFI Contracts', report by the Comptroller and Auditor General, HC 205, Session 2007-08.
New South Wales Government (1991), 'A Framework for National Performance Monitoring of Government Trading Enterprises', report to Special Premiers Conference prepared by the Task Force on Monitoring Performance of Government Trading Enterprises, Treasury, Sydney.
New South Wales Parliament (2006), 'Cross City Tunnel Inquiry, Final Report', Sydney.
OECD (1985), 'The Role of the Public Sector, Causes and Consequences of the Growth of Government', *OECD Economic Studies*, **4**, Special Issue, Spring.
Productivity Commission (2007), 'Financial Performance of Government Trading Enterprises 2004–05 to 2005–06', Productivity Commission Research Paper, Canberra, July.
Regan, M. (2007), 'The Economics of the South East Queensland Infrastructure Plan and Program 2007–2026, a Report to the Department of Infrastructure, Government of Queensland', Robina: Bond University.
Regan, M. (2010), 'Australian Infrastructure Report Card 2010', paper presented at the International CFO Forum, 23 September, Westin Hotel, Melbourne.
Selanie, B. (2005), *The Economics of Contracts*, 2nd edn, London: MIT Press.
Smith, B. (2007), 'Built to Serve: The Benefits of Service-Led PPPs', London: Serco Institute.
Sturgess, G. (2003), 'Competition: A Catalyst for Change in the Prison Service', report on behalf of Public Services Strategy Board, Confederation of British Industry, London.
Thompson, J. (2002), 'Intergenerational Equity: Issues of Principle in the Allocation of Social Resources Between this Generation and the Next', Research Paper No. 7, 2002-03, Department of the Parliamentary Library, Canberra, Victoria Guidance Material, Melbourne.
Winston, C. (2006), *Government Failure versus Market Failure, Microeconomics Policy Research and Government Performance*, Washington, DC: AEI-Brookings Joint Center for Regulatory Studies.
Wolf, C. (1993), *Markets or Governments, Choosing between Imperfect Alternatives*, 2nd edn, Cambridge, MA, USA and London, UK: MIT Press.

# 9. Rethinking the state through the lens of regulatory governance

**Graeme A. Hodge**

## 9.1 INTRODUCTION

There is much talk of how today's state functions and how it could perform better. But rethinking the state requires answers to many of the fundamental questions considered throughout history. We may also dress this up in the language of 'modernising', of 'reinventing' and of 'commercialising', or perhaps use the lingo asserting that government ought to be more 'joined up', more of a 'partner' or act with a more 'networked' capability. Such suggestions promise new models and fresh approaches. They also cover a huge amount of ground, implying new approaches to the resolution of political conflict, and to the capacity and ability of public management to better meet the needs of today's more demanding citizens and consumers. Any reading of history, however, suggests that legitimate government has traditionally needed to successfully reconcile a wide range of conflicting values and interests amongst multiple constituencies and simple assertions to 'reinvent' government, to 'commercialise' it or to 'modernise' it, have usually not been met with obvious success. This is not to say that there is not a need to do so, only that simple recipes which have succeeded in bringing immediate success to government have not been a feature of Western history over the last several decades. So how we might ensure that governments better serve the needs of today's citizens and other interest groups remains a profound challenge. This chapter argues that the lens of regulatory governance is a potentially useful one in contemplating the various themes of globalisation, reinvention and modernising the state. Section 9.2 of this chapter argues that the very notion of regulation has been rethought over the past few decades and this new conception, as well as the idea of regulatory governance, both challenge us in several ways. The implications of regulatory governance are presented in sections 9.3 and 9.4. Section 9.5 of the chapter then offers an example of how we might rethink a popular thrust of modern governments, the public–private partnership

(PPP), through the regulatory governance lens. Some conclusions are then drawn in section 9.6.

## 9.2 RECONCEPTUALISING REGULATION

The concept of regulation has itself been heavily contested, and there are a wide variety of concepts and definitions for regulation. To begin with, it can be viewed from ideologically extreme vantage points. At one extreme, regulation can be 'a dirty word representing the heavy hand of authoritarian governments and the creeping body of rules that constrain human or national liberties', whilst at the other extreme, it can be viewed as 'a public good, a tool to control profit-hungry capitalists and to govern social and ecological risks' (Levi-Faur, 2010, p. 4). Some have viewed regulation only with reference to the work of governments, whilst others have gone beyond this. Moreover, disciplines have traditionally viewed regulation differently: legal scholars have emphasised legal instruments, whilst sociologists have emphasised other forms of control; economists have viewed regulation as a tool used only when necessary to deal with market failures; and public administration scholars have emphasised the authority of the state and its formal regulatory organisations (Levi-Faur, 2010, pp. 4–5). Our fundamental conceptions of regulation therefore range from seeing regulation as a strict legal concept in which laws and regulations are determined through the legislative processes of Parliament, through to a more fluid behavioural concept in which regulation is seen as a focused attempt at controlling the behaviour of others. Thus, at one end of the scale, we are presented with a narrow, top-down 'command and control' view of regulation; whilst at the other, an extraordinarily broad view of regulation exists that incorporates everything including the ability of parents to 'regulate' the behaviour of their children.

These competing notions of regulation have been progressively subject to cross-disciplinary analysis. And indeed early narrow ideas of regulation have been completely reconceptualised. Contemporary regulation is now viewed as covering multiple disciplines, as 'decentred' and as crossing all sectors. Industry and civil society both 'regulate', as does government. The traditional 'command and control' concept of regulation has thus been broadened to include instruments and activities which extend well beyond the law. According to Black (2002, p. 19) for example, regulation is:

> the sustained and focused attempt to alter the behaviour of others according to defined standards or purposes with the intention of producing a broadly identified outcome or outcomes.[1]

Broad definitions of regulation such as this have, of course, challenged the traditional thinking of legal and public administration scholars alike. But while narrower conceptions may be easier to digest, they are less helpful and do not explain the broad range of modern efforts designed to influence behaviour. This reconceptualisation of regulation has led to several important insights, not only for the language of regulation, but for fundamental ideas concerning rethinking, modernising and reinventing the state.

Firstly, today's concept of regulation includes a wide variety of regulatory mechanisms and tools. These range from government Acts and regulations through to codes, guidelines, standards, contracts, grants, economic incentives, information usage, markets, licences and accreditation schemes. There are a multitude of regulatory tools and techniques now at our disposal, with black-letter law being just one of these options.

Taking an institutional perspective, the second insight is that the locus of regulation may be from inside government, through independent institutions or through hybrid mechanisms. It may also occur through co-regulation, self-regulation or even 'meta' regulation, where regulatory bodies oversee others (as occurs with accreditation bodies for the professions, for example) who themselves do the detailed oversight. The last two decades have seen the rise of the independent regulator, as noted by Jordana et al. (2009) in relation to certain jurisdictions and sectors. They found that the increase in the number of independent regulators across 48 countries through the 1990s was two and a half times that over the previous three decades. Importantly too, this phenomenon has been observed not only in relation to economic regulation but also to the social arena.

This brings us to the third insight. We have come to understand that regulation has not simply been a phenomenon which has occurred as a result of the frequent privatisation of essential public services – it has come to represent a more fundamental reordering of societal priorities and power. Regulation, as argued by Majone (1999, p. 1), has essentially been recognised as 'a distinctive mode of policy making' and has become an 'alternative mode of public control'. This is a powerful insight. Braithwaite et al. (2007) push this notion further, suggesting that the regulatory role of government is not only an important one, but one which is increasing. They noted that the work of governments broadly includes three functions: providing, distributing and regulating, and they observed that whilst the government's role in directly providing services is currently decreasing (through for example, outsourcing and privatisation), and its role in distributing (or redistributing) wealth will continue unabated through time, the government's role in regulating is increasing in a myriad of ways. Indeed, regulation has now become a policy preference of government.

The fourth insight stems from the numerous regulatory instruments now available. Freiberg (2010), for example, lists six different modes of regulating for government,[2] with each of these modes typically having dozens of different tools within it. He explains that states may act through economic tools (such as through making markets, or by influencing markets via taxing, quotas or pricing), through transactional tools (where governments influence behaviour through contract or grant conditions for minimum wages, for example), through authorising tools (of registration, licensing, permission, accreditation or litigation), through informational tools (such as product labelling or disclosing interest rates), through structural tools (of physical design, or processes such as Australia's 'pay as you go' tax arrangements) or through the more traditional and familiar legal tools (where laws, rules and regulations are made). What is clear here is that there are a range of regulatory tools available to the government and that traditional 'command and control' instruments, where government acts as a legislature, constitute only one of these tools. Perhaps less clear, but equally important, is the sense that regulation activities may be either positive (so that particular behaviours are encouraged through incentives) or negative (where behaviours are discouraged through disincentives). Figure 9.1 outlines a range of examples of the tools within each of these six modes of regulating.

Accordingly, rather than focusing on the degree of perfection achieved in the text of legislative instruments, scholars and decision-makers have shifted their attention to questions of how regulatory systems can be best designed, what tools and mechanisms work most effectively in particular circumstances and the degree to which citizens and other stakeholders see regimes as having legitimacy and credibility (see, for example, Bartle and Vass, 2007; Black, 2008). Also, scholars now rightly concern themselves with the responsiveness of regulators to dynamic environments and the overall effectiveness of the regimes in practice.

Fifthly, the extent to which regulatory activity includes a range from hard law through to soft law has been described in frameworks such as the enforcement pyramid first articulated by Ayres and Braithwaite (1992). The implication of this is that much regulatory time is spent on measuring and monitoring, in assessing and in reporting, and in regulatory conversations as opposed to formal court proceedings. And many of these activities are inherently cross-disciplinary rather than belonging to one specific group. Regulation has quietly become a cross-disciplinary professional pursuit, albeit not yet widely acknowledged as such.

The sixth insight is that regulatory activity has remained – despite what some commentators care to argue – an inherently political activity. Whether governments choose to regulate directly through, for example,

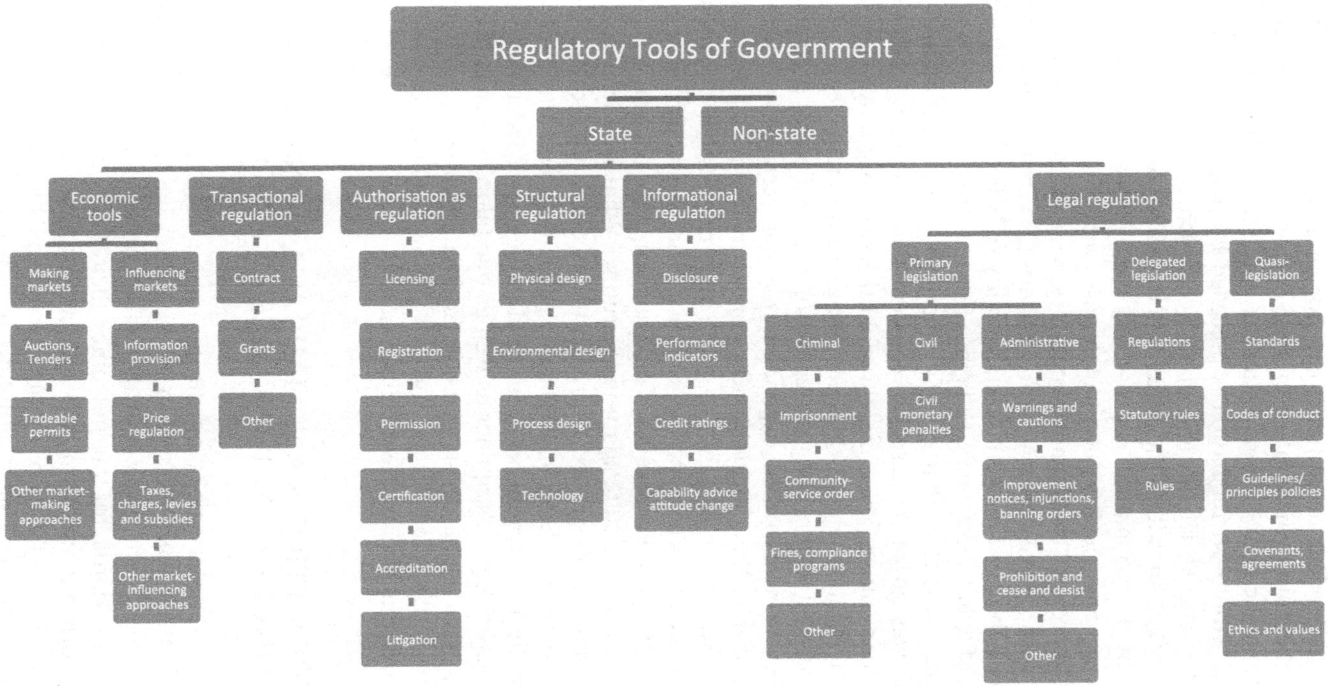


*Source:* Adapted from Freiberg (2010).

*Figure 9.1 The regulatory tools of government*

legislation, independent institutions, monitoring and reporting regimes, markets or the employment of incentives or contracts, the choice of mechanism and the content comprising the regulatory fabric are political decisions. Moreover, regulation is preceded by policy choices in the face of public interest debates and discussion. Such choices involve, by definition, conflicts in values. Indeed as Van de Walle (2009, p. 45) states, government by its very nature 'is constantly dangling in an uneasy equilibrium between competing values'. As a consequence, there is rarely one single 'best approach' to organise regulatory regimes to the advantage of citizens. Such choices on regulatory activity also involve discussions which continually move between today's reality of 'what is', to differing conceptions of 'what should be' in a better, future world.

Overall, then, it is clear that today's conceptions of regulation are far broader than was earlier the case. But so what? Discussion on 'modernising' and on 'reinventing government' should therefore begin by acknowledging that regulation means different things to different people, that regulation spans all sectors and that regulation is both a policy preference of modern governments and an expanding role in governing. But there is also more to it than that. These broader conceptions of regulation bring with them observations of how we have been progressively changing governance structures and how the state itself has been reshaping and adapting over the past few decades. These, in turn, have real implications for how we may see the state adapt in the future. What is now needed is a richer and more sophisticated approach to discourse around issues of reinventing, commercialising and reforming the state. One that marries together equally the breadth, emotion and values of broad policy discourse through multiple disciplines as well as one that is informed by an evidence base from regulatory scholarship. So what observations might be made on this broader idea of regulation? And how might the concept of regulatory governance assist these deliberations?

## 9.3 OBSERVATIONS AND IMPLICATIONS FROM RECONCEPTUALISING REGULATION

There are several observations worthy of note, having reconceptualised regulation. Firstly, if our conception of regulation has been broadened to one where regulation involves sustained attempts to alter behaviour according to standards for an outcome, then the role of regulation involves far more than simply those people employed in formal regulatory agencies. As Levi-Faur (2010, p. 10) put it, 'while only few of us are acting as professional regulators, most, if not all, of us act as regulators in some

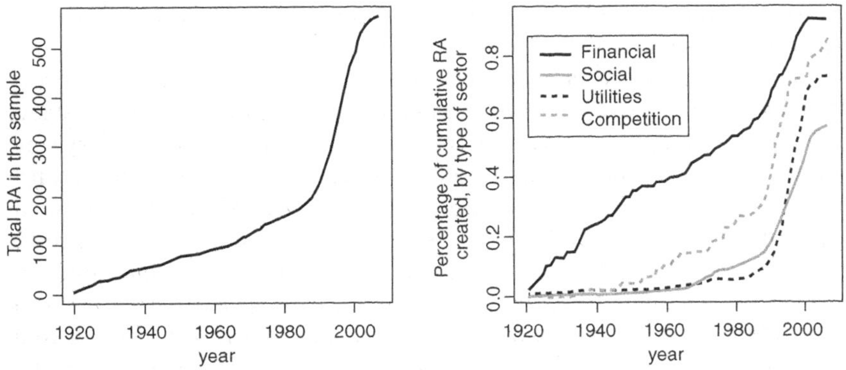


*Source:* Adapted from Jordana et al. (2009).

*Figure 9.2 Cumulative annual creation of regulatory agencies (RA) across 48 countries and 16 sectors over 88 years: 1920–2007*

capacity'. The point being made here is profound: if we aim to change behaviour in a sustained way, we are regulating.

Secondly, the very notion of the state as the centre of regulation is seen as a misconception. Regulatory space is always more complex than that, and the state competes with others for regulatory influence. As hinted earlier, the three sectors (the state, market actors and civil actors) potentially regulate each other as well as themselves. Businesses regulate other businesses (through contractual standards for food manufacturing or processing throughout the world, for example), and parts of government regulate other parts of government. Non-governmental organisations (NGOs) accredit codes of conduct to assure clean or green business practices, and so on. The practice of auditing and the growth of ombudsmen can also be viewed as regulatory tools.

Thirdly, the substantial growth in the number of independent regulatory agencies around the world observed by Gilardi et al. (2006) and Jordana et al. (2009) was both a significant and visible sign of growing regulatory interest. And whilst regulatory agencies were not strictly speaking, a new feature of modern systems of governance, they became a highly popular form of governing throughout the 1990s (Levi-Faur, 2010, p. 15). Not only was it essentially a global phenomenon, but it was also observed across both economic sectors (electricity, telecoms, competition) and social sectors (food safety, pharmaceuticals, media, environment). This is shown in Figure 9.2. What is clear from this expansion is that the regulatory phenomenon was in practice far broader in its application than narrow notions of regulation only being applicable to instances of market failure, for example.

Fourthly, reconceptualised ideas of regulation suggest its crucial relevance to modern governing systems and invite questions as to the existence of the 'regulatory state'. We certainly live in the era of the regulatory state (Majone, 1994) and as Jordana and Levi-Faur (2004, p. 8) remind us, it is a popular and convincing label capturing the essence of changes in governing capitalist economies. But what is the regulatory state? At one extreme we might view it as a 'sort of intellectual brazier around which [scholars of regulation] can all gather, to warm our hands and speak to each other, in a world of increasingly fragmented professionalism' (Moran, 2002 cited in Jordana and Levi-Faur, 2004, p. 8). The alternative view is to see it as the major aspect of the transformation in governing capitalist economies since the 1980s and replacing the welfare state. Jordana and Levi-Faur (2004) suggest that neither extreme is accurate and that a more prudent view of the regulatory state might be somewhere in the middle. They argue that the term 'regulatory state' 'suggests [that] modern states are placing more emphasis on the use of authority, rules and standard setting, partially displacing an earlier emphasis on public ownership, public subsidies, and directly provided services. The expanding part of modern government, the argument goes, is regulation' (Jordana and Levi-Faur, 2004, p. 8). This view is accompanied by some warnings: that multiple forms of control are employed in governing capitalist economies with several modes often co-existing; that the state does not operate as the sole source of regulatory control in any event; and that the regulatory state probably has a certain 'multi-levelness' to it both within one country as well as internationally. Levi-Faur (2010, p. 17) also observes that three elements in particular characterise this conception of the regulatory state:

- bureaucratic functions of regulation are separated from service delivery;
- regulatory functions are separated from policy-making (and therefore are placed at arm's length from their political masters); and
- regulation and rule-making emerge as a distinct stage in the policy-making process, and therefore, a distinct profession and administrative identity.

Allied to this 'regulatory state' idea, and fifth in this list of insights, is the concept of 'regulatory governance'. Again contested, Minogue and Carino (2006, p. 4) argue that 'regulatory governance is now fully accepted as a significant part of the literature on regulation in general and privatisation and post-privatisation regulatory reforms in particular'. To them, it is:

> an attempt to go beyond the formal rules that govern relationships between the public and private sectors, to the broader framework of state-market relations, and drawing on disciplinary contributions that range across economics, law, politics, and public policy and management.

This view therefore sees regulatory governance as aiming to examine regulatory arrangements in relation to the general public policy process, and as 'looking behind the institutional façade to grasp the "real world" of public action' as Minogue and Carino (2006) nicely put it. In doing so, it acknowledges fully that 'independence from political control does not mean independence from public accountability'.

Sixthly, in order to understand how any one single actor is regulated, we need to look well beyond the state to multiple overlapping 'webs of influence'. Indeed Grabosky (1995) goes so far as to suggest that 'it is perhaps more useful nowadays to regard a regulatory system as consisting of layered webs of regulatory influence, of which conventional activities of regulatory agencies constitute but a few strands'. So regulatory regimes are complex and overlapping, with governments being only one of the influential players.

Even more broadly again, and point number seven, is the arrival of the phrase 'regulatory capitalism'. Braithwaite (2008) explains that whilst many people saw the state running fewer things and regulating more, some analysts started talking about the regulatory state. He continues that:

> then it was recognised that many other organisational actors beyond the state were also doing a lot more regulating of other organisations than in the past, so some analysts . . . spoke of a regulatory society. Along came David Levi-Faur and Jacint Jordana to point out that capitalist markets had become more vibrant at the same time as regulation of markets had become more earnest.

Not only did they coin the phrase 'regulatory capitalism', they also produced a large body of data showing that privatised markets and regulatory institutions had expanded beyond the West to around the world, and that markets themselves had been used as a regulatory mechanism of choice. To Braithwaite's mind, then, we therefore saw not only 'freer markets' with 'more rules' as Vogel (1996) had earlier pointed out, but: 'more capitalism, more regulation'; a proliferation of new technologies of regulation; increased delegation to business and professional self regulation and to civil society, to international networks of experts, and to increased regulation of the state by the state (particularly for competition).

More formally, Levi-Faur (2010, p. 23) described regulatory capitalism as:

- the growth in scope, importance and impact of regulation at the national and global levels;
- the growing investments of political, economic and social actors in regulation in general and regulatory strategies in particular; and
- the emergence, extension and consolidation of hybrid forms of regulation which shape diverse and more complex forms of regulatory regime.

To him, the idea of regulatory capitalism took regulatory thinking beyond national boundaries and beyond formal state-centred rule-making. It also denoted a world where regulation was increasingly a hybrid of different systems of control, where statist regulation evolved with civil regulation, where national regulation expanded with international and global regulation, where private regulation expanded with public regulation, and where voluntary regulation existed with coercive regimes. Not only were we dealing with the growth of the regulatory state but also the growth in the number of civil and business actors that invested in regulation and their own business-to-business regulatory institutions and instruments (Levi-Faur, 2010, p. 23). The implications of this notion of regulatory capitalism have been profound. Braithwaite (2008), for example, argues that this notion was a challenge to traditional social science disciplines which were 'preoccupied with geographically bounded political systems, legal systems and cultures'. He also argues that the oft-told story of the triumph of neoliberalism at the end of the twentieth century (and, to him, widely believed on the far left and far right) is a 'fairy tale'. Neoliberalism (defined as 'a program for destroying collective structures which may impede the pure market logic') and its Hayekian prescriptions of small government, privatisation and deregulation, did not occur. Government typically got bigger in terms of spending power and employment numbers and was not hollowed out, the state was still seen as vital to long-term economic growth prospects, and changes from state ownership to private led to more regulation, not less. Likewise the cousin of neoliberalism, the Washington Consensus, stalled after disastrous privatisations in jurisdictions such as Russia, and the Washington Consensus became the 'Washington Consensus plus good governance and the rule of law' (Braithwaite, 2008).[3] To Braithwaite, then, regulatory capitalism triumphed, whilst neoliberalism lost the war for the hearts and minds of the world's policy-makers.

All of this is interesting, but again, what are the implications of these ideas as we rethink the state?

## 9.4 SOME THOUGHTS MOVING FORWARD

The broader modern notion of regulation and the idea of regulatory capitalism both have a bearing when we contemplate the reshaping of future governance and regulatory arrangements. Thoughts might turn to broader systemic or societal level issues or towards narrower policy or technical concerns.

To begin with, we have adopted a broader idea of regulation – one which recognises that much regulation occurs without rules – through economic incentives to steer business, moral suasion by shaming, and architecture (Parker and Braithwaite, 2003, p. 119). This view challenges traditional legal perspectives in three fundamental ways (Morgan and Yeung, 2007). Firstly, it challenges our assumption that the state is the primary locus for articulating community goals (compared to the social influence of multiple non-state, civil society and business organisations). Secondly, it challenges the assumption of hierarchy that the state has final authority (compared with multiple sites of governance operating in overlapping ways rather than simply vertically). And thirdly, it challenges the assumption of centrality of rules – or in other words commands as the primary mode of shaping behaviour (compared to the real limitations of legal rules and potential for alternatives).

These ideas around a 'decentred' view of regulation have not dislodged either the state or the law. But they do generate 'new questions about the relationships between the state and the range of other actors, institutions, and techniques highlighted by a decentred approach' (Morgan and Yeung, 2007, p. 4). They remind us that decentred regulatory questions span all three sectors and thankfully also invite continued questions on the role of the state. They encourage us to think of public ownership as a mode of regulation rather than as an end in itself. They suggest that when we view history, we consider the possibility that the rise of the regulatory state was associated with rising complexity, and with an increasing trend for credibility to replace coercive power as the essential resource of policy-makers. And they invite the paradoxical historical observation that the delegation of regulatory power to extra-political institutions enabled elected representatives to maintain political credibility (Flinders, 2008). They also remind us to continue asking questions about the effectiveness of traditional command-and-control (law) based approaches to regulation compared to alternative 'non-law options'.

As a consequence it is perhaps little surprise in many ways for regulatory scholars to read that international transactions, in which payment is made to purchase manufactured products, rely on corporate financial accounts and on electrical standards, both of which are governed by 'transnational private regulation'. Looking at accounting regulation and standards setting for major global product markets (using ISO – International Organization for Standardization, or electrotechnical standards), Buthe and Mattli (2011) conclude that today's global rulers are 'new' and that there has been a 'privatisation of regulation in the world economy' – if we believe their book title. But to those considering regulation through a broader lens, this analysis, whilst impressively detailed and analytical, simply continues earlier themes from work such as Ayres and Braithwaite (1992), whose regulatory pyramid model and ideas of regulatory responsiveness are now accepted globally, and Braithwaite and Drahos (2000, p. 5), who surprisingly found that NGOs often prevailed in ratcheting up regulatory standards rather than powerful corporations racing to the bottom.[4]

Of course in any conversation on public sector issues, language has always had a prized position. Indeed phrases such as 'reinventing' and 'rethinking' as a diagnosis for improving governing systems have been almost magical. What is meant by 'magic'? Pollitt and Hupe (2011) suggest that magic terms in government are highly abstract, but carry an overwhelmingly positive connotation: it is hard to be 'against' them. They imply a certain consensus and are able to dissolve previous dilemmas and binary oppositions (such as democracy versus efficiency, or public versus private interests.) They also seem to have a global marketability, carry effortlessly across domains and are known by practitioners and academics alike.[5] On these criteria, the terms 'reinventing' and 'rethinking' appear to have magical properties. The advantage of magic terms such as these is that they help to set agendas, and provide a vocabulary for debates. They stimulate, mobilise, enthuse and excite. The multiple meanings and ambiguities also mean, though, that they may be used as much for 'white magic' as for 'black magic'. So such concepts should not be glorified. They usually imply that a better world is achievable through more: more 'reinvention' or more 'rethinking'; and few ask questions which go in the opposite direction. To see magic concepts as having direct prescriptions for practice, however, 'is to misinterpret their capacity'. Importantly too, Pollitt and Hupe (2011) remind us that:

> magic concepts do *not* reconcile the oppositional proverbs and doctrines which previous generations of public administration scholars painstakingly documented and discussed. Rather, they rise above them – to a higher level of abstraction – or, if one prefers, they avoid them.

Pollitt and Hupe (2011) further warn that practitioners 'should not be seduced into thinking that these apparently unopposable ideas actually solve previous dilemmas or resolve awkward trade-offs . . . Little wonder then that they conclude 'magic' is entertaining . . . [and] excites discussion, but when the show is over many hard choices remain'.

The 'reinventing government' movement of the 1990s might be one historical example of 'magic' here. Osborne and Gaebler's (1993) paperback was reportedly the only text on public administration ever to reach bestseller lists in the United States, and was also no doubt a highly influential book in practical terms.[6] But the magic title aside, the academic credentials of this book were minimal. The observations of Fox (1996) on the 'reinventing government' movement left no room for doubt as to its scholarly credibility. To him, ideas such as 'steering not rowing' were 'breathless in their salesmanship', despite what he described as their 'clear inconsistencies', 'bizarre logic' and 'linguistic manipulations'. Likewise, the observations of De Carvalho (1998) on the notion of 'steering not rowing' remind us that such rhetoric is not value-free. What exactly is meant by rowing, asked De Carvalho? Rowing may, for instance, be undertaken in the style of the huge Roman trireme, as depicted in the movie *Ben Hur*. This Roman version of rowing saw galley slaves, so little trusted that they were chained to their posts, the admiral standing on the deck above the rowers, and with rowing undertaken under the beating (benchmarking) of a monotonous drum. The contrast with Viking rowing was stark. Viking vessels were open-decked, with room for feedback between the rowers and the admiral of the ship as well as between the rowers themselves. Being free men rather than slaves, the rowers were not chained to their posts, thus enhancing cooperation. So rowing was hardly a neutral activity and the efforts of those providing the motive force to go forward was on some vessels valued equally with the efforts of those setting the direction.[7] Debates on the various interpretations as to just what is meant by the notion of steering (rather than rowing), and the relative importance of the two functions, continue to inflame passion even in today's policy debates.

More substantively, despite our new conceptual framework, there is still no resolution as to the optimum design of regulatory regimes. So when we might best adopt traditional tools and when others might best serve us remain open questions, as do many issues around the effectiveness and legitimacy of the multiple alternative options. Such questions deserve full consideration.

Perhaps more useful than broad systemic considerations however, might be some reflection on a popular modern practice of governments nowadays – that of public–private partnership. It is to this matter that I now turn.

## 9.5 LOOKING AT PUBLIC–PRIVATE PARTNERSHIP THROUGH A REGULATORY LENS

Public–private partnership (PPP) is a popular phenomenon, with many meanings.[8] Authors such as Weihe (2005) and Hodge and Greve (2007) have indeed noted that partnerships encompass several different families of activities. One visible form of recent partnership has been the long-term infrastructure contract partnership (LTIC) family. The LTIC is organised around a design–finance–build–own–operate–transfer model and often involves private sector financing and private sector project management capabilities. There are multiple options for the precise partnership arrangements, however.

There is much that could be said on the form, the politics and the performance of LTIC PPPs. Only a few salient points will be made here, and then we will use a regulatory lens to gain some insights into this technique. There have been many policy promises made by governments in adopting PPP. The initial rationale under John Major's United Kingdom (UK) government was to get around restrictions on formal public sector debt levels. Private financing promised a way to provide infrastructure without increasing the public sector borrowing requirement (PSBR). This was followed by the promise that PPPs would 'reduce pressure on public-sector budgets'.[9] The third promise of PPPs was that this delivery mechanism provides better value for money for taxpayers. This is a policy promise most worthy of examination and one that has also formed the primary PPP rationale in countries such as the UK and Australia. Added to these three initial promises have been several more – some explicit, such as reduced risk to government from projects, better accountability, better on-time and on-budget delivery and greater innovation; and some implicit, such as encouraging a more innovative public sector, improved business confidence, improved palatability for user funding for infrastructure, provision for long-term infrastructure life-cycle costs and boosted sales of professional PPP services abroad. To these 13 PPP objectives, we might nowadays also add two more objectives following the recent credit market failures and stock market downturns. Governments may wish to broadly support businesses and preferentially adopt the PPP mechanism in difficult market circumstances (that is, the objective of business assistance) or pursue a broader societal objective of economic development. Furthermore these objectives have also altered over time, and today still remain slippery in the rough and tumble of government policy speak.

It is not, of course, surprising that the delivery of major public infrastructure facilities can be controversial. Public infrastructure provision has a long historical pedigree, and some things are not new at all; the involvement of private sector contractors, the size of funds at stake and the long-term nature of the commitment. But the new long-term contractual form of partnership (LTIC) has three new characteristics that deserve close attention. These include the preferential use of private finance, high-level complexity through bundled contracts, and new accountability and governance assumptions.

Many questions have haunted global assessments investigating LTIC PPP performance. These questions have broadly covered matters of technical performance – including assessments of, for example, value for money (VfM), on-time or on-budget delivery – as well as issues of governance such as transparency and accountability. Issues of technical performance are not central to this chapter, and readers are referred to Hodge (2010) where I presented a recent international review of performance results. Focussing solely on the VfM objective, I summarised the mixed results of some 28 evaluations and reviews from the past decade. I noted as well that 'statistically solid evidence on LTIC type PPPs is weak', that the counterfactual of traditional procurement is both 'horribly vague and also largely unquantified', and that 'nearly all studies are business cases' before contracts are signed or early on in the project.

Issues of governance were likewise judged on another earlier occasion to have been just as mixed. Indeed, in Hodge (2006) I argued that on all three of the characteristics seen above as new to LTIC PPP provision (the preferential use of private finance, high-level complexity through bundled contracts, and new accountability and governance assumptions), the PPP tool lacked legitimacy in the eyes of the citizens on whose behalf it was being employed. This was a strong charge. On the matter of complexity, I noted that this was not simply a matter of narrow legal concern, but of parliamentarians not fully understanding the deals, and of citizens not being able to get a clear picture of their worth underneath either the veil of complexity or the cloak of 'commercial-in-confidence'. Moreover, scrutiny of PPP arrangements had too often become not an issue of how to create improved accessibility for citizens, but a concern that a shield had been created behind which governments could shelter and avoid public accountability.

Also, whilst we have instituted a 'regulatory state' of independent regulators, ombudsmen and audit review bodies in order to disperse power away from political quarters after the privatisation of state utility businesses, this had not occurred with these infrastructure deals. PPPs had essentially continued to be two-way government–business deals rather than also involving the community or any other independent accountability or representative bodies. They had also been handled on a case-by-case basis, by the government itself in the face of multiple conflicts of interest, with government simultaneously acting as policy advocate, economic developer, steward for public funds, elected representative for decision-making, regulator over the contract life, commercial signatory to the contract, and planner. To my mind, then, the potential for the interests of the government and business partners to dominate over the public interest had become palpable. Early drafts of Victoria's PPP guideline materials did not even mention the 'public interest' notion and treated government solely as if it were a commercial contractual partner in a private business deal. This is reminiscent of past centuries.[10] Clearly communities need far more discussion and debate as to how we might better ensure that the public interest is met through PPP deals, as well as meeting the needs of the two legal parties to the deal.

The implications of shortfalls observed were argued as profound. To the extent that new infrastructure contract delivery arrangements have reduced existing accountability arrangements and altered longstanding governance assumptions with little democratic debate, new PPP arrangements lacked legitimacy to my mind. Little wonder that I saw PPPs as they were operating in Australia as very much an illegitimate child of the historical partnership family. The evidence from parliamentary inquiries underway and completed around this time was also referenced. It was noted that 35 of the 46 recommendations made by the committees fell into the three categories above (financial, complexity, accountability and governance concerns). Also, the largest two categories of these recommendations concerned PPP accountability and governance, and issues stemming from the implications of the private finance preference. We might observe that with the Premier and ministers of the NSW government refusing to attend the Cross City Tunnel Parliamentary Committee to explain their perspectives (NSW Parliament, 2006), this was arguably a further testament to the fact that ministerial accountability for PPP transactions was almost non-existent. The illegitimacy of one government being happy to sign up the next dozen governments to multi-billion-dollar contract payments, with subsequent elected representatives then not participating in a fundamental public accountability mechanism to explain decisions, was argued as being 'an all time low in our traditional democratic polity' (Hodge, 2006).

Moreover, taxpayers' interests were not being served according to Tomazin (2006), who stated that 'State Government secrecy surrounding billions of dollars worth of projects done in partnership with the private sector means Victorians have no idea whether they provide value for money'. And clearly 'the obligatory public interest test for each PPP does not automatically guarantee the public interest is served'. The possibility of a coalition of political interests operating against the public interest of citizens is a more sinister logic. But the confluence between political and business interests is clear. Political interests can enjoy better party funding for elections, and see both the promise of early delivery of big infrastructure projects and the promise of shifting blame to other parties if anything goes awry. The private financial interests of financiers, consulting firms, advisors and infrastructure companies see a slice of the financial transactions, or 'deal flow' as it is openly labelled.

Overall we could conclude that whilst PPPs can have some potential advantages over traditional project arrangements, their legitimacy is questionable. As Collins (2004) noted, 'contract law is now being called upon to play a more pivotal role in the governance mechanisms of the post-regulatory state'. But whether this rule-setting mechanism is sufficiently democratic and accountable is at issue. The future legitimacy of PPPs will depend on such a deficit being overcome. Daintith (1979) also remarked that the use of contracts as a governing tool can amount to 'the power to rule without Parliament'. Perhaps we have now reached this stage? In any event, with little practical oversight from administrative law, Australian public–private partnerships need, at a minimum, to become more transparent and democratic before their legitimacy is acceptable.

Of course, on top of any such performance and governance concerns, the use of political rhetoric is always bound to be colourful. Indeed partnership notions have long been as much a public policy language game as they have been anything of real substance (Greve and Hodge, 2005; see also Edelman, 1985; Linder, 1999). A clear example of this has been the UK government, which has explicitly acknowledged that its Private Finance Initiative (PFI) was simply an equivalent form of privatisation (Treasury, 2003), whilst in Australia the reformist Victorian state government worked hard to differentiate PPPs from the privatisation activities of the former Kennett administration (Sheil, 2003; see also Greve and Hodge, 2005, pp. 1–21). Another example is the very label 'partnership' for large private finance contracts – which is a nonsense. Infrastructure finance construction deals are no more partnerships than when citizens sign a house mortgage with their local bank. A further example is the use of terminology such as 'value for money' (VfM). A crucial linguistic concern here is the point made by Davies (2008, p. 200) who studied alliance contracts and argued that Australian governments 'all provide directions for managers to achieve value for money, but are silent on how value for money should be measured'. Moreover he saw VfM as 'a nebulous concept' which 'frightens auditors' as they move from traditional certification-based checking into areas requiring greater judgement (Davies, 2008, pp. 242, 216). The point here is that public policy language games are used in the partnership arena to suit local political objectives, and such games obscure meanings rather than clarify and sharpen our understanding of the phenomenon. In Australia, the warm glow of partnership language is likely to be employed for some time yet in preference to the harsher-sounding imagery of privatisation, private finance deals and unit costs.

What then might we conclude overall? Firstly, the contract itself is the regulatory tool. This is supplemented by the use of market tendering in the bidding process (albeit that there are often few bidders) and the use of post-project auditing (again, which has tended to be nervous of VfM assessments.) Also, there is now sufficient concern around the value for money being achieved through these arrangements to investigate whether or not the ad hoc contract by contract agreements ought to be streamlined and regulated through institutional arrangements in much the same way as independent utility regulators now operate. Looking forward, there is little doubt that the partnership ideal (or getting the best from the public sector as well as the best from the private sector) will continue over coming decades. And as a consequence the role of information as a regulatory tool may provide a new weapon for public accountability.

## 9.6 CONCLUSION

The lens of regulatory governance is potentially useful in contemplating societal themes of globalisation, reinvention and modernising the state. Regulatory governance ideas bring new meaning to regulation itself and also have implications for how the state is likely to be rethought in the future. Rather than replacing traditional lenses, it encourages new questions around the role of the state, the crowded and contested regulatory landscape, the wide range of available regulatory tools, and the effectiveness of these tools. In the example of PPP, the ad hoc contract is viewed as the regulatory tool itself, and it is concluded that the governing arrangements for this regulatory technique are insufficient to guarantee high public legitimacy at present.

## NOTES

1. Note that this particular definition of regulation does not even include the usual criteria of 'rules' which is most commonly taken as the central criteria for definition.
2. Freiberg's six modes of regulation parallel the governance observations of Bell and Hindmoor (2009), who see the modern state as operating through modes such as persuasion, markets, and via community or other networked arrangements as well as through traditional government hierarchy.
3. To Braithwaite, this description showed that despite regulatory capitalism having

occurred rather than the neoliberal prescription, the neoliberals still could not use the dirty word 'regulation'.

4. Likewise, the early ideas of Parker (2002) are profound. She argued that corporate self-regulation could be successful and that regulators needed to focus more on 'meta-regulating' corporate systems if democratic control was to be established.
5. Pollitt and Hupe (2011) nominate 'governance', 'accountability' and 'networks' as three magic concepts in current public sector work.
6. Personal testimonials to the author confirm this point. One first-hand anecdote tells of Osborne and Gaebler's 'reinventing' paperback book being given to every incoming minister of the Kennett Government, in the state of Victoria, Australia, in 1992. All ministers were reportedly told to 'go and read this because that was the way government was going to be done in Victoria!'.
7. Note also that the 'steering not rowing' catch phrase was first coined by Steve Savas, one of the most ardent privatisation advocates in the US, but subsequently popularised through Osborne and Gaebler's popular bestseller *Reinventing Government: How the Entrepreneurial Spirit is Transforming the Public Sector* (1993).
8. NAO (2009) noted that there were hundreds of partnership types existing throughout the United Kingdom, ranging from the London Underground, to various Private Finance Initiative projects through to many local government arrangements.
9. We might reflect that the private financing of a long-term infrastructure does not strictly reduce the call on the budget. A mechanism through which governments may turn a large, one-off capital expenditure into a series of smaller, annualised expenditures has simply been provided. And like any domestic credit card or mortgage arrangement, this does not reduce pressure on the family budget, because all debts must be repaid in the end, at hopefully minimum interest rates to ensure efficiency. The one important exception to this is the case where a government enters an infrastructure deal requiring users or citizens to pay directly, such as tolls on a new road. Here, such an arrangement does reduce pressure on public sector budgets, because government has essentially purchased the infrastructure through the commitment of funds from future (private) road users rather than using its own resources.
10. Feedback to this effect resulted in the development of a 'public interest test' within the Department's guidance material which – if the boxes were ticked – guaranteed (at least in the minds of advocating bureaucrats) that the public interest had been 'defined' and met.

## REFERENCES


Ayres, I. and J. Braithwaite (1992), *Responsive Regulation: Transcending and Deregulation Debate*, New York: Oxford University Press.

Bartle, I. and P. Vass (2007), 'Self Regulation Within the Regulatory State: Towards a New Regulatory Paradigm?' *Public Administration*, **85**(4), 885–905.

Bell, S. and A. Hindmoor (2009), *Rethinking Governance: The Centrality of the State in Modern Society*, Port Melbourne, Australia: Cambridge University Press.

Black, J. (2002), 'Critical Reflections on Regulation', *Australian Journal of Legal Philosophy*, **27**, 1–36.

Black, J. (2008), 'Constructing and Contesting Legitimacy and Accountability in Polycentric Regulatory Regimes', *Regulation and Governance*, **2**, 137–164.

Braithwaite, J. (2008), *Regulatory Capitalism: How It Works, Ideas for Making It Work Better*, Cheltenham, UK and Northampton, MA, USA: Edward Elgar.

Braithwaite, J., C. Coglianese, and D. Levi-Faur (2007), 'Can Regulation and Governance Make a Difference?' *Regulation and Governance*, **1**, 1–7.
Braithwaite, J. and P. Drahos (2000), *Global Business Regulation*, Cambridge: Cambridge University Press.
Buthe, T. and W. Mattli (2011), *The New Global Rulers: The Privatization of Regulation in the World Economy*, Princeton, NJ: Princeton University Press.
Collins, H. (2004), 'Regulating Contract Law', in C. Parker, C. Scott, N. Lacey and J. Braithwaite (eds), *Regulating Law*, Oxford: Oxford University Press, pp. 13–32.
Daintith, T. (1979) 'Regulation by Contract: The New Prerogative', *Current Legal Problems*, **32**(1), 41.
Davies, J. (2008), 'Alliance Contracts and Public Sector Governance', PhD thesis, Griffith University, August, unpublished.
de Carvalho, D. (1998), 'The Captain is a Schizophrenic! Or Contradictions in the Concept of the Steering State', *Australian Journal of Public Administration*, **57**(2), 107–114.
Edelman, M. (1985), 'Political Language and Political Reality', *Political Science*, **18**, 1–19.
Flinders, M. (2008), *Delegated Governance and the British State*, Oxford: Oxford University Press.
Fox, C. (1996), 'Reinventing Government as Postmodern Symbolic Politics', *Public Administration Review*, **56**(3), 256–262.
Freiberg, A. (2010), *The Tools of Regulation*, Sydney: Federation Press.
Gilardi, F., J. Jordana and D. Levi-Faur (2006), 'Regulation in the Age of Globalization: The Diffusion of Regulatory Agencies across Europe and Latin America', in G. Hodge (ed.), *Privatisation and Market Development: Global Movements in Public Policy Ideas*, Cheltenham, UK and Northampton, MA, USA: Edward Elgar, pp. 127–147.
Grabosky, P.N. (1995), 'Using Non-Governmental Resources to Foster Regulatory Compliance', *Governance*, **8**(4), 527–550.
Greve, C. and G. Hodge (2005), 'Introduction', in G. Hodge and C. Greve (eds), *The Challenge of Public–Private Partnerships: Learning from International Experience*, Cheltenham, UK and Northampton, MA, USA: Edward Elgar, pp. 1–21.
Hodge, G. (2006), 'Public–Private Partnerships and Legitimacy', *University of New South Wales Law Journal*, Forum, **29**(3), 318–327.
Hodge, G. (2010), 'Reviewing Public–Private Partnerships: Some Thoughts on Evaluation', in G. Hodge, C. Greve and A. Boardman (eds), *International Handbook on Public–Private Partnerships*, Cheltenham, UK and Northampton, MA, USA: Edward Elgar, pp. 81–112.
Hodge, G. and C. Greve (2007), 'Public–Private Partnerships: An International Performance Review', *Public Administration Review*, **67**(3), 545–558.
Jordana, J. and D. Levi-Faur (2004), 'The Politics of Regulation in the Age of Governance', in J. Jordana and D. Levi-Faur (eds), *The Politics of Regulation: Institutions and Regulatory Reforms for the Age of Governance*, Cheltenham, UK and Northampton, MA, USA: Edward Elgar, pp. 1–28.
Jordana, J., D. Levi-Faur and X.I.M. Fernandez (2009), 'The Global Diffusion of Regulatory Agencies: Channels of Transfer and Stages of Diffusion', Working Paper no. 28, Institut Barcelona d'Estudis Internacionals.

Levi-Faur, D. (2010), 'Jerusalem Papers in Regulation & Governance', Working Paper no. 1, Hebrew University, Israel.

Linder, S. (1999), 'Coming to Terms with the Public–Private Partnership: A Grammar of Multiple Meanings', *American Behavioural Scientist*, **43**, 35–51.

Majone, G. (1994), 'Rise of the Regulatory State', *West European Politics*, **17**(3), 77.

Majone, G. (1999), 'Regulation in Comparative Perspective', *Journal of Comparative Policy Analysis: Research and Practice*, **1**(3), 309–324.

Minogue, M. and L. Carino (2006), 'Introduction: Regulatory Governance in Developing Countries', in *Regulatory Governance in Developing Countries*, Cheltenham, UK and Northampton, MA, USA: Edward Elgar, pp. 3–16.

Moran, M. (2002), 'Review Article: Understanding the Regulatory State', *British Journal of Political Science*, **32**, 391–413.

Morgan, B. and K. Yeung (2007), *An Introduction to Law and Regulation: Text and Materials*, Cambridge: Cambridge University Press, pp. 16–78.

National Audit Office (NAO) (2009), 'Private Finance Projects', a paper for the Lords Economic Affairs Committee, October, UK.

NSW Parliament (2006), 'First Report: Cross City Tunnel', Joint Select Committee on the Cross City Tunnel, Tabled according to Legislative Council Standing Order 231.

Osborne, D. and T. Gaebler (1993), *Reinventing Government: How the Entrepreneurial Spirit is Transforming the Public Sector*, Reading, MA: Addison-Wesley.

Parker, C. (2002), 'Regulating Self-Regulation: The ACCC, ASIC, Competition Policy and Corporate Regulation', in S. Bell (ed.), *Economic Governance and Institutional Dynamics*, South Melbourne, Australia: Oxford University Press, pp. 244–261.

Parker, C. and J. Braithwaite (2003), 'Regulation', in P. Cane and M. Tushnet (eds), *The Oxford Handbook of Legal Studies*, Oxford: Oxford University Press, pp. 119–145.

Pollitt, C. and P. Hupe (2011), 'Talking about Government: The Role of Magic Concepts', *Public Management Review*, **13**(5), 641–658.

Sheil, C. (2003), 'Privatisation, Politics and Public–Private Partnerships', in D. Hayward and P. Ewer (eds), *Visions for Victoria*, Carlton North, Australia: Vulgar Press.

Tomazin, F. (2006), 'Secrecy Shields Bracks' Deals from Scrutiny', *Age*, 5 October.

Treasury, HM (2003), 'PFI: Meeting The Investment Challenge', Norwich, UK: HMSO.

Van de Walle, S. (2009), 'International Comparisons of Public Sector Performance: How to Move Ahead', *Public Management Review*, **11**(1), 39–56.

Vogel, S.K. (1996), *Freer Markets, More Rules: Regulatory Reform in Advanced Industrial Countries*, New York: Cornell University Press.

Weihe, G. (2005), 'Public–Private Partnerships: Addressing a Nebulous Concept', Working Paper no. 16, International Centre for Business and Politics, Copenhagen Business School, Denmark.

# 10. Developments in central banking after the GFC: central banks, the state, globalisation and the GFC

**Louise Parsons***

## 10.1 INTRODUCTION

There is general consensus that central banks are entering a new chapter in their history after the global financial crisis (GFC), and that they are in fact on the brink of a new era in central banking (see for example Goodhart, 2010, p. 15). The GFC highlighted the need for a broader responsibility for and oversight of financial stability, not only in domestic economies, but in the world as a whole (G-20, 2010). This responsibility may become the primary responsibility of central banks, as they may be the best institutions to oversee financial stability generally, or at least play an important or lead role in financial stability. The predominant focus of central banks currently is monetary policy. A change in the mandate of central banks to include or prioritise a responsibility for financial stability will result in a number of changes in central banking. In fact, central banking may never be the same again (Mishkin, 2010, p. 50). A changed responsibility may also affect the relationship between the central bank and the state (Goodhart, 2010, p. 15). This chapter focuses on how, after the GFC, the relationship between the central bank and the state may change, and how a greater responsibility for financial stability on the part of central banks may impact on central bank independence and the relationship between the central bank and the state.

## 10.2 CENTRAL BANKS BEFORE THE GFC

Historically the general functions of central banks have been to produce and distribute notes and coin, act as banker to government, hold foreign reserves, conduct open market operations, provide lender of last resort assistance to banks, and set interest rates in furtherance of monetary policy objectives (Bank for International Settlements, 2009, p. 19). Central banks have at times also been responsible for providing loans to governments to fund government projects and even war (Otahal, 2011, p. 1). Some were tasked with secondary responsibilities such as the maintaining of full employment. More recently, central banks have also assumed responsibilities for payment systems. For example, the Reserve Bank of Australia was made responsible for payment system oversight in July 1998, after the introduction of real-time gross settlement systems in Australia through the Payment Systems (Regulation) Act 1998.

In the second half of the 1970s, as inflation became a worldwide problem, the key focus of central banks started to shift to combating inflation and preserving price stability. Over time it was accepted generally, however not universally, that central bank independence was a prerequisite for effective monetary policy operations (Lamfalussy, 2010, pp. 6–7). Only an institution that was mostly independent of the political pressures affecting government could effectively implement monetary policy for the common good (Goodman, 1991, p. 329). Politicians or government departments may serve predominantly political agendas, whereas independent central banks may be more inclined 'to subordinate other goals, such as growth and employment, to the fight against inflation' (Goodman, 1991, p. 329). It is therefore important to examine the concept of 'central bank independence' in more detail.

## 10.3 CENTRAL BANK INDEPENDENCE: A BRIEF HISTORICAL PERSPECTIVE

The relationship between the central bank and the state has not been constant, and central bank independence has often been reviewed in the aftermath of a financial crisis (see Goodhart, 2010). In fact, the changing relationship between the central bank and government involves 'a political process that moves in cycles between various degrees of acceptance and rejection of the idea of . . . central bank independence' (James, 2010, p. 17). Central bank independence ultimately depends on political will.

Early in the twentieth century, the actions of some central banks, notably the Bank of England, the Bank of France and the Federal Reserve Bank of New York, were criticised (James, 2010, p. 12) specifically for not using their independence and autonomy appropriately. The Great Depression and the collapse of the gold standard later were construed as evidence of the failure of central banks (Goodhart, 2010, p. 2). Central banks lost their 'mystique' through 'theoretical confusion, indecision and policy errors', and in the process, the gold standard and central bank independence became associated with mass unemployment and deflation (Singleton, 2010, p. 25). Consequently, governments relieved central banks of their monetary policy functions and took those responsibilities on themselves (Goodhart, 2010, p. 2). In fact, after the Great Depression and the Second World War, the International Monetary Fund (IMF) was created and most central banks lost whatever independence they previously had (James, 2010, p. 12). The German central bank, the Bundesbank, was however, a notable exception to post-Depression central banks (James, 2010, p. 12). It was established in 1957 and was structured as an institution largely independent from government. The Bundesbank achieved great success as a central bank, with the Deutsche Mark becoming the most stable currency. The Bundesbank subsequently became the model for central bank independence in the second half of the twentieth century (James, 2010, p. 12).

The mid-1970s effectively marked a new beginning with an increase in central bank independence, a trend which continued and increased in the 1980s. Economic research highlighted the benefits of managing inflation, and evidence for industrial countries suggested that good economic performance, including lower inflation and positive growth, correlated with an independent central bank (James, 2010, p. 13). It became accepted generally that the best institution to conduct monetary policy is one that feels strong enough to resist political pressures (Shirakawa, 2010). In the mid-1990s, some countries increased the independence of their central banks in order to raise their commitment to price stability (Eijffinger and De Haan, 1996, p. 1). It constituted a 'quiet revolution' (Blinder, 2004) and a 'quantum upward jump' (Cukierman, 2009, p. 70), after the previous approximately 40 years in which there was little, if any, reform in central banking. The independence of the Bank of England, however, increased in the early 1990s even though there was no change in its founding legislation (Cukierman, 2009, p. 74). Gordon Brown gave the Bank of England operational independence from government in 1997 (Goodhart, 2010, p. 5) (although it should be noted that at that stage the Bank of England had already adopted an inflation-targeting model). Central bank independence also became important for developing countries. For example, the independence of the South African Reserve Bank was enshrined in the new South African Constitution in 1994.

To summarise, in the last 20 to 30 years of the twentieth century – the period that is now referred to as the 'Great Moderation' (Bernanke, 2004) or the 'triumph of the markets' (Goodhart, 2010, p. 5) – central banks earned, and gained, respect and significant prestige. The Great Moderation was characterised by a 'substantial decline in macroeconomic volatility' (Bernanke, 2004) and exhibited a neoliberal approach, focussing on central bank independence, the combating of inflation through inflation-targeting, and the use of indirect methods in the conduct of monetary policy (Epstein, 2006, p. 1). At this point in history, central banks were significantly more independent, both factually and legally, than previously (Cukierman, 2009, p. 68). The Great Moderation came to an end in 2007 with the onset of the GFC.

## 10.4 WHAT DOES 'CENTRAL BANK INDEPENDENCE' MEAN?

It is not clear exactly what the phrase 'central bank independence' means (Eijffinger and De Haan, 1996, p. 1), but it refers to the relationship of the central bank vis-à-vis the state. Some writers have equated that relationship to the relationship between the judiciary and the government (Eijffinger and De Haan, 1996, pp. 1–2). Just as an independent judiciary is important for the 'correct and lawful implementation of rights and freedoms' (Ferejohn, 1999, p. 353), so an independent central bank is in the best position to ensure the optimal implementation of monetary policy. Judicial independence and central bank independence are also similar in that they are not ends in themselves, but fulfil important social goals. In the case of the judiciary, its independence is justified 'by the necessity of enabling judges to fulfil their roles as guardians of the rights and freedoms of the people' (Ferejohn, 1999, p. 353). Central bank independence is justifiable because of its contribution to the common economic good.

It should be borne in mind that central banks are generally creatures of the legislature. The state legislates to provide the bank with a certain mandate, purpose, structure and independence. Consequently, the degree of central bank independence depends to an important extent on the state, as expressed in the legislative framework or founding statute of a central bank.

During the 1970s, there was considerable debate as to how the relationship between central banks and governments should be regulated, specifically with regard to the conduct of monetary policy. Although many models were proposed and at times adopted, 'inflation-targeting', a model first implemented by the Reserve Bank of New Zealand, became the most widely used method of regulating the relationship between the state and the central bank (Goodhart, 2010, p. 5). In the inflation-targeting model, setting an inflation target is the prerogative of government (usually the Treasury or the Department of Finance) and the central bank then selects the appropriate approved instruments to achieve that target within its broader mandate (Eijffinger and De Haan, 1996, pp. 2–3). The central bank is accountable to parliament (or government) in respect of meeting the inflation target through periodic addresses by the central bank governor. A central bank generally does not incur direct punitive measures for failing to meet the inflation target, although there may be some indirect negative repercussions, and for example central bank governors may feel under pressure to resign if the target is not met. In reality, most central banks only have 'instrument' independence. They can choose the manner in which monetary policy is conducted and the instruments to be used. They do not however have 'goal' independence, which would include the actual setting of the inflation target (Eijffinger and De Haan, 1996, p. 2).

An alternative characterisation of the relationship between the central bank and the state is the agency or contracting model. In this model, the central bank has a contract with government in terms whereof the central bank acts as an agent of government (Eijffinger and De Haan, 1996, pp. 10–11). Even if the central bank is not explicitly created as an agent of government, its mandate as set out in legislation may point to an agency relationship. Whilst the central bank is created as an independent entity, the state or government 'instructs' the central bank as an agent to direct its policies at a specific goal, for instance price stability, for the benefit of the state (Eijffinger and De Haan, 1996, p. 10).

Notwithstanding the legal foundations of central bank independence, it should be recognised that there may be a significant difference between legal independence, and actual or factual independence. Legal independence refers to the manner in which the independence of the central bank is guaranteed, protected or described in its founding (or other) legislation. Factual independence refers to how independent the central bank is in reality, notwithstanding the legal parameters.

There is some consensus on the factors that influence legal independence. In this regard, James highlights the following (James, 2010, pp. 13–15):

- explicit guarantees of independence;
- the manner of appointment of governors, and the removal of governors from office (how and by whom);
- the internal governance structures of central banks;
- reporting requirements of the central bank, and the rights of the government to request information from the central bank;
- the involvement of government officials in any decision-making in the central bank, in particular the monetary policy committee;
- responsibilities and mandates for setting monetary policy, including the setting of any inflation targets, where used;
- the institutional structure of the central bank, for example if it

has private shareholders, or is government owned, whether it is a corporation or not; and
- the role of the central bank as banker to government, and the ability or responsibility of the central bank to provide the executive arm of government with loans.

Factual independence, however, depends on:

> various formal and informal institutional arrangements such as the type of exchange rate regime, the ability of the bank to engage effectively in open market operations, the stance of fiscal policy and the existence of explicit institutional arrangements beyond the law that make the price-stability objective a recognised . . . objective of the [central bank]. (Cukierman, 2009, p. 73)

Factual independence can be judged by, for instance, the turnover of governors or other chief executives, especially where those positions are filled by persons appointed by the governing political party (James, 2010, p. 14). Clearly, however, viewed in isolation, the frequency of change in persons in executive positions, even if it correlates with changes in government, may not lead to decisive conclusions about factual independence. Factors such as the length of time for which governors are appointed, their pension arrangements and the possibility of reappointment are also important. Factual independence can also be judged by how a central bank views itself (James, 2010, p. 14). For example, in the eyes of an outsider, the presence of a government official on the board of a central bank may be an indication of a lack of central bank independence. In reality, the independence of the central bank may be unaffected because of conventions observed by both the central bank and the government. In fact, the entire political and social setting within which the central bank operates should be examined (James, 2010, p. 15). This may reflect, for instance, public sentiment, and general public support for the independence of the central bank (Eijffinger and De Haan, 1996, p. 51).

Important work has been done to measure central bank independence through complex indices, using different factors that indicate the extent of central bank independence. A well-known example is the Cukierman Index. Although there is evidence that legal and factual independence do not necessarily correlate in reality, the statutory nature of central banks still means that the key to their independence lies in their founding legislation, as the expressed 'will' of government. Specific powers or objectives can be clearly stipulated in legislation, or may be inferred or implied from general stipulations. In the alternative, in the absence of a specific prohibition, it can be inferred that the central bank has a specific power (BIS, 2009, p. 65). The level of central bank independence can be influenced further by the nature and status of its founding legislation. For example, better protection of independence can be derived from a 'superior' law, such as a constitution, that has additional requirements for its amendment (BIS, 2009, pp. 61–62).

The nature of the obligations placed on a central bank by legislation also influences its independence. For example, a central bank that is not obliged to lend money to the state is generally more autonomous and independent, as its monetary policy objectives will not be undermined by such loans (which are frequently given at low interest rates) (BIS, 2009, p. 67). Other factors evident in the legislation itself that have an influence on the level of independence include the clarity with which a specific mandate is given to the central bank (the more specific, the more independent the central bank will generally be).

The actual legal organisational structure and ownership of a central bank (for example whether it is a company or an incorporated association) do not appear to have a meaningful impact on the independence of a central bank (BIS, 2009, p. 65). By contrast, the nature of the state may however have a bearing on central bank independence. It has been argued that higher levels of central bank independence correlate with political structures such as federations, whilst republics may have central banks with less independence (James, 2010, p. 15). This view is however not widely accepted, and it has been suggested that constitutional factors influence central bank independence less than external economic factors (Gudmundsson, 2010, p. 26).

## 10.5 IS CENTRAL BANK INDEPENDENCE DESIRABLE?

The functions performed by central banks, in particular the conduct of monetary policy, make the independence of the central bank desirable. As referred to earlier, one of the key arguments in favour of central bank independence is that an independent monetary authority is less likely to yield to political pressure, such as pressure to lower interest rates (Eijffinger and De Haan, 1996, p. 4). Political neutrality provides a general public benefit. Ben Bernanke explains the need for and benefit of central bank independence as follows (Bernanke, 2010):

> To achieve both price stability and maximum sustainable employment, monetary policymakers must attempt to guide the economy over time toward a growth rate consistent with the expansion in its underlying productive capacity. Because monetary policy works with lags that can be substantial, achieving this

> objective requires that monetary policymakers take a longer-term perspective when making their decisions. Policymakers in an independent central bank with a mandate to achieve the best possible economic outcomes in the longer term, are best able to take such a perspective.

Furthermore, the independence of a central bank works in the public interest, because unlike the government, the central bank can more easily avoid money-creation to fund public spending (Eijffinger and De Haan, 1996, p. 5). Accordingly, higher levels of central bank independence have been linked to lower inflation, higher growth, increased investment and an improved distribution of real and nominal rates of interest (Cukierman, 2009, p. 76). An independent central bank will also be able to ward off pressures and potential temptations from the private sector better (Cukierman, 2011, p. 34).

Central bank independence however also has its critics. The most important argument against central bank independence is based on the so-called democratic deficit (Eijffinger and De Haan, 1996, p. 15). When an independent central bank is responsible for monetary policy, this function is 'socially and politically constructed as lying beyond the scope of democratic oversight and control' (Polillo and Guillén, 2005, p. 1807). Monetary policy can be said to be in essence no different from fiscal policy. Therefore monetary policy could and should also be conducted by democratically elected officials (Eijffinger and De Haan, 1996, p. 15). Whilst such criticism is valid, it is still a democratically elected parliament that in the first place drafts and approves the legislation that forms the legal framework of the central bank. In that way, fundamentally, the formation of the central bank is democratically decided (Eijffinger and De Haan, 1996, p. 15), and parliament (or the state) has ultimate control as it can change the legislation. In addition, the problem of the democratic deficit of central banks, especially in the conduct of monetary policy, can be at least partially overcome by making the central bank accountable to the democratically elected officials – for instance to parliament (or its equivalent). According to Cukierman, the 'delegation of authority to a non-elected institution should be accompanied by accountability and transparency' (Cukierman, 2009, p. 69), and this is often the case with central banks. The terms 'accountability' and 'transparency' however only became frequently used in the early 1990s when central bank independence increased generally (Cukierman, 2009, p. 69). Central bank accountability is therefore frequently considered as a necessary counterbalance to central bank independence (see generally Eijffinger and De Haan, 1996). Legislation may also divide certain tasks between the government and the central bank (Eijffinger and De Haan, 1996, p. 16), and may require the central bank to consult with government.

## 10.6 THE IMPACT OF THE GLOBAL FINANCIAL CRISIS ON CENTRAL BANKS

The GFC started on the watch of the world's central banks, and developed and intensified not only in their 'back yards', but also in their front yards (Cecchetti, 2010). The GFC ended the Great Moderation.

As the GFC unfolded, central banks were in the first line of defence against the crisis using not only their balance sheets, but also their access to money and financial markets (Lamfalussy, 2010). Responding to a financial crisis is a crucial role of central banks, a role similar to that of a firefighter (Cukierman, 2011, pp. 27, 31). Central banks are responsible for maintaining liquidity and protecting the credibility of the financial institutions, and the system as a whole (Cukierman, 2011, p. 31). This has been one of central banks' most fundamental functions since the Great Depression (Cukierman, 2011, pp. 27, 31).

As part of this response, central banks used monetary policy in an attempt to stabilise the economy. Even though interest rates were already low, they were eased further. In fact, a number of central banks simultaneously, and in consultation with each other, reduced interest rates in September 2008 (BBC, 2008) thereby demonstrating the willingness of central banks to adopt an international perspective. In fact, central banks were praised for their 'swift and internationally coordinated action' (Borio, 2011, p. 1).

Central banks also acted as lenders of last resort by providing emergency liquidity assistance to institutions. Overall in the GFC, however, central banks were forced to deviate from the classic Bagehot formulation of the lender of last resort function, according to which a central bank should, in a crisis, lend freely against good security at a high interest rate (Bagehot, 1873). In particular, central banks were obliged to lend against commercial paper (or securities) that were not of the high quality envisaged by Bagehot. Central banks were also required to use their balance sheets to an unprecedented extent, as shown by the sudden and significant change and increase in central bank balance sheets after the GFC (Cecchetti, 2010, p. 12).

The sheer size of the GFC pushed central banks into new territory.

> The result has been an increasing variety of 'non-conventional' central banking interventions . . . [T]his has led not only to the spectacular expansion of the balance sheets of central banks, but also to the radical change in the composition of their assets, which implied the acquisition of risky assets. As a result, the key central banks have started navigating in unchartered waters, in terms of both operational techniques and their relations with governments. (BIS, 2010, p. 8)

Whilst there may have been a popular expectation that central banks should have stopped the crisis, and should have done more to preserve financial stability, the reality was that central banks could not. One of the problems for central banks during the GFC was the limited range of instruments and tools at their disposal to deal with the crisis. Central banks sometimes extended the application of their instruments beyond their original limits, for example, by providing support to institutions for which they were not responsible (Mayes, 2009, p. 40).

Goodhart points out that the role of central banks in the GFC raised a number of issues (Goodhart, 2009, p. 5). Firstly, the stigma attached to banks that borrow from the central bank was again highlighted during the GFC. Fears of reputational risk may prevent banks from borrowing from the central bank (Goodhart, 2009, p. 5). Such actions may increase systemic risk and do not augur well for financial stability. Secondly, in the GFC it transpired that the liquidity needs of banks were frequently not for overnight cash, but more for one to three months' funds. It appears as if there is currently no provision for such short-medium term liquidity assistance in the toolkit of central banks (Goodhart, 2009, p. 5). Thirdly, commercial banks have in recent years started to hold less high-quality, liquid public sector assets. They relied increasingly on wholesale money markets leading to problems in the GFC when these markets dried up. Consequently commercial bank assets that were less liquid, not always of good quality, and at times even included private mortgages, were given as security for central bank liquidity assistance. Central banks virtually had no choice but to accept such security, because the alternative would be not to assist commercial banks with their liquidity shortages at all (Goodhart, 2009, p. 5).

The GFC has altered the perceived roles and functions of central banks, most notably their roles in the prevention and resolution of financial crises, and consequently, their role in ensuring financial stability (BIS, 2009, p. 5). Even though central banks were not responsible for many of the factors that contributed to the GFC, they still take pride in their expertise in relevant areas (Cecchetti, 2010, p. 1). It would be 'discordant to suggest that there is little need for [central banks] to consider a change in approach' after the GFC (Cecchetti, 2010, p. 1).

In particular, the GFC raises two significant issues in relation to central banks: (1) whether the primary responsibility of central banks should be financial stability; and (2) whether a change in primary responsibility from price stability to financial stability will result in a change to their independence and their relationship with the state (BIS, 2011, p. 7). Through their active involvement in managing the GFC, central banks may have placed two of their main achievements in jeopardy: the priority given to monetary policy (specifically price stability) and their independence (BIS, 2011, p. 7). It is however evident that the proper conduct of monetary policy did not yield financial stability (Goodhart, 2010, p. 8).

## 10.7 A POSSIBLE CHANGE TO THE ROLES OF CENTRAL BANKS: A NEW OR ADDITIONAL RESPONSIBILITY FOR FINANCIAL STABILITY

The most contentious issue faced by central banks currently is whether, and to what extent, they should be responsible for financial stability, given that their main focus is price stability. One of the key difficulties is that a responsibility for financial stability may encompass a responsibility for systemic regulation (prudential supervision of financial institutions) (Cukierman, 2011, p. 31), and not all central banks are also prudential supervisors and regulators.

### 10.7.1 What is 'Financial Stability' and Why is it Important?

It is important to first consider what the phrase 'financial stability' means. Financial stability can be defined as 'a state of affairs in which an episode of financial instability is unlikely to occur, so that fear of financial instability is not a material factor in economic decisions taken by households or businesses' (Allen and Wood, 2006, p. 160). The European Central Bank describes financial stability as 'a condition whereby the financial system is able to withstand shocks without giving way to cumulative processes, which impair the allocation of savings to investment opportunities and the processing of payments in the economy' (see ECB, n.d.). The objectives of financial stability accordingly include the strengthening of the resilience of the financial system (Jordan, 2010), and the prevention of the build-up of excesses or imbalances on asset and credit markets by actively leaning against the financial cycle (Jordan, 2010).

There is now general consensus that insufficient emphasis had been placed on financial stability before the GFC. In fact, 'achieving and preserving financial stability has now become a key policy objective in our societies' (Praet, 2011), and financial stability has come to be regarded as 'not only a national but an international public good' (Blankart and Fasten, 2009, p. 50).

The extent of financial instability that occurred in the GFC (that is, through the involvement of non-bank institutions, a severe credit crunch, and the international spread of the crisis) was not generally foreseen or anticipated. After the GFC, there has been rising support for the notion that appropriately accountable organisations should be responsible for financial stability on both a national and an international scale. Even if financial stability may result from central banks pursuing price stability, financial stability should be pursued as an objective in itself (Gran, 2010).

The reinvention of the Financial Stability Forum as the Financial Stability Board (FSB) by the G-20 displays the importance of a focus on financial stability at an international level. The G-20 have widely acknowledged the importance of financial stability, for example in their Paris Communiqué in February 2011 (G-20, 2011). At their Seoul Summit in November 2010, the G-20 demonstrated the importance of appropriate structures and authorities for financial stability when it requested the FSB to consider its own structure as well as any increased need for additional resources. The role of the IMF has also been adjusted to provide for a focus on international financial stability. In this regard, the IMF cooperates with the FSB in tasks such as country reports and early warning reports (IMF, 2011).

### 10.7.2 Do Central Banks already have a Responsibility for Financial Stability?

Many argue that there is already an obligation for financial stability on central banks (Hicks, 2009, p. 450; Group of Thirty, 2009, pp. 1–2). This may be the case even if it is not an express obligation, as is for instance the case with the European Central Bank and the Reserve Bank of New Zealand (Bollard and Delbruck, 2011, p. 8).

Goodhart and Cukierman are of the view that central banks have always had two objectives: price stability and financial stability (Goodhart, 2010, p. 1; Cukierman, 2009, p. 69). The conventional view has long been that financial stability is a by-product of price stability, and that an effective monetary policy would result in financial stability. However, achieving price stability does not automatically ensure macroeconomic stability (Shirakawa, 2010). Also, central banks may assume responsibility for financial stability (even though this may not be their explicit legal mandate) (McCracken and Everett, 2009, p. 24) in order to ensure that they may give effect to their monetary policy mandate. In reality, the effective conduct of monetary policy depends on financial stability. Financial stability can therefore be seen as an implied obligation.

A responsibility for financial stability is not only linked to the monetary policy obligation. The lender of last resort function of central banks also implies that central banks have a responsibility for financial stability. The provision of emergency liquidity assistance (as lender of last resort) is an instrument that could promote or secure financial system stability by preventing or counteracting systemic risk created by a failing institution (Shirakawa, 2010).

Judging by the large number of financial stability reports published by central banks, one may conclude that they have accepted or assumed that they in fact do have a financial stability responsibility, perhaps as an inherent power. For example, on its website the Reserve Bank of Australia (RBA) highlights its role in monitoring the health of the Australian financial system and the publication of the findings in the *Financial Stability Review* published twice a year, as well as the contribution to financial stability it makes through managing crisis situations (RBA, 2011).

### 10.7.3 Should Central Banks be Responsible for Financial Stability?

Notwithstanding differences of opinion as to whether central banks are already responsible for financial stability, there appears to an overwhelming emerging consensus that they should be responsible for financial stability (see BIS, 2011, pp. 1, 12 and further). The so-called 'Jackson Hole consensus', according to which central banks had a minimal role to play in financial stability by maintaining price stability and minimising the effects of burst bubbles, has broken down (Praet, 2011).

The view that central banks should be responsible for financial stability is shared by a number of influential central bankers, including Stefan Ingves, Governor of the Swedish central bank (Sveriges Riksbank), Masaaki Shirakawa, Governor of the Bank of Japan, Charles Goodhart (previously attached to the Bank of England), and Lucas Papademos (former Vice-President of the European Central Bank, ECB). Academics and economists such as Otto Hieronymi also support this view.

It is important to note that Goodhart, one of the most influential thinkers in central banking, has always maintained that price stability was the first core purpose of a central bank, with the lender of last resort function and financial stability as secondary objectives (Goodhart, 2009, p. 35). Recently though, Goodhart concluded that financial stability, and not price stability, is the key function of a central bank (Goodhart, 2010, p. 19). He argues that the function of conducting and setting monetary policy can be outsourced to a specialist committee or a government department, such as the Ministry of Finance (Goodhart, 2010, p. 5). It is however only the central bank that, by using its balance sheet, can enhance financial stability (Goodhart, 2010, p. 19).

The importance of a financial stability function for central banks is emphasised in the reports from both the US Government Accountability Office, Financial Regulation, and the Group of Thirty (US GAO, 2009;

Group of Thirty 2009; Hicks, 2009, pp. 450, 454). These two reports however emphasise different points. The first adopts a strong domestic focus, and argues that the Federal Reserve should maintain financial stability internally within the United States, whilst the second emphasises the importance of the role of central banks in financial stability in global financial markets. (Hicks, 2009, pp. 450, 454).

In some jurisdictions, central banks have already been more involved in financial stability after the GFC. In the European Union, for example, the European Systemic Risk Board (ESRB) was created as a direct response to the GFC, following recommendations by the de Larosière report that it was necessary to focus on the stability of the entire financial system (ESRB, n.d.). The ESRB has 'the sole task of monitoring macro-prudential developments and risks' (BIS, 2011, p. 23). The ESRB is strongly supported by central banks, in particular the ECB, as the majority of the members of its General Board are in fact central bankers (Praet, 2011).

In the United States, the Financial Stability Oversight Council (FSOC) was established as a federal body by the Dodd–Frank Wall Street Reform and Consumer Protection Act, 12 USC (2010) (Dodd–Frank Act). The FSOC is charged with identifying and mitigating threats to financial stability in the United States. The Chairman of the Board of Governors of the Federal Reserve, as one of the voting members on the FSOC, gives the Federal Reserve an important role on the FSOC (US Treasury, 2010). In addition, the Dodd–Frank Act also places other important financial stability responsibilities directly on the Federal Reserve. These include additional oversight responsibilities and the adoption of a macro-prudential approach to supervision and regulation, which considers the risks to 'overall financial stability in addition to the safety and soundness of individual firms' (Bernanke, 2011).

In the United Kingdom, the Bank of England now has an objective for financial stability, encapsulated in the Bank of England Act 1998 under which it must 'contribute to protecting and enhancing the stability of the financial systems of the United Kingdom' (Bank of England Act 1998, Section 2A). In addition, the United Kingdom (UK) government established an interim Financial Policy Committee (FPC) in the Bank of England in 2011. The FPC is predominantly staffed by the Bank of England and should contribute to the financial stability objective of the Bank of England by 'identifying, monitoring, and taking action to remove or reduce, systemic risks with a view to protecting and enhancing the resilience of the UK financial system' (Bank of England website, http://www.bankofengland.co.uk/financialstability/fpc/index.htm). In particular, the FPC is charged with identifying risks to financial stability in the UK and making recommendations as to how to deal with those issues (Kohn, 2011).

Lastra however holds a contrary view, that financial stability should not be the primary responsibility of central banks. In her opinion, ensuring financial stability is a function of the state (government). Accordingly, the central bank's responsibility for financial stability would only be a delegated responsibility with the ultimate responsibility remaining that of government (De Haan and Oosterloo, 2006, p. 262).

It would be possible for the responsibility for financial stability to be shared between the central bank and other institutions (Cukierman, 2011, p. 32). Practically, however, modern-day central banks have extensive research departments populated with experts, and central banks are well placed to monitor systemic risk. Nevertheless, the central bank will have to be provided with appropriate instruments to ensure financial stability, and the role of the central bank in financial stability will have to be clearly defined (Goodhart, 2010, p. 9).

### 10.7.4 What would the Consequences be of Mandating Central Banks with a Financial Stability Responsibility?

#### Financial stability should be an express legal obligation

A central bank's responsibility for financial stability should, ideally, be expressly included in the founding legislation of the central bank and be stated as a key task (De Haan and Oosterloo, p. 260). One of the difficulties requiring attention is the vague language used to describe existing financial stability obligations. Verbs such as 'contribute to' or 'promote' are often used (De Haan and Oosterloo, 2006, pp. 261, 268) but terminology that clearly establishes the obligation should be adopted.

As referred to above, the obligation for financial stability is seen as being implied in the founding legislation, or as inherent to the functioning of a central bank. The position of the RBA is a case in point. The Reserve Bank Act 1959 does not explicitly confer a responsibility to ensure financial stability on the RBA, but it is accepted by the Australian Federal Government that the RBA is responsible for financial stability (De Haan and Oosterloo, 2006, p. 261). This opinion is shared by academics (McCracken and Everett, 2009), and the RBA itself (RBA website, http://www.rba.gov.au/fin-stability/about.html). Another example is the European Central Bank (ECB). The wording of both the Maastricht Treaty and the Statute of the European System of Central Banks and of the European Central Bank have been criticised for being vague (Lamfalussy, 2010, p. 7). For instance, in terms of the Treaty, the ECB 'shall contribute to the smooth conduct of policies pursued by the competent authorities relating to the prudential supervision of credit institutions and the stability of the financial system' (Maastricht Treaty, Article 105 (5); and Lamfalussy, 2010, p. 7). In terms of the Protocol on the Statute of the European System of Central Banks and of the European Central Bank (ESCB Statute), the ECB 'may offer advice to and be consulted by' various parties 'on the scope and implementation of Community legislation relating to the prudential supervision of credit institutions and to the stability of the financial system' (ESCB Statute Art. 25.1; and Lamfalussy, 2010, p. 7).

In the case of some central banks, their financial stability obligation is not mandated in legislation at all. The Bank of England was such an example. Although the Bank of England had previously accepted financial stability as one of its objectives, until recently, it was charged with the 'overall stability of the financial system as a whole' merely by way of a letter from the Chancellor of the Exchequer directed to the Governor of the Bank (De Haan and Oosterloo, 2006, p. 261). This obligation was confirmed in a non-binding memorandum of understanding between the Bank of England, HM Treasury and (what was then) the Financial Services Authority (De Haan and Oosterloo, 2006, p. 268). The Financial Policy Committee (FPC) within the Bank of England was initially established by agreement between the Bank and the government, and the FPC itself is to advise the government on the tools it requires for financial stability (Kohn, 2011).

Failing to provide an express and explicit legislated responsibility and authority for financial stability has important implications. Gaps in the legal framework may lead to suboptimal functioning and a failure to meet the legislative intent. Vague goals also create operational difficulties for institutions, and it may be very difficult to hold an institution accountable for failing to meet an obligation that is not clearly stipulated. If an obligation to ensure financial stability is merely implied, the performance of the responsible institution cannot be adequately evaluated or monitored (De Haan and Oosterloo, 2006, p. 262). This is an important consideration as central banks should be held accountable. In addition, a poorly described legislative objective or duty may be open to incorrect interpretation, and the concept of 'financial stability' should therefore be clearly defined or described. From the point of view of good governance, it is preferable to establish a clear legal basis for central bank actions relating to financial stability, and to formulate the functions and powers of the central bank with regard to financial stability clearly (see for example BIS, 2011, p. 1 and further).

Part of the difficulty lies in the fact that financial stability as such is harder to define than price stability, and objectives for financial stability are more difficult to set than those for monetary policy (De Haan and Oosterloo, 2006, p. 267). A monetary policy framework generally sets one goal, provides one instrument and gives the responsibility to one institution. It is, however, more challenging to formulate clear objectives for the financial stability function. Also, the manner in which central bank legislation is drafted may not allow for a very specific formulation of such objectives (BIS, 2009, p. 3). In addition, there is no single 'financial stability instrument' (rather, there are several, including prudential supervision, the provision of emergency liquidity assistance, and the dissemination of financial stability information through financial stability reviews).

**The relationship between a responsibility for financial stability and the supervision of financial institutions**

Allocating a responsibility for financial stability to an institution cannot be done without consideration of who carries the responsibility for macro-prudential regulation and supervision. The GFC highlighted the difficulties for central banks if they are not also the supervisors of banks, and emphasised that if the central bank is not the supervisor, then it needs a very close relationship with the supervisor (Mayes, 2009, p. 40). For example, the United States (US) has adopted the so-called 'integrated model' (Mayes, 2009, p. 40), and the bank supervision function is housed inside the Federal Reserve. The Bank of England will also be responsible for bank supervision (again) from 2013 (see HM Treasury, 2010).

**Appropriate tools for managing financial stability**

If a central bank is made responsible for financial stability, regardless of the exact ambit of the responsibility (whether the central bank has to 'monitor', 'supervise', 'promote', 'create', 'contribute to' or 'ensure' financial stability), it will need appropriate tools to give effect to its mandate and responsibilities.

It is likely that central banks will also need additional macro-prudential instruments that target financial stability goals (Bollard and Cassino, 2011). Further, if the central bank is not also the micro-prudential supervisor, appropriate measures should be in place to provide access to information of supervised institutions, preferably in the founding legislation of the central bank. For example, the RBA's right to access to such information is not legislated. The resultant gap is filled by the Memorandum of Understanding between the RBA, the Australian Prudential Regulation Authority (APRA) and the Australian Securities and Investments Commission (ASIC) (McCracken and Everett, 2009, pp. 26–27), although its effectiveness has never been tested in practice. In addition, some of the tools available for improving financial stability including the setting of capital requirements, liquidity ratios and leverage ratios for financial institutions (Goodhart, 2010, p. 9) are micro-prudential in nature and not within the powers of a central bank if it is not also the bank supervisor. Such a potential gap should be addressed.

At the start of, and during, the GFC the difficulty for central banks was not insufficient information, but rather that they lacked effective tools to maintain financial stability (Goodhart, 2009, p. 30). However, Goodhart does not provide an immediate answer to his poignant question as to what can be done to give central banks 'balls' (Goodhart, 2009, p. 31).

Nevertheless, some of the existing tools of central banks can be used, even if only indirectly, to further financial stability. In fact, a number of existing core central bank tasks already promote the safeguarding of financial stability. Whilst lending ratios are widely used, other tools also include:

- the provision of liquidity to the financial system, including payment and settlement system oversight,
- the formulation of macro-prudential policies aimed at preventing and mitigation systemic risks; and
- the regulation and supervision (including micro-prudential supervision) of financial institutions. (BIS, 2010, p. 26)

Furthermore, the ability of the central bank to act as lender of last resort and provide emergency liquidity assistance is also considered one of the tools that the central bank can use to manage financial stability (Hicks, 2009, p. 450). Monetary policy, however, does not appear to be the ideal tool to promote financial stability (Mishkin, 2010, p. 47).

The publication of a financial stability report can also be considered as an existing tool for procuring financial stability as it publicly communicates the central bank's assessment of financial stability and informs decision-making (De Haan and Oosterloo, 2006, p. 265). An increasing number of central banks now publish a separate financial stability report, irrespective of whether they have a legislated mandate for financial stability (De Haan and Oosterloo, 2006, p. 263). Fundamentally, however, a report has no coercive power and is, at best, only persuasive.

## 10.8 A CHANGE IN THE RELATIONSHIP BETWEEN THE CENTRAL BANK AND THE STATE: CAN CENTRAL BANK INDEPENDENCE BE AT RISK?

A responsibility for financial stability cannot be seen, either in focus or in effect, as a purely domestic responsibility. Such was one of the important lessons of the GFC: systemic risk is a global issue. The recent focus internationally on the regulation of systemically important financial institutions bears testimony to the heightened awareness globally not only of the importance of financial stability, but also of the connectedness and inter-relationships of the global financial system.

A new or more explicit responsibility for financial stability may impact on the existing relationship between the central bank and the state, as a financial stability responsibility may radically change the functions of a central bank (Goodhart, 2010, pp. 9, 10). In fact, central bank independence may be at risk:

> The risk arises from the obvious fact that having to comply with two distinct mandates pushes the central bank into a much more complex world. The modalities of their independence in their monetary policy function may be debatable, but, once agreed, the terms of independence can be reasonably well defined. In the case of the macro prudential mandate . . . this is much more difficult. Once it appears that an initial liquidity problem is mutating into a solvency problem, and especially when the latter implies the risk of a systemic meltdown, the central bank has to operate hand in hand with the government. (BIS, 2011, p. 11)

It is therefore likely that central bank independence 'is likely to come under increasing threat' (Borio, 2011, p. 1). If central banks are responsible for financial stability and fulfil the more far-reaching financial stability function, the democratic deficit may become more obvious, because of potential threats to public funds. Ultimately, prudential supervision and the provision of lender of last resort assistance are 'very hard to depoliticise' (Singleton, 2010, p. 28). In response, political pressure may lead to a reconsideration and reduction of the independence of central banks. This threat may arise if central bank actions appear to be or are similar to the fiscal actions of governments.

> [T]he current controversy surrounding central bank independence within informed circles has little to do with monetary policy independence . . . and very much to do with the ability of the central bank to engage in unconventional market interventions which bear a high similarity to fiscal policy. (Stella, 2010, p. 14)

In uncertain times (such as when decisions regarding financial stability have to be made) politicians will likely resist central bank independence, and may even resort to making the decisions themselves (Singleton, 2010, p. 28). Central banks may also experience more government pressure after a crisis (Cukierman, 2011, p. 34).

Further, central banks may be forced to lose their international focus if, in response to the GFC, they are forced to adopt a singular domestic focus (Hieronymi, 2009, p. xiv). In order to protect domestic financial stability, it may be necessary to focus on and strengthen 'monetary nationalism' (Hieronymi, 2009, p. xiv). In this manner, the international characteristic of central banks that have always increased their independence may be reduced, or lost.

An independent central bank which is highly important through its sheer impact, importance and responsibilities, especially if it has not only the monetary policy objective but also the key role in ensuring financial stability, may appear to be a political threat. A perception that the democratic deficit may become larger or more significant may result in central bank independence being reduced by government in an attempt to protect state power and sovereignty. However, contrary to what may have been expected, and notwithstanding criticism of the actions of central banks before and during the GFC, the responsibilities of some central banks such as the Federal Reserve and the Bank of England have in fact been increased after the GFC.

A pragmatic resolution of the problem of the independence of central banks with additional financial stability mandates would be to develop a range of definitions of central bank independence, based on functional distinctions. Central banks already fulfil a variety of functions, which correspond to different levels of interaction with the state. Although such a situation may be complex, it is not improbable that it could result. The RBA, for example, currently has two boards based on functional distinctions: the Reserve Bank Board and the Payment Systems Board (with the latter being subservient to the Reserve Bank Board in the event of a conflict). It is therefore theoretically possible that a 'Financial Stability Board' could be created in a central bank that would function alongside the Monetary Policy Committee or Board.

Globalisation and internationalisation may also impact on the future independence of central banks, and their relationship with the state. Generally, the international focus of central banks enhances their independence (see James, 2010), and an explicit responsibility for financial stability will require domestic central banks to increase their international focus. Other aspects of globalisation and the internationalisation of finance also point to an increase in central bank independence, which may meet with political resistance. For example, the collaboration between central banks through the Committee of Central Bank Governors at the BIS, and perhaps even at the G-20, increases the level of independence of central banks from the state. Furthermore, '[t]he globalisation of financial systems also affects the role of central banks in the *design of financial regulation and supervision*. This role is played by central banks because they either have a direct supervisory responsibility or act in an advisory capacity to governments' (Trichet, 2007). The role of regulators may have to be enlarged as there is an increasing need globally for a consistent approach (Trichet, 2007). When central banks perform this role to a greater extent, the likely impact on the relationship between the central bank and the state cannot be ignored. Sceptics may even point out that a conflict of interest between national and international interests could arise. Ultimately, political pressure because of a perceived threat to state sovereignty may lead to a reduction or redefinition of the independence of central banks.

## 10.9 LESSONS LEARNT?

During a crisis, there may not be sufficient time or opportunity for theoretical musings. It is necessary that, at the end of the GFC and its immediate aftermath, the theoretical underpinnings of the financial system, and also of the role of the different public authorities including central banks, should be reconsidered. In fact it is common for a theoretical revolution to follow a financial crisis (see generally Goodhart, 2010). It is important to redevelop the theoretical framework that will include central banks, their roles and their relationships to government. Central bank independence will likely be an important consideration in such a debate. A discussion of the mandate, role and function of central banks is important because it facilitates the necessary thorough understanding of the long-term implications of the GFC (BIS, 2011, p. 2). As Hieronymi (2009, p. 25) points out, one should however, with central bank independence, as with most other things, always be careful of letting the pendulum swing too far too fast.

## NOTE

* The assistance of Professors John Farrar and David Mayes in the preparation of this chapter is gratefully acknowledged. Also, this chapter was significantly improved by the comments from Assistant Professor Tammy Johnson, together with feedback and comments received at the Conference on Globalisation, the GFC and the State, held at Bond University in July 2011.

## REFERENCES

Allen, W.A. and G. Wood (2006), 'Defining and Achieving Financial Stability', *Journal of Financial Stability*, **2**(2), 152–172.

Bagehot, Walter (1873), *Lombard Street*, London: Henry S. King.
Bank for International Settlements (BIS) (2009), 'Issues in the Governance of Central Banks: A Report from the Central Bank Governance Group May 2009', electronic version, contains minor updates up to 25 May 2009, http://www.bis.org/publ/othp04.pdf, accessed 10 April 2012.
Bank for International Settlements (BIS) (2010), 'The Future of Central Banking under Post-Crisis Mandates', BIS Working Paper No. 55, Bank for International Settlements Monetary and Economic Department, 24–25 June, http://www.bis.org/publ/bppdf/bispap55.pdf, accessed 10 April 2012.
Bank for International Settlements (BIS) (2011), 'Central Bank Governance and Financial Stability', report by a Study Group chaired by Stefan Ingves, May, http://www.bis.org/publ/othp14.pdf, accessed 10 April 2012.
BBC (2008), 'Central Banks Cut Interest Rates', *BBC News*, 8 October, http://news.bbc.uk/2/hi/business/7658958.stm, accessed 10 April 2012.
Bernanke, Ben S. (2004), 'The Great Moderation', speech delivered at the meetings of the Eastern Economic Association, Washington, 20 February.
Bernanke, Ben S. (2010), 'Central Bank Independence, Transparency, and Accountability', speech delivered at the Institute for Monetary and Economic Studies International Conference, Bank of Japan, Tokyo, 26 May.
Bernanke, Ben S. (2011), 'Dodd–Frank Implementation: Monitoring Systemic Risk and Promoting Financial Stability', testimony before the Committee on Banking, Housing, and Urban Affairs, US Senate, Washington DC, 12 May.
Blankart, Charles B. and Erik R. Fasten (2009), 'Financial Crisis Resolution – The State as a Lender of Last Resort?' *Economic Affairs*, **29**(3), 47–52.
Blinder, Alan S. (2004), *The Quiet Revolution: Central Banking Goes Modern*, New Haven, CT: Yale University Press.
Bollard, Alan and Enzo Cassino (2011), 'Economic Surveillance after the Crisis: Reflections from a Small Full Service Central Bank', speech delivered at the Sim Kee Boon Institute Conference on Financial Economics, Singapore, 5 May.
Bollard, Alan and Felix Delbruck (2011), 'The Crisis and Monetary Policy: What We Learned and Where We Are Going', background paper, Bank of New Zealand, 29 January, http://www.bis.org/review/r100202a.pdf, accessed 10 April 2012.
Borio, Claudio (2011), 'Central Banking Post-Crisis: What Compass for Unchartered Waters?' Bank for International Settlements, Working Papers No 353, September, http://www.bis.org/publ/work353.pdf, accessed 10 April 2012.
Cecchetti, Stephen G. (2010), 'Introductory Remarks', Ninth Bank for International Settlements Annual Conference, Basel, 24–25 June, published in Bank for International Settlements Papers No. 55, http://www.bis.org/publ/bppdf/bispap55.pdf, accessed 27 August 2012.
Cukierman, Alex (2009), 'Central Bank Independence and Monetary Policy-Making Institutions Past, Present and Future', in David Mayes and Geoffrey E. Wood (eds), *Designing Central Banks*, Abingdon: Routledge.
Cukierman, Alex (2011), 'Reflections on the Crisis and on its Lessons for Regulatory Reform and for Central Bank Policies', *Journal of Financial Stability*, **7**(1), 26–37.
De Haan, Jakob and Sander Oosterloo (2006), 'Transparency and Accountability of Central Banks in their Role of Financial Stability Supervisor in OECD Countries', *European Journal of Law and Economics*, **22**(3), 255–271.
Eijffinger, Sylvester C.W. and Jakob De Haan (1996), 'The Political Economy of

Central-Bank Independence', Special Papers in International Economics No 19, International Finance Section, Department of Economics, Princeton University, http://www.princeton.edu/~ies/IES_Special_Papers/SP19.pdf, accessed 10 April 2012.

Epstein, Gerald (2006), 'Central Banks as Agents of Economic Development', Research Paper No 2006/54, United Nations University, http://www.wider.unu.edu/publications/working-papers/research-papers/2006/en_GB/rp2006-54/_files/78091779622373109/default/rp2006-54.pdf, accessed 10 April 2012.

European Central Bank (ECB) (n.d.), 'Financial Stability Review', http://www.ecb.int/pub/fsr/html/index.en.html, accessed 10 April 2012.

European Systemic Risk Board (ESRB) (n.d.), 'Establishment of the ESRB', http://www.esrb.europa.eu/about/background/html/index.en.html, accessed 10 April 2012.

Ferejohn, John (1999), 'Independent Judges, Dependent Judiciary: Explaining Judicial Independence', *Southern California Law Review*, **72**, 353–384.

G-20 (2010), 'Seoul Summit Leaders' Declaration', http://www.g20.org/images/stories/docs/eng/seoul.pdf , accessed 10 April 2012.

G-20 (2011), Paris Communiqué, Communiqué Meeting of Finance Ministers and Central Bank Governors, Paris, 18–19 February, http://www.g20.org/images/stories/canalfinan/docs/08comu.pdf, accessed 10 April 2012.

Gnan, Ernest (2010), 'Are Price Stability and Financial Stability Complementary or Contradictory Mandates? Four Issues' (Speech delivered at the 38th Economics Conference 2010, Oesterreichische Nationalbank, 2010).

Goodhart, Charles A.E. (2009), *The Regulatory Response to the Financial Crisis*, Cheltenham, UK and Northampton, MA, USA: Edward Elgar.

Goodhart, Charles A.E. (2010), 'The Changing Role of Central Banks' (Bank for International Settlements Working Paper No 326, November 2010), http://www.bis.org/publ/work326.pdf, accessed 10 April 2012.

Goodman, John B. (1991), 'The Politics of Central Bank Independence', *Comparative Politics*, **23**(3), 329–349.

Group of Thirty (2009), 'Financial Reform: A Framework for Financial Stability', http://fic.wharton.upenn.edu/fic/policy%20page/G30Report.pdf, accessed 10 April 2012.

Gudmundsson, Már (2010), 'Comments on Harold James's Paper "Central Banks: Between Internationalisation and Domestic Political Control"', Bank for International Settlements Working Papers No 327, November, http://www.bis.org/publ/work327.pdf, accessed 10 April 2012.

Hicks, Rebecca (2009), 'A Potential New Role for Central Banks: A Comparison of Expert Proposals for Reform, Developments in Banking and Financial Law', *Review of Banking and Financial Law*, **28**, 448–457.

Hieronymi, Otto (ed.) (2009), *Globalization and the Reform of the International Banking and Monetary System*, New York: Palgrave Macmillan Studies in Banking and Financial Institutions.

HM Treasury (2010), 'A New Approach to Financial Regulation: Judgement, Focus and Stability', United Kingdom, Cm 7874, 26 July, http://www.hm-treasury.gov.uk/d/consult_financial_regulation_condoc.pdf, accessed 10 April 2012.

IMF (2011), 'Factsheet FSB Early Warning Exercise, 13 April 2011', http://www.imf.org/external/np/exr/facts/ewe.htm, accessed 10 April 2012.

James, Harold (2010), 'Central Banks: Between Internationalisation and Domestic

Political Control', Bank for International Settlements Working Papers No 327, November, http://www.bis.org/publ/work327.pdf, accessed 10 April 2012.
Jordan, Thomas J. (2010), 'The Interaction of Monetary and Macro-Prudential Policy', speech delivered at the Bank of Japan Conference, 27 May.
Kohn, Donald (2011), 'The Financial Policy Committee at the Bank of England', speech delivered at the US Department of the Treasury Conference, 2 December.
Lamfalussy, Alexandre (2010), 'Keynote speech', Ninth Bank for International Settlements Annual Conference, Basel, 24–25 June; published in Bank for International Settlements Papers No 55, http://www.bis.org/publ/bppdf/bispap55.pdf, accessed 27 August 2012.
Mayes, David (2009), 'The Role of Central Banks in Financial Supervision and Regulation', *Economic Affairs*, **29**(3), 40–46.
McCracken, Sheilagh and Anna Everett (2009), *Everett and McCracken's Banking and Financial Institutions Law*, 7th edn, Pyrmont, OH: Lawbook Co.
Mishkin, Frederic S. (2010), 'Monetary Policy Strategy: Lessons from the Crisis', CB Central banking Conference, Monetary Policy Revisited: Lessons from the Crisis, Frankfurt, 18–19 November, http://rse.anu.edu.au/seminars/documents/10ecbnber.pdf, accessed 28 August 2012.
Otahal, Tomas (2011), 'Rent-seeking Origins of Central Banks: The Case of the Federal Reserve System', MEDELA Working Papers in Business and Economics, No 8/2011, Model University in Brno, http://ideas.repec.org/p/men/wpaper/08_2011.html, accessed 10 April 2012.
Polillo, Simone and Mauro F. Guillén (2005), 'Globalisation Pressures and the State: The Spread of Central Bank Independence', *American Journal of Sociology*, **110**(6), 1764–1802.
Praet, Peter (2011), 'The (Changing) Role of Central Banks in Financial Stability Policies', speech delivered at the 14th Annual Internal Banking Conference, Federal Reserve Bank of Chicago and European Central Bank, Chicago, IL, 10 November.
Reserve Bank of Australia (RBA) (2011), 'About Financial Stability', http://www.rba.gov.au/fin-stability/about.html, accessed 10 April 2012.
Shirakawa, Masaaki (2010), 'Future of Central Banks and Central Banking', Opening Speech delivered at the International Conference of the Bank of Japan, Tokyo, 26 May.
Singleton, John (2010), 'The Winds of Change for Central Banks', *Central Banking*, **20**(3), http://www.centralbanking.com/central-banking-journal/feature/2043798/winds-change-central-banks, accessed 10 April 2012.
Stella, Peter (2010), 'Minimizing Monetary Policy', conference paper at the Bank for International Settlements Conference, 24 June, http://www.bis.org/events/conf100624/stellapaper.pdf, accessed 10 April 2012.
Trichet, Jean-Claude (2007), 'The Role of Central Banks in a Globalised Economy', speech delivered on the occasion of the 13th Conférence de Montréal, Montreal, 18 June.
United States Government Accountability Office (US GAO) (2009), 'Report to Congressional Addressees January 2009, Financial Regulation: A Framework for Crafting and Assessing Proposals to Modernize the Outdated US Financial Regulatory System GAO-09-216', http://www.gao.gov/new.items/d09216.pdf, accessed 10 April 2012.
US Treasury (2010), 'Financial Stability Oversight Council Created Under the Dodd–Frank Wall Street Reform and Consumer Protection Act: Frequently

Asked Questions', October, http://www.treasury.gov/initiatives/Documents/FAQ%20-%20FinancialStabilityOversightCouncilOctober2010FINALv2.pdf, accessed 10 April 2012.

## LEGISLATION

Australia (Commonwealth)
Payment Systems (Regulation) Act 1998
European Union
Protocol on the Statute of the European System of Central Banks and of the European Central Bank.
Treaty of Maastricht, formally the Treaty on European Union, signed on 7 February 1992
South Africa
Constitution of the Republic of South Africa Act 1996 (South Africa)
United States of America (Federal)
Dodd–Frank Wall Street Reform and Consumer Protection Act, 12 USC (2010).

# 11. The euro crisis*

**David G. Mayes**

## 11.1 INTRODUCTION

The third phase of the global financial crisis (GFC) has been focused on the fears of sovereign default in Europe and the attempts that are being made to manage the problem in ways that will not have an unnecessarily severe impact on the real economy. The structure of Economic and Monetary Union (EMU) in the European Union (EU) has contributed both to the problem and to the difficulty in finding a lasting solution. This experience has revealed fundamental problems in the process of integration and the role of the state. This chapter focuses on the nature of the problem and the plausible ways out – not simply to end this phase of the GFC but to provide a sustainable future path for EMU and continuing integration in Europe and elsewhere round the world. The GFC has emphasised the extent of interconnection among economies through globalisation and the advantages of international cooperation and coordination in the avoidance and management of crises.

The common response has been to suggest that either increased integration is required, particularly at the political level, or that some countries should leave the euro area. This chapter suggests, however, that the original concept was workable, even in the face of shock as large as the GFC, had the agreed rules been applied. It is now more difficult to follow this path, given the poor fiscal discipline of many of the participating countries, but a revised pact, involving not just a more plausible procedure for correcting potential excessive deficits but also a stronger procedure for improving the debt position of all members steadily – the so-called preventative arm – could still work. It is this route which was chosen in the 21 July 2011 agreement. By the time of the next agreement on 26 October 2011, it had become clear that the position of Greece, the most heavily indebted country, was only recoverable with a considerable write-down of privately held government debt, agreed at 50 per cent (and since increased), and a recapitalisation of European banks. A package of six measures to try to ensure future stability had also been agreed. By March

2012, the write-down of debt had been agreed by the holders of Greek bonds and the Greek Parliament had passed all the measures that the EU and International Monetary Fund (IMF) had demanded of the government to help move towards a sustainable fiscal position.

These measures and attempts to 'leverage' the European Financial Stability Facility (EFSF) by allowing it to take the first loss rather than underwrite all new debt from troubled countries still did not convince markets and the outside world that Greece or the other potential problem countries, Ireland, Italy, Portugal and Spain could be handled. It is difficult to decide whether the chosen recipe will work, not least because it is not clear whether Greece will accept it over the coming years. The present government has agreed all that is needed but political turmoil and public discontent brought the previous government down and a technocratic government had to be appointed under the leadership of a former vice-president of the European Central Bank to try to shift the problem above politics. However, the problems are not ended by this as it depends whether the changes implemented are sufficient to return to a sustainable financial position.

The political pressure exists in all five member states and the governments have all changed. In Italy the prime minister resigned on 8 November 2011 and was also replaced by a technocrat regime headed by a former EU commissioner. As a result most of the measures desired by the EU have been agreed. The new Spanish government passed a major austerity package, but as in Ireland where the economy still appears to be in recession it is not clear that recovery path will work.

Success is also debatable because the willingness of the other member states to contribute more is limited – as evidenced by the difficulty in getting agreement to the previous 21 July measures and then to what has been described as a 'fiscal treaty' in March 2012 (Treaty on Stability, Coordination and Governance in the Economic and Monetary Union). However, the countries have agreed, at least for the time being to keep both the EFSF and the ESM (European Stability Mechanism) in being.[1]

These pressures from the GFC have affected the role of the state in the euro area in at least seven obvious ways:

- Countries with difficulties in funding their debts have had to seek relief from their partners and the IMF, which has entailed conformity with strict conditions – in common with earlier IMF support.
- The other partners have had to offer funding despite a no-bail-out clause.
- Countries have proved very susceptible to spillover effects from others in financial markets and have not been able to address these

fully on their own, thereby enhancing the degree of cooperation in financial markets.
- Cross-border banking problems have revealed that cross-country cooperation agreements are inadequate and that interests can conflict.
- Previous means of trying to limit fiscal spillovers in the euro area through the Stability and Growth Pact (SGP) have been inadequate.
- The expected problems posed by the single monetary policy for countries in difficulty have fully materialised.
- The limits of the willingness to pay for other countries' actions have been exposed.

All of these concerns have an impact on economic sovereignty. Whether they represent a loss of sovereignty or whether in any sense the joining of the euro area represents an increase in sovereignty are complex questions to answer. Small countries did not have much sovereignty beforehand and were highly dependent upon the decisions of large countries, the views of financial markets and shocks to the system that were beyond their control. The degree to which any one country with a specific problem has control over the operation of common policies in the euro area is normally almost zero. Until, that is, they become a threat to the system. Some larger countries, such as France, Spain and Italy, now have more control over their destiny than was the case where in the earlier years of the European Monetary System (EMS) Germany effectively determined the general alignment of policy for its own domestic benefit. Germany consequently must therefore have less sovereignty than before.

The system is not completely lopsided, otherwise small countries would not have joined. If they are not to subject to idiosyncratic shocks, they gain through the lower interest rates and greater stability of being part of the wider area – in part from being able to diversify their wealth in the larger euro area and hence provide a greater measure of self-insurance. All gain from lower transaction costs and reduced barriers but the small countries have a serious problem in the event of an idiosyncratic downward shock, as illustrated by Ireland (and the Baltic States) in the GFC. Here the trade-off between the years of gain and the years of harsh adjustment comes into play. No doubt electors are revisiting the judgements they made before deciding to join the euro area – if they were given a choice, that is.

The main issue is that the process is highly asymmetric. Not only do the states with the fiscal problems have to make the adjustment themselves to return to prudence, but a downward adjustment is immensely more difficult than an upward one.

The subsequent sections deal in turn with the nature of the predicament the euro area faces; how the system was intended to work; and how the fiscal and financial problems might be addressed, before concluding. However, the primary concern here is not with solution to the crisis per se but with the implications that the crisis and its likely resolution have for the role of the state.

## 11.2 THE CURRENT PREDICAMENT

The problem that the euro area faces at present is that a number of countries, Greece, Ireland, Italy, Portugal and Spain (unkindly referred to as the PIIGS in the popular press) have accumulated levels of public sector debt that, in combination with present fiscal deficits, lead lenders to think that they may not be repaid in full. As a result the spreads that most of these countries are being asked to pay on new debt and rolling over the existing debt are such that the burden would be so high that the default that is feared would be triggered. Other than Greece, the countries themselves are convinced and have thus far succeeded in persuading both their EU colleagues and the IMF that they can manage to reorganise their budgets in such a way that they can service the debt in the short run and run down the excess so that it is sustainable in the long run. Provided, that is, that the EU and the IMF offer rates of interest that reflect normal times and not the panic rates that have precipitated the crisis. Even the 21 July 2011 agreement over the handling of Greece did not involve writing down any of the debt, but a rescheduling. The 26 October 2011 agreement went further and wrote down privately held debt by 50 per cent in a negotiated settlement with the banks holding the debt, in the hope that this will keep the country's debt ratio down to 120 per cent by 2020, which may be manageable.[2] However, all this is predicated on a whole package of structural reform and increased competitiveness through lowering real wages and the net fiscal cost in Greece. For all countries concerned the problem is that they cannot simply make changes today that will solve the problem, but have to continue to follow policies that keep debt sustainable over several decades.

Offering a plausible commitment involves turning the current budgets from strong deficits into surpluses with a believable prospect that the position will be maintained over the future. Cutting expenditure and raising taxes at a time of difficulty will make the present recession deeper in the short run and it is not surprising that the Greek government for example has opted to meet as much as possible of the shortfall by asset sales. Being members of the euro area, the troubled countries cannot undertake the usual stimulus to recovery by devaluing their exchange rate, and their competitiveness can only be improved by deflation (or inflation clearly less than that of their competitors, which is clearly difficult when inflation levels are near zero).[3]

Making all these changes requires a substantial public and political commitment. Not only do the budgetary measures have to be agreed by parliaments, but also wage bargainers have to agree to wage levels falling relative to competitors if the outcomes are to be sustainable. It is not surprising therefore that governments have fallen in countries faced with such pressure, and that the public is reluctant to accept the austerity involved as they do not feel it is their fault but that of politicians and financial institutions that have allowed them to get into this mess in the first place. In any case such a route to adjustment, especially if applied slowly, runs the risk of progressive difficulty with rising taxes and falling expenditures leading to lower taxable incomes and greater demands on the welfare system. Rapid turnarounds are possible under fixed exchange rates without ramping up debt, as demonstrated by Estonia, but traditionally the exchange rate has formed an important pillar of the recovery from a severe fiscal and financial crisis, as demonstrated by the Nordic countries in the early 1990s and the Asian countries in 1997–98.

The idea behind the EU and the IMF stepping in for the interim is that it gives the countries time to implement the changes and start the recovery, so that the longer-term future looks feasible to private sector lenders who will then be prepared to lend to these countries at rates of interest that are not crippling. This has been the normal outcome of IMF intervention in the past, although countries quite naturally have not liked the harsh restructuring terms the IMF have imposed. Sometimes it has taken rather longer and subsequent programmes of IMF lending have been required. It has normally been a feature of such lending that it is offered at a rate of interest reasonably close to that at which the lender itself raises the funds, hence providing a considerable improvement over what could be obtained in the market. In the present case, up until the 21 July agreement, Greece, Ireland and Portugal were paying penalty rates, thereby making their short-run cash flow problems worse. (The reasoning behind this penalty was difficult to understand. If it reflected perceived risk, then the other countries should not have been lending in the first place.) While temporary lending programmes are usually only of a size sufficient to finance new debt and debt that comes up for repayment, it is possible to use the facility to buy back debt in the market at a very substantial discount and hence reduce the nominal value of debt outstanding.

This approach of replacing market lending by EU/IMF lending 'temporarily' represents Plan A, although duration of the EU lending in the case of Greece can be as long as 30–40 years. If Plan A cannot be applied, because no convincing budgetary reorganisation can be found or agreed, then the alternative is to reduce the amount that the governments have to spend on interest or the repayment of principal to lenders.[4] If this can be agreed with the lenders, as appears to be the case with Greece, then this can be arranged without triggering a technical default.[5] However, this is not normally possible because of the collective action problem. It would pay some lenders to opt out of the agreement as then they could get repaid under the previous schedule. Collective action clauses exist in some bond contracts in order to make just such reorganisations feasible.[6] It is planned for them to become normal practice in EU debt in 2013. The 21 July agreement included a degree of voluntary rollover by the private sector, but the 26 October agreement included a voluntary write-down of 50 per cent, slightly increased in the eventual terms. Collective action has been rather easier than in many circumstances as most of the holders of the debt are euro area banks in other countries.

Defaults bring with them other unwelcome consequences as they bring all of the country's transactions into question at the same time, triggering close-out clauses and claims for early repayment, thus bringing the financing system to a halt. This would create a much worse recession and would make it very difficult to raise external finance for quite some time subsequently, until the position of all the debt holders has been worked out.

One of the difficulties that European governments railed against in the 21 July measures over Greece was that ratings agencies made the problems more difficult.[7] This highlights that having a credible proposal is key to the solution. The parties involved may have no problem persuading themselves, but it is others that they have to convince for market prices and ratings to change. The lack of success in Greece in particular of reining in the problem means that claims that such changes will happen in the future are not very persuasive, particularly given the lack of enthusiasm in the EU for a Plan B that involves avoiding default by other member states writing down Greek debt and thereby bearing some of the loss.[8]

The dilemma at present is that the governments of some of the lending countries feel that a default in the future may occur anyway and they are unwilling to step in and take over from private lenders, as their own taxpayers will then have to bear some of the loss. However, if there is a default in the short run they will also face losses, as some of the lenders to the troubled countries are their banks, which might fail as a consequence, either facing the governments with the need to organise a bailout or with disruption to their own financial systems. It is difficult to have much sympathy for these lenders, as the risks were well known. Well before the crisis, surprise was expressed at the smallness of the risk premium in the market (Mayes and Viren, 2007).

Furthermore, the European Central Bank (ECB) is holding many of the bonds and it would need recapitalising by the member governments according to its capital key if there were to be a default.[9] There is thus no easy way out. Indeed the ECB is now buying debt in the market in an effort to reduce interest rates on Spanish and Italian debt, thus expanding its balance sheet and increasing the potential exposure to loss. However, it is of the view that the market is exaggerating the default risk and that these bonds are still of high quality.

High in governments' minds are the consequences of the insolvency of Lehman Brothers, where world financial markets froze and asset prices fell dramatically as counterparties could not assess who was going to bear the losses, thereby constituting stage two of the GFC. The ECB has also fought very strongly to ensure that it only accepts unimpaired collateral in its operations. As a result the July 21 agreement entailed that Greek debt would be effectively underwritten by the euro area and this position was maintained in the October 26 agreement.

In this instance it appears to be rather easier to sort out who the bondholders are, but the extent of the losses will be difficult to establish for a while.[10] Despite the existence of the Paris and London Clubs for sorting out bond write-downs, this process takes time if there is a default and meanwhile international financial markets would return to distress.[11] Thus the European problems would become problems for everybody. With collective-action clauses the process would be smoother. Having such a plausible route to manageable sovereign default will be one of the better incentives for more prudent fiscal policy (Von Hagen, 2010).

To quite an extent the euro area countries have already been placing far more of the potential burden on themselves than was the case with the sovereign defaults in the 1980s (Buchheit and Gulati, 2011). Then the problem was also the overexposure of banks to the debt. The solution used was first to roll over the debt and even increase it to enable interest payments without default, during the period of IMF lending and restructuring – the Baker Plan. Then, when this proved insufficient, the debt was written down and new longer-term bonds issued – Brady bonds. Thus eventually it was the lenders who bore the loss rather than the taxpayers in the lenders' countries, but the process was sufficiently drawn-out and the loss recognition carefully timed so that it could be borne without a crisis. Some similar delay in recognition might help weaker banks survive in the present crisis but the authorities have taken the view that they should seek recapitalisation (estimated at €106 billion in the 26 October agreement) as soon as possible since a write-down of the debt has been agreed. However, in the interim, interest rates have to be low enough that default is not triggered.

It is important not to place all of the troubled countries in the same basket. Italy's debt, for example, is largely domestic. However, because of the size of the Italian economy the foreign holdings are more significant than the whole of Greek debt. It seems likely that Ireland has already put in place a recovery plan that will work unless there is another important downwards shock.[12] Similarly, while Spain faces substantial economic difficulty, it is not clear that it would be overwhelming. If the problem of possible default only really applies to Greece and perhaps Portugal, then these countries are sufficiently small that the rest of the euro area could afford to bail them out – ignoring the moral hazard consequences of doing so – and hence could make a credible commitment that would calm markets.[13] In the same way, allowing the default would have very limited impact on the euro area as a whole, unless markets believed that this would push other larger countries into default as well. Whichever way the process plays out, people do not like the prospect of losses and in crises they become very risk-averse and jittery. Solutions have to take this into account however irrational the behaviour might seem.

Marimon (2011) shows that, in many respects, the problem is most worrying for Portugal, as it has not managed to stop its debt from rising over the last decade, expects continuing slow growth rates and has relatively high tax rates. Greece had stabilised but not reduced its debt, while Ireland and Spain were on falling trajectories. The primary balance in Greece has been no worse than that in the euro area as a whole. The problem is the size of debt interest.

The key issues for the euro area countries are, firstly, that they need to be committed enough to overcome the fears of financial markets. Secondly, they have to negotiate agreements with each other in order to find an equitable sharing of the burden, as just letting a default happen will be worse.

## 11.3 THE INTENDED RULES

The primary issue for the euro area countries is that they should not have been having these problems at all in the first place. Under the terms of the Maastricht Treaty which laid out the agreement on EMU, to qualify for membership the ratio of government debt should not exceed 60 per cent of gross domestic product (GDP) 'unless the ratio is sufficiently diminishing and approaching the reference value at a satisfactory pace'. Furthermore, under the terms of the Stability and Growth Pact (SGP) debt positions should have been slowly improving, because not only were governments to avoid excessive deficits amounting to more than 3 per cent of GDP in any year, except in the event of a substantial recession, but they should also

*Table 11.1 Euro area government debt/GDP (%)*

| Country | 1995 | 1999 | 2007 | 2010 |
|---|---|---|---|---|
| Euro area | 72.1 | 71.6 | 66.3 | 85.3 |
| Belgium | 130.4 | 113.7 | 84.2 | 96.8 |
| Germany | 55.6 | 60.9 | 64.9 | 83.2 |
| Estonia | 8.2 | 6.5 | 3.7 | 6.6 |
| Ireland | 82.0 | 48.5 | 25.0 | 96.2 |
| Greece | 97.0 | 94.0 | 105.4 | 142.8 |
| Spain | 63.3 | 62.3 | 36.1 | 60.1 |
| France | 55.5 | 58.9 | 63.9 | 81.7 |
| Italy | 121.5 | 113.7 | 103.6 | 119.0 |
| Cyprus | 51.4 | 58.9 | 58.3 | 60.8 |
| Luxembourg | 7.4 | 6.4 | 6.7 | 18.4 |
| Malta | 35.3 | 57.1 | 62.0 | 68.0 |
| Netherlands | 76.1 | 61.1 | 45.3 | 62.7 |
| Austria | 68.3 | 67.3 | 60.7 | 72.3 |
| Portugal | 59.2 | 49.6 | 68.3 | 93.0 |
| Slovenia | na | na | 23.1 | 38.0 |
| Slovakia | 22.1 | 47.9 | 29.6 | 41.0 |
| Finland | 56.6 | 45.7 | 35.2 | 48.4 |

*Source:* Eurostat.

have been aiming for a budgetary position that was close to balance or in surplus (Breuss and Roeger, 2007). Even with the slower-than-hoped-for rates of growth attained over the period since the third stage of EMU started at the beginning of 1999, this would still have meant that debt ratios should have fallen in most years. As it was, in many countries they crept up (see Table 11.1).

The reasons have been widely debated (Heipertz and Verdun, 2010), with some blame falling on the SGP itself, in that it did not attempt to try express the strategy in terms of cyclically adjusted budgets. However, in part that reflects the underlying problem of fiscal budgeting. The cyclically adjusted position is not known until after the event. There is an inherent tendency for forecasts to be optimistic, where some of any upturn in the growth rate is likely to be attributed to lasting changes – the information technology (IT) revolution and the 'new economy' being an obvious case in point – and some of any downturn to be attributed to one-off factors. This generates a fundamental asymmetry in the budgetary process, manifested in the euro area in a tendency to cut tax rates too far when the economy is doing well (Mayes and Viren, 2011). The asymmetry is often referred to as 'deficit bias', for which there are many explanations.[14]

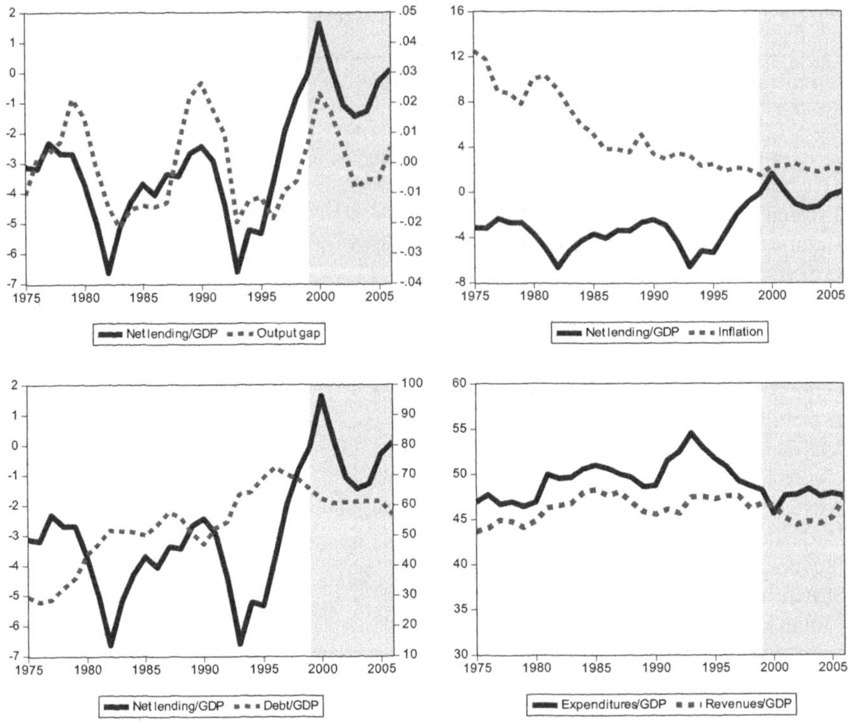


*Source:* Mayes and Viren (2011).

*Figure 11.1 Debt and fiscal balance in the euro area (medians)*

In Figure 11.1 (drawn from Mayes and Viren, 2011) it is clear from the lower-left quadrant that fiscal prudence increased substantially in the run-up to EMU and has only weakened slightly since the euro area started. Thus while there was only one year in surplus, deficits became much smaller for the same position in the economic cycle (shown in the upper-left quadrant). Debt ratios had stopped their long rise and begun to turn down, a process that did not end after 1999. It is also clear from the lower-right quadrant that the main contributor to the slight worsening in deficits was not expenditure but the decline in revenue. Thus the degree of adjustment required by the euro area as a whole was small and only a modest improvement in fiscal prudence would have led to clearer reduction of the debt ratio in each year. However, it is not just the overall behaviour which matters in this instance but that of the most vulnerable member states.

This experience means that through the cycle, setting of the budget should take this inherent bias into account. There are a number of ways in which this might be accomplished, for example by requiring that the target for improvement be somewhat harsher. However, any rules that are self-imposed are unlikely to get over the forecasting bias unless the computation is somehow above politics and open to ready verification. Sweden has offered an example of how to do this with its independent Fiscal Policy Council set up in 2007, establishing the budgetary position (Calmfors and Wren-Lewis, 2011):

> The council assesses the extent to which the Government's fiscal-policy objectives are being achieved. These objectives include long-run sustainability, the budget surplus target, the ceiling on central government expenditure and that fiscal policy is consistent with the cyclical situation of the economy. The council also evaluates whether the development of the economy is in line with healthy long-run growth and sustainable high employment. Additional tasks are to examine the clarity of the Government's budget proposals and to review its economic forecasts and the economic models used to generate them. Finally, the Council should try to stimulate public debate on economic policy.[15]

In the same way the Office of Budgetary Responsibility in the UK should help reduce the asymmetry.[16] It is not that the government is compelled to adopt the independent body's views but that it needs to have a very well-articulated reason for disregarding them. Seven other EU countries have independent assessments of the budgetary outlook, the Central Plan Bureau being the longest-serving, since 1947 (Calmfors and Wren-Lewis, 2011). Von Hagen (2010) suggests that having such councils would be one of the few changes to the system that could have a marked effect on behaviour.

In any case the problem is that budgetary forecasts, like any other forecast, even if undertaken with excellent models and principles, will be subject to substantial error. While an independent body may avoid some of the errors of bias, the fact that its forecasts can turn out to be well off the mark may in fact damage its credibility. A body that merely comments on the official projections may retain greater credibility (Calmfors and Wren-Lewis, 2011).

It is somewhat surprising that there is no fiscal equivalent of the fan charts used for monetary policy to show the likely distribution of forecast outcomes,[17] nor a strategic approach to reacting to forecasting errors once they are made. In part this is because monetary policy can be altered at regular intervals during the year if necessary, without causing undue disturbance to the economy, but short-run management of tax rates, value-added tax (VAT) being the usually quoted candidate, has never been popular.[18] Trying to do much management of expenditure programmes during the year is also difficult. The European Semester, while the name might imply a six-monthly review, is an annual process that takes place in the first six months of the year.[19] In any case it is normally argued that sharp changes in tax rates should be avoided and that smoothing is likely to be socially optimal (Leith and Wren-Lewis, 2000). In which case, the transition paths for debt ratios will tend to be slow – emphasising the importance of maintaining adequate cushions below any limiting ratios. On 4 October 2011, the EU agreed a package of six measures (five regulations and one directive)[20] to try to establish a new framework for better economic governance, including institutionalising the European Semester, and this is discussed in the next section.

The core problems were, however, twofold. The EU chose to make a very liberal interpretation of the Treaty when deciding on the initial membership of the euro area in 1998, admitting Belgium and Italy which had debt ratios substantially above 60 per cent. This was compounded in 2000 with the admission of Greece. Not only has it now been shown that the statistics were incorrect and that Greece did not qualify, but even on the published statistics there has been no other period since the signing of the Maastricht Treaty in 1992 that Greece would have qualified. Despite the rhetoric relating to longer-term stability, in qualification it was clearly not applied in practice.

Furthermore the euro area abandoned the credibility of the SGP in 2003 when it decided to suspend its operation when France and Germany were found by the Commission to be running excessive deficits.[21] The weakened version of the Pact agreed in 2005 not only increased the chance of excessive deficits but made the suggestion that effective sanctions would be taken against errant members, whether in the form of a non-interest bearing deposit or ultimately a fine of up to 0.5 per cent of GDP, thoroughly unlikely. Had France and Germany been contrite and taken the necessary steps, then it would have been possible to take more credible measures against the debt pressures in other member states. The Commission's conclusions after the ECOFIN Council decided to hold the EDP in abeyance for France and Germany in November 2003. Council Document 14492/03 summarises the key point clearly: 'Only a rule-based system can guarantee that commitments are enforced and that all Member States are treated equally'.

According to Heipertz and Verdun (2010) most countries did not take the medium-term objective (MTO) of getting budgets close to balance or in surplus (CTBOIS) seriously. Projections would show this occurring in the future but without a firm programme of how it would be achieved in the event that budgetary outcomes were insufficiently favourable. The argument during the review of the SGP in 2003–05 emphasised the importance of getting countries facing deficits back to better growth paths. However, the deterrent value of the EDP stemmed from just the fact that having to tighten fiscal policy when the economy was doing badly would be politically unattractive. Hence it was thought that member states would want to aim the trajectory of their fiscal policy through the cycle, such that the chances of an excess deficit in a downturn were small. To take the example of monetary policy, central banks tighten when the threat of inflation breaching the target becomes unacceptably large – not that simply that inflation is expected to breach the target in the absence of a policy change. In the absence of major shocks, central bank projections normally show inflation clearly within the target over the policy horizon.

It is the combination of admitting countries with high debt ratios and managing to do little to ensure their steady reduction which has proved the undoing of the euro area. Adherence to their own rules would have restricted the problems. Of the high-deficit countries, Belgium made substantial progress despite political difficulties and has thus far managed to weather the GFC despite major problems with two of its largest banks, Dexia and Fortis.[22] The terms of EMU membership in no way prevented member states from improving their debt position if they chose to do so. Finland for example virtually halved its debt ratio from just below 60 per cent of GDP to close to 30 per cent over the period 1997 to 2008.

However, even if the Maastricht criteria had been applied rigorously, they were still open to wide criticism as they did not reflect the prevailing view in economics of the criteria for an Optimum Currency Area (OCA) (Mundell, 1961; Edwards, 2006). The Maastricht criteria were agreed following the work of the Delors Committee in 1989, which while chaired by Jacques Delors as President of the European Commission was composed of the central bank governors of the member states and two advisors. This Committee followed, instead, what has been labelled the 'monetary' approach to integration, requiring that the members converge to conditions for stability in financial markets both domestically through the long-run rate of interest and internationally through the exchange rate and that they converge on an acceptably low inflation rate.

This approach has four main disadvantages. Firstly, by concentrating on inflation it ignored the fact that the member states had very different price levels. Member states with low price levels would expect to see above-average inflation as their price levels converged; countries with higher price levels would be likely to adjust far less, as lowering price levels is very difficult without a clear recession. Any such adjustment would tend to come from increasing competitiveness through productivity and reductions in real rather than nominal wages in a rather subdued economic environment.

Secondly, the monetary approach ignores the main concerns of the OCA criteria, namely that countries should not be subject unduly to idiosyncratic shocks that affect just them and not the rest of the area to which they belong, and that they should have the necessary flexibility through labour markets, wages and fiscal policy to respond to any such shocks that did occur.[23] In the event of an idiosyncratic shock, the area-wide monetary policy will not respond, nor will the exchange rate move. Hence other policies will have to compensate for this rigidity.

This is not an impossibility as most large countries, such as the United States (US), Canada or even Australia, do not meet the OCA criteria in terms of exposure of some parts of the country to idiosyncratic shocks, but they do have adequate responses in place to absorb the shocks, whether by people moving away from adversely affected areas or by trying to regenerate the local economy. The most important deficiency in this need for other sources of flexibility is that there is no significant ability to make fiscal transfers to the adversely affected regions in the euro area. This means that a member state with a problem has to rely far more on its own resources, which makes adjustment much more difficult. However, this was all predictable, and the chapter discusses in the next section the provisions that Finland within the euro area, and Sweden outside it, have made in order to have the necessary resources to handle these shocks.[24]

The third issue that was set on one side was that many countries would be able to qualify only occasionally, mainly when they happened to be out of phase with the rest of the euro area. Estonia is a good example. It has become the most recent member of the area at the beginning of 2011. Since it has been a member of the EU it has shown real convergence, with trivial public debt, and has normally run a surplus each year. Since it had a currency board based on the euro it has met the criterion of exchange rate convergence automatically. The problem was inflation. As a low-income and low-price-level country it expected higher inflation than that in the lowest three inflating members of the EU much of the time. It only qualified because it was much worse hit by the GFC than most of the EU, with a 20 per cent decline in GDP. The resulting collapse in price pressures meant inflation fell to 0.2 per cent and hence the country qualified.[25]

While Estonia will no doubt be an excellent member of the euro area with the most prudent fiscal policy in the whole area (possibly Finland excepted) and a highly flexible economy (Mayes, 2010), some of the other newer members of the EU and the obvious case of Greece would not necessarily meet the longer-term requirements for sustainable membership even though they can (fleetingly) meet the Maastricht criteria and be admitted.

Fourthly, financial markets adjusted on the basis of the likelihood of membership of the euro area actually occurring, and not on a judgement of suitability for joining EMU. Thus the convergence of long-term interest rates to the German level only indicated that the countries were expected to join. Now this close relationship between all the members and the most stable countries, primarily Germany, has been broken and signals from the market about individual countries will be of more value.

Interest rate convergence was itself a contributor to the disequilibrium within the euro area as countries that were previously an inflation risk and hence attracted high interest rates got a major gain on entry to Stage 3 through the interest rate reduction.[26] This helped stimulate faster growth. By the same token that the single monetary policy cannot respond to individual country adverse shocks, so it is true for these positive shocks. As a result, not only do countries grow faster but they also experience greater inflation than they would if they had a domestic monetary policy that could respond to domestic pressures.[27] Thus positive as well as negative shocks have disadvantages in EMU although in the former case it takes a lot longer for them to emerge. With a positive shock there is a very clear benefit at the outset with improvements in GDP per head and reductions in unemployment, but the downside is that the increasing real wages tend to overshoot, reducing competitiveness and meaning that regaining competitiveness has to be achieved by deflation, at least in relative terms, which is a painful process.

Ireland is perhaps the most important exception to the general picture as it did not start the crisis with a debt problem but encountered a debt problem as a result of the great cost of bailing out its failing banks. In part this was a self-imposed cost as Ireland issued a blanket guarantee in September 2008, thereby protecting all creditors and not just depositors (Honohan, 2010; Lane, 2010). This has proved hugely expensive and nearly brought the country down as well as the government. Nevertheless, the fact that it does appear possible for Ireland to survive shows that shocks can be absorbed under the euro area system and that it is prior fragility from high debt which brings countries down, not the EMU rules per se.

## 11.4 ADDRESSING THE FISCAL PROBLEM

There are two levels at which the fiscal issues can be addressed in the EU framework. The first is for the euro area countries to agree a revised preventative arm to the SGP, which members actually adhere to. This is the route chosen in the 21 July 2011 agreement and forms part of the 'six-pack' of measures. Building prudence into the constitution or law and having independent fiscal councils also forms part of the measures. The worsening in the debt position in the euro area is general so a clear downward path in the medium term is required. At present, the members are required to get back inside the excessive deficit procedure by 2013, that is, to have an actual and projected deficit of less than 3 per cent of GDP by then, although some will clearly not be able to make it by then. Thereafter they need to move at least to balance if they are to start repaying debt. The problem is that the faster they grow, the faster the debt ratio will fall for any given financial balance. On top of that for any given structure of the fiscal system, the faster the growth rate, the higher will be the surplus and the lower the deficit. The proposal of introducing mandatory good budgeting principles into the law (constitution) of each member state would help prudence, somewhat along the lines of the balanced budget legislation in many US states (Poterba, 1995; Hou and Smith, 2010).

The second level would be to move towards greater fiscal integration. If the EU were more politically integrated then there would probably be a significant EU-level budget that enabled fiscal transfers to be made to states troubled by high debts and adverse shocks. However, one of the reasons that the EU has developed the way it has, rather than following the precepts of the MacDougall Report (1977) which set out how to organise a low-cost redistributive system, is that this was thought to encourage fiscal laxity – at that stage relating only to Italy although Belgium was building up problems. Fiscal federalism can develop where richer regions accept that those that have lower revenue-raising ability or higher costs are not in a position to do anything about it. In the case of the member states with debt problems at present, it is in the main not a question of fiscal capacity or higher burdens from commonly agreed expenditure programmes. Ireland has above-average GDP per head and the debt problem has been caused largely by poor financial policy and a non-sustainable budgetary stance (Honohan, 2011; Lane, 2010). It is difficult to see why fiscal transfers would be thought appropriate in these circumstances. The current arrangement of only going as far as providing access to loans at near the finest rates and negotiating a plan for recovery is understandable in the circumstances. (There are limits even to this process as at some point those raising the debt at the finest rates will find that their own credit rating falls because of the size of the commitments.)

While there are many who would like to go down the road of closer economic integration, it is not on the political agenda and would contravene what is labelled as the 'no bailout clause' in the Lisbon Treaty.[28] In circumstances where each part of the euro area follows good fiscal standards then it might be possible to consider a measure of fiscal transfers beyond those inherent in the use of structural and cohesion funds. At present inequalities across the EU are addressed by co-financed investment projects in both physical and human capital. This approach has proven extremely successful in advancing Ireland from the bottom of the EU GDP per capita rankings when it joined, to well above the average before the GFC. Spain, Portugal, Greece, Italy and all the new member states have similarly benefited extensively. It does not, however, address the problem of short-term asymmetric shocks which heavily affect one area compared to the others.

There is of course a further dimension to either approach, which is to ensure that the costs of a sovereign default for the rest of the euro area and to the country itself are manageable, hence bringing the position in line with defaults by non-federal government entities in the United States.

The conditionality being imposed on the states borrowing from the EFSF follows standard practice in trying to encourage all the facets of the economic system that would lead to greater flexibility, some of which is under the general label of structural reform. By bringing the IMF into the lending programmes, the euro area countries have not merely managed to increase the funds available but have added credibility to the restructuring imposed and the process of monitoring its implementation over the future.

What is required for a successful and sustainable fiscal stance is not simply that debt is low enough but that countries have a sufficient insurance against shocks. The simplest example is the development of a sovereign wealth fund so that should a country find that foreign markets are effectively closed to it, it can nevertheless continue to finance a countercyclical deficit through running down assets.[29] Such financial assets are likely to be much easier to sell than the real assets that are to be sold by Greece. It is only in the event of a broader international crisis that such assets might fall substantially in price and hence make avoiding the need to raise new debt in the crisis impossible. The pension and unemployment buffer funds that exist in Finland and Sweden are a smaller-scale example (Mayes, 2009).

Pursuit of fiscal rules on their own is not enough. The United Kingdom (UK) applied two main rules over the period from 1997 up to the crisis. The first was to limit the debt ratio to 40 per cent of GDP, thereby building in a cushion for shocks, and the second was to limit borrowing to investment.[30] Similar such attempts to avoid using debt finance for current expenditure over the course of the cycle have existed elsewhere before, in Japan for example. However, the underlying rationale that the investment will bring in future revenues, whether through taxation of increased incomes and activity or user charges, does not always follow as some investment, while socially meritorious, does not generate much in the way of an income flow. Indeed it may well generate increased streams of expenditure. Vulnerability to a shock and to over-optimism about sustainable expenditures in the face of good growth was very clearly illustrated in the UK despite the existence of such rules, with debt approaching 70 per cent of GDP and likely to double over the course of the crisis.

The experience of some of the more distressed euro area countries in the GFC is likely to make some of the new member states which are yet to join the euro more cautious about doing so. The debate is reflected very clearly in that which went on in Finland and Sweden before the euro was introduced (Mayes and Suvanto, 2002). Both countries launched an expert commission of enquiry into the likely outcomes (published as Calmfors et al., 1997 in the case of Sweden; and Pekkarinen et al., 1997 for Finland). Both concluded that there was no conclusive evidence one way or the other, but Sweden concluded that in the light of this the sensible route was to delay entry until the country had reduced unemployment to low levels and established sufficient fiscal buffers that they could withstand a severe economic shock. As a result Sweden is still outside as the performance of the economy has been at least as good as that of the euro area and flexibility in the exchange rate has been valuable. Finland on the other hand, which was rather further away from meeting the OCA criteria, argued that membership would force a change in wage setting and other labour market behaviour and hence the country should enter at the outset and then adjust rapidly thereafter. Finland's performance has been even better than that of Sweden and it is clear that it has been the beneficiary of two facets of membership: lower interest rates and an initially low exchange rate, leading to good competitiveness. Finland has indeed adjusted, with, until the immediate run-up to the crisis, moderation in wage growth and steadily falling unemployment, albeit from very high levels. Finland has also been a model of fiscal rectitude, bringing down its debt from close to 60 per cent of GDP to nearly 30 per cent so that it could withstand a severe shock – which indeed it received in the GFC with a 9 per cent fall in GDP – and establishing buffer funds for both unemployment expenditures and pensions.

Finland thus shows that by following the spirit of the Maastricht rules it is possible to succeed in the euro area, while Sweden shows that fiscal prudence outside and inflation targeting can also lead to a satisfactory outcome, with smaller real losses in the downturn. The key question, therefore, is whether the EU can devise a set of incentives that will be sufficient for states to comply with the new SGP rules.

One problem with the current rules is that they are asymmetric. Countries face constraints on their fiscal actions with the threat of fines in the event of non-compliance but they receive no prizes for prudence. This asymmetry is continued in the 'six-pack' of measures to improve economic governance approved on 4 October 2011. Overall a country that decreases a surplus by €1 billion has exactly the same impact on the area's total debt as one that increases its deficit by the same sum. Prudent countries will get some benefits in terms of lower interest rates but once they attain AAA status further gains are rather limited. Hence motivation to improve on not just the minimum required but the general target for longer-term debt is limited. This was not addressed in the 'six-pack' measures. Indeed the only sorts of ways that this could be implemented would be to give prudent member states some benefit through the EU budget, perhaps in terms of some rebate. A straight piece of symmetry with the idea of interest-free deposits in the case of an excessive deficit would be the ability to borrow from the other member states at below the market rate. This does not sound a very likely proposition either.

Secondly, it is very difficult to get round the problem that fiscal projections are highly inaccurate as they depend on growth assumptions. Furthermore any attempt to estimate 'through the cycle' measures can only be verified after the event. Hence it will be difficult to get over the inherent bias that falls in the actual rate of growth are viewed as being temporary, whereas increases are quickly rationalised as being more permanent. Having an independent assessment, as in Sweden and the UK, may help, whether these are at the national level or performed by the European Commission.

One suggestion which has some appeal[31] is to issue euro area bonds for the first x per cent of a country's debt. Such bonds would be guaranteed by all the member states. Beyond that all debt would be on national responsibility only. In current circumstances, the more indebted countries would pay a sharp premium on this national debt. This would cut the borrowing costs for states in difficulty without impacting on the interest rates of the most prudent borrowers. If one wanted a strong incentive for prudence, then choosing x to be a fairly low value, such as 30 per cent, would make sense. However, several of the existing member states with AAA ratings have more debt outstanding than that and hence might find that their own borrowing costs rose at the margin.[32] Choosing too high a value would threaten the credit rating of the entire system and would be counterproductive.

Strong arguments have been advanced (Issing, 2011, for example) that debtor countries have a sufficiently strong hold over the rest of the member states because of the strength of the wish to avoid defaults that they will effectively be able to impose costs on the others. This is not immediately clear from the nature of the bargaining that has gone on thus far, including the 21 July and 26 October agreements. What has been imposed on the borrowers is at the limit of what is politically achievable; pushing them much further is likely simply to trigger the default. It is not clear what more could be achieved by closer economic integration. Clearly such integration cannot involve harsher restraint on these countries. It would have to offer some attraction to the prudent countries that would actually reduce the pressure on the indebted countries. That is difficult to spell out.

The European Commission (2010) has argued that as well as tackling fiscal imbalances through an enhanced SGP, the EU should consider the emergence of both internal and external imbalances among countries, and this is implemented through the 'six-pack' measures. Thus the Commission will consider the savings and investment and current account balances on an annual basis, as part of the European Semester, with a view to deciding whether such imbalances were excessive. In line with the SGP there is a preventative arm drawing attention to imbalances and encouraging action, and a corrective arm where such corrections became mandatory through the agreement of the Council. It is difficult to make such a scheme as transparent and rule-bound as the SGP and the idea has been widely criticised (Giavazzi and Spaventa, 2010, for example). Imbalances might be picked up rather better through the process of macro-prudential supervision that has begun with the European Systemic Risk Board. Although such measures are inherently financial and do not relate directly to the real economy, sources of imbalance such as declining competitiveness and rising real exchange rates would be clearly identified. Such a framework would look more deeply at structural and other fundamental features of macroeconomic policy.

However, what has been decided through the 'six-pack' of measures on 4 October is to reinstate the more compulsive side of the SGP, augmented by a similar requirement for adhering to a stable medium-term outlook and a requirement to avoid excessive macroeconomic imbalances as described in European Commission (2010). This is labelled the Euro Plus Pact. There are other requirements for greater transparency and statistical standards to ensure that the other member states are not so easily misled as they were in the case of Greece. The medium-term requirement is essentially a balanced budget requirement for countries that comply with the maximum 60 per cent ratio of government debt to GDP, and a declining ratio requirement for those whose debt is higher.[33] Failure to comply with any of these requirements, including the statistical standards, can result in a fine, in the form of a non-interest bearing deposit initially, which can be forfeited in the event of a continuing lack of compliance. In the case of excessive deficits and statistical infringements the deposit or fine can be up to 0.2 per cent of GDP, and in the case of the macro-imbalances up to 1 per cent. An Excessive Imbalance Procedure (EIB) is thus added to the Excessive Deficit Procedure. The balance of effort is thus firmly on trying to stop problems emerging. Imposing penalties on those in difficulty simply makes the problem of correcting the difficulty worse.

One feature of the 'six-pack' that should help credibility is that to prevent recommendations for action and the imposition of sanctions, a qualified majority of states, excluding the one involved, must vote for this. Under the previous arrangements, member states had to vote in favour for such measures to be introduced. Reversing the nature of the majority required makes it much less likely that a weakening of the system can occur, as in 2003 with the SGP.

It is obvious from the lack of response by financial markets and the widening spreads, particularly for Italy, that this set of changes is not yet convincing for the countries at risk. Unfortunately, while troubled countries look for immediate reductions in interest rate spreads so that they can reduce the interest burden on their budgets while they struggle to restructure and return to a sustainable long-run trajectory, convincing evidence on how the revised measures are likely to operate will only be generated over a sustained period of time. That evidence would involve either compliance with all of the requirements despite difficult budgetary consolidation on the part of those who appear otherwise likely to breach the rules, or the actual imposition of sanctions leading to change. Given the experience of 2003, seeing France and Germany actually pay sanctions or make unpleasant adjustments would help restore confidence.

Macroprudential supervision at an EU level is now being addressed through the European Systemic Risk Board (ESRB) but it is not planned to give the ESRB operational tools to alter the behaviour of the member states. Actions will be limited to advice and moral suasion.

It is likely therefore that the EU will continue to operate with what can perhaps be described as a 'fair weather' system. Provided the pressures are not too great, countries will move towards a lower debt burden when the area is growing satisfactorily. But when problems arise they will tend to run deficits through the automatic stabilisers at least, in a way which is not symmetric with periods higher than average growth.

As it is inherent in the asymmetry facing the system that debt is run up much more rapidly than it is run down, this implies an optimistic view of the economic cycle if the position is to continue to improve over the longer run. Countries will accept hardship in a crisis but it becomes rapidly difficult to apply this in normal times or for long periods. With the implicit adjustment period for Greece being 30–40 years from the framing of the 21 July agreement this implies considerable strength of will. Even with the reductions in the burden implied by the 26 October agreement similar requirements apply, as the restructuring requirements for Greece have increased, not diminished. (What has changed is that the other member states, the IMF and bondholders have become much more pessimistic over the expected stream of debt servicing payments that following these requirements will generate.[34])

Efforts for such long periods are not impossible. Germany did not complete the reparations for the First World War until long after the end of the Second, and the UK's repayment programme of debt to the US accumulated during the Second World War took half a century to complete. Deciding at the outset whether this will happen is a combination of an act of faith and an assessment of whether the adverse consequences from failure to comply are likely to ensure compliance. History is clearly important and countries that get into difficulty tend to have an unfortunate history, so the process is reinforcing – in the negative direction.

## 11.5 CONCLUDING REMARKS

The various proposals that are being put forward by the EU jointly, such as the 21 July and 26 October agreements, and by individual member states, such as the Franco-German proposals of 18 August, are not as yet convincing the markets.[35] Whether the March 2012 agreement on the 'fiscal treaty' will do better remains to be seen and there has been no great response in financial markets. One of the main reasons for this lack of confidence is that the measures to put the problem right are being drip fed and reflect obvious reluctance on the part of the participants. Convincing measures are usually sweeping in character and reflect an observable willingness to do whatever is necessary to address the problem.[36] The initial May 2010 measures with respect to Greece fell in that category. It was by no means clear at that date that over €0.5 trillion would be required to address the problem.

In many respects therefore it is not that the agreed measures or likely developments in trying to enforce structural change and fiscal prudence and recovery will not work. It is that outsiders are not convinced that they will be fully implemented and sustained. Insiders are also not convinced, with Finland demanding collateral from Greece for its own contribution to the bailout fund. The history of the SGP suggests that unless there is a fundamental change in attitudes towards fiscal prudence, most of the changes envisaged in its structure will have only a limited effect (Von Hagen, 2010). Although it is currently the Southern European countries that are most at risk, it is the large countries' actions in the past, particularly those of France and Germany, which have weakened the pressure for correcting and preventing problems and indeed have contributed most to the increasing total of euro area government debt.

In some respects the euro area countries have made the problem worse for themselves by in effect taking so much of the troubled countries' debt onto their own books, either through the official EFSF and EFSM (the European Financial Stabilisation Mechanism that was set up with ability to lend just €60 billion in the early days of the debt crisis) lending or through the purchases of the ECB. Even the IMF debt is potentially a burden for the euro area (through either the ESM or a write-down of the outstanding privately held debt) as the IMF is a preferred creditor and hence will get paid out first.

It is thus likely that if current proposals are seen through, the debt position in the euro area countries can return to sustainable levels. Although the intention is to try to rein in deficits by 2013 or more likely by 2015 if growth does not pick up, the downward path for debt ratios could easily take 20 years to achieve. Some form of relatively crude fiscal rules that are easy to monitor and difficult to evade will no doubt help, as would independent fiscal councils to ensure that there is a good public debate and that some of the causes of deficit bias are restrained. The 'six-pack' of measures agreed on 4 October are a step in that direction. The concern is with the extreme cases. However, even if the process should fail at some point for Greece or another heavily stressed country, this will be more a comment on overenthusiasm for euro area membership in the past than the indication of a fundamentally flawed mechanism for countries starting with a compliant deficit. The fiscal shocks experienced in the global financial crisis are unusual but even so the well-prepared countries look able to see themselves through without incurring downgrades from the rating agencies.

The nature of the bailout process over the crisis is, however, more open to question. It appears that there has been a considerable transfer of potential loss from the lenders, who knowingly took it on, to the taxpayer. This reflects a lack of preparedness. But the introduction of collective action clauses in sovereign bonds is likely to offset some of the moral hazard this has caused. The ironic consequence, however, is that raising debt will become more expensive at a time when budgets are already strained.

## NOTES

* This chapter was drafted in late 2011 and updated in early 2012 during the editing process. It is inevitable therefore that some remarks will become outdated as the Euro Crisis continues.

1. The EFSF is a temporary facility set up by the euro area countries as a private company in Luxembourg to provide lending initially for Greece. By this device it did not require a formal treaty change or full ratification through the European Parliament. The ESM was intended as a formal longer-term replacement to come into force in 2013.
2. This was finally agreed in March 2012, with slightly larger write-down, by a sufficient proportion of the lenders that the remainder could be forced to accept through collective action agreements. However, the debt ratio is expected to be noticeably higher.
3. Devaluation of course increases the burden of foreign currency debt in domestic currency terms.
4. Buchheit and Gulati (2011) provide a very clear exposition of the range of unattractive options that the other members of the euro area face.
5. This technicality matters as it would trigger the credit default swaps that the bondholders have undertaken, thereby shifting the losses, quite possibly outside the banking system. In the case of Greece the default has only been partial and the write-down agreed by most lenders so the swaps have not been triggered.
6. Some sort of agreement is required, because there is no court that can compel a particular course of action by a sovereign borrower. Lenders are of course in a strong position as the defaulting country needs such a reorganisation if it is to re-enter financial markets. Drelichman and Voth (2011) show that the history of organised defaults and restarting borrowing is very long by considering the case of Philip II of Spain, who was a serial defaulter in the second half of the sixteenth century.
7. Von Hagen (2010) argues that seeking more favourable ratings will not affect the views of those who might invest in the debt.
8. Confidence in the 26 October agreement has also been weak because of the inability of the member states to agree how to 'leverage' the EFSF so that it effectively covers €1 trillion of debt despite having funding of only €440 billion by taking the first loss rather than issuing the security outright. By combining the EFSF and the ESM the resources available would be around €750 billion.
9. As it is, without a default, the ECB is likely to make a profit on its purchases as it is buying when prices are low and the haircuts large. The ECB's holdings of Greek debt have not been written down as part of the present agreement.
10. Fifty per cent was the view at the 26 October meeting, but this would still only reduce Greek debt to 120 per cent of GDP by 2020 on current projections of Greek growth and restructuring. (Both of which have shown signs of overoptimism, thus far.) A larger write-down automatically decreases the potential debt to GDP ratio as it not merely reduces the debt but also reduces the required stream of interest payments over future years
11. Currently the position has been a little easier as the Institute of International Finance (IIF), the international association covering banks, has been able to negotiate on behalf of the industry.
12. Although Ireland's primary problem was the exposure to bank losses through issuing a guarantee, the budget was also out of longer-term sustainability and thus restructuring was required even before adding in that needed to service the markedly increased debt (Whelan, 2011).
13. The commitment would need to be very large – JSFRC (2011) estimated this to be at least €2 trillion at the time of the 26 October agreement – because it has to cover all plausible eventualities and not just current known losses.
14. Calmfors and Wren-Lewis (2011) offer six: a lack of information, which permits governmental optimism; impatience to get things done; the ability to exploit future generations; electoral competition; the common pool problem – external consequences of budgetary decisions neglected; and time inconsistency.
15. http://www.finanspolitiskaradet.se/english/swedishfiscalpolicycouncil/abouttheswedishfpc.4.6f04e22 2115f0dd09ea8000950.html.
16. In New Zealand this should already be built into the system, as under the terms of the Fiscal Responsibility Act 1994 the New Zealand Treasury is required to provide

impartial – and public – advice for ministers. Although it is of course up to them whether they choose to accept it and they could choose an optimistic stance, as was in fact the case in the run-up to the GFC. In practice, however, opposition parties do not feel that they are told enough to make a full appraisal.

17. Fancharts were pioneered by the Bank of England but now can be found in many other central banks' monetary policy statements as well, including Norway and Sweden.
18. The setting of monetary policy can of course be altered at any time should the need arise.
19. The European Semester is explained by the European Commission in http://europa.eu/rapid/pressReleasesAction.do?reference=MEMO/11/14.
20. Labelled the 'six-pack' (Council of the European Union, 2011).
21. Heipertz and Verdun (2010) provide a very rich description of the debate and the actions of the major players.
22. Dexia and Fortis had to be bailed out in October 2008, following the Lehmans collapse, but Dexia got into further difficulty as a result of holding impaired Greek debt and on 10 October 2011 was broken up, with its Belgian banking operations being bought by the government, some of its French operations being sold and its impaired assets being swept into an asset management company from which creditors will be repaid.
23. Edwards (2006) suggests there are ten criteria that should be borne in mind:

    - factor mobility, and in particular labour mobility, across the members of the potential union;
    - high level of trade in goods across the members of the union;
    - different (or diversified) composition of output and trade across countries;
    - price and wage flexibility across members of the union;
    - similar inflation rates across countries;
    - financial markets should be integrated across countries;
    - absence of 'fiscal dominance' in the individual countries;
    - low, and similar, levels of public sector debt in the different countries;
    - similarity (or synchronisation) of external shocks to which the different countries are exposed to; and
    - political coordination across countries.

24. One of the reasons that Ireland is managing to cope with the massive downturn and fiscal restructuring it is facing is that there has been a major exodus of the population since 2008, thus *inter alia* easing the potential demands on social benefits.
25. With such low public debt it was quite difficult to come up with a reference ten-year bond rate to compare with the other countries to establish convergence under the interest rate criterion.
26. One might also argue that some of the interest rate premium was because of default risk, which also fell to near zero on the expectation of EMU membership, because lenders expected that the system would avoid defaults by one means or another.
27. Most countries also experienced a property price boom, which was ended by the GFC. This generated a rapid asset price decline which exacerbated the problems of trying to adapt to losses.
28. To confuse matters, some of the participants have labelled the 'six-pack' measures as 'fiscal union' simply because they entail restraints to fiscal activity by the member states, but those constraints fall far short of what would be considered a fiscal union in the context of federal states such as Australia, Canada, Germany and the US.
29. The Irish sovereign wealth fund was readily swallowed up by the scale of the crisis but did reduce the need to borrow (Whelan, 2011).
30. Having rules with a fixed ratio of debt to GDP only make sense if the taxing capacity remains constant. Large demographic changes can alter the sustainable budget balance considerably. Indeed, Calmfors and Wren-Lewis (2011) argue that there are no good simple rules.

31. Although not to the French and German governments according to their 18 August 2011 communiqué http://www.reuters.com/article/2011/08/21/us-eurozone-germany-schaeuble-idUSTRE77K0SW20110821.
32. An alternative solution offered is that Eurobonds should only be used by countries that have excess borrowing. While enabling them to pay lower interest rates, the incentives this would involve would not encourage prudence but present a moral hazard.
33. These take the form of medium-term budgetary objectives and are linked to an annual growth assessment by the European Commission.
34. Even after a 50 per cent write-down in privately held debt the debt ratio is still expected to stabilise at as much as 120 per cent of GDP in 2020.
35. Indeed some remarks, such as the Franco-German statement in Deauville on 18 October 2010 actually made matters worse by making bond holders fear that a compulsory bail in would be imposed at some date in the future (http://www.elysee.fr/president/root/bank_objects/Franco-german_declaration.pdf).
36. Von Hagen (2010) argues, for example, that most of the proposed changes to the SGP are limited in character and while moving in the right direction will not achieve a lot. Establishing fiscal councils might however change the nature of the political discussion towards debt, and the adoption of a framework for managing defaults smoothly would act as a major incentive.

# REFERENCES

Breuss, F. and W. Roeger (2007), 'Sluggish Growth and the SGP Fiscal Rule: Model Simulations', in F. Breuss (ed.), *The Stability and Growth Pact: Experience and Future Aspects*, Vienna: Springer Verlag, pp. 191–242.

Buchheit, L.C. and M. Gulati (2011), 'Greek Debt – the Endgame Scenarios', in F. Allen, E. Carletti and G. Corsetti (eds), *Life in the Eurozone With or Without Sovereign Default*, Philadelphia, PA: FIC Press, pp. 83–96.

Calmfors, L. et al. (1997), *EMU – A Swedish Perspective*, Report of the Calmfors Commission, Dordrecht: Kluwer.

Calmfors, L. and S. Wren-Lewis (2011), 'What Should Fiscal Councils Do?' University of Oxford Economics Discussion Paper, no. 537.

Council of the European Union (2011), 'Council Confirms Agreement on Economic Governance', press notice 14998/11, 4 October, http://www.consilium.europa.eu/uedocs/cms_data/docs/pressdata/en/ecofin/124882.pdf, accessed 4 April 2012.

Drelichman, M. and H.-J. Voth (2011), 'Lending to the Borrower from Hell: Debt and Default in the Age of Philip II', *Economic Journal*, **121**(557), 1205–1227.

Edwards, S. (2006), 'Monetary Unions, External Shocks and Economic Performance', Austrian National Bank Working Paper 126.

European Commission (2010), 'Surveillance of Intra-euro-area Competitiveness and Imbalances', *European Economy*, 1/2010.

Giavazzi, F. and L. Spaventa (2010), 'The European Commission's Proposals: Empty and Useless', VoxEU.org, 14 October, http://www.voxeu.org/index.php?q=node/5680, accessed 1 November 2011.

Heipertz, M. and A. Verdun (2010), *Ruling Europe: The Politics of the Stability and Growth Pact*, Cambridge: Cambridge University Press.

Honohan, P. (2010), 'The Irish Banking Crisis Regulatory and Financial Stability Policy 2003–2008' A Report to the Minister for Finance by the Governor of the Central Bank, http://www.bankinginquiry.gov.ie/The%20Irish%20Banking%20

Crisis%20Regulatory%20and%20Financial%20Stability%20Policy%202003-2008.pdf, last accessed 4 April 2012.
Hou, Y. and D.L. Smith (2010), 'Do State Balanced Budget Requirements Matter? Testing Two Explanatory Frameworks', *Public Choice*, **145**, 57–79.
Issing, O. (2011), 'Slithering to the Wrong Sort of Union', *Financial Times*, 8 August.
Lane, P.R. (2010), 'The Irish Crisis', IIS Discussion Paper no. 356, Trinity College Dublin.
Leith, C. and Wren-Lewis, S. (2000), 'Interactions Between Monetary and Fiscal Policy Rules', *Economic Journal*, **110**, 93–108.
MacDougall, G.D.A. (1977), 'Report of the Study Group on the Role of Public Finance in European Integration Chaired by Sir Donald MacDougall', Economic and Financial Series, no. A13, Commission of the European Communities, Brussels, April.
Marimon, R. (2011), 'The Current Situation: The Euro Area, a Crisis of PIGS?' in F. Allen, E. Carletti and G. Corsetti (eds), *Life in the Eurozone With or Without Sovereign Default*, Philadelphia, PA: FIC Press, pp. 1–8.
Mayes, D.G. (2009) 'How Much Have the Financial Crises in the Nordic Countries Helped Them Cope with the Current Financial Turmoil?' *Journal of Common Market Studies*, **47**(5), 995–1013
Mayes, D.G. (2010), *The Microfoundations of Economic Success: The Case of Estonia*, Cheltenham, UK and Northampton, MA, USA: Edward Elgar.
Mayes, D.G. and A. Suvanto (2002), 'Beyond the Fringe: Finland and the Choice of Currency', *Journal of Public Policy*, **22**(2), 161–82.
Mayes, D.G. and M. Viren (2007), 'The SGP and the ECB: An Exercise in Asymmetry', *Journal of Financial Transformation*, **19**, 159–75.
Mayes, D.G. and M. Viren (2011), *Asymmetry and Aggregation in the Euro Area*, London: Routledge.
Mundell, R. (1961), 'A Theory of Optimum Currency Areas', *American Economic Review*, **51**, 657–665.
Pekkarinen, J. et al. (1997), *Finland and EMU*, publication 1997/26, Helsinki: Prime Minister's Office.
Poterba, J.M. (1995), 'Balanced Budget Rules and Fiscal Policy: Evidence from the States', *National Tax Journal*, **48**(3), 329–336.
Von Hagen, J. (2010), 'The Sustainability of Public Finances and Fiscal Policy Co-ordination in the EMU', Case Network Studies and Analyses, no. 412/2010.
Whelan, K. (2011), 'Ireland's Sovereign Debt Crisis', in F. Allen, E. Carletti and G. Corsetti (eds), *Life in the Eurozone With or Without Sovereign Default*, Philadelphia, PA: FIC Press, pp. 41–58.

# APPENDIX

## A The 21 July 2011 Agreement

The agreement set out in the communiqué from the heads of state or government of the euro area (available at http://www.consilium.europa.eu/uedocs/cms_data/docs/pressdata/en/ec/123978.pdf) has seven main ingredients:

1. A doubling of the size of the funding support programme for Greece from €109 billion to €218 billion.
2. An extending of the term of the facility from 7.5 years to 30 years with a ten-year further transition period.
3. A reduction in interest rates (also applies to Portugal and Ireland) so that the premium over the EFSF's borrowing rates is not so large.
4. A voluntary roll-over programme by the private sector amounting to €36 billion after the cost of credit enhancement by the EFSF (a figure of €106 billion up to 2019 is also quoted).
5. A task force to help Greece make maximum use of the structural funds for economic growth and recovery.
6. Widening of the terms of the EFSF (and ESM) ability to intervene by permitting purchases in the secondary market in exceptional times.
7. A strengthened preventative arm for the SGP.

## B The 26 October 2011 Agreement

This agreement, which is summarised at http://www.consilium.europa.eu/uedocs/cms_data/docs/pressdata/en/ec/125644.pdf, has seven main elements:

1. Additional financing for Greece up to €100 billion
2. An agreement to discount Greek government debt held by private investors by 50%, in part financed by €30 billion from the other member states.
3. A gearing of the EFSF to around €1trillion (by methods to be announced later) involving credit enhancement and increased funding.
4. Recapitalisation of the banking system by June 2012 to a 9% Core Tier 1 ratio – financing to be provided by governments should banks need or wish it (without deleveraging).
5. A new restructuring package in Italy following on the packages in Greece, Spain, Ireland and Portugal.

6. Further enhancement to the 'six-pack' measures to ensure better economic governance, in particular a set of ten measures to ensure the better functioning of the Eurogroup, including twice-yearly summits at heads of government level and an enhanced secretariat.
7. Further measures, perhaps including treaty changes, to be proposed by December 2011.

# 12. The governance and regulation of sovereign wealth funds and foreign exchange reserves in a post-GFC world*

**Mohamed Ariff and John H. Farrar**

## 12.1 INTRODUCTION

In recent years, largely as a result of globalisation, states have been building up substantial portfolios of assets in other countries. Most of these holdings have been of bonds and marketed equities but some are direct ownership. These funds are normally labelled sovereign wealth funds (SWFs). The initial growth in such funds came from oil-rich countries which wanted to convert at least some of the sales of their oil into other assets that could be used in the future rather than simply into current consumption. A well-managed fund of that form might be able to sustain living standards once oil was depleted. In the early years such funds were small compared with global assets and their holders tended to spread their ownership so they were not a threat to the management of firms or countries and could be treated like any other institutional investor (Truman, 2010; Xu and Bahgat, 2010; Shemirani, 2011)

Nowadays the funds are no longer trivial and in some cases result in control of foreign enterprises. Furthermore such funds have become a form of strategic development for some countries, allowing them to exploit the openness of other countries while protecting their own firms through restrictive entry conditions. While foreign ownership through foreign direct investment (FDI) is long-standing, and host countries have come to terms with the potential threats this could pose to their economic and political stability, the idea that a foreign state is the owner raises further concerns. Foreign state-owned firms have had foreign subsidiaries in the past but these portfolio holdings are new.

One facet which exacerbates the concerns over these funds is the very substantial foreign exchange reserves (FERs) that have been built up in a few countries. These reserves are the result of imbalance in the financial system and lead to a potential threat of further instability to the world economy. The major motivation for holding such large balances was the impact of the Asian crisis in 1997–98 and other examples of sudden stops in emerging markets. If a country without foreign exchange reserves is subject to a major adverse shock it may well need to approach the International Monetary Fund (IMF) for temporary lending to give the space for the results of structural reform to emerge. In 1997–98 the IMF imposed harsh conditions for loans which many of the countries thought unnecessary, a view that has won considerable support (Chweiroth, 2009). With major reserves countries are not only much safer from speculative attack but they are less likely to have to go to the IMF in the event of difficulty. However, more recently it has become clear that such funds are simply the consequence of running a policy designed to hold exchange rates down to permit continuing production growth and gain market share at the expense of those who do not manage their exchange rates in the same way. Taken together these reserves with SWFs pose a potential threat to international stability and hence raise concerns in host countries. They also point to an asymmetry in behaviour in the international trading and investment systems. It would be unfortunate for development if the way symmetry is regained is by the currently open countries returning to the control of exchange rates and restricting investment inflows.

The purpose of this chapter is to consider some of these questions. It looks at the nature of SWFs and FERs, policy issues to which they give rise, the impact of the global financial crisis (GFC) and issues of governance and regulation. Governance and regulation involve discussion of both domestic and international regulation as well as systems of legal and self-regulation (Gilson and Milhaupt, 2007–08). This chapter aims to explore the governance issues in the context of the political economic debate on SWFs and FERs in a world of asymmetric behaviour of some key players.

## 12.2 THE NATURE OF SOVEREIGN WEALTH FUNDS

SWFs are a mixture of funds and entities which are set up for various purposes by states. Hence it is difficult to prescribe similar goals or to generalise about the operational processes of all funds. Operating within market capitalism, they represent examples of state ownership of savings set aside for future consumption from current incomes of resource-rich nations, such as Saudi Arabia from high current incomes due to oil and gas prices since 1978, or small nations such as Singapore and Hong Kong which have less expenses than larger countries and so are able to invest the surplus (Rose, 2008–09a, 2008–09b).

The US Government Accountability Office (GAO) defines SWFs by four criteria:

- They are government-chartered or government-sponsored investment vehicles.
- They invest some or all of their funds in assets other than sovereign debt outside the country that established them.
- They are funded through government transfers arising primarily from sovereign budget surpluses, trade surpluses, central bank currency reserves or revenues from the commodity wealth of a country.
- They are not actively functioning as a pension fund.

The International Working Group (IWG) on SWFs defines them as follows in the Generally Accepted Principles and Practices (GAPP):

> SWFs are special-purpose investment funds or arrangements that are owned by the general government. Created by the general government for macroeconomic purposes, SWFs hold, manage, or administer assets to achieve financial objectives, and employ a set of investment strategies that include investing in foreign financial assets. (IWG, 2008, p. 3)

Certain types are excluded from the latter: foreign exchange reserves, state-owned enterprises and public servant pension funds. According to the IMF, SWFs can be grouped into five categories:

- stabilisation funds;
- savings funds;
- reserve investment funds;
- development funds;
- pension reserve funds. (IMF, 2008)

The impact of SWFs has entered public discussion: see Truman (2010) and Avendano and Santiso (2009). In the West, there has been increasing concern about the governance of SWFs, which led to an initiative in 2010 culminating in the agreement adopting the Santiago Principles to provide some governance guidelines for these state entities. The latest wave of SWFs is arguably a product of the financial instability caused by Western financialisation and Eastern neo-mercantilism. At the same time they are funds which are recycling global financial flows rather than acting as the sources of new funds. Apart from the need to adopt some degree of disclosure on how such large sums of money are deployed, there is also public debate on whether some nations with large SWFs could use these assets for political purposes. An Organisation for Economic Co-operation and Development (OECD) document raises this latter issue, and concludes that that is a matter of grave concern: see Avendano and Santiso (2009, pp. 29–30).

As a result of the way some SWFs are managed, their longer-term impact is likely to be similar to the great experiments of state capitalism of Indonesia, Japan and Mexico in the twentieth century, where state-sponsored firms lost a lot of money. A public debate on this issue is found in *The Economist* (21–27 January 2012). An argument is made that investment decisions made by the politicians or politician-selected protégés who make investment decisions of where and how the SWF assets should be deployed are vastly untrained in such tasks.

Data available from World Bank and OECD sources suggest that 44 nations hold about US$4800 billion which is 7.5 per cent of the world gross domestic product (GDP) in SWFs. Of these nations, those having substantial assets as SWFs are few. Seven nations with ten funds (each of which is larger than US$100 billion) account for 75 per cent of the total SWF assets. The countries are: China with $1130 billion in three funds; the UAE between $372 billion and $627 billion; Norway $570 billion; Saudi Arabia $520 billion; Singapore $405 billion; Hong Kong $320 billion; Kuwait $296 billion. The US has no federally controlled SWFs although four of its resources-rich states control $60 billion in SWF assets. Another approach looks at SWFs from the point of view of liability. The total value of SWF assets is $4800 billion of which the top seven nations own 75 per cent while 35 other nations account for 25 per cent; see Figure 12.1.

*The Economist* (2012) notes with concern the rise of state capitalism in a revised form under the guise of market capitalism, when history has shown that state capitalism in whatever form can lead to poorly judged investments, and resulted in wasted assets in the first half of the last century, and in the case of Indonesia and Mexico in the second half of the last century. Cases like Singapore tend to be the exception rather than the norm.

This is especially an issue if there are also continuing doubts about the quality of disclosure, and governance, as discussed earlier. During the GFC, when financial firms lost a lot of value, these firms attempted to prop themselves up with funds obtained from several SWFs. The SWFs were motivated to acquire significant interests in these firms, so they provided funds only to suffer huge losses as the financial firms either collapsed or lost more value as the crisis persisted. The governance issue for the host country is the control SWFs would exercise over these key firms after the crisis. For the country of origin of the SWFs, the issue is poor governance

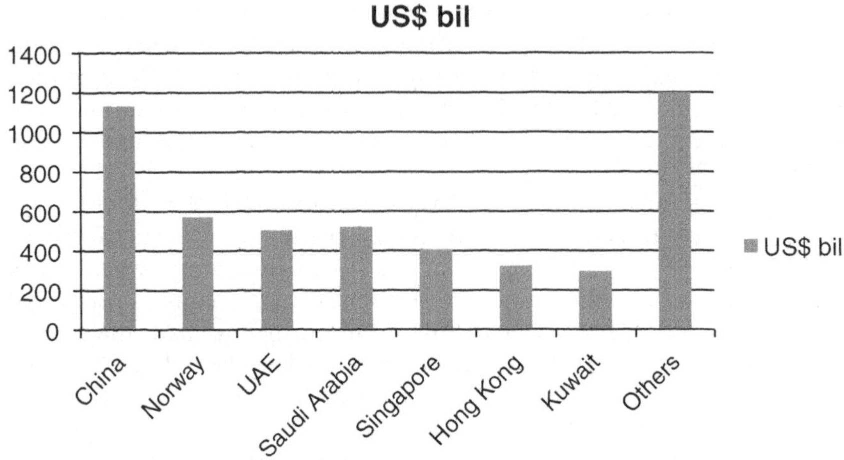


*Figure 12.1 Asset values in US$ of sovereign wealth funds, 2011*

decisions that led to losses reported in the financial firms for such adventures by SWFs. Because of the poor disclosure culture in many SWFs, the extent of the loss to the home-country taxpayers is yet to be documented.

The mutual funds that are owned by individual investors (as opposed to the SWFs controlled by the state) have better process for investment decisions: significant statute laws, and regulatory frameworks exist as well as reporting and monitoring by independent investment analysts. This is not the case with SWFs. Most of these SWFs are managed under less disclosure while most mutual funds with small amounts of assets are required to disclose more information on how assets are deployed and how the funds perform each year. Many SWFs are not transparent and some data may be a rough estimate. The financial press often quotes different data.

## 12.3 THE FUNCTIONS OF SWFS

Gordon Clark and Ashby Monk (2012, p. 16) in their paper 'Sovereign Wealth Funds: Form and Function in the 21st Century', list the main functions as follows:

- SWFs are a means of realising a long-term premium on a nation's wealth over and above the projected real rate of national economic growth. This premium is realised through financial assets invested in a broad portfolio of

assets, representing the potential of global economic integration rather than the potential of one country or region.
- SWFs are a means of separating a portion of a nation's accumulating wealth from the real economy by placing those assets 'outside' of the economy so as to promote long-term macroeconomic stability.
- SWFs are a means of insuring the future economic prosperity of a sovereign entity in the context of global economic and financial instability and the limits of nation-state power in the international community of nations.
- SWFs are a means of storing a nation's wealth separate from the short-term exigencies and political commitments that characterise the life of a sovereign nation; in this sense, SWFs are an endowment fund for the conservation of wealth.
- SWFs are a means of distributing current national wealth, often due to the exploitation of finite resources, to future generations either through discounting the value of accumulated liabilities or by maximising the future value of current assets.

In addition, they mention an underwriting function and insulation function.

## 12.4 PUBLIC POLICY ISSUES OF MANAGING SWFS

SWFs seem to go against the Washington Consensus group of policies which favour the shrinking of the state and privatisation, and arguably to threaten the free market system. The total SWF assets of 44 nations amount to 7.5 per cent of the world GDP; that of foreign reserves amount to 19 per cent of the 2011 world GDP. The asset value of worldwide mergers is also about 7.5 per cent of the GDP of major countries. Mergers are regulated by many countries in the West. The basic Companies Acts of modern states specify the manner in which takeovers and mergers take place. At the height of the GFC in the last quarter of 2007, SWFs were working to prop up top financial firms, attracted by the prospect of cheaply acquiring a controlling interest in these firms. There were huge losses incurred in the process as documented in the financial press, so the purpose of the SWF acquisitions appear to be control rather than reasonable investment returns.

Some critiques (Truman, 2010) advance an argument that SWFs cannot be managed independently and free of political influences and will hence be effectively arms of commercial policy, exercising the sorts of nineteenth century style economic imperialism that the post-Second World War international system sought to eliminate. This concern is particularly felt about many of the major SWFs and especially the Chinese SWFs because of the role SWFs play in the rise of state capitalism in recent decades.

The state capitalism of different shades practised by Russia, Japan, Mexico, Korea, Indonesia and several others in the twentieth century led to huge losses of public wealth. Thus, one argument advanced by *The Economist* is that the current use of state resources such as the SWFs resembles the erstwhile wastage of state assets in the twentieth century, all in the name of creating faster growth.

Also of concern is the fact that in several countries with large SWFs there is state control of significant industries. The energy industry is owned 67 per cent by state firms in countries such as Russia, Libya, Saudi Arabia and Iran; 55 per cent in utilities in several key developing countries; 35 per cent in communications across the world; 33 per cent in financial firms in developing countries. These industries are a source of monopolistic pricing as cartels. Despite the cheapening of communication technology, telcos earn huge amounts by maintaining their monopoly of communication networks under state control.

Other concerns are lack of transparency and accountability of some SWFs and the difficulties this presents to the target entities in the West in which they invest, and to national security. There is a wide range of differing disclosure regimes, many of which are not adequately policed particularly when the SWF is directly controlled and managed by the state. The most transparent SWFs are owned by Norway, New Zealand, Singapore and Japan, and the least by countries such as Russia, China and Saudi Arabia. When these SWFs seek to invest in key financial services or industries which are relevant to national security there is cause for concern. (Gilson and Milhaupt, 2007–08; Xu and Bahgat, 2010; Shemirani, 2011).

SWFs are similar to hedge funds in some respects. They are stand alone, unregulated pools of capital. They are different in that they use less leverage. They are normally less aggressive for short-term results. Some SWFs are now investing in hedge funds and add to the problems of regulating them.

## 12.5 THE NATURE OF FOREIGN EXCHANGE RESERVES

SWFs are distinguished from foreign exchange reserves. The purposes of the latter are described by the Centre for Central Banking Studies of the Bank of England as follows:

1. Formal backing for the domestic currency
2. A tool of exchange rate or monetary policy
3. Funds for servicing foreign exchange liabilities and debt obligations

4. A source of funds for payment for government expenditure overseas
5. A defence against emergencies or disaster
6. An investment fund for financial gains.

Clearly (6) overlaps with SWFs (Nugee, 2012).

Foreign exchange reserves in the post-war era are the result of two great movements in economic ideology – the promotion of development and world trade. The idea of providing support for underdeveloped economies through state-supported plans such as most-favoured nation status, and assisted World Trade Organization (WTO) membership led to some states pursuing a self-interested policy of: (1) open free trade with the developed nations; while (2) restricting entry to the home markets; and (3) use of managed currency as the tool to make domestic production continually cheaper than would be the case with freer trade and investment.

Take for instance the cases of South Korea and Japan, which, under the favoured era following the Second World War, did exactly the three things highlighted above. While having free access to the world markets, the domestic markets were difficult to enter for foreign firms and the central banks pursued a policy of managed currency to obtain trade advantages. While these two countries were reined in to drop the policy freedom under item (3) through the Plaza Accord of the 1984, they still practice unbalanced trade while the rest of the world has taken more steps to let foreign goods enter a country with little tariff or hidden regulation. Some Japanese economists (Ozawa, 2005, is one of them) created a theory of Flying Geese paradigm to justify the export-led growth which is a path to global imbalances. In this paradigm, Asian nations will catch up with the West where the production of goods will move from the more advanced to less advanced nations.

The result of these policies helped Japan and South Korea (and several other countries) to amass foreign reserves disproportionate to the size of the economy. The world's foreign reserves total US$12313 billion. This sum is approximately twice world trade, which the foreign reserve is supposed to serve. As a proportion of world GDP this number is 19 per cent. If we take the world's total assets in SWFs of some US$8 trillion, it appears that the states have total resources as SWFs and foreign reserves amounting to 30 per cent of the world GDP.

Drilling down to the countries that hold most of these resources, we find that 12 nations account for two-thirds of the total reserves: China, Japan, Saudi Arabia, Russia, Taiwan, Brazil, Switzerland, South Korea, Kyrgyzstan, Hong Kong, Germany and Singapore. These 12 countries have foreign reserves totalling US$8000 billion while the rest of the

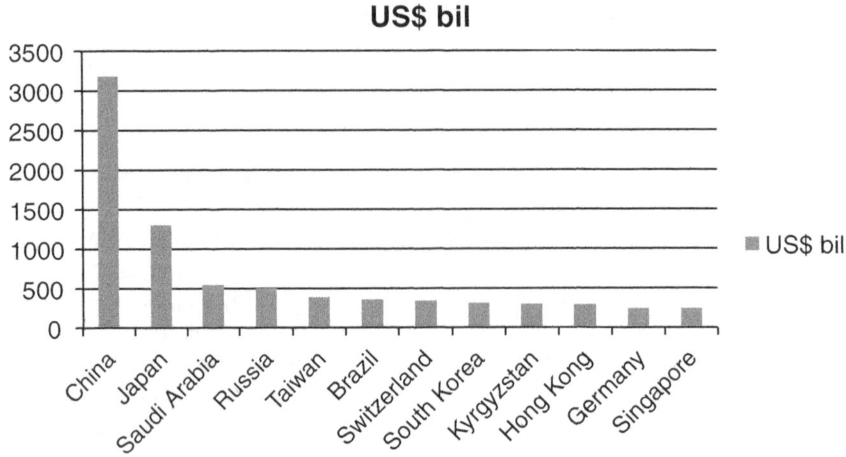


*Figure 12.2 Foreign reserves of 12 largest holders each with above US$ 200 billion*

world has just about 35 per cent of the reserves. Some small countries such as Kyrgyzstan, Singapore and Hong Kong have huge reserves, while major more balanced growth countries such as Germany (US$239 billion), the United Kingdom (US$122 billion) or France (US$172 billion) each have much smaller reserves although these are also large trading nations. The giants with large reserves are either small countries or countries practicing trade protection and managed exchange rates to gain trade advantages.

Therefore, it appears that unbalanced development policies of some countries are aimed at creating large pools of foreign reserves to secure a high rating so that a managed exchange rate policy can protect the currency at the managed exchange rate. Except for Germany, Japan and Switzerland, the other countries with large reserves have a managed flotation of their currencies, which gives them advantages to manage foreign reserves to support the artificially low exchange rates. If one takes into account the free access to exports these countries enjoy while practicing strict barriers for imports, there is a double advantage that plentiful foreign reserves provide advantages to keep the currency low, and trade surplus up.

Once the foreign reserves become large there is an incentive to treat these as state resources. As long as foreign exchange reserves are about the size to support a year's worth of trade, then there is no temptation to use this resource for other than supporting international trade as designed by the IMF. Once a country has too large an amount of foreign reserves, then the state can deploy the resource for local development purposes. For instance, China has deployed some large parts of the reserves to build water diversion from rivers to arid areas and for building roads. From the home-country point of view this enlarges the available resources for development. The public policy issue is whether uneven resource mobilisation by exchange rate management as against free floating of currencies and barriers to free trade – which have created imbalances in the world economy – should be used in this manner instead of trade for which the IMF designed the reserve management; see Nugee (2012).

## 12.6 THE IMPACT OF THE GFC

The GFC had a serious impact on SWFs like every other investor. It also gave rise to opportunities. Firstly, SWFs incurred heavy losses, and this led to a move to less risky, more liquid and balanced portfolios. It also led to a re-evaluation of SWF governance and management, particularly as regards to risk management (Balin, 2010, p. 2). Secondly, it slowed investment by governments in SWFs and the availability of SWF finance. In an uncertain investment climate since the global crisis, there was a need for greater caution (Balin, 2010, pp. 3–4).

Thirdly, it led to the first major use of SWF funds to aid sovereign stabilisation measures. These included capitalisation of banks, the purchase of domestic real estate, and the financing of budget deficits and fiscal stimuli. To stall the potential effect of the 2007–08 crisis, all seven major SWF nations dipped deep into the funds to undertake not just saving financial institutions but also to invest in infrastructure, spur manufacturing, etc. to counter the reduced economic activities.

Fourthly, SWFs were able to acquire controlling interests in major Western companies at bargain basement prices. This is the most controversial impact and led to calls for reform (Balin, 2010, pp. 5–6). Fifthly, it has led to increased cooperation with other SWFs and institutional investors (Balin, 2010, pp. 6–7).

Lastly, there has even been discussion amongst some SWFs about holding IMF Special Drawing Rights (SDRs) to shift the general economy from dependence on the US dollar. This can be compared in some respects with Keynes's idea of the Bancor as an international currency based on a basket of commodities. However SDRs are not a global reserve currency at the moment (UN, 2009).

## 12.7 GOVERNANCE AND REGULATION OF SWFS

The governance and regulation of SWFs can be discussed under two main headings: domestic and international regulation; legal and self-regulation. We set out in Figures 12.3 and 12.4 diagrams contrasting corporate governance with the governance of SWFs.

In essence corporate governance is a symbiosis of legal and self-regulation. The self-regulation takes a variety of forms from quasi law such as Stock Exchange Listing Rules and Statements of Accounting Practice, to institutional codes such as the Corporate Governance Principles and Practice, companies' own codes and business ethics. These are supplemented by the OECD's Principles of Corporate Governance (Farrar, 2008). By contrast there is limited legislation in respect of SWFs, and now the Santiago Principles as a code of self-regulation.

Many countries impose restrictions on FDIs but vary in the operation of them. Thus China is seeking to actively invest its surplus overseas while it operates a strict regime at home. Australia by contrast has tended to operate a fairly liberal approach to foreign investment in the past but has taken a stricter approach to recent bids by Singapore and China.

The Australian regime is implemented through the Foreign Acquisitions and Takeovers Act 1975. The Treasurer is responsible under the Act and reviews proposals on a case-by-case basis to decide if they are contrary to Australia's national interest. The Treasurer acts on the advice of the Foreign Investment Review Board.

The US enacted the Foreign Investment and National Security Act 2007 (FINSA) for stricter controls. FINSA requires the President to conduct a national security investigation of certain proposed investment transactions. Congress has a broad oversight role, but only the President has the power to suspend or prohibit transactions. Key transactions which have been vetoed are China National Offshore Oil Corporation's attempted acquisition of UNOCAL in 2005 and Dubai Ports World's attempted acquisition of P&O.

The international approach has been through treaties and systems of self-regulation. An attempt at a multilateral approach failed but there have been bilateral treaties between some countries. One approach would be to attempt comprehensive regulation applicable to all, treating SWFs like other investors. This does not seem practicable. Another approach would be a prohibition of specific investments or activities. A third approach would be to insist on reciprocity.

The two main systems of self-regulation are the Santiago Principles adopted by the International Working Group in October 2008, and the OECD's Declaration and Guidelines. Earlier work had been done by

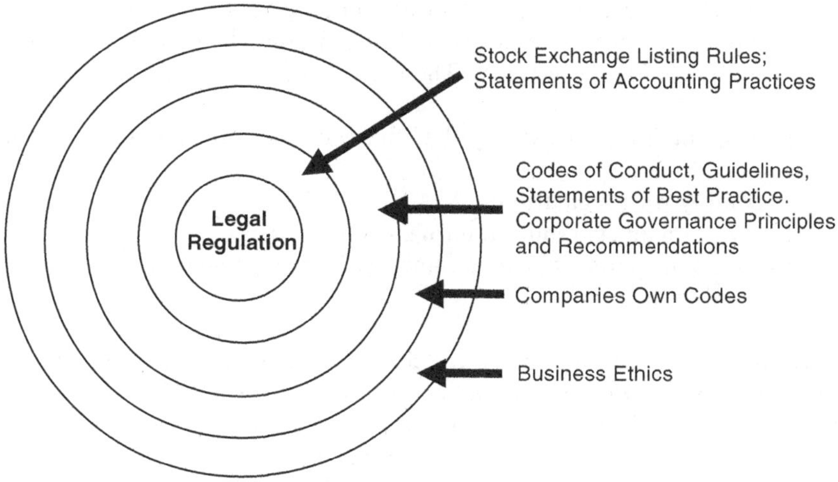


*Figure 12.3 Corporate governance*

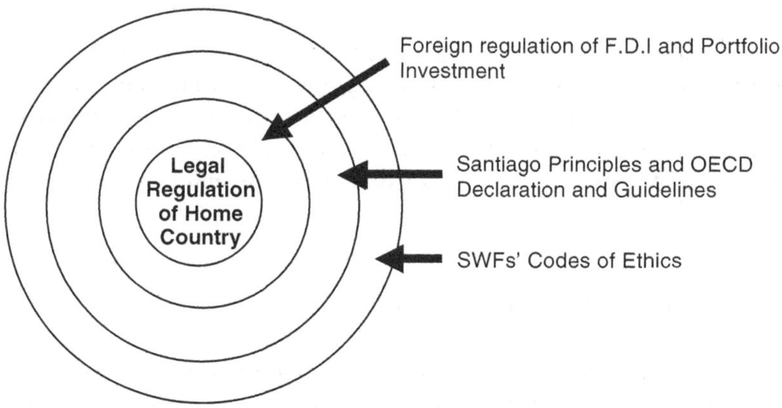


*Figure 12.4 The governance of SWFs*

Edwin Truman for the Peterson Institute for International Economics in the form of the SWF Scoreboard in 2007 (Truman, 2010).

The Santiago Principles or Generally Accepted Principles and Practices of SWFs (GAPP) are set out in the Appendix to this chapter and we shall concentrate on six aspects. See generally Das et al. (2010). The purposes of the Principles are: (1) to identify a framework of accepted principles and practices reflecting governance and accountability; (2) to enable better understanding of SWFs; and (3) to bring mutual benefit from SWFs. There are five guiding objectives. These are:

1. to help maintain a safer global financial system and free flow of capital;
2. to comply with regulation;
3. to invest on an economic and financial risk basis;
4. to have transparency in governance, risk management; and
5. accountability.

Governance and accountability are dealt with in a number of the principles. Principle 2 requires the 'policy purpose' of the SWF to be defined and disclosed. This is usually in the relevant legislation. The legal framework and reporting systems must be in place (Principles 1, 7, 10–12 and 23). Public disclosure of the policy objective and framework must be made (Principle 16). Proper management and voting procedures should be in place (Principles 9, 13, 16, 19, 21 and 22). Most but not all the SWFs have requirements of minimum competency for governing body members.

Like all self-regulation, the Santiago Principles and the OECD Declaration and policies are well-meaning but somewhat bland, aspirational documents which lack legal force. On the other hand they probably represent as much progress as we can reasonably expect at this stage. One of the main problems is to take SWFs in isolation from overall strategies and policies.

## 12.8 POLICY COORDINATION

Policy coordination between the SWF and the domestic fiscal and monetary authorities must be carried out (Principle 3). The SWFs investment policy must be clear and consistent with the policy objective and based on sound portfolio management principles (Principle 18). Most of the SWFs are accountable to and report to their legislatures.

### 12.8.1 Investment Management

Other principles dealing with investment management are 18, 19 and 21–23. All SWFs are seeking to maximise the long-term risk-adjusted return but the relevant objectives differ. Most disclose their investment policy on their websites and in their reports.

### 12.8.2 Commercial Conduct

Transparency through statement of policy purpose and refraining from pursuit of collateral objectives combined with disclosure are required to reassure recipient countries (Principles 2, 4, 16, 19 and 21). In practice there seems to be considerable variation in compliance with these principles.

### 12.8.3 Competition

SWFs must comply with the competition rules of host countries and not take unfair advantage of information (Principles 15 and 20).

### 12.8.4 Financial Market Stability

A number of the principles aim at financial market stability. These deal with adequate disclosure, voting policies, and investment policy (Principles, 17, 18, 21 and 22). Principle 17 requires disclosure of relevant financial information so as to contribute to stability in international financial markets and enhance trust in recipient countries. This should be strengthened as it goes to the root of the matter.

The implementation of the Santiago Principles has been uneven. A small group mainly from democratic countries have been highly committed to them. A second larger group have partly complied and a third group have not yet complied. It has been argued by Edwin Truman of the Peterson Institute that the Santiago Principles fall well short of the international standards of best practices as he defines them (Truman, 2010).

In a report prepared by the International Forum of SWFs of 7 July, 2011 the following particulars were given about compliance:

- 95 per cent (404 of the 426 responses given) of Member's practices are fully or partially consistent with the Santiago Principles;
- 80 per cent (340 of the 426 responses given) of Members' Santiago Principles consistent (partially or completely) practices pre-date the Santiago Principles
- 15 per cent (64 of the 426 responses given) of Members – consistent (partially or completely implemented) practices post-date issuance of the Santiago Principles; and
- 4 per cent (18 of the 426 responses given) of Members have identified one or more instances of not having implemented Santiago Principles – consistent practices.

In a Policy Brief of August 2011 Sarah Bagnall and Edwin Truman compare compliance with the Santiago Principles from the IFSWFs' Report with their SWF Scoreboard and the results are shown in Table 12.1.

The OECD Investment Committee produced a report on Sovereign Wealth Funds and Reciprocal Countries Policies in April 2008 which summarised existing policies of relevance to SWFs and supported the work of the IWG leading to the Santiago Principles. The resulting work consists of a Declaration on SWFs and reciprocal country policies, guidance reaffirming the relevance of long-standing OECD investment principles and Guidelines for recipient-country investment policies relating to national security. These are backed up by a peer review system.

## 12.9 THE GOVERNANCE AND REGULATION OF FERS

FERs are the subject of domestic laws which differ from state to state. They are also subject to Article IV of the Articles of Agreement of the International Monetary Fund (IMF). The present version was incorporated into the Articles by the Second Amendment in 1978 as a result of the collapse of the par value system. This system linked the member state's ability to modify the value of the currency against a common denominator expressed in gold either directly or through the US dollar. The new system legalised freedom to choose exchange arrangements. Article IV Section 1 sets out the general obligations of members. Each member shall:

1. endeavour to direct its economic and financial policies toward the objective of fostering orderly economic growth with reasonable price stability, with due regard to its circumstances;
2. seek to promote stability by fostering orderly underlying economic and financial conditions and a monetary system that does not tend to produce erratic disruptions;
3. avoid manipulating exchange rates or the international monetary system in order to prevent effective balance of payments adjustment or to gain an unfair competitive advantage over other members; and
4. follow exchange policies compatible with the undertakings under this Section. (IMF, 2011)

Section 3 provides for surveillance over exchange arrangements by the IMF. This has not been effective as major countries such as the US have ignored it. Martin Wolf in his paper 'Surveillance by the International Monetary Fund' has argued that there are six reasons for its ineffectiveness: ignorance by economists, insularity, ideology, incentives,

*Table 12.1 Compliance with the Santiago Principles by principle*

| Principle | Compliance | | |
|---|---|---|---|
| | IFSWF Report | SWF Scoreboard | Difference |
| Legal Framework, Objectives, and Coordination with Macroeconomic Policies | | | |
| 1. Legal framework | 88 | 87 | 1 |
| 2. Policy purpose | 88 | 98 | −10 |
| 3. Integrated with macroeconomic policies | 55 | 80 | −25 |
| 4. Source of funds and use of earnings | 86 | 79 | 7 |
| *Subtotal* | 79 | 86 | −7 |
| Institutional Framework and Governance Structure | | | |
| 6. Division of roles | 88 | 88 | 0 |
| 7. Role of government | 88 | 88 | 0 |
| 8. Role of governing body | 88 | 90 | −2 |
| 9. Decisions made by managers | 86 | 76 | 10 |
| 11. Annual report | 88 | 88 | 0 |
| 12. Audit | 83 | 82 | 1 |
| 13. Internal ethical standards | 76 | 51 | 25 |
| 17. Financial information disclosure | 83 | 76 | 7 |
| *Subtotal* | 85 | 80 | 5 |
| Investment and Risk Management Framework | | | |
| 18. Investment policies | 79 | 57 | 22 |
| 19. Investment principles | 74 | 24 | 50 |
| 21. Corporate responsibility policy | 52 | 31 | 21 |
| 22. Risk management framework | 71 | 57 | 14 |
| *Subtotal* | 69 | 42 | 27 |
| Total (16 principles) | 80 | 72 | 8 |
| Non-overlapping Principles | | | |
| 5. Statistical data | 83 | | |
| 10. Accountability framework | 90 | | |
| 14. Third party procedures | 71 | | |
| 15. Disclosure in host countries | 74 | | |
| 16. Governance framework | 86 | | |
| 20. Avoid conflict of interest | 64 | | |
| 23. Investment reporting standards | 76 | | |
| 24. Self review of Santiago Principles implementation | 48 | | |
| *Subtotal* | 74 | | |
| Total (24 principles) | 78 | | |

*Note:* IFSWF – International Forum of Sovereign Wealth Funds.

*Source:* Truman 2010, Bagnall and Truman 2011, IFSWF 2011.

intimidation by members, and impotence of the IMF. He makes some telling criticisms. There are now proposals to enhance the role of the IMF as mediator (Wolf, 2011).

Wolf argues that the IMF needs to be humbler yet braver and more open to outside ideas, seeking a role as a central player with the G-20 group (Wolf, 2011). The Palais Royal Initiative (2011) recommended that Article IV be amended to reflect a strengthened commitment to ensuring policies are conducive to the stability of the global economic, monetary and financial system. Strong consideration should be given to graduated remedial actions which could include financial penalties and freezing of part or all of a country's voting rights. It also mentioned the activation of WTO procedures and trade sanctions based on IMF'S assessment (Palais Royal Initiative, 2011). However, the IMF lost ground in the Asian financial crisis and GFC and has yet to recapture it. We are unlikely in fact to see any stronger criticisms of members' conduct or a system of international sanctions on FERs issues such as exist under the WTO system in trade issues.

## 12.10 CONCLUSION

SWFs are becoming significant players in the global economy and differ from institutional investors. They represent a hybrid between market and state capitalism as they are pockets of state capitalism in market capitalist systems. The transparency of most SWFs is below Western standards which gives cause for concern. The lack of openness and reciprocity in the home countries of SWFs is another concern, and should cause Western countries to err on the side of caution in handling inward investment by SWFs. The Santiago Principles are a step in the right direction but have only had limited success. The OECD Declaration relates only to its members.

China and Singapore are pursuing active SWF policies which include long-term investment. The Australian Treasury Secretary's view at the moment is that the focus should be on delivering a surplus and reducing net debt. The superannuation system in Australia already acts as a series of 'mini wealth funds' (Williams, 2011). This is not quite so, as these are not sovereign funds. The idea of a new fund is not without merit, but there is a need to be clear as to what role it should play. More attention needs to be given to this. Western countries currently seem to concentrate on portfolio management and to lack the strategic vision which characterises Singapore and China which are actively using SWFs. This lack of perspective at this important time of transition is unfortunate.

The imbalances in foreign exchange reserves resulting from

neo-mercantilist policies of some Asian countries are a threat to the balanced growth needed in a globalised economy. Surveillance by the IMF has been weak and the situation is unlikely to change unless and until there is reform of quota shares and voting power. The IMF seems to be in search of a role in the post-GFC world, and there is a risk that the centre of gravity will move elsewhere.

In the meantime SWF activities when combined with exchange rate manipulation and a highly unbalanced trade position raise serious problems of unfair competition in both trade and investment. Globalisation was not supposed to work like this. Globalisation is not an inexorable natural force but complex human activity, and to control it needs strong leadership and a collective act of will. We have not seen this since 1944.

## NOTE

* The authors wish to thank David Mayes for constructive criticism of earlier drafts of this chapter.

## REFERENCES

Avendano, R. and J. Santiso (2009), 'Are Sovereign Wealth Funds' Investments Politically Motivated? A Comparison with Mutual Funds', OECD Development Centre Working Paper No. 283, Paris.

Bagnall, S. and E. Truman (2011), 'IFSWF Report on Compliance with the Santiago Principles: Admirable but Flawed Transparency', Policy Brief, August, Peterson Institute for International Economics.

Balin, B. (2010), 'The Impact of the Global Economic Crisis on Sovereign Wealth Funds', *Asian Pacific Economic Literature*, **24**, 1.

Chwieroth, J.M. (2009), *Capital Ideas: The IMF and the Rise of Financial Liberalization*, Princeton, NJ: Princeton University Press.

Clark, G.L. and A.H.B. Monk (2012), 'Sovereign Wealth Funds: Form and Function in the 21st Century', *CAPCO Journal*, **33**, 17–27.

Das, U.S., A. Mazarei, H. van der Hoorn (2010), *Economics of Sovereign Wealth Funds*, Washington, DC: IMF.

Farrar, J.H. (2008), *Corporate Governance: Theories, Principles and Practice*, 3rd edn, Melbourne: Oxford University Press.

Gilson, R. and C. Milhaupt (2007–08), 'Sovereign Wealth Funds and Corporate Governance: A Minimalist Response to the New Mercantilism', *Stanford Law Review*, **60**, 3145.

International Forum of Sovereign Wealth Funds (IFSWF) (2011), 'IFSWF Members' Experiences in the Application of the Santiago Principles', 7 July.

International Monetary Fund (2008), 'Sovereign Wealth Fund – A Work Agenda', 29 February.

International Monetary Fund (2011), *Articles of Agreement of the International Monetary Fund, 2011 Edition*.
International Working Group of Sovereign Wealth Funds (IWG) (2008), *Sovereign Wealth Funds Generally Accepted Principles and Practices 'Santiago Principles'*, Washington
Nugee, J. (2012), Bank of England, *Centre for Central Banking Studies Handbook Foreign Exchange Reserves Management*.
Ozawa, T. (2005), *Institutions, Industrial Upgrading, and Economic Performance in Japan – The 'Flying-Geese' Paradigm of Catch-up Growth*, Cheltenham, UK and Northampton, MA, USA: Edward Elgar Publishing.
Palais Royal Initiative (2011), 'Reform of the International Monetary System: A Corporate Approach for the Twenty First Century', http://www.global-currencies.org/smi/gb/telechar/news/Rapport_Camdessus-integral.pdf, accessed 12 April 2012.
Rose, P. (2008–09a), 'Sovereign Wealth Fund Investment in the Shadow of Regulation and Politics', *Georgia Journal of International Law*, **40**, 1207.
Rose, P. (2008–09b), 'Sovereigns as Shareholders', *North Carolina Law Review*, **87**, 83.
Shemirani, M. (2011), *Sovereign Wealth Funds and International Political Economy*, Farnham: Ashgate.
Truman, E. (2010), 'Sovereign Wealth Funds – Threat or Salvation', Washington, DC: Peterson Institute for International Economics.
United Nations (UN) (2009), 'Report of the Commission of Experts on Reforms of the International Monetary and Financial Systems', New York, 21 September.
Williams, R. (2011), 'Treasury Chief Way Wary of Wealth Fund Zeal', http://www.smh.com.au/business/treasury-chief-wary-of-wealth-fund-zeal-20111109-1n7ds.html, viewed 18/01/2012, accessed February 2012.
Wolf, M. (2011), 'TSR External Commentary: Surveillance by the International Monetary Fund', http://www.imf.org/external/np/pp/eng/2011/081511.pdf, accessed 12 March 2012.
Xu, Y.C. and G. Bahgat (2010), *The Political Economy of Sovereign Wealth Funds*, Basingstoke: Palgrave Macmillan.

## APPENDIX

The Santiago Principles provide as follows:

**GAPP 1. Principle**
The legal framework for the SWF should be sound and support its effective operation and the achievement of its stated objective(s).

**GAPP 2. Principle**
The policy purpose of the SWF should be clearly defined and publicly disclosed.

**GAPP 3. Principle**
Where the SWF's activities have significant direct domestic macroeconomic implications, those activities should be closely coordinated with the

domestic fiscal and monetary authorities, so as to ensure consistency with the overall macroeconomic policies.

**GAPP 4. Principle**
There should be clear and publicly disclosed policies, rules, procedures, or arrangements in relation to the SWF's general approach to funding, withdrawal, and spending operations.

**GAPP 5. Principle**
The relevant statistical data pertaining to the SWF should be reported on a timely basis to the owner, or as otherwise required, for inclusion where appropriate in macroeconomic data sets.

**GAPP 6. Principle**
The governance framework for the SWF should be sound and establish a clear and effective division of roles and responsibilities in order to facilitate accountability and operational independence in the management of the SWF to pursue its objectives.

**GAPP 7. Principle**
The owner should set the objectives of the SWF, appoint the members of its governing body(ies) in accordance with clearly defined procedures, and exercise oversight over the SWF's operations.

**GAPP 8. Principle**
The governing body(ies) should act in the best interests of the SWF, and have a clear mandate and adequate authority and competency to carry out its functions.

**GAPP 9. Principle**
The operational management of the SWF should implement the SWF's strategies in an independent manner and in accordance with clearly defined responsibilities.

**GAPP 10. Principle**
The accountability framework for the SWF's operations should be clearly defined in the relevant legislation, charter, other constitutive documents, or management agreement.

**GAPP 11. Principle**
An annual report and accompanying financial statements on the SWF's operations and performance should be prepared in a timely fashion and in accordance with recognized international or national accounting standards in a consistent manner.

**GAPP 12. Principle**
The SWF's operations and financial statements should be audited annually in accordance with recognized international or national auditing standards in a consistent manner.

**GAPP 13. Principle**
Professional and ethical standards should be clearly defined and made known to the members of the SWF's governing body(ies), management, and staff.

**GAPP 14. Principle**
Dealing with third parties for the purpose of the SWF's operational management should be based on economic and financial grounds, and follow clear rules and procedures.

**GAPP 15. Principle**
SWF operations and activities in host countries should be conducted in compliance with all applicable regulatory and disclosure requirements of the countries in which they operate.

**GAPP 16. Principle**
The governance framework and objectives, as well as the manner in which the SWF's management is operationally independent from the owner, should be publicly disclosed.

**GAPP 17. Principle**
Relevant financial information regarding the SWF should be publicly disclosed to demonstrate its economic and financial orientation, so as to contribute to stability in international financial markets and enhance trust in recipient countries.

**GAPP 18. Principle**
The SWF's investment policy should be clear and consistent with its defined objectives, risk tolerance, and investment strategy, as set by the owner or the governing body(ies), and be based on sound portfolio management principles.

**GAPP 19. Principle**
The SWF's investment decisions should aim to maximize risk-adjusted financial returns in a manner consistent with its investment policy, and based on economic and financial grounds.

**GAPP 20. Principle**
The SWF should not seek or take advantage of privileged information or inappropriate influence by the broader government in competing with private entities.

**GAPP 21. Principle**
SWFs view shareholder ownership rights as a fundamental element of their equity investments' value. If an SWF chooses to exercise its ownership rights, it should do so in a manner that is consistent with its investment policy and protects the financial value of its investments. The SWF should publicly disclose its general approach to voting securities of listed entities, including the key factors guiding its exercise of ownership rights.

**GAPP 22. Principle**
The SWF should have a framework that identifies, assesses, and manages the risks of its operations.

**GAPP 23. Principle**
The assets and investment performance (absolute and relative to benchmarks, if any) of the SWF should be measured and reported to the owner according to clearly defined principles or standards.

**GAPP 24. Principle**
A process of regular review of the implementation of the GAPP should be engaged in by or on behalf of the SWF.

# Index

12th Five-Year Plan 86–89
21 July 2011 Agreement 270
26 October 2011 Agreement 270–271

Abbot Point Coal Terminal 131–132, 135–136
Accord 174
accountability 31, 210–212, 215, 225, 284
accounting standards 5, 75
accreditation 200
acquisitions 72
activism 32
administrative law 38
affirmative action 46
African Union 58
Air New Zealand 140, 149
airports 127
alternative dispute resolution 50
Amersham International 154
Anti-Dumping Agreement 60
apartheid 43, 45, 47, 57, 65
arbitration 57
Asian financial crisis 7, 82–83
asset
  management 181
  values 164
Association for the Taxation of Financial Transactions and Aid to Citizens 95
asymmetry 245, 261
Attorney General 33
audit 292
  review bodies 211
Auditor General 45
Australia 7, 17, 29, 117–137, 173–176, 178–179, 184–188, 193, 210, 213–214, 219, 256, 282, 288
Australian
  Securities and Investment Commission 118, 124, 234
  Prudential Regulation Authority 234
  Taxation Office 122
autonomy 31

bailout 250
balance sheets 226
balanced budget 262
  legislation 258
Baker Plan 249
Bancor 281
bank 248–249
  failures 64
  for International Settlements 58
  of England 220, 231, 233, 237, 267
Basel Committee on Banking Supervision 56–57, 65
Basic Law 98–100, 102–104, 109–112
Belgium 254
best practice 161
BHP Billiton 135
bidding criteria 179
bilateral investment treaties 56
Bill of Rights 28, 45, 48–52
blanket guarantee 257
board of directors 119
bonus shares 140
Bowen Basin 127
Brady bonds 249
branding 77
brands 78
Brazil 165
BRICS 12, 58–60, 70, 89
Brisbane Airport 127
British Telecom 154
Broad-Based Black Economic Empowerment 46, 57, 66, 68
budget deficits 281
buffer funds 259
build-own-transfer 174–175, 185–186, 189
Bundesbank 220

Bundesrat 110–112
Bundestag 98, 101–104, 106, 110–112
bundled contracts 211
bureaucracy 30
business case 187

Cable and Wireless 154
California energy crisis 165
Canada 106, 256
Cape Town 52
Capital 2
  Market Development 167
    Task Force 150
  markets 149, 164, 166
  mobility 56
capitalisation 151, 156
  of banks 281
capitalism 16
carbon pollution 132
cash flows 142
Catalonia 13
central
  bank 15, 218–238, 255
    independence 219–225
  Plan Bureau 253
  planning 80
certainty 187–188
China 7, 9, 12–13, 44, 72–90, 275, 281–282, 288
  -ASEAN FTA 82
  Federation of Trade Unions 3
  Mobile 78
  National Offshore Oil Corporation 282
  Telecom 78, 81
  Unicorn 78, 81
chrome 44
City of London 2
civil
  organisations 87–88
  rights 32
  society 88, 198
clean water 37
Cleaner Energy Strategy 126
Clinton administration 2
close to balance or in surplus 251, 254
coal 44, 125, 134
cohesion funds 259
Cold War 2–3
collective action
  clauses 249
  problem 248
colonisation 3, 22
comity 33, 37
commercial
  conduct 285
  discipline 167
commercialisation 7
Committee of
  Central Bank Governors 237
  Nine 103–104
common law 48–49, 68
Communist Party 83
community service obligations 120–121
company law 75
comparative advantage 66, 74, 79
competition 157, 285
  Commission 70
  laws 63
  Tribunal 62–63
Competitive
  Neutrality Fee 120
  tender 177
competitiveness 85, 246–247, 255, 257, 260
compliance 264, 287
confidence 31
confidentiality 104
conflict of interest 165, 211–212
constitution 44–45, 48, 51–54, 66, 68
  Act 28, 68–69
constitutional
  arrangements 28
  Court 45–46, 49–50, 52–55, 61, 68–69, 97–104, 107–108
  democracy 43
constitutionalism 55, 94
contagion 4, 96
contestability 30
contracts 30
convergence 255
Corfu Channel 105
corporate
  governance 10–11, 282–283
  plans 123
Corporations Act 118–119, 121
corporatisation 117–137
corporatism 88
corruption 66, 69

cosmopolitanisation 2
Court of Appeal 33
credibility 226, 253, 259
credit
  crunch 228
  default swaps 266
  insurance 186
  rating 186
    agencies 5, 9
  wrapping 186
Cross-City Tunnel 183, 185
Crown 29
CS Energy 133
Cukierman Index 223
customary law 48
cyclically adjusted budgets 251

de Larosière 231
debt 14, 246, 259, 2
  crisis 101
  ratio 252, 254–255, 265
decision-making 34
default 248–249, 262
  risk 142, 249, 267
deficit bias 251, 265
deflation 247, 257
deleveraging 143
Delors Committee 255
democracy 94, 97, 100–101, 107–108
democratic
  deficit 47, 57, 65, 113, 225, 237
  formative action 98
  right 35
demographic dividend 44
deregulation 17, 56, 164, 174
derivative products 4
Deutsche Mark 220
devaluation 246, 266
Dexia 255, 267
Directorate of
  Priority Crime Investigation 49–50
  Special Operations 49
discounts 153
dispute resolution 66, 186
distribution networks 77
dividend 122
Dodd-Frank Act 231
Doha Round 84
Dubai Ports World 282
Dudgeon Point 136
dumping 61
dynamic
  efficiency 166
    gains 148–149
  stochastic general equilibrium 10

e-tolling 181
EastLink 185
ECOFIN 254
economic
  growth 84, 89, 150
  infrastructure 173–174
  Partnership Agreements 60
  policy 24
  reform 84
  sovereignty 245
economies of scale 81
education 37, 65
efficiency 117, 156
Electoral
  Act 28, 36
  Finance Bill 33
  system 36
electricity 132, 151, 158
emergency liquidity assistance 226, 229, 235
emerging strategic industries 86
Employment Contracts Act 11
EMU 250
ENERGEX 126
environment 37
environmental protection 180
equity research 155
Ergon Energy Corporation 126
Estonia 247, 256
euro 97, 99, 243–268
  area 96–97
    bonds 261, 268
  crisis 12, 16
  Plus Pact 262
Eurogroup 95, 109, 271
Europarechtsfreundlichkeit 98
European
  Central Bank 228–229, 232–233, 249, 265
  Commission 254, 262, 268
  Council 97
  Financial
    Stabilisation Mechanism 265

Stability Facility 94, 96–97, 109, 244, 259, 265–266, 270
Monetary System 245
Parliament 108, 266
Semester 254, 262, 267
Stability Mechanism 94, 96–97, 109, 244, 265–266, 270
Systemic Risk Board 231, 262–263
Union 9, 12–13, 17, 60, 94–113
Eurosystem 15
excessive
deficit 250, 254
procedure 255, 258, 263
imbalance procedure 263
exchange rate 246–247, 255–256, 260, 273
Executive 28–29, 31, 37–38
expropriation 57
external imbalances 262
extractive industries 64

factual independence 223
fair weather system 263
fan chart 253, 267
Federal Reserve 231, 237
fertility rate 68
financial
advisors 143
inclusion 59
literacy 152
market stability 285
Markets Authority 11
Policy Committee 231, 233
Services Authority 10
stability 5–6, 218, 227–237
Board 5, 57–58, 65, 229
Oversight Council 231
financialisation 274
Finland 16–17, 256, 259–260, 264
first
in Africa 58
past the post 33
fiscal
buffers 260
cost 83
council 258, 268
deficit 246
discipline 243
federalism 258
integration 158
Policy Council 253
Responsibility Act 266
sustainability 102, 190
transfer 256, 258
treaty 244, 264
flexibility 168, 186, 259–260
flipping 152
Flying Geese 279
foreign
direct investment 44, 56, 64, 73, 78, 149, 272, 282
exchange reserves 16, 272–289
Investment
and National Security Act 282
Review Board 282
forestry 129
Plantations Queensland 129
Fortis 255, 267
Fourth Labour government 25, 28, 37
France 245, 254, 263–264, 280
Franklin D Roosevelt 3
Future Investment Fund 140

G-20 4–6, 58–60, 84, 89, 94–95, 229, 237, 288
gas 134
gateway
procurement 193
to Africa 58
GATT 58, 60
GDP 44, 68
Geely 72
gender-based discrimination 49
Genesis Power 140
gentailers 148–149
German
Constitutional Court 94, 108
Parliament 95, 103–104
Germany 12–13, 35, 37, 94–113, 165, 245, 254, 257, 263–264, 280
Ghana 54
Gini coefficient 44
Gladstone Ports Corporation 135
Glenister 49–50
global
administrative law 57
financial crisis 4–6
governance 22
human community 112

globalisation 1–3
go abroad policies 73
goal independence 222
gold 44
  standard 219
golden shares 165
governance 30, 206, 211–212, 283
  deficit 47
government owned corporations 117–134
  Act 119–120, 162
gradualism 9, 79
great
  depression 219–220
  moderation 15, 220–221, 226
Greece 16, 24, 95–96, 99, 243, 246–248, 250, 254, 256, 259, 262–266, 270
Greek
  bonds 244
  debt 248, 250
Greenspan standard 10
guanxi 80
G.W. Bush administration 3

Haier 83
Hancock Queensland Plantations 129
harmonisation 9
health and safety 134
healthcare 51
hegemony 2–4, 10, 22
Hilmer review 117
Hong Kong 145, 274–275, 280
housing 37, 51
Huawei 78
human
  capital 46
  dignity 100
  Rights 32
    Act 28
    Commission 45
    obligations 38

IBM 75
identity 38
ideology 24
idiosyncratic shock 245, 256
IMF 5–7, 56–58, 82, 84, 94, 109, 220, 229, 244, 247, 249, 259, 264–265, 273, 281, 286, 288–289
imperialism 2, 3
incentive 153, 155, 188–190
  structures 30
incomplete contracts 161, 186, 189, 193
independence 227–228
independent
  adjudicative institutions 63
  Electoral Commission 45
  fiscal councils 265
India 146
Indonesia 275
Industrial
  Development 125–126
    Council 65–66
  policies 86
  relations 134
inequality 23
inflation 219–221, 225, 255–256
  targeting 220–222, 260
information 214
  and communications technology 77
infrastructure 211–213
  procurement 191
initial public offerings 74
innovation 12, 148, 185
  policy 85
insolvency 249
instalments 153
Institute for International Finance 266
instrument independence 222
intellectual property 85
  rights 87
interest rates 245, 257, 260
intergenerational equity 190
intergovernmentalism 95
internal imbalances 262
International
  Centre for the Settlement of Investment Disputes Tribunal 69
  Court of Justice 105
  environmental law 105
  Financial Reporting Standards 75
  Labour Organisation 22
  law 50
  obligations 32
  trade
    Administration Commission 60–61
    agreements 38
internationalisation 1

investment 2
  bankers 143
  options 151
IOSCO 5
IPOs 152
Ireland 96, 244–247, 250, 257–259, 266, 270
ISO 208
Italy 244–246, 254, 259, 263, 270
iwi 163–164

Jackson Hole consensus 230
Japan 275, 278–279
jobless growth 70
joint ventures 85, 87
judicial review 61, 99

keiretsu 73
key performance indicators 184, 189
knowledge processes 87
Korea 279
Kuwait 275
Kyrgyzstan 280

labelling 200
landmark design 181
League of Nations 22
legal
  advisors 143
  independence 223
  infrastructure 42
  system 31–33
legislation 37
Legislative Council 28
legitimacy 22, 67, 79, 101, 211–213
Lehman Brothers 106, 249
lender of last resort 218, 226, 229–230, 235
Lenovo 75
leveraged democratic legitimisation 102
liberalisation 9, 26
licensing 200
life-cycle cost 177, 181, 188, 191–192, 210
light touch regulation 11
liquefied natural gas 132, 134
liquidity 155–156, 226
Lisbon Treaty 94, 108, 258
listing 77
litigation 50
local authorities 54
London
  Club 249
  Underground 215
long-term infrastructure contract 210–211
Luxembourg 266

Maastricht
  criteria 255–256
  rules 260
  Treaty 15, 232, 250, 254
macroeconomic stability 277
macroprudential
  frameworks 5
  supervision 262
  tools 5
majoritarian democracy 55
managed exchange rate 280
management consultants 143
manganese 44
manufacturing 26
Maori 11, 29, 35
  Council 32, 163
  Party 13, 164
market
  failure 198
  pressures 42
  size 150
Mauritius 70
mechanistic state 172
Medium to Long-Term Plan 86
Melbourne 184, 190
Memorandum of Understanding 234
mergers and acquisitions 62, 74–75
Meridian Energy 140
Mexico 275
Mighty River Power 140
Millenium Development Goals 59
mining 134
minority shareholder 165
mixed ownership model 141
MMP 33, 35–37
Model Laws on Arbitration and Conciliation 50
monetarism 7
monetary
  nationalism 237

policy 218–221, 224–225, 227–229, 235–236, 245, 253, 255, 267
committee 222, 237
money creation 225
monitoring 200, 202, 259
monopolistic behaviour 81
monopoly capitalism 56
moral
hazard 268
suasion 263
most-favoured nation 279
multilayered governance 113
multinationals 12, 72–90
mutual funds 276

national
airlines 158
Development and Reform Commission 81
Intellectual Property Strategy 86
Patent Development Strategy 86
Planning Commission 65–66
security 159
Tax Equivalent Regime 122
treatment 67
nationalisation 64, 67
natural monopolies 157
neoliberal principles 56
neoliberalism 7, 24–25, 31, 34, 37, 206, 215
neo-mercantilism 274, 289
networks 22
net worth 142
New
Growth Path 65–66
imperialism 3
management 11
public management 30
South Wales 7, 184, 212
Zealand 7, 10–11, 13, 17, 21–38, 140–168, 266, 278
Post 161
Treasury 141
no bailout clause 258
non-
adversarial contracting methods 190–191
governmental organisations 54, 59, 203, 208

North Queensland Bulk Ports Corporation 131, 135–136
Northern
Queensland Basin 125
Territory 179
Norway 267, 275, 278
NWQ Minerals Province 136
NZ Rail 149
NZX 150

obligations 51, 53
Occupy movement 24
Wall Street 95
OECD 7, 44, 58, 282
Declaration and Guidelines 283–284, 288
Office of
Budgetary Responsibility 253
Government Owned Corporations 120
oil 44
ombudsmen 203, 211
open market operations 218, 223
openness 26
optimal currency area 16
optimism bias 174, 179, 181
Optimum Currency Area 255
criteria 256, 260, 267
organised crime 49
outbound foreign direct investment 72–78, 82, 85, 88–90
outsourcing 6
outward foreign direct investment 159

Palais Royal Initiative 288
Paris Club 249
parliament 28, 31–32, 34, 45
parliamentary sovereignty 45, 48
partial privatisation 140–168
participation 152, 154–155
participatory principle 45
Partnerships Victoria 183, 188, 193
path dependency 79
patronage risk 189
Payment System
Board 237
oversight 219
performance-based management 185
Philippines 83
platinum 44

Plaza Accord 279
pluralism 48
policy
  advice 30
  coordination 284–286
  quality 164
  stability 164
polis 192
political
  decision-making 28
  interests 213
polity 47
polycentricity 51
Port of Brisbane 130
portfolio management principles 284
Portugal 96, 244, 246–247, 250, 259, 270
price
  level 255
  stability 15, 219–220, 224, 227–230
principal-agent models 30
principle of proportionality 103
Private Finance Initiative 182, 213, 215
privatisation 6, 11, 13, 30, 54, 56, 79, 174, 199, 206, 211, 213
Privy Council 33
procedural rules 102
procurement 187, 189, 192–193
productivity 23, 174, 255
profitability 145, 157
project
  evaluation 191
  Finance Initiative 172
  Risk 180
property rights 6, 164
protectionism 67
public
  choice theory 188
  goods 6, 157–160, 172
  interest 30, 62–63, 172, 212
    test 180, 215
  investment 173
  private partnerships 6, 14–15, 172–193, 197, 209–214
  procurement 172–193
  Protector 45
  sector
    borrowing requirement 210
    comparator 180
  service 29–31
  Values Survey 34

Q Port Holdings 131
QIC 131
QR National 129–130
quasi-
  nationalisation 7
  public goods 173
Queensland 7, 13, 117–137
  Fuel Subsidy Scheme 128
  Motorways Ltd 131
  Rail 125

R&D 12, 77, 81, 85–86, 148–149
Radio New Zealand 163
rating agencies 265
real wages 257
reasonableness 52, 69
redistribution 64
referendum 35–36
regional cooperation 84
regionalism 82, 90
registration 200
regulation 90, 198–206
regulatory
  agencies 203
  capitalism 205–207, 214
  governance 14, 197–215
  instruments 200
  standards 208
  state 204, 211
  tools 201, 214
renewable energy 151
Representation Commission 35–36
rescue package 106
Reserve Bank of
  Australia 219, 230, 232, 234, 237
  New Zealand 221, 229
residual risk 193
restructuring 26
Review of the Centre 31
Right to life 69
rights of
  the individual 38
  women 49
risk 178, 181, 187
  transfer 180
  weighting 179, 181, 191
role of the state 6–10
Roman Empire 175
Royal Commission on the Electoral System 35

rule of law 206
Rules of Procedure 103
ruling party 43
Russia 278

safety net 96
sanctions 254
Santiago Principles 274, 282–288, 290–293
Saudi Arabia 273, 275, 278
SCAW 60–61
Schick Report 31
Scotland 13
Scottish Parliament 175
securitisation 4
select committee 35
self-
  insurance 245
  regulation 282, 284
Seoul Consensus 4, 12, 59, 70
separation of powers 46, 51, 60–61, 65
sequencing 26
service delivery 178, 180, 185–186
shadow banking 5
share ownership 167
short-termism 188
Sichuan Tengzhong Heavy Industry Machinery Co. 72
Singapore 159, 274–275, 278, 280, 282, 288
six-pack 258, 261–263, 265, 267, 271
Soccer World Cup 70
social
  infrastructure 173–174
  policy 24–25
  protection 23, 30, 37
  responsibility 160–165
  security 51
  stability 64, 80
  values 1
  welfare state 26, 37
  wreckage 43
societal engineering 46
socio-economic rights 51–55
Solid Energy 140
South
  Africa 11–12, 42–70
  African Reserve bank 220
Southern
  African
    Customs Union 58
    Development Community 58
    Police Services Act 69
  Cross Station 185
sovereign
  budget rights 106
  debt 64, 96
    crisis 94, 111
  default 249, 259
  wealth funds 7, 16, 259, 267, 272–289
sovereignty 28, 42
Spain 24, 244–246, 250, 259, 270
Special Drawing Rights 281
spillover 158
stability 31
  and Growth Pact 16, 245, 250, 254–255, 257, 260, 262–264, 268, 270
standardisation 1
standards 207–208
Stanwell Corporation 133
State
  Administration of Foreign Exchange 76
  capitalism 7, 16, 56, 275, 277–278
  corporatism 88
  enterprises 56
  intervention 80–81
  Owned Enterprises Act 30, 160
  ownership 64, 273
  participation
  Services Commission 230
state-owned enterprises 30, 74, 76, 79, 81, 88–89, 140–168
Statement of Corporate Intent 119, 121, 123
static efficiency 166
  gains 143
step-in rights 185
stimulus package 83
stock markets 77, 150
strategic
  expectations letters 123
  investment 159
structural
  deficit 101
  funds 259
  reform 246, 273

subprime mortgages 4
subsidiarity 108
substantive law 102
Sumeria 175
SunWater 134
supranationalism 94–113
Supreme Court 33
surveillance 289
sustainability 66, 180
Sweden 17, 253, 259–261, 263, 267
Sydney 184
  Airport rail link 184
systemically important financial institutions 5

Tanzania 54
Target 2 109
technology 37, 77
telecommunications 146
Telstra 130
Temasek 159
Theodore Roosevelt 3
timeliness 180
toll roads 173
tolls 183
too big to fail 108
totalitarianism 192
TOWSE Act 164
toxic debt 7
trade agreements 37
Trail Smelter 105–106
training 83
transaction costs 245
transfers 162
transformation 46
transparency 4, 7, 31, 37, 167, 211, 225, 284–285
Transurban City Link 184
Treasury 142–144, 147, 150, 155–159, 166–168
treaty
  compliance 67
  making 65
  of Waitangi 11, 29, 32, 163

UAE 275
UN Convention against Corruption 69
UNCITRAL 50
unelected 15
unemployment 26, 65
Uniform Tariff Policy 121
United
  Kingdom 2, 4, 10, 172, 174–175, 179, 185, 187, 193, 210, 231, 253, 259–261, 264, 280
  States 2–4, 44, 77–78, 231, 256, 275
unlisted public companies 123
user
  amenity 181
  pays 190

value
  added tax 253
  chain 81
  for money 179–184, 211, 213–214
    test 177
vertical integration 81
Victoria 15, 175, 184, 188, 212
Vision for 2030 66
Volvo 72

wage bargainers 247
wages 156
Waitangi Tribunal 163–164
Walmart 62–63, 70
war against terrorism 7
Washington 106
  Consensus 1–2, 9–11, 25, 56, 59, 67, 82, 206, 277
water 51, 53–54
whole-life costing 179
wholesale money markets 227
Wiggins Island Coal Export Terminal 135
World
  Bank 5, 57
  Trade Organisation 58, 60–61, 66, 75, 83–84, 95, 279, 288
    dispute resolution 66
written constitution 27

Xstrata 136

youth dependency rate 68